How
the French
Think

How
the French
Think

An Affectionate Portrait of an
Intellectual People

SUDHIR HAZAREESINGH

BASIC BOOKS
A Member of the Perseus Books Group
New York

Published by Basic Books
A Member of the Perseus Books Group

Designed by Jeff Williams

Library of Congress Cataloging-in-Publication Data

Hazareesingh, Sudhir.
   How the French think : an affectionate portrait of an intellectual people / Sudhir Hazareesingh.
      pages cm
   Includes bibliographical references and index.
   ISBN 978-0-465-03249-5 (hardcover)—ISBN 978-0-465-06166-2 (e-book)
   1. Philosophy, French. 2. France—Intellectual life. I. Title.

B1801.H39 2015
194—dc23

                                                            2015022738

10 9 8 7 6 5 4 3 2 1

For Karma,
who makes everything beautiful

CONTENTS

PREFACE

I began observing French public life as an adolescent in my native island of Mauritius in the 1970s, when I was drawn to the country's culture, history, and politics by a variety of influences. First, my secondary school, the Royal College Curepipe, where we were served a copious diet of French classics, from Molière and Racine to Saint-Exupéry, Gide, "hell is other people" Sartre, and the inevitable (and already somewhat irksome) Camus. The family setting was essential, too, notably because of my father, Kissoonsingh, a Cambridge- and Sorbonne-trained historian who worked as principal private secretary to the prime minister of Mauritius, Sir Seewoosagur Ramgoolam. He cultivated close ties with politico-literary elites in France and Africa, in particular the Gaullist writer and France's first minister of culture André Malraux and the Senegalese president Léopold Sédar Senghor. Another inspiring figure was my brother, Sandip, a devotee of Napoleonic history, thanks to whom I plunged with relish into all aspects of the emperor's legend.

There was also the French cultural attaché in Mauritius, Antoine Colonna, a close friend of the family who was a native of Corsica (and thus a living link with the mythical birthplace of the emperor). Antoine provided us with subscriptions to French weekly periodicals such as *Le Nouvel Observateur*, *Le Point*, and *L'Express*, enabling me to remain closely attuned to French political and intellectual life. The French like to divide things into two, and the bifurcation of the time was between those who gathered around the liberal president, Valéry Giscard d'Estaing, and those who favored the left-wing parties of the Union de la Gauche. My sympathies were very much with the latter, especially with the Stalinist French communists, whose valiant past and unrelenting dogmatism appealed to my adolescent sensibility. I absorbed the writings of communist economists on the noxiousness of state monopoly capitalism, devoured the poems of Louis Aragon and Paul Éluard, and idolized communist martyrs and heroes such as Gabriel Péri, the antifascist campaigner who was executed by the Nazis at the Mont-Valérien fortress in 1941, and the Resistance leader Henri Rol-Tanguy, who launched the insurrection against the occupying forces in Paris in August 1944 from his underground bunker in Denfert-Rochereau. Yet I remember reading Giscard's pamphlet *Démocratie française* with quiet fascination; indeed, I could not help admiring its clinical elegance and programmatic ambition.

Just as vital in nurturing my Francophilia were television shows such as Bernard Pivot's *Apostrophes*, which introduced me to the contemporary French literary scene and allowed me to savor its delicately rarefied atmosphere. I vividly recall a discussion between Pivot and the writer Marguerite Yourcenar in 1979 about whether good and evil were "necessary." The exchanges were not particularly profound or conclusive. But it all *sounded* wonderful. Even though there was something slightly comical about all this preciosity, especially when viewed from the hazy distance of a little tropical island in the Indian Ocean, no one else at the time could rival the French in terms of sheer intellectual energy and panache—not the United States, still mired in its post-Vietnam maelstrom, and especially not Britain, with its industrial strife, shambling public finances, and bitterly factionalized Labour Party. In hindsight, my lifelong passion for the politics and history of France was clearly a product of those heady years.

Since the early 1990s, while teaching at Oxford, I have also lived in Paris for part of the year, and I associate with a variety of intellectual communities, from those within institutions of higher education and the editorial boards of journals and publishing houses to research networks, literary juries, and historical associations. These sustained interactions grant me an excellent vantage point from which to observe French thinking in all its glories, complexities, and idiosyncrasies. I thus came to realize that French traditions of thought are translated into concrete ways of life in which ideals and values are affirmed through social, cultural, and academic rituals—festivals, anniversary celebrations, *rentrées littéraires*, demonstrations, marches, petitions, even doctoral examinations. The intimate connection between thought, practice, and performance is vividly brought home to me whenever I am invited to serve on a doctoral jury in France and observe the magnificent rhetorical style of my French colleagues.[1]

My deeper immersion in the intellectual life of France has impressed upon me the powerful influence of literature in both reflecting and shaping the nation's mindset—one of the striking features of French culture. Voltaire's *Candide* and Rousseau's *Nouvelle Héloïse* (*The New Héloïse*) were essential vehicles for disseminating Enlightenment ideals of autonomy and authenticity, just as in the nineteenth century Alexandre Dumas's novels gave the French people more of an impression of their royalist past than all the historians of the age. More recently, there are few more illuminating pathways into the complex experiences of occupation, resistance, and collaboration in France between 1940 and 1944 than Joseph Kessel's *Army of Shadows*, Vercors's *Silence of the Sea*, and Louis-Ferdinand Céline's *Castle to Castle*. These literary works underscore, too, some of the key (and admirable) elements of the French spirit: a willful predisposition to deviate from the beaten path, a cult of sentiment and mystery, and a resistance to all conformism.

The principal aim of this book is to identify the cultural distinctiveness of French thinking—a cosmology that is as much a matter of content as of temperament, style, and idiom. As we shall see, French thought is pervaded by religious concepts, images, and metaphors. Though secular in its public institutions and the collective beliefs and practices of its people, France continues to live under the shadow of its once-dominant Catholicism. I was already aware of this in Mauritius in the 1970s when I began to immerse myself in French political and intellectual culture: good and evil were not only subjects of literary and philosophical discussion but also concepts that were regularly used in political intercourse. Indeed, one of the classic works I first encountered, toward the end of the decade, was Alain Peyrefitte's *Le Mal français*, the title of which astutely combines organic and religious themes (*mal* carries connotations of both physical disorder and sinfulness).

Despite the official separation of spiritual from temporal matters in France, this neo-religious sensibility is everywhere visible. One of the modern French words for an intellectual is *clerc* (a member of the clergy), and the positions held by an intellectual have been consistently defined through concepts such as faith, commitment, heresy, and deliverance. Likening his experiences in the French Communist Party during the 1940s and 1950s to a form of "religious mysticism," the philosopher Edgar Morin admitted that his affiliation to communism had been a "search for salvation through collective redemption." French thinkers have also been constantly fascinated by the occult and by the appeal of providential figures, from Napoleon to Charles de Gaulle. Likewise, there remains to this day a sacred and quasi-messianic dimension to French views of the nation. Republicanism, France's dominant political tradition, long operated as a civil religion, with its own cults, martyrs, missionaries, and holy texts—and it is no coincidence that the hallowed Parisian cenotaph for national heroes, the Panthéon, is a deconsecrated church. There is still much truth in the philosopher Alfred Fouillée's early twentieth-century observation about his fellow citizens: "France is always in search of an ideal form of inspiration whose illumination may cause all sincere souls to rejoice."[2]

A Yearning Toward Universality

Le Style Français

In February 2003, French foreign minister Dominique de Villepin delivered a speech at a Security Council debate at the United Nations in New York on whether to sanction the use of force against Saddam Hussein's regime in Iraq. Speaking in the name of an "old country" and an "old continent" that had experienced "wars, occupations and barbarity," Villepin declared—prophetically—that a war against the Iraqi regime would have catastrophic consequences for the region's stability: "The option of war may appear a priori the most effective. But let us not forget that, after winning the war, peace has to be built." Stressing that "the use of force [was] not justified," he ended by expressing his faith in the capacity of the international community to build a more harmonious world: "We are the guardians of an ideal, the guardians of a conscience. The heavy responsibility and the immense honor which is ours should lead us to give priority to peaceful disarmament."[1]

Villepin's speech was broadly welcomed across the world, typifying as it did a shared collective aspiration for a different kind of politics, one which was grounded in humanism rather than force. And yet in his vision, and in the way in which it was elaborated, there was also something very recognizably, unquestionably French: a seductive masculinity and rhetorical verve that drew on the nation's finest traditions of public oratory; an appeal to reason and logic, with the issue under discussion being neatly framed into binary oppositions (conflict and harmony; self-interest and the common good; morality and power politics); a sense of articulating an age-old wisdom resting on centuries of often painful historical experience; and a confident optimism, underpinned by a belief in France's cultural superiority. Although it did not do so explicitly—and was all the more compelling for it—the speech threw down the gauntlet to George W. Bush's America and its complaisant ally, Great Britain, and held up the actions of these nations to the court of international public opinion as threats to peace and stability. This silent demonization of the dastardly "Anglo-Saxons" was the climax of Villepin's oratorical artistry, along with his characteristically French claim to be speaking in the name of universal principles—all the more sincerely so, one felt, because these happened to coincide exactly with French national interests.

Villepin's ideas were not simply reflections of the modern Gallic view of the world but were steeped in wider traditions of French thinking about international peace that can be traced back to the eighteenth century. His speech carried a subtle but forceful echo of the eighteenth-century author Abbé de Saint-Pierre's idealistic proposition that a confederation of like-minded states (led by France, naturally) provided the best guarantee of a peaceful world. The foreign minister's high-minded eloquence was also reminiscent of the style of Aristide Briand, the mercurial statesman of the interwar period who sought to promote international peace through diplomacy and interstate cooperation. In short, it was embedded in a rich and complex pattern of French thinking.

In this book I will explore the different facets of this intellectual universe, highlighting its long-term characteristics and its evolution over time as well as its continuing cultural manifestations today, and showing how (and why) the activities of the mind have occupied such a special place in French public life. Beyond identifying the many and varied ways in which the French have represented themselves and imagined the world, my ultimate ambition here is to try to explain *how* the French think—in other words, to make sense of their preferred concepts, frameworks, and modes of thought as well as their particular stylistic fetishes. These include such classic characteristics as a belief in their innate disposition toward creative thinking, as when the writer Blaise Pascal observed of his compatriots, "I do not speak of fools, I speak of the wisest men; and it is among them that imagination has the great gift of persuasion." Also pervasive is the sense of an exceptional Gallic aptitude for lucidity, a crisp clarity that has been attributed to the very properties of the French language: "What is not clear," affirmed the writer Antoine Rivarol imperiously, "is not French." This precision could be accompanied by a certain hedonistic levity, as acknowledged by the critic Hippolyte Taine: "All that the Frenchman desires is to provoke in himself and in others a bubbling of agreeable ideas." Typically French, too, is an insouciance of manner—"doing frivolous things seriously, and serious things frivolously," as the philosopher Montesquieu put it, and also a contrarian and impertinent tendency, as when the historian Ernest Lavisse noted, "We are not born to be docile or respectful." Jules Michelet (another historian) regarded this disputatiousness as one of the singular attributes of the French educated classes: "We gossip, we quarrel, we expend our energy in words; we use strong language, and fly into great rages over the smallest of subjects." Above all, the French style of thinking is famous for its love of general notions. For the essayist Émile de Montégut, "There is no people among whom abstract ideas have played such a great role, whose history is rife with such formidable philosophical tendencies, and where individuals are so oblivious to facts and possessed to such a high degree with a rage for abstractions." Or, in the more positive gloss of the writer Julien Benda: "A truly enriching thought is the one which engages with a general and not an individual matter, and indeed which may not correspond rigorously to reality."[2]

All these manifestations of the *esprit français* will be encountered in the following pages along with many others: most notably, the French predilection for conducting arguments about the good life around idealized metaphysical concepts such as monarchy, reason, the general will, the proletariat, and the nation. In fact, such is the French fondness for metaphysics that the term has even been deemed appropriate to describe the difficulties of buying freshly baked bread during the summer holiday season. Equally prevalent is a passion for holism, for considering questions in their totality as opposed to looking at their contingent manifestations. As the philosopher Philippe Corcuff observed, this essentialism is integral to French thought, framing collective discussion on all matters, from the Republic and the state to multiculturalism, security, and America. The philosopher Michel Lacroix provided a good example of this way of thinking when he described his patriotism as resting on "an ontological understanding" of Frenchness. This holism is also evident in the Gallic urge to subject everything—from constitutions and bills of rights to political programs—to exhaustive codification (even if the provisions in question are then blithely ignored). The French style of thought is noteworthy, too, for its capacity to give theoretical and existential properties to all aspects of social life, from speaking, dressing, and eating to the celebration of rituals and the use of language itself. Hence the quintessentially French *Festival du Mot* (Festival of the Word), whose tenth incarnation took place at La Charité-sur-Loire (Nièvre) in early summer 2014 under the patronage of the academician Érik Orsenna. According to its organizers, its purpose was to "make words resonate so that we may reflect on their magic and their power, with the conviction that words have to be shared with the greatest number."[3]

Just as prevalent is the French attachment to questions of presentation and form. This tendency finds expression in the belief in the aesthetic quality of intellectual activity, in a fondness for taxonomies and neologisms, and, as a student from the Lycée Poincaré in Bar-le-Duc, Meuse, triumphantly declared to her local newspaper after finishing her examination, in the idea that any good piece of writing should be structured around the "dialectical plan" of thesis, antithesis, and synthesis. Her dissertation addressed the question of whether human choices are based on "reason" or on "passion," which brings up perhaps the greatest of all French stylistic traits, already brilliantly illustrated by Villepin: the obsession with dividing things into two. As a seasoned observer of Parisian intellectual life has noted, the French have a habit of structuring public debate around a small number of recurring themes: openings and closures, stasis and transformation, freedom and determinism, unity and diversity, civilization and barbarity, and progress and decadence.[4]

An Exceptional Nation

If the modern self-image of the British is one of a practical community, "solid and not given to chasing bubbles," as Keir Hardie, one of the founders of the British Labour Party, once put it, that of the French is typically of a reflective people whose attachment to the realm of ideas is both intense and demonstrative. An Egyptian cleric visiting Paris in the late 1820s found the French to be distinctive "by their keen intelligence, profound perceptiveness and depth of mind when treating recondite issues." More than a century later, trying to prepare its servicemen for the singularities of the natives, a British Army manual issued before the Normandy landings in 1944 observed, "By and large, Frenchmen enjoy intellectual argument more than we do. You will often think that two Frenchmen are having a violent quarrel when they are simply arguing about some abstract point." The French devotion to culture is reflected in the weight given to the written word—hence France's long history of the repression of writers, symbolized in the nineteenth century by the prison of Sainte-Pélagie in Paris, where many of the nation's most eminent thinkers, poets, and other writers were detained because of what they had published. Hence, also, the impressive cohort of creative figures who rest in the Panthéon: philosophical giants Voltaire and Rousseau, classic examples of the ideal of the *grand homme* as a pedagogue of virtue during the Enlightenment; Victor Hugo and Émile Zola, symbols of the nation's attachment to literary excellence; and more recent entries, such as the progressive Martinique poet Aimé Césaire and the ethnologist Germaine Tillion.[5]

There are many other signs of this French fixation with culture, beginning with the lasting preoccupation with linguistic precision and the rules of syntax; as Bishop Bossuet once sternly told the heir to the French throne, "He who ignores the laws of grammar spurns the precepts of reason." There is also the association, in the French progressive tradition, of the idea of citizenship with learning: the philosopher Nicolas de Condorcet wrote that the "first duty of society towards its citizens is public education." Another illustration is the claim to superior intelligence by political groups: in the first half of the twentieth century, both the extreme right Action Française and the extreme left Communist Party referred to themselves as the "party of intelligence." Equally noteworthy is the treatment by French towns and cities of even their most obscure literary luminaries as sources of civic pride—not to mention the celebrity status accorded to men and women of ideas and their continuing (and at times envied) capacity to shape national domestic and foreign policy. (A recent example is the philosopher Bernard-Henri Lévy's determining role in France's military intervention in Libya in 2011.) The notion that "culture" should be assigned its own specific department in government is a modern French invention that has now spread across the world. Last, but not least, there is the creation of special schools for the training of French elites. Villepin is emblematic in this respect, too: a product of the École Nationale d'Administration, he typifies the technocracy that has captured France's political and administrative hierarchy in the modern age. With his aristocratic origins and haughty contempt for universal suffrage (he has never stood for election, despite having occupied the highest public offices), Villepin perfectly fits the sociologist Pierre Bourdieu's description of this new ruling class as the "nobility of State."[6]

All great nations think of themselves as exceptional. France's distinctiveness in this regard lies in its enduring belief in its own moral and intellectual prowess. These visions of excellence have often been crystallized in French depictions of Paris. In Louis-Sébastien Mercier's *Tableau de Paris* (*Panorama of Paris*, 1799), the capital is seen as a bastion of modern creativity, a city regarded across the world as "the most astonishing city in the universe." The thinker Auguste Comte believed that Paris was the center of humanity because "the philosophical spirit" was more developed there than anywhere else in the world. Hailed as a magnificent symbol of freedom and revolutionary endeavor since the nineteenth century, because of repeated insurrections against its various governments, Paris is also (paradoxically) idolized by the champions of the principle of state centralization, defined by the nineteenth-century philosopher Charles Dupont-White as "the power of reason expressed through law."[7]

Above all, Paris is captivating because of its intellectual ebullience. Hence the extraordinary appeal of its cultural life as evoked in an 1878 letter by the future socialist leader Jean Jaurès, who had just arrived at the Lycée Sainte-Barbe from his native town of Castres, Tarn, to prepare the entrance examination for the École Normale Supérieure:

> There are ten of us here, preparing for the École, each with different tastes and ambitions: the one prefers literature, the other history, and another philosophy. We tell each other about our readings, our ideas, our enthusiasms, our discoveries, our systems (these days every nineteen-year-old has a system); and these constant exchanges stimulate a prodigious activity in the mind, which is subjected to an incessant barrage of thoughts which interact with each other, are then combined, and come to maturity; add to this the events in the fields of politics, literature, and theater, which always have a powerful echo in the colleges of Paris so that on Sundays, when we are allowed out, we rush to the newsstands to read the latest publications, we stop off in the museums, we hurry to the matinee and evening performances of the latest plays. Such is the life of intense and sustained thought which is the joy and privilege of Parisian life.[8]

How all these different—and contrasting—ideals of French greatness emerged and became entrenched will be examined in the first half of the book. From the seventeenth century (known as the "Grand Siècle"), which marked the golden age of French monarchical absolutism, the French *génie* dominated European artistic and cultural life, be it through the triumph of classicism in literature, painting, and architecture; the Cartesian correlation of existence with thought; or the association of the French language with precision, civility, and feminine refinement. France was also noted for its scientific advances, the fertility of its utopian imagination, and its relish for plunging into ideological disputes of an often scholastic quality: the French ardently embraced Montaigne's maxim "There is no conversation more boring than the one where everybody agrees."[9]

What makes this sense of intellectual greatness even more portentous is the French belief that they have a duty to think not just for themselves but also for the rest of the world. Ernest Lavisse thus noted in 1890 that whereas Rome's mission had been to conquer the world, and Germany's calling was to harness the power of all things Germanic, his nation was "charged with representing the cause of humanity." This is a secularized version of an older religious ideal that, since the rule of Charlemagne, has portrayed

France as the "eldest daughter of the Church." Hence the inescapably messianic dimension shared by all the great modern French political doctrines: from the revolutionaries' aspiration to regenerate humankind through Napoleon's celebration of the *grande nation* to Charles de Gaulle's "certain idea of France" as a country destined for *grandeur*—one of the underlying assumptions of Villepin's United Nations speech. For the academician Jean d'Ormesson, such lofty aspirations remain an integral feature of the French national character: "There is at the heart of Frenchness something which transcends it. France is not only a matter of contradiction and diversity. She also constantly looks over her shoulder, toward others, and toward the world which surrounds her. More than any nation, France is haunted by a yearning toward universality."[10]

The French Revolution provided a powerful and lasting inspiration for the emergence of these messianic ideals. All the key concepts in modern French political culture—liberty, equality, and fraternity; the rights of man; popular sovereignty; patriotism; the general interest; the division between Left and Right—first entered the mainstream in the aftermath of the events of 1789. Two of the most recognizable representations of Frenchness across the world, the tricolor flag and the Marseillaise, were devised during the Revolution. Likewise, the nation's central ideals and myths were forged in the light of early revolutionary landmarks. The overthrow of despotism was symbolized by the Storming of the Bastille on July 14. The sovereign unity of the people was expressed three weeks later in the abolition of feudalism by the Constituent Assembly on the night of August 4.[11]

The centralization of power was the defining principle of the dominant political force of the early 1790s, the Jacobins. The tradition of defensive patriotism against foreign invaders was exemplified by the French victory at the Battle of Valmy in September 1792 and the ensuing revolutionary wars against the European monarchies. The moral regeneration of the citizenry, and the elimination of impurity from the body politic, were reflected in the execution of the king and the violent phase of revolutionary government known as the Terror (1793–1794). The principle of civil equality was promulgated in the Civil Code, and the norms of heroic virtue and providential leadership were exemplified in such figures as Maximilien Robespierre and Napoleon Bonaparte. For the next two centuries, most of the fundamental arguments among the French—about the nature of their regime, the obligations of citizenship, the possibility and desirability of progress, the claims of social justice, the devolution of power to the regions, the place of religion in public life, and the legitimacy of sectional interests—continued to revolve in one way or another around this revolutionary heritage.[12]

It is precisely the length of this revolutionary shadow which accounts for the fratricidal quality of modern French political debate, with its momentous battles between (binary oppositions, again) monarchists and revolutionaries, social reformers and conservatives, representatives of the bourgeoisie and of the working class, supporters of church and of state, centralizers and believers in local autonomy, advocates of parliamentarianism and presidentialism. These conflicts and the divisions they spawn defined the contours of political argument for much of the modern era. Yet behind these antagonisms there were elements of convergence and even a shared sense of what it meant to be French: a belief in the ideals of duty and public service, a defiance of fate, a contempt for materialism, a cult of heroism, and an attachment to the enabling and civilizing powers of the state: France is one of the few countries in the world (perhaps along with North Korea) where a short book can plausibly be published bearing the title *We Must Love the State*. The French also coped with their intellectual fractures by cultivating the art of synthesis. This power is often underestimated: from Comte's bold combination of positivistic science and religious mysticism to the blending of republican absolutism and provincial skepticism by philosopher Émile Chartier (also known as Alain), and all the way through to the fruitful tension between the *petite* and the *grande patrie* (little and great homeland), French thought (in its most creative moments) has succeeded in harmonizing apparently opposing values.[13]

Despite the rhetorical attachment to the idea of *rupture*, French culture possesses a fundamental unity, which manifests itself in the reproduction across generations of certain basic assumptions and styles of thought. This type of continuity is especially visible in French patterns of rationalist and utopian thinking and in the underlying intellectual approaches of different historical schools. Within the Left and the Right, too, despite the numerous changes in nomenclature since the late eighteenth century, there are remarkable elements of stability. The dominance of communism between the 1930s and the late 1970s was a modern manifestation of an older Jacobin revolutionary tradition that first emerged in 1789. Likewise, Bonapartism, a doctrine that favors a strong state, a charismatic leader, and an ardent form of nationalism, was a central force on the Right for much of the nineteenth century, and in the revived form of Gaullism it was a decisive feature of French politics in the second half of the twentieth century.[14]

These doctrines, with their emphasis on the concentration of power in the hands of a providential leader, also provide the foundation for France's ongoing fascination with its tradition of royal majesty. Elected by universal suffrage, yet towering over all other political institutions and insulated from external constraints to a degree unknown in any other democracy, the president of the Fifth Republic has been rightly likened to a "republican mon-arch." In the 1960s in the satirical weekly *Le Canard enchaîné*, the cartoonist Roland Moisan represented President de Gaulle as the king and his entourage as courtiers in a successful pastiche of the memoirists of the seventeenth- and eighteenth-century French court. This tradition continued with his succes-sors: Valéry Giscard d'Estaing was described as "the man who wanted to be king" by *Le Nouvel Observateur*; François Mitterrand's regal demeanor often elicited remarks comparing him to absolute monarchs; and Nicolas Sarkozy's abrasive style (and short stature) reminded some of Napoleon Bonaparte. In-deed, Louis XIV's precepts on the art of kingship provide more insight into the ethos of the modern French presidency than any manual of constitutional law—notably, his injunction to "bring together in his person all the authority of the ruler" and "never to show any attachment to anyone."[15]

These conceptual juggling acts have produced delicious oxymorons and nourished yet another cherished feature of Gallic thinking: the love of para-dox. Thanks to this trait, France has given us passionate rationalists, conserva-tive revolutionaries (and revolutionary traditions), violent moderates, secular missionaries, spiritual materialists, *spectateurs engagés* (committed observers), patriotic internationalists, conflictual allies, and collective-minded individ-ualists—and, by virtue of the sometimes unfortunate fate of French armies on the battlefield, from Vercingétorix to the Battle of Waterloo, perhaps the most exquisite paradox of all: the glorious defeat. This fondness for reconciling opposites has sometimes confused even the most well-meaning outside ob-servers. When the novelist Julien Green delivered a lecture on the nationalist writer Maurice Barrès at Oxford in 1950, he ordered it around three radically divergent facets of Barrès's thought. After concluding his exposition of the "three Barrèses," he asked whether there were any questions. A hand went up: "Could you tell us the names of Barrès's two brothers?"[16]

Sociability and Imagination

Writing a book about the substance and style of French ideas across eras presents significant challenges. The literature on modern French thought is of course compendious, and it contains wonderful works on specific periods (Norman Hampson on the Enlightenment, Patrice Higonnet on revolutionary Jacobinism, Theodore Zeldin on the formative years between 1848 and 1945, Tony Judt on the decades after World War II) and on particular themes, such as the revolutionary and republican legacies, the sources of nationalism, the ideologies of Left and Right, and the French "passion" for communism. This book attempts to put together all the pieces of this gigantic puzzle to make a single, integrated account, both serious and playful, of the French way of thinking across different subjects and epochs, from René Descartes to Jacques Derrida and from abstruse moral and philosophical issues to the question of the survival of French culture in a globalized world.[17]

How the French Think combines close attention to texts with an explanation of the wider historical and cultural settings in which they are embedded. As the intellectual historian Quentin Skinner has reminded us, concepts have a dual quality: they can be understood only within broader intellectual frameworks, and they are also tools that are deployed for particular purposes that may vary quite significantly over time. "Thought" is taken here to include formal doctrines and informal systems of belief, general theories and particular constructs, detailed visions of the good life as well as allusive symbolic representations. In my endeavor to capture the richness and creativity of French thinking, I have drawn upon as wide a variety of sources as possible: the writings of political elites and intellectual eminences; works of historical erudition and slender pamphlets; fiction, paintings, and songs; articles in the national and local press; police reports, memoirs, and private correspondence; aphorisms, advertisements, and self-help manuals; even a book on how to communicate with the dead. At the same time, I pay attention to the institutional underpinnings of French thought: educational structures such as the Grandes Écoles and their (increasingly contested) role as the producers of national elites; the Académie Française, the stern guardian of national linguistic and cultural orthodoxies; the major disseminators of mass culture, such as newspapers, journals, and museums; and the institutions and places that promote cultural sociability across the land, from parties, think tanks, and pressure groups to Masonic Lodges, taverns, and cafés. The association of the café with intellectual life was already well entrenched in modern French culture by the mid-nineteenth century, as the writer Alfred Delvau acknowledged: "The first time I drank beer and heard of Kant, Hegel and Schiller, it was in a Paris brasserie." This legacy continues to this day: in April 2014 an editorial in the daily newspaper *Libération* celebrated the bistro as a key provider of "direct social links" among French people.[18]

What, then, makes it possible to speak of the collective frame of mind of the "French"? The short answer is that, to an extent which is unique in modern Western culture, the nation's major intellectual bodies—from the state to the great educational institutions, academies, publishing houses, and organs of the press—are concentrated in Paris. This cultural centralization helps to explain why French ways of thought exhibit such a degree of stylistic consistency—and why even countercultural groups and movements adopt modes of thinking that often seem to replicate those of their adversaries. Hence the

Enlightenment radicals' notion of popular sovereignty, the exact mirror of the precept of absolutist power; the holistic abstraction of nineteenth-century counterrevolutionary thought, which matched the essentialism of its republican rivals; and the irreducible nationalism of the communists in the modern age, despite their doctrinal opposition to this "bourgeois" doctrine. This commonality is also the product of shared collective experiences. Systems of ideas and intellectual currents such as republicanism and Gaullism have often represented the maturation of existing social and cultural practices, or the reactions of particular generations to defining (and traumatizing) episodes such as revolutions, civil conflicts, and wars. But French thought also changed in the process of being disseminated, particularly in light of the resistance it encountered on the ground. For these reasons, I have deliberately moved beyond the conventional repertoire of canonical thinkers to pay attention to the wider cast of characters in French thought: authors of books and pamphlets, editorialists, newspaper readers and journal subscribers, political activists, members of associations, and teachers and students.

Intellectual life in France is also distinctive in its organization around particular patterns of sociability. The classic example of this phenomenon is the *salon*, a private cultural gathering, the aim of which was to entertain, to exchange ideas, and to promote the values of civility and politeness. These meetings flourished in French high society from the seventeenth century on, contributing to the circulation of philosophical and artistic ideas, the breakdown of social barriers, and the empowerment of women. The *salon* was often a site for the development of pioneering ideas and social practices: thus, it was one of the privileged arenas in which women could engage in philosophical debate—notably, by critically confronting the work of Descartes. (Hence, the word *cartésienne* rapidly became incorporated into the language of educated society in the seventeenth century.) These intellectual exchanges later took on more overtly political dimensions, preparing the way for the modern democratic era. A Russian diplomat stationed in Paris in the 1840s was startled by the range of opportunities available for political chat: "Here we have political *salons*, literary *salons*, legitimist *salons*, *salons* of the *juste milieu* (moderate factions), diplomatic *salons*, and finally, neutral *salons*."[19]

But, arguably, the most important cultural function of the *salon* was its refusal to be tied down by what we would today call disciplinary boundaries. Nowhere was this exuberant intellectual eclecticism more radiantly displayed than at the *salon* hosted in the Bibliothèque de l'Arsenal between 1824 and 1834 by its curator Charles Nodier. His famous Sunday evening *causeries* (talks) left an indelible imprint on his audience, not only because of his charm and wit, but also because of his dazzling capacity to roam across subjects, themes, and epochs. In the admiring summary of the literary critic Sainte-Beuve:

> Nodier loves and caresses with his imagination the banished exiles, the heroic outlaws, the prematurely ended destinies, the small invisible goblins, the anonymous books that need an interpretive key, the illustrious authors concealed behind an anagram, the local dialects that resist the sovereignty of national languages, all the dusty or bloody corners of singular events and mysteries, many valuable leftovers, and many ingenious paradoxes that contain fragments of truth, freedom of the press before Louis XIV, literary publicity before the era of the printing press, French spelling before Voltaire.[20]

Nodier's salon attracted men and women of indomitably conservative spirit as well as revolutionaries and utopian dreamers, and in this respect, too, it symbolized one of the great Gallic intellectual curiosities: the contrast between the venerable character of some of the nation's most prestigious cultural institutions and the enduring emphasis on transformation in French thinking. Humanist centers of learning have been fixtures in the Parisian intellectual landscape for centuries: the Collège de France was founded in 1530, the Académie Française in 1635, and the École Normale Supérieure in 1793. Yet the ideal of innovation has been at the heart of modern French thought. After his move to Paris in 1831, the German poet Heinrich Heine was particularly struck by this trait, describing the French as "lovers of vanities, parades, fashions and novelties."[21]

In the modern era, the concepts of revolution and rupture have become familiar tropes across the French human sciences, whether in politics, history, literature, philosophy, sociology, linguistics, psychology, or anthropology. The period between the early 1950s and the late 1970s alone gave us the *nouveau roman* (new novel), the *nouvelle vague* (in cinema), the *nouvelle histoire*, the *nouvelle philosophie*, the *Nouvelle Gauche* and the *Nouvelle Droite*, and, let us not forget, *nouvelle cuisine* (although that concept dates back to at least 1742 and the publication of the third volume of cookbook author Menon's *Nouveau traité de la cuisine* (New treatise on cuisine). For the ethnologist Claude Lévi-Strauss, one of the most influential French thinkers of the twentieth century, the explanation of this thirst for novelty is simple: "The great speculative structures are made to be broken. There is not one of them that can hope to last more than a few decades, or at most a century or two."

The idea of knowledge as continuous and cumulative, which is such a central premise of Anglo-Saxon epistemology, is alien to the French way of thinking. One of the reasons for this (and Lévi-Strauss's observation is helpful here, too) is the emphasis on the speculative quality of thought in France. French intellectual constructs are speculative in that they are generally the product of a form of thinking that is not necessarily grounded in empirical reality. This method finds expression in the classic French saying "Tant pis pour les faits" (So much the worse for the facts), and in the celebrated Gallic attachment to the deductive method of reasoning, immortalized by Descartes, which starts with a general, abstract proposition and then proceeds to a particular conclusion or proposition. Working the other way round, Anglo-Saxons often bemoan the specious and trivial results of this French mode of reasoning; it was in this spirit that the Chichele Professor of Social and Political Theory at Oxford, Gerry Cohen, once penned a piece on "Why One Kind of Bullshit Flourishes in France."[22]

Universality and Fragility

This book appears at a moment when France is in a particularly troubled state. The nation is grappling with a growing sense of unease about its present condition and its future prospects. Just as I finished writing, this anxiety was heightened by the violent attacks on the satirical magazine *Charlie Hebdo* and a kosher supermarket in Paris in January 2015, in which cartoonists, hostages, and police officers were killed by three young French men of immigrant descent. Despite the remarkable public response—over a million men and women demonstrated in the "republican march" in the streets of the French capital on January 11—these incidents highlighted ongoing French fears about insecurity, the integration of postcolonial minorities, and the economic and social fractures in French society.

The events of January 2015 also played into a broader malaise that was reflected in recent years in widespread concerns about France's place in a globalized world order, the viability of the republican social and political system, and the preservation of the French way of life. A telling symptom of this disorder is the declining level of trust in French elites, which has plummeted to record depths in recent years. As the columnist Alain Duhamel soberly observed, "Parties are condemned, leaders are contested, elected representatives inspire contempt, and journalists, disdain." He might have added intellectuals to the list, as the other major sign of this malaise is the loss of confidence by the French in the creativity of their thinkers and in their cultural singularity. In

2012, the *Magazine littéraire* even dared to raise the ultimate question: "Does France Still Think?"[23]

This book seeks to understand not only why this pessimism has come about but also what it tells us more generally about French styles of thinking. A key consideration here is the changing pattern of interaction between French ideas and the wider world. An enduring source of the French pride in their thought is that their history and culture have decisively shaped the values and ideals of other nations. Versailles in the age of the Sun King was the unrivaled aesthetic and political exemplar for European courts, and Caraccioli, the eighteenth-century Italian author of *L'Europe française* (French Europe), expressed a common view when he enthused about the "sparkling manners and lively vivacity" of the French before concluding, "Every European is now a Frenchman."[24]

Ideas from France have traveled much further: for example, the Civil Code was a model for newly independent states across Latin America during the nineteenth century. The first generation of Russian Bolsheviks was obsessed by the analogies between their own revolution and the overthrow of the French *ancien régime*; the early actions of Lenin and Trotsky were fashioned less by ideology than by their perceptions of how their circumstances fitted with the French precedent. Thanks to its colonial empire, the second largest in the world after Britain's, France projected its *mission civilisatrice* (civilizing mission) across its Asian and African dominions. The Statue of Liberty, which has become such an iconic emblem of Americanness, was designed by the French sculptor Frédéric Bartholdi. And, to this day, Poland's national anthem celebrates Napoleon Bonaparte, and Brazil's flag bears the motto of Comtian positivism: "Order and progress."[25]

An equally compelling measure of the French impact on modern thinking is the way in which particular episodes in the nation's history have resonated across the globe. Revolutionary ideas have been an inspiration to national liberators throughout the world, from Wolfe Tone in Ireland and Toussaint Louverture in Haiti to Simón Bolívar in Latin America, and José Rizal, one of the Philippines' emblematic national heroes, was an admirer of Victor Hugo. Similarly, Napoleon's military campaigns and his art of war were celebrated not only by writers and poets across Europe but also by Japanese samurai warriors and Tartar tribesmen (a folk song celebrated "Genghis Khan and his nephew Napoleon"), and even by the Vietnamese revolutionary hero Võ Nguyên Giáp. In the late 1930s, when he was a history teacher at the Thang Long School in Hanoi, Giáp gave lectures on the French revolutionary and imperial eras. One of his students later recalled the "mesmerizing" effect of the lectures on his students.[26]

At the same time as it traveled across epochs and continents, French thought consistently engaged with the world, drawing inspiration from events and intellectual trends abroad. The critique of monarchical absolutism was partly elaborated under the universal gaze of writer Guillame-Thomas Raynal's *Philosophical and Political History* . . . , a scathing indictment of European colonialism that placed the French struggle for a more democratic society in a global context. Early French liberalism was nourished by the cosmopolitan exchanges of Germaine de Staël's "Coppet Circle" *salon* and François Guizot's admiration for England, "the beacon of dignity and human freedom," because of its "Protestant Christianity and parliamentary government." Kantian ideals of moral autonomy played a major role in the transformation of French republicanism in the second half of the nineteenth century, while Friedrich Nietzsche, Martin Heidegger, and Sigmund Freud were decisive influences on existentialist and structuralist thinkers in the post-1945 decades. Communist doctrine in France in the twentieth century cannot be understood without reference to its international dimensions—notably, its ideological and emotional attachments to the Soviet Union. Yet even at their most inspiring, these outside experiences and modes of thinking were assimilated through an irreducibly Gallic prism: as Tocqueville candidly acknowledged of his *Democracy in America* (1835), "although I rarely spoke of France in that book, I did not write a page without thinking of her and without always having her, as it were, before my eyes." This principle was taken to the extreme by the writer Édouard Laboulaye, who published a three-volume *History of the United States* (1855–1866) without ever bothering to cross the Atlantic. Paying tribute to the valiant spirit, generosity, and moral excellence of the Poles, Jules Michelet described their nation as "the France of the North." A century later, this splendid ethnocentrism was alive and well, as when André Malraux traveled to Beijing to inform a no doubt nonplussed Mao Zedong that the Chinese were "the French of Asia."[27]

French universalism, in other words, was as much concerned with Frenchness as with universality—as attested by the ways in which outside ideas have been received in France. Foreign concepts and systems of thought acquired different intonations as they made their way to Paris, at times becoming difficult to recognize by their originators. Karl Marx was so dismayed by the way in which his ideas were traduced by French socialists (not to mention by his three daughters falling in love with Frenchmen) that he declared, "Je ne suis pas Marxiste." This ambiguous rapport with the wider world shines through in the intellectual representations of France's principal neighbors and rivals. Revolutionary America rapidly went from being a bucolic Rousseauist paradise to the place that, in the French diplomat Talleyrand's celebrated formula, had "thirty-two religions and only one dish." Germany, likewise, moved from being a haven of idealism in the nineteenth century to the epitome of a nation "lacking in tact and charm," according to the philosopher and historian Ernest Renan. (This observation was made, admittedly, after the Prussians had annexed Alsace-Lorraine.) Speaking at a time when Germany was divided into two states, the writer François Mauriac was more subtle, but no less dismissive, when he declared, "I love Germany so much that I am glad there are two of them." And England? She might have appeared to be an enticing land of liberty, where the creative genius of a Francis Bacon or a John Locke could flourish and where "even the people commonly think," as Voltaire generously put it in his *Lettres anglaises* (*Letters on England*). For the moderate tradition in French thought, from Montesquieu through Jacques Necker to Benjamin Constant, England even acquired the status of a "political model." And English soil also readily offered respite from the tempestuous politics of France: Victor Hugo's exile during the years of Napoleon III's imperial rule became a symbol of the defiance of despotism.[28]

But the visitor from France who crossed the Channel nevertheless found a land inhabited by a strange and impenetrable people. In her widely read *Promenades dans Londres* (Walks in London, 1840), the feminist Flora Tristan observed, "The Englishman is under the spell of his climate and behaves like a brute"; she found the general atmosphere in London so melancholic that it created "an irresistible desire to end one's life by suicide." Indeed, treacherous Albion has been one of the recurrent images in modern French demonology. It proved all the more enduring because this concept could be deployed to justify a variety of grievances, both real and imagined: murderous and ungallant behavior (the massacre of French knights at Agincourt, the burning of Joan of Arc), religious apostasy (the piously Catholic Jacques-Bénigne Bossuet's lament about "perfidious England"), vindictiveness (governor Sir Hudson Lowe's petty treatment of Napoleon during his captivity on Saint Helena), colonial treachery (a late nineteenth-century poem accused the English of "stealing France's most prized conquests"), and duplicitousness (de Gaulle's belief during World War II that the "Anglo-Saxon" tandem of Winston Churchill and Franklin D. Roosevelt were plotting against him behind his back). In the most extravagant versions, these heinous traits were combined, as in Georges Colomb's comic strip *La Famille Fenouillard* (The Fenouillard family, 1893)—one panel showed the English "burning Joan of Arc on the rock of Saint Helena."[29]

This capacity to shift swiftly from positive to negative representations is one of the notable characteristics of French thinking. As we will discover, the syndrome lies at the heart of France's contemporary pessimistic sensibility.

Analyzing the rhetorical style of the nation's modern political leaders, the liberal intellectual Jean-François Revel once observed that they seemed caught between "the fantasy of omnipresence and the fear of claustrophobia." The point subtly captures a wider trait of French thought that is often concealed by a bombastic style and grandiose declarations of intellectual and cultural superiority: a nagging, almost ineffable fragility of spirit. This trait manifests itself in a certain defensiveness, in a casual dismissiveness of outside ideas, and, above all, in a tendency to fall back on stereotypes, negative fantasies, and conspiracy theories. Hence the French predilection for mythological narratives—affirming not only idealizations of progress, virtue, and sacrifice but also darker tropes of betrayal, dispossession, and death. The march of modern French thought has gone from a confident and often brazen optimism to a mood of increasing introspection that is marked by a sense of unease with the world and a sentimental attachment to the heroes and glories of the past.[30]

This book will show that French thought over the past four centuries has been distinctive in several key ways—first in its historical character, meaning both its substantive continuities over time and its references to the past as a source of legitimation or demarcation. Second, French thought stands out in its fixation with the nation and the collective self, which provide an enduring focus of public debate and the philosophical underpinning of assorted conceptions of the good life. It is, third, striking in its extraordinary intensity (ideas are believed not only to matter but, in existential circumstances, to be worth dying for), and fourth, in the belief that communicating specialized forms of knowledge to a wider public is an integral feature of intellectual activity. Finally, French thought is notable for its constant interplay between the themes of order and imagination—or, to put it in terms of specific thinkers, between the cold linearity of Descartes and the unbridled expansiveness of Rousseau. Just as fundamentally, it will be assumed here that it is possible to make meaningful generalizations about the shared intellectual habits of a people as diverse and fragmented as the French—a nation whose fetish for singularity de Gaulle once summed up derisively by citing the country's production of 246 varieties of cheese.

CHAPTER 1

The Skull of Descartes

For the three hundredth anniversary of the death of René Descartes, the French journalist Pierre Dumayet traveled in 1950 to La Haye, where the philosopher had been born in 1596. This village in the Indre-et-Loire had been renamed La Haye–Descartes in his honor in the early nineteenth century, and Dumayet was keen to find out what the locals thought of their most illustrious son, whose seminal work had laid the foundations of rationalist thought. Dumayet's most memorable interviewee was an elderly inhabitant whose name, appropriately enough, was Madame Raison. She affirmed that the inhabitants were delighted to honor their *grand homme*, for he had not only been one of the iconic figures of his age, universally admired for his scientific achievements, but also the "lover of a queen." Intellectual excellence combined with sexual prowess: the cult of Descartes was still flourishing in this remote corner of central France.[1]

In the eighteenth century, the Abbé de Saint-Pierre hailed Descartes not just as an eminent Frenchman but as "one of the greatest men who ever lived" on account of "the remarkable advances he procured to human reason." That Descartes should have played such a central role in French thought is in many respects paradoxical, in view of his life. His early interests were not especially philosophical: he was fascinated by warfare, and his first piece of writing was on the rules of fencing; he spent the period between 1620 and 1627 traveling around Europe and living the life of a gentleman in Paris. Even when he devoted himself to philosophy, he read little: he was fascinated by mathematics and was contemptuous of the classics. For the last two decades of his life, largely to avoid the scrutiny of his work by religious authorities in France, he chose to live in Holland, where he was noted for his "passion for solitude"—not a typically French trait at the time (or, for that matter, since).[2]

Descartes's eminence as a philosopher rests largely on his *Discourse on Method* (1637), one of the most famous texts in the French language. Its fourth part concisely summarizes his notion of philosophical rationalism: a belief in the separation of mind and matter (dualism), the identification of the essence of the soul with thought, and the deductive certainty of existence through the skeptical method of reasoning. The passage in which he presented the latter conclusion was characteristic of Descartes's style, both engaging and intimate:

> I resolved to pretend that nothing which had ever entered my mind was any more true than the illusions of my dreams. But immediately afterwards I became aware that, while I decided thus to think that everything was false, it followed necessarily that I who thought thus must be something; and observing that this truth: *I think, therefore I am* [*cogito ergo sum*], was so certain and so evident that all the most extravagant suppositions of the sceptics were not capable of shaking it, I judged that I could accept it without scruple as the first principle of the philosophy I was seeking.[3]

This notion that thought was the defining attribute of humankind was the cornerstone of Descartes's rationalism. It was a metaphysical proposition, and less an affirmation of particular substantive principles than an invitation to order one's thinking according to clear logical rules—with the potential implication that doing so might elicit different, and possibly conflicting, patterns of reasoning. Hence one of the abiding paradoxes of the Cartesian tradition is that even among his own devotees, the interpretations of Descartes's legacy were enormously varied. The philosopher Jean Le Rond d'Alembert held Descartes as the inspiration for French resistance to tyranny; for the critic Désiré Nisard, he was the force behind French literary genius; the republican thinker Edgar Quinet viewed him as a symbol of Christian humility; and the playwright Marcelle Joignet was only one in a long retinue who lauded him as the progenitor of feminism.[4]

Like all canonical thinkers (and this, of course, added to his renown), his work also provoked criticism and hostility. From the outset, many Catholics believed that his insistence on the primacy of individual reason was a tacit encouragement of irreligiosity and even atheism—hence his work being put by the Vatican on the Index of Prohibited Works. Voltaire thought his science was wrong on all major counts, and that his conception of man was "far removed from reality." Some of his critics deplored his abstraction and rootless universalism; others deemed him a shallow thinker, citing Blaise Pascal's terse dismissal of his philosophy as "useless and uncertain." To this day, Descartes is lambasted for his ruthless determination to provide experimental proof that animals were not sentient beings. Summarizing his seminal influence on the history of Western cruelty to animals, a pet-loving Descartophobe claimed that the philosopher "cut open his [own] wife's poodle."[5]

To exacerbate this glorious cacophony further, the habit also developed of using Cartesianism as a shorthand to describe a range of French cultural traits. For the essayist Charles Péguy, who saluted Descartes as a "cavalryman who set out at a good stride," Cartesian thought was irreducibly Christian (and French) because of its spiritual quality, notably its ability to convey a sense of the experience of God. However, Cartesian skepticism was also associated with more negative collective attitudes, as indicated in one writer's frustrated account of his compatriots' temperament: "Just as Descartes rested his method on his *cogito ergo sum*, whoever wishes to devise the political system which suits us best should start from this premise: we are French, therefore we are born to oppose. We love opposition not for its results, but despite its results: we love it for its own sake. Our mood is combative, and we always need an enemy to fight, a fortress to capture. We like to launch the assault, not so as to enjoy the spoils of victory, but for the pleasure of charging up the ladder."[6]

Nothing more perfectly symbolizes France's obsessive passion for its national philosopher than the fate of Descartes's remains. His body was brought back to his native land from Sweden (where he died) and reburied in 1667, whereupon he became a celebrity even among occultists: a poem refers to a young woman conversing with "the illustrious and learned ghost" of Descartes. The revolutionaries joined in the exchanges a century later, with several abortive attempts to transfer his remains into the Panthéon in the 1790s. After a brief transit at the convent of the Petits Augustins in Paris, his ashes were eventually reinterred in the Saint-Germain-des-Prés Church in 1819—where they remain to this day. But two years later, there was a further twist, as the Institut de France received a skull purporting to be that of Descartes, complete with the signatures of all its former Swedish owners (including a certain Arngren, who, no doubt in honor of the philosopher's mathematical accomplishments, had allegedly displayed it in his gambling den). For the next hundred years, the skull was an object of scientific controversy. Successive generations of French anatomists, phrenologists, and anthropologists argued vigorously about its authenticity. The results fell somewhat short of Cartesian certainty, but were conclusive enough to allow the relic's temporary exhibition in the Jardin des Plantes collection. No doubt to enhance its credibility, the skull was placed next to another cranium bearing the inscription, "Subject who indulged in excessive self-abuse, died an imbecile."[7]

A Broad Church

If, as will be seen in the following chapter, occultism reflected the French penchant for mystery, and the uncovering of what was hidden from plain sight, the Cartesian heritage represented the opposite inclination: a form of reasoning based on logical clarity and the search for certainty. A key aspect here was the rejection of arguments based on religious faith. As the revolutionary playwright Marie-Joseph Chénier put it, Descartes's primary contribution was to "accustom men increasingly to found their knowledge on *examination* rather than *belief*." And so, particularly from the nineteenth century onward, the adjective "Cartesian" ceased to be a purely philosophical term and was increasingly used to denote a style of reasoning deemed to be distinctively Gallic. It was a style that emphasized the importance of providing a fixed and unvarying meaning to concepts; expressing the truth in clear and distinct ideas; arguing with precision and elegance; moving from simple to complex forms; cultivating a sense of moral autonomy and intellectual audacity; and overcoming one's passions and instead approaching issues rationally.[8]

Not that these attributes were always welcomed: a fetish for precision could easily turn into a love of formalism for its own sake; deductive thinking could lead one away from knowledge based on experience; too much autonomy could undermine the benefits of moral solidarity; and excessive boldness could degenerate into the "intoxication of superiority." It was precisely this double-edged quality that the sociologist Émile Durkheim had in mind when he affirmed that Cartesian thinking was "profoundly rooted in [France's] national spirit," before concluding, "Every French person is to some degree, whether consciously or not, a Cartesian."[9]

Part of the appeal of this shared sensibility lay in its flexibility, and indeed its somewhat hazy quality. This fluidity allowed the Cartesian flag to be flown by thinkers and philosophical movements that interpreted rationalism in different ways. During the first half of the nineteenth century, one of the most original standard-bearers of Cartesianism was Auguste Comte, the founder of positivism, whose wider thought will be explored in Chapter 4. Such was Comte's intellectual identification with Descartes (and such, too, was his immodesty) that he compared one of his own early works to the *Discourse on Method* and hailed Descartes as the master of modern philosophy; he also shared Descartes's view that common sense was the best guide to practical morality.[10]

Comte's philosophy was geared toward one overriding goal: the completion of the scientific revolution in human understanding, a revolution he believed had been initiated by Descartes (along with Francis Bacon and Galileo). Comte continued to profess his admiration for Cartesianism in his later, more spiritual works, notably, when he suggested that women were drawn to his philosophy, as they had been to Descartes's, because of their capacity for empathy and their practical common sense. Comte admired Descartes because he had elaborated a new scientific method based on geometric certainty—an approach that had constituted the most decisive breakthrough in modern knowledge and paved the way for Comte's own "social physics." In overall terms, Comte's Cartesianism represented the dogmatic side of the tradition—especially in its search for a unifying, homogeneous doctrine of human understanding and its attachment to the notion of internal discipline and self-mastery, the necessary condition for reconciling man with the objective laws of nature.[11]

A different but no less authoritarian (and metaphysical) form of Cartesian rationalism was invoked by the Doctrinaires, a collection of thinkers who shaped the conservative politics of the July Monarchy, the regime that governed France under the reign of King Louis-Philippe between 1830 and 1848. For François Guizot, one of its principal intellectual figures, Descartes was the symbol of a particular kind of French common sense that was both practical and philosophical: "This common sense is reason, and the French spirit is both rational and reasonable." Against those who viewed skepticism as a potentially subversive philosophical method, the Doctrinaires hastened to quote the first moral maxim of the *Discourse*, in which Descartes stressed the virtue of obeying the laws and customs of one's country and governing oneself "in all other matters according to the most moderate opinions and those furthest from excess." More generally, they emphasized that the purpose of Cartesian doubt was to produce certainty. The Doctrinaire intellectual Charles de Rémusat thus observed that "Cartesian doubt is the method of a genius full of confidence and youthfulness, marching toward the conquest of the new world of the human spirit."[12]

A key element of this modern vision was the separation of philosophical thinking from religious belief: as Victor de Broglie, another of the leading Doctrinaire thinkers, noted, "Descartes set himself and attained the goal of establishing the absolute independence of philosophy from religion, without which there can be neither a philosophy worthy of the name, nor a religion which is solidly grounded." To the extent that the Doctrinaires sought to secularize public life and establish a political system resting on purely rational philosophical foundations, their conception of reason was progressive.

However, their cloistered liberalism was neither egalitarian nor individualistic: its central purpose was to enshrine the ideal of bourgeois rule and to discredit any idea of radical political change.[13]

This agenda left no room for utopian daydreaming: as the quasi-official philosopher of the July Monarchy, Victor Cousin, put it, Descartes's thinking was to be cherished for its "absence of chimeras and illusions." Cousin was Descartes's most enthusiastic and effective nineteenth-century champion, producing a new edition of his works and reorganizing the teaching of philosophy in educational curricula so as to anchor it around his sanitized and ideologically neutered version of Cartesianism: a doctrine whose purpose was to "reveal known truths" about human psychology, spirituality, and the existence of God, and thus justify the status quo.[14]

From the mid-nineteenth century onward, alongside these elitist Comtian and Doctrinaire sensibilities, there also emerged more distinctly democratic versions of Cartesian rationalism. Describing his initiation into Rousseau's thought in his youth, Jules Michelet compared it to "that disposition toward uncertainty and doubt which Descartes requires for the search of the truth." At the time of the 1848 Revolution, which overthrew the July Monarchy and founded the democratic government of the Second Republic, Claude Husson, a philosophy teacher from Caen, hailed Descartes's *cogito* as the dawn of a new age of freedom because it had opened the path toward human enlightenment: "Thought, the spirit, the human self had at last become the defining principle of politics." This Cartesianism, too, was grounded in a metaphysical conception of man. But this was not an egotistical self, retrenched in private contemplation, but rather an individual at one with the universe and imbued with the true spirit of God. By liberating humanity from its false idols, Husson wrote, Descartes's *cogito* had thus "proclaimed the true republican principle."[15]

The philosopher Étienne Vacherot concurred, hailing Descartes (somewhat exaggeratedly) as the initiator of the "complete and absolute emancipation of the human mind." In the opening of his *Politique radicale* (Radical politics) in which he paid fulsome tribute to Descartes, the republican thinker Jules Simon was just as emphatic: "I believe only in my own reason, I submit only to its evidence. Prophecy, tradition, majority have to appear before my reason, as before their supreme judge." The republican statesman Jules Ferry appealed to this humanist conception of rationalism centered around the notion of moral autonomy when he placed his education reforms "in the tradition of Descartes and Bacon, who two centuries ago secularized human knowledge and philosophy."[16]

Yet this Cartesian pedagogy could also be interpreted conservatively. An edited collection of philosophical texts for schoolteachers in the late nineteenth century gave a prominent place to Descartes's "provisional moral-ity," stressing the imperatives of deference to national laws and customs and "self-improvement rather than changing the order of the world"; this was a logical continuation of Victor Cousin's authority-loving Cartesianism. But there were also more combative interpretations. Freemasons of the Grand Orient de France (the largest Masonic organization in the country) struggling to secularize their movement invoked the spirit of Cartesianism (there was a Descartes lodge in Tours).[17]

For those of a more robustly anticlerical disposition, Descartes became a symbol of religious persecution. According to the socialist freethinker Maurice Barthélemy, the philosopher had been a "martyr" of the rationalist cause, as throughout his life he had been "tormented and slandered by religious big-otry." Above all, Cartesian reason could inspire the ideal of a justice based on evidence and rigorous proof, as during the Dreyfus Affair, the case of a Jewish army officer who in 1894 was wrongly convicted of spying for Germany (he was later exonerated). In his memoirs, the socialist leader Léon Blum explained the writer Anatole France's support for the "Dreyfusard" cause as an expression of his "rationalist faith," which he summarized in these terms: "[Anatole France] was a Dreyfusard because the methodical and scientific work of the intellect was in his eyes the only certain reality."[18]

The sheer breadth of this Cartesian rationalism—its positivist celebration of science, its Doctrinaire association with the essence of reason, and its re-publican emphasis on moral autonomy—naturally invited controversy. In his writings on the Dreyfus Affair, the nationalist Maurice Barrès accused the republicans' obsessive Cartesianism of undermining tradition: in this view, which was widely shared among French conservatives, true reason was not an individual but a collective property. From within the education system, some voices criticized the teaching of Cartesian skepticism, saying it led to a partic-ular type of facile French mentality and ultimately produced "rebellious minds without a will to act, quibblers rather than hard workers, critics and dreamers rather than men of action."[19]

The most wide-ranging attack on this type of rationalism came in the first volume of the historian Hippolyte Taine's *Les Origines de la France contempo-raine* (The origins of contemporary France), in which Descartes was identified as the source of a mode of reasoning that had perverted the entire modern French way of thinking. This "classical spirit" purported "to follow in all in-quiry, in all confidence, and without any restraint or precaution, the methods of mathematics; to extract, circumscribe, and isolate a few very simple and general notions, then, without any reference to experience, to compare and combine them, and from the artificial compound thus obtained, to deduce by pure reasoning all the consequences which it contains." For Taine, a critic of the French revolutionary tradition, this Cartesianism had exercised its baleful influence far beyond the confines of pure rationalism: Rousseau and his disciples had fallen under the influence of this mode of reasoning while they were deducing an entire set of political institutions from an abstract theory of human nature.[20]

The Republican Patriot

As the historian Claude Nicolet observed, "Descartes was not a republican, but one could not be a republican without Descartes." The first half of the twentieth century marked the apogee of this republican rationalism, with the tricentenary of the *Discourse* in 1937 turning into a national celebration. The French government issued a special commemorative stamp in Descartes's honor, and the philosopher Henri Bergson came up with his very own Cartesian maxim: "We must act as men of thought, and think as men of action." Commenting on the impact of Descartes's works on his generation, the philosopher Gérard Milhaud observed that "there exists in France a sort of Cartesian mystique which makes of our man a 'hero of the nation.'"[21]

Descartes biographer Charles Adam was barely exaggerating when he noted that "in France today, not a week, indeed not a day passes without someone publicly proclaiming his adhesion to the Cartesian method, or the Cartesian spirit." Adam's Descartes was an imaginative reinvention, a genial philosopher who had founded the "great charter of modern society" and foreshadowed the republican principles of solidarity and fraternity. Likewise, Adam presented Descartes's belief in the universality of common sense as an anticipation of the Third Republic's educational reforms in the late nineteenth century. All the branches of the republican family found a place for Descartes in their pantheon: in his *Descartes social* (The social Descartes), the progressive writer Maxime Leroy sought to demonstrate that the philosopher's concern for social hygiene anticipated the French Saint-Simonian and socialist traditions.[22]

The figure who helped to popularize this republican version of the Cartesian spirit the most was the philosopher Émile Chartier (Alain), whose Radical movement dominated the politics of the later Third Republic. Alain regarded Descartes as the father of modern French thought, "the Prince of Understanding." Through his skeptical method, he said, Descartes had invented a form of reasoning that was centered around the reflective, thinking individual: "No man is more whole than Descartes, no one is less open to fragmentation, no one has thought better from the perspective of the self." (Alain's anthropocentrism extended to embracing the Cartesian postulate that animals were incapable of thought.) In his *Propos* (Commentaries), short and pithy pieces published in the French press and aimed at a general audience, Alain elaborated a practical moral code that drew heavily on Cartesian maxims; he often repeated that there was something Cartesian in every man. Among the values celebrated in this ethic were the spiritual quality of freedom; the importance of self-understanding and of containing one's negative passions; the avoidance of irresolution and the cultivation of self-confidence; the quest for happiness through optimism; the intellectual rewards of solitude; and, above all, the formation of judgment through patient and careful reflection.[23]

Alain's rationalism, too, was highly metaphysical. He likened the justification of republicanism to Descartes's geometry: "an a priori truth and an established rule, to which experience has to be bent." Yet this apparent dogmatism was tempered by a strong dose of individualism, which also was inspired by Cartesian skepticism. Thus Alain's concept of "civic distrust," the cornerstone of his political philosophy, was an extrapolation of Descartes's method of doubt. He believed that citizens should constrain their rulers not by trying to govern in their place, but by subjecting their utterances and deeds to systematic scrutiny in the same way as a logician would treat a philosophical proposition. This "power of refusal" (and this concept, too, was very Cartesian) was to be forged away from large gatherings, where individual judgment could too easily be swayed by wider groups. Instead, it was ideally exercised by the "solitary" citizen "seeking not to harmonize his thought with that of his neighbor." Alain's conception of citizenship was an original synthesis of Cartesianism with republicanism: "If we wish a public life which is worthy of Humanity, the individual must remain the individual everywhere. Only the individual is capable of thought."[24]

The culmination of this celebration of Descartes as the emblem of republican rationalism was his coronation as symbol of the nation. One of the philosopher's most valuable assets in the later nineteenth century, in the context of the heightened salience of German thought in the wake of the Franco-Prussian War of 1870–1871, was precisely his Frenchness: he was incontrovertibly Gallic in his catholic spirit as well as in his literary genius, which was "embedded in the French language, proceeding from the same order and following its movement and rhythm." World War I was a turning point in this nationalist metamorphosis. Alain, who was a combatant, made a number of pointed references to Descartes's "swordsmanship" in his postwar writings.[25]

Others were less subtle. In a study published in 1921, the philosopher Jacques Chevalier credited Descartes with inspiring France's victory. He described the supreme military commander Marshal Ferdinand Foch as the highest embodiment of the Cartesian spirit. The heroism of the peasants who had fought to defend their land against German barbarity was also deemed "Cartesian," as it expressed the philosopher's cherished virtues of hard work, common sense, and dedication to the common good. The textual basis of the latter claim was slim, but this was no time for literary nuance. The *Discourse on Method* represented the "essence of French spirit," a judicious synthesis of dualities: "realism and idealism, aptitude for action and taste for contemplation, the cold audacity of thought and the burning flame of sentiment, a cult of positivity, which always subjects its conclusions to the light of evidence, and a passionate belief in spiritual reality, which constantly drives humanity to transcend nature and surpass itself." And just in case this lengthy catalog was somehow deemed insufficient, Chevalier also recruited Descartes's philosophy to spearhead a supremely patriotic objective: "the liberation of French thought from the yoke of German thinking."[26]

As World War II approached, this Cartesian nationalism resurfaced, as when the writer Georges Duhamel referred to the French cultural presence in Europe as the "Descartes Line," an intellectual extension of the Maginot fortifications. The historian Henri Berr invoked Descartes's spirit as the inspiration for the French values of "reason, truth and humanity," which contrasted with Hitler's Machiavellian spirit of "savagery and barbarity."[27]

Further Cartesian echoes were heard between 1940 and 1944 as France endured military defeat and as resistance groups both inside and outside the country challenged the occupying forces and their collaborationist allies in the Vichy regime. Many conservative antirepublican intellectuals were quick to blame France's swift capitulation to Hitler on its cult of rationalism, which they claimed had sapped the nation's spiritual heritage and diverted the people from the sincerity and openness of the Catholic tradition. Approving the Vichy government's ban on secret societies in 1940, an editorial in a conservative newspaper observed that Freemasons were devotees of the Cartesian maxim "I advance wearing a mask." Another writer added, "We will have to turn our backs on Descartes if we wish to live and endure as a nation." More chillingly, the Vichy education minister, Abel Bonnard, demanded that Descartes be "thrown out of the window."[28]

In 1941, in a powerful echo of Taine's negative view of the French revolutionary tradition, an article in the reactionary *Nouvelle Revue Française* lambasted what it termed the "Cartesian ideal of clarity" for its perversion of French thought since the eighteenth century. It was responsible, according to the author, for the introduction of democracy, the undermining of religious beliefs, the rejection of traditionalist values, and the elimination of patriotism. The consequences of this intellectualist mode of reasoning had been devastating: the French had become obsessed with individualism, which had corroded both public and private spheres; the defeat of 1940 had been a direct consequence of the blindness of French elites, which stemmed from their fetish for a priori reasoning.[29]

Resistance groups did not engage with, let alone respond in detail to, such broadsides: as the historian Henri Michel noted, this was primarily a time for action, and indeed there was a reluctance to engage in theoretical and philosophical reflection during the war years. But it was not too difficult to find Cartesian presences, both symbolic and substantive, among those French patriots who refused to surrender in 1940—such as the communist Georges Politzer, who before the war had celebrated Descartes as the incarnation of a "rationalism in movement." Another emblematic hero of the French Resistance was the Sorbonne philosopher Jean Cavaillès; his colleague Georges Canguilhem later explained Cavaillès's commitment to the armed struggle against the Nazis as the logical consequence of his philosophical rationalism. When Cavaillès was asked to give a lecture to his fellow detainees in November 1942 during his internment in the camp of Saint-Paul-d'Eyjeaux, he spoke on "Descartes and His Method." In the first issue of *L'Université libre* (The free university), a clandestine communist journal aimed at a highly educated readership, the editorial affirmed, "In the country of Descartes, reason will remain victorious!"[30]

Descartes's spirit also haunted the collective imagination of the French Resistance for a deeper reason. In the early years of the conflict, France's moral and spiritual condition was frequently compared to a *tabula rasa* (blank slate)—there was a sense that all moral and political certainties had been invalidated; one observer spoke of the "undoing of all norms." Everything had to be reconstructed from scratch, hence the Cartesian undertones of General de Gaulle's Appeal of June 18, 1940, which called on the French people to continue the struggle against Germany. This proclamation rested not on a universal moral imperative, but rather on an appeal to the conscience of each individual citizen—a point noted by many members of the Resistance. There was also an undeniably Cartesian quality to the general's own frame of mind during the war years: in his elevation above and retrenchment from the world (what he would later describe as "the need to reach the summit and never descend"); in his skeptical refusal to take anything for granted, even (and, indeed, especially) the support of his immediate allies; and in his repeated intention to follow the "straight path" to national liberation—a direct echo of the second moral maxim in the *Discourse*, which Descartes had expressed in the form of advice to travelers lost in a forest: "They must always walk as straight as they can in a given direction, and not change direction for weak reasons."[31]

The Existentialist Hero

In his diaries from the early years of World War II, the philosopher Jean-Paul Sartre recalled how reading Descartes had been one of his principal refuges from the dullness of the philosophy taught at the École Normale Supérieure. Along with his intellectual comrades Paul Nizan and Raymond Aron, he embraced Descartes as an "explosive thinker," a "revolutionary who ripped and slashed while leaving to others the task of stitching things up again." This was a doubly appropriate comment for the period 1939–1940: it bore witness to the disintegration of French collective values as well as the beginning of Sartre's personal quest to redefine the concept of freedom. The major product of this enterprise was existentialism, a new form of philosophical rationalism that would dominate French intellectual life in the postwar years, under the impetus of Sartre, his companion the writer Simone de Beauvoir, and the novelist and philosopher Albert Camus. Disseminated in a range of literary forms—from complex philosophical texts to shorter works of nonfiction, journal articles, plays, and novels—existential ideas attempted to make sense of an era of moral and political uncertainty, seeking a solution to the apparent meaninglessness of existence. In Camus's words: "The world in itself is unreasonable, and the absurd lies in the confrontation of this irrationality with the unrelenting desire for clarity whose call emanates from deep within man." Theirs was a quest to define an authentic self, a self for which there was no blueprint, but which nonetheless had to withstand the test of universality. As Sartre put it in *Being and Nothingness*, "Man being condemned to freedom carries the weight of the entire world on his shoulders."[32]

Sartre's existentialism was largely derived from his readings of the phenomenology of the German idealist philosopher Edmund Husserl, but there was also a distinct Cartesian premise to his thinking. Although it displayed some continuity with its pre-1940 rationalist and republican predecessors, this Sartrian Cartesianism was also strikingly different. In 1944 Sartre published an edited collection of Descartes's philosophical texts. In the introduction, he hailed the inventor of the *cogito* as the founder of the notion of free will as well as the architect of modern democracy ("For one could not base universal suffrage on anything other than the universal capacity to say yes or no"). Above all, the Sartrian Descartes had anticipated existentialism, for he had understood that the concept of liberty was at the heart of human self-realization, and that freedom "contained within itself the imperative of absolute autonomy." Sartre returned to this metaphysical theme a year later in his public lecture on existentialism: "There can be no other truth, from the outset, than this: *I think therefore I am*, this is the absolute truth of consciousness coming to a realization of itself." His critics pointed out that it was no accident that Sartre chose to base his ideal of the human yearning for freedom in Descartes: as a pure property of the mind, Cartesian freedom seemed to require no form of political action, and could thus legitimize Sartre's lack of active participation in the Resistance.[33]

Existentialism was pilloried in the postwar years for its seeming lack of good cheer: the characters in existentialist fiction (Roquentin in Sartre's *Nausea*, or Meursault in Camus's *The Stranger*) seemed more inclined to adopt the false and socially contrived values of *mauvaise foi* (bad faith) than to embrace their "authentic" or true selves. Sartre's emphasis on the irreducible individuality of consciousness also led some progressives to regard existentialism as merely a spruced-up version of the democratic and republican traditions of Cartesianism. There were some superficial similarities: there was a certain echo of Alain, for example, in Sartre's paradoxical comment of 1944 that "we were never more free than under German occupation." By this he meant that the extreme circumstances of the occupation, and the possibility that certain individual choices could result in death, brought about a true appreciation of the meaning of freedom. In this sense, Sartre's existentialism attempted to jettison what he perceived as the more cumbersome elements of the classical rationalist heritage. It held up the prospect of a radical and creative form of freedom, but in a moral universe in which there was no God or teleology, no agreed normative ideals of the kind upon which the Comtian and Doctrinaire accounts relied, and not even the reassuring fiction of a progressive human nature to underpin republican rationalism. From his ethereal vantage point, Sartre concluded, "We are alone."[34]

Despite their best efforts to offer a collective (and optimistic) horizon for their doctrine, existentialist thinkers struggled to define their conception of the free life and the ensemble of values and virtues they thought desirable. The "humanism" to which Sartre appealed in 1945 was essentially a reprise of German idealism, and in the ensuing years he abandoned his project of constructing a system of morality. The solution eventually came through a progressive ethic of liberation—an obvious philosophical extension of the experiences of the Resistance. This ideal was formulated in different ways. The Sartrian notion of *engagement* was centered on a universalist norm of intellectual responsibility. Writing thus became a form of action, an intervention in the collective search for freedom, with the novelist henceforth assuming the task of "taking a stand against all injustices, wherever they come from."[35]

Camus adopted a similar premise in his concept of "revolt," which brought with it the possibility of overcoming the absurd through the practice of collective solidarity: as he put it in a strikingly neo-Cartesian formula, "in the daily ordeal we face, revolt plays the same role as the *cogito* in the order of thought: it is the first principle. But this principle removes man from his solitude. It is a common theme which gives value to all human endeavors. I revolt, therefore we exist." Camus was careful to distinguish this humanist revolt, which had modest and concrete objectives, from the concept of "revolution," which in contrast aspired to an impossible harmonization of humanity: such an enterprise could only, in his view, end in mass murder and oppression.[36]

Simone de Beauvoir's writings also described the difficulty of finding a positive existential ethic "beyond the consolation of falsehood and that of resignation." Comparing existentialist philosophy to Descartes's revolt against the *malin génie* ("evil demon" or "evil genius," whose aim is to provide a completely misleading account of the world, a figure deployed by Descartes as part of his method of using systematic doubt to arrive at certain knowledge), she attempted to define a "morality of ambiguity" in which freedom was achieved "by the realization of each individual existence as an absolute."[37]

In her philosophy Beauvoir drew considerably from the Resistance (like Sartre, she did this partly as an overcompensation for her political inactivity during the war years). The heavy potential cost of freedom was illustrated in her 1945 novel *Le Sang des autres* (The blood of others), where the character Blomart, the head of a Resistance network, wrestles with the dilemma of sending those under his command to their deaths. He eventually assumes the burden, even though it leads to the demise of Hélène, the woman he loves: "Formerly, he had dreamt of justifying his acts with strikingly logical reasons; but this would be too easy. He had to act without any guarantees." Another hypothetical example from the Resistance was used to illustrate the notion of responsibility: "It is up to us to decide whether we must kill one man to save ten, or let ten die in order not to betray one; neither in the heavens nor on earth is the decision written down. However I choose, I shall betray my profound desire to respect human life. And yet I have to make a choice." Beauvoir later acknowledged the intellectual limitations of such reflections as the basis for a theory of moral action.[38]

The most convincing articulation of existentialism (and the one with the most far-reaching consequences) came in Beauvoir's *Le Deuxième Sexe* (*The Second Sex*, 1949), a seminal work that applied the doctrine's insights to the feminine condition. Rejecting the classic view of gender as constituted by human nature, Beauvoir argued that sexual character was "ambiguous" and not biologically determined: "One is not born, but one becomes a woman." This conditioning, she claimed, is a cultural construct, a product of myths and experience combining to create an "imperialism of consciousness" that maintains the domination of men over women. The book ends by opening up the horizon of sexual liberation, which she believed would be achieved through women reappropriating their bodies and helping to forge a new relationship with men based on the ideals of equality and fraternity.[39]

Descartes Joins the Communist Party

"Some would have us believe that these decadent aesthetes and existentialists represent the authentic French spirit, whereas they only express the ideological decomposition of the bourgeoisie. In philosophy as in literature, these forces of reaction are trying to undermine the old optimistic and conquering spirit of our nation, which goes from Descartes to Paul Langevin, and which exalts human dignity, reason, and liberty." Published in a French communist philosophical review in 1947, this diatribe summed up the party's manifest contempt for existentialism. Its perceived bleakness and parochialism were contrasted with the communists' luminous conception of reason, which is represented here by Descartes and the renowned physicist Paul Langevin, who had spent the war years under Vichy house arrest before joining the communist fold in 1946. (This was also a carefully coded swipe at Sartre's less salubrious war record.)[40]

Descartes became one of the principal standard-bearers of French communist rationalism from the mid-1930s, and the qualities he symbolized bore witness to its versatile character. His name was frequently conjured up as proof of the historical depth of the radical tradition in French culture and its continuing embodiment in the Communist Party. In the words of the party daily *L'Humanité*, Descartes "had inaugurated the independence of human thought from all dogmas"; he was thus "one of the most eminent representatives of human progress." This grandeur was lavishly displayed in communist publications and rituals. During annual commemorative marches to honor the memory of past revolutionary martyrs, for example, communist militants carried the portraits of writers who had been "the glory of France." Descartes featured prominently in this pantheon, alongside Rousseau, Voltaire, Denis Diderot, Émile Zola, and Victor Hugo. In the aftermath of the Resistance, as the party prepared to join General de Gaulle's French provisional government in the wake of the liberation of Paris in 1944, Descartes was also deployed to underscore communism's impeccable national credentials: communist ideology was thus presented as the inheritor of a tradition of excellence beginning with "Montaigne, Rabelais and Descartes."[41]

As part of this progressive lineage, Descartes symbolized the communist attachment to the defense and dissemination of high culture within France. From the mid-1930s, the party created the "Descartes Circle," a cycle of public lectures whose purpose was to stimulate discussion of scientific and philosophical issues as well as major questions of international politics. The philosopher's name was also repeatedly used to promote the ideal of mass education—in notable contrast to conservative and fascist conceptions of culture. For the three hundredth anniversary of Descartes's death in 1950, the communists organized an exhibition on the philosopher; it started in Paris and was then staged in Marseille, Grenoble, Lyon, and Montpellier. And when the communist publisher Éditions Sociales launched its series of "popular classics," Descartes's *Discourse* was, naturally, among the first titles to be released. The qualities associated with this communist Cartesianism included clear thinking and analytical lucidity as well as a robust nationalist spirit. In 1955 the communists waged a vigorous campaign to oppose the French government's attempts to introduce the teaching of the English language in secondary schools. Arguing that such projects were merely "an attempt to enslave the French nation to American imperialism," one communist intellectual claimed that the continuing study of French writers such as Descartes was integral to a sound education, as it helped the nation form citizens who "embraced the ideals of peace and freedom, and would not wish to become slaves or docile mercenaries."[42]

This humanist Descartes, the symbol of French national genius, was given its most emphatic depiction by the communist leader Maurice Thorez in a speech at the Sorbonne in May 1946: "He teaches us hope and confidence, faith in human intelligence, a love for the all-conquering power of labor. His philosophy inspires us to action and tells us that we can forge our own destinies. The world loves France because in our country, it recognizes Descartes and those who have continued his oeuvre." But there also emerged more doctrinal communist representations. The philosopher Henri Mougin claimed that the scientific contribution of Cartesianism stemmed less from Descartes's substantial discoveries than from his method, which rested on a distinct epistemology: "The unity of intelligence is both the symbol and the instrument of a larger unity: the unity of thought."[43]

This assertion went to the heart of the French communist conception of reason, which was fundamentally monistic and made no distinction between the humanities and social sciences, on the one hand, and the natural sciences, on the other. Furthermore, in opposition to idealist interpretations, this communist philosophical reading treated Descartes's thought as essentially materialist, claiming that the main purpose of his science was to make sense of the objective world. Although Mougin recognized an element of ambivalence in Descartes's philosophy with respect to the relationship between mind and matter, he insisted on a resolutely materialist interpretation of Cartesianism:

far from celebrating the solitary character of human thinking, the fundamental thrust of the *cogito* was "the installation of thought in the world." The philosopher Henri Lefebvre completed the picture. Although it had failed to escape completely from the clutches of idealism, Descartes's geometric reason had constituted a revolution in modern thinking: it had paved the way for Marx's practical reason, as it had been geared toward understanding and resolving the problems of the modern age. Buttressed by excerpts from Marx and Engels's *Holy Family*, this scientific and materialist interpretation turned Descartes into one of the intellectual progenitors of the French revolutionary tradition.[44]

There was a certain tension among these different communist conceptions of reason. The humanist version reflected the party's genuine belief in the value of learning and its commitment (through its extensive network of associations) to the popular dissemination of French high culture; in this respect, the communists were the true inheritors of the republican tradition. The "scientific" Descartes, however, was potentially problematic, as he tapped into the party's dogmatic instincts on fundamental moral and philosophical questions. This variety of Cartesianisms opened the door to some risqué adaptations, as when an article on the civic achievements of Soviet communism (published as the Stalinist purges were getting under way in 1937) claimed that "the Cartesian formula 'I think therefore I am'" had been replaced in Russia by this new ideal: "I exist, therefore I have rights."[45]

More mundanely, Descartes was recruited to enhance the communist electoral turnout: in 1946, to the surprise of its author, an article on Descartes's philosophy was used to call for a positive vote in a forthcoming constitutional referendum (the author later humorously summed up this campaign as "Descartes Votes Yes"). As the postwar French communist cult of the Soviet Union reached its zenith, rationalism degenerated into mysticism and then into outright religiosity. But thanks to Descartes, this spiritualism could at least be rendered *aux couleurs de la France* (in French colors): as the novelist Jean-Richard Bloch put it, in a fetching anachronism: "When I started to examine Stalin's life, his actions and his works, I was struck by their transparency, their lucidity, their precision. Had Stalin been French, we would use the expression 'Cartesian logic' about his thinking. There is no one more 'Cartesian' than Stalin."[46]

A Triumphant Reason

Nationalism and universality, individualism and the collective spirit, spiritualism and science, cerebral Parisian elitism and contented provincial modesty:

Descartes's method and maxims have been appropriated as a source of legitimation by a range of cultural sensibilities in the modern era. This phenomenon may be taken as evidence of the creative ambiguity of his thought, an essential precondition of philosophical *longue durée*. But it also underscores its irreducible Frenchness. The contrast with Britain is particularly striking here: none of the great philosophers of the empiricist tradition is celebrated as a national symbol in Britain; the only comparable figure in British culture would be Shakespeare, but he was not what the French would call an intellectual. Above all, the heritage of Descartes bears witness to France's enduring fascination with a certain mode of thinking that he typified—bold and ambitious in its aspirations; fluent but controlled in its style; deductive and essentialist (not to say dogmatic) in its form; combative and oppositional in its instincts; while also, paradoxically, wedded to the ideals of clarity and certainty.

For, notwithstanding its variations, there was real substance to the notion of an *esprit cartésien*. Associated with the concept of a detached, skeptical, and critical self, it expressed the belief that reason was the defining feature of the human condition, and that reason was, moreover, the only source of our ability to make moral judgments and impose a durable conceptual order on the world. From the Doctrinaires to the communists, French rationalists also shared the view that reason was an invigorating, empowering attribute: both negatively, as a way of shaking off established temporal and spiritual dogmas (even if only to replace them with others), and positively, in providing an instrument for dominating nature and improving the human condition. Cartesianism was especially important in defining a sense of Frenchness that rested on an essentialized and undivided conception of the self. It is no accident that Descartes furnished the philosophical underpinning of modern republican nationalism; indeed, as we shall see later, his holistic metaphysic remains at the heart of the implacable French hostility to multiculturalism. In this sense, the Cartesian legacy highlights something important about modern French culture: behind the political instability and frequent changes of regime in the century and a half that followed the Revolution, there were strong underlying elements of philosophical unity in French elite thinking.

In the 1960s, this rationalism started to come under increasing strain as its conception of the individual thinking subject was contested (notably, by "structuralist" philosophers who questioned key rationalist assumptions, such as the very possibility of a fixed and unchanging notion of meaning). Yet these challenges only demonstrated (yet again) the adaptative capacities of Cartesianism. In 1987 the philosopher André Glucksmann, one of the leading figures in the anti-Marxist "new philosophy" movement, published his *Descartes, c'est la France* (Descartes is France), in which he argued that the real spirit of

Cartesianism lay not in the bombastic rationalism of the French progressive tradition but in a much more sober, tempered, and prudent conception of reason—a rationalism without illusions. (Glucksmann also made much of the fact that Descartes's philosophy had been known as "the new philosophy.")[47]

Contemporary devotees have readily embraced this more modest "Descartes-lite." The philosopher Pierre Guenancia thus argued that Descartes was the most effective antidote to the excesses of state power and the rising tide of communitarian thinking, both of which threatened to undermine the sovereignty of individual reason. His colleague Denis Moreau commended Descartes for helping him confront practical dilemmas: overcoming his sense of disorientation, remaining faithful in his marriage, reconciling his rationalism with his Christian faith, and even understanding the conceptual limits of television. Even as radical a critic of Descartes's philosophical individualism as the sociologist Bruno Latour, who believes that thought is irreducibly collective and that it is "precisely *because* we are numerous, supported, instituted and instrumented that we accede to the truth," could not help ordering his analysis around the Cartesian *cogito*.[48]

Further evidence of Descartes's enduring value as a national symbol is the revival of the (admittedly undecorous) saga concerning his remains. In 2009, François Fillon (who was then prime minister) sought to have the philosopher's skull moved from the Musée de l'Homme (where it was at one point exhibited next to a cast of the French soccer player Lilian Thuram) to his electoral stronghold in the *département* of the Sarthe; a few years later, some Radical parliamentarians proposed that his body be moved to the Panthéon. Yet Descartes is also still celebrated for the literary qualities of his writings; in this sense, perhaps the ultimate accolade for the creator of the *cogito* is his continuing capacity to inspire the musings of French playwrights, novelists, poets, and scriptwriters, all of whom find something (different) to celebrate in his life and philosophy: his capacity to be "at home in all of Europe while truly belonging to no place"; his devotion to God; his love for his daughter, Francine, whose tragic early death left him "distraught"; his contempt for verbosity and useless agitation and his embodiment of "virtuous humility"; his ability to inspire a sense of "pathological doubt"; his sense of adventure and anticipation of romanticism as "a knight of the impossible, brother of d'Artagnan." In a four-part drama filmed in Brittany and based on Celtic legends, Descartes's *oeuvre* provides a fictional computer technician, Chris, with the means of overcoming a malevolent force springing from a rock.[49]

There are no limits to these Descartes fantasies and appropriations, notably when the satirical journalist Frédéric Pagès suggested, with tongue firmly in cheek, that the real reason for Descartes's domiciliation in Holland was his penchant for hallucinogenic drugs. In 2012 the horticulturist Guy André created a rose of an apricot-pink shade in the national philosopher's name; inaugurating it in the public gardens of the town of Descartes, he described it as "an international rose, serious in its behavior and Latin in its color." Not to be outdone, long-serving manager of the Lorient Football Club, Christian Gourcuff, declared at the end of his final season that his "4-4-2 technique" was "Cartesian." The painter Brigitte Clamon, who frequently uses geometrical figures in her art, made the same claim about her technique—though she conceded, upon further questioning, that she also allowed her lines to flow "spontaneously." She concluded, "This is paradoxical." And the deductive qualities of the Cartesian mind could not fail to inspire crime writers. In *L'Échelle de Monsieur Descartes* (The ladder of Monsieur Descartes), a mysterious murder set in Paris in 1648 is solved by the intrepid Inspector René, who is armed with nothing more than a pencil, a few sheets of paper, and "his triumphant reason."[50]

CHAPTER 2

Darkness and Light

As the rule of President François Mitterrand drew to a close, and in the immediate aftermath of his death in January 1996, the French people made a number of discoveries about this enigmatic figure, the first socialist to be elected to the presidency under the Fifth Republic. It emerged that Mitterrand had shown some sympathy for the nationalist extreme right in the 1930s, and that he had been quietly supporting a second family (at the state's expense) for the previous two decades.[1]

Just as unsettling, however, was the revelation that Mitterrand, an intellectual politician, a man of the Left and therefore an inheritor of France's distinguished tradition of philosophical rationalism, had been holding regular meetings with the astrologer Élizabeth Teissier at the Élysée Palace. The author of widely consulted (if not unerringly accurate) horoscopes, Teissier became Mitterrand's trusted confidante between 1989 and 1995. According to her best-selling memoirs, she found that he exuded a "very strong magnetism." His career, she said, fell under the aura of the "Black Moon," the source of soul-searching and renewal in astrological lore. Indeed, she claimed to have unearthed "mysterious but powerful cosmic connections" between his destiny and that of the Fifth Republic. The president took her counsel not only about private issues concerning his family and his health, but also on matters of state, great and small. During the Gulf War, Mitterrand would sometimes call her twice a day. He asked her to draw up astrological profiles of his prime ministers and senior ministers and sought her advice about the timing of his political initiatives. Thus—in a first in modern French constitutional history—it was at the astrologer's explicit behest that a date was chosen for an important referendum: the September 20, 1992, vote ratifying the Maastricht Treaty that created the European Union.[2]

Teissier was awarded a doctorate in sociology by the Sorbonne in 2001. This might be dismissed as a minor aberration of the French university system, just as it could be tempting to write off Mitterrand's sudden interest in astrology as an unconventional response to the collapse of the Cold War order in Europe—or simply as an eccentricity of an aging—and increasingly ailing—European leader. The same might be said to explain how this leader could declare to his perplexed compatriots, during his final New Year's broadcast in 1994, "I believe in the forces of the spirit, and I will not leave you." Yet the president was merely the most recent in a long line of modern French rulers, from the 1789 Revolution onward, who have believed that supernatural forces were shaping their destiny and the fate of the French nation.[3]

Maximilien Robespierre, the implacable leader of the Terror, celebrated a mystical deistic cult and was hailed as a messiah by a group of devotees, the Theotists; some of his supporters could even discern a "Robespierre constellation" in the night sky. Napoleon Bonaparte was not as superstitious as his first wife, Joséphine, who regularly consulted one of the great fortune-tellers of the era, Madame Lenormant. But the emperor nevertheless frequently referred to his "good star," which he claimed he could precisely locate in the firmament, often pointing it out to his bemused entourage. Ahead of the Battle of Waterloo, as he sensed the tide turning against him, he traveled to the Malmaison Palace in a desperate (and vain) attempt to catch another sight of his celestial talisman. A few decades later, in 1857, his nephew Napoleon III invited the renowned medium Daniel Dunglas Home to the Tuileries Palace. Home conjured the appearance of a little white hand, which the Empress Eugénie recognized as that of her deceased father. However, the hand reappeared at a later session and this time carefully signed the name of Napoleon Bonaparte.[4]

The era of republican democracy since the late nineteenth century has done little to contain this passion for celestial guidance and metaphysical communion with the afterlife. On the contrary, some of the greatest figures of the Third Republic are believed to have called upon the services of fortune-tellers, including Jean Jaurès, Aristide Briand, Raymond Poincaré, and Georges Clemenceau. After World War II, the trend continued, again cutting across political divides, with devotees including the socialist president Vincent Auriol and the conservative prime minister Antoine Pinay. In addition to President Mitterrand, a striking recent example of this political stargazing is Charles de Gaulle, the Resistance leader and founder of the Fifth Republic. It is a little-known fact that the general discreetly consulted astrologer Maurice Vasset throughout his presidency. Vasset was a major in the French Army, and the two men first met in Toulon in August 1944; de Gaulle praised Vasset as "a good soldier and a good astrologer." This information perhaps puts a new complexion on one of the concluding sentences of the general's *War Memoirs*, when he declares, "Gazing at the stars, I take the full measure of the insignificance of things."[5]

From the late Middle Ages onward, starting with the apocalyptic divinations of the French apothecary Nostradamus, whose *Prophecies* were published in a series of installments in the mid-sixteenth century, there has been a consistent French interest in combining the observation of stars with magic and history in order to uncover the hidden meaning of the universe. A doctoral dissertation on the commercial practice of occultism in 1934 found the trade to be flourishing across the country, with clients from all walks of life; in 1954, it was estimated that France had 50,000 fortune-tellers. This belief in some form of mystical, transcendental order remains widespread in contemporary France: it is estimated that around 10 million French men and women consult an astrologer every year. Major bookstores, such as the FNAC chain, have well-stocked sections of esoteric literature; according to official trade figures, just over 6 million copies of such books were printed in France in 2011—more than on religion, and nearly as many as on history. Sociologists have attempted to explain the phenomenon as a response to the isolation produced by modern individualism, the survival of superstitious beliefs, and the destruction of traditional religious myths by science. Yet these explanations are too simple, overemphasizing the contrast between past and present, between positive knowledge and esoteric belief, and, most notably, between secular and religious thought. For between the poles of theology and materialism there lies a rich hinterland combining a commitment to rationalism with a faith in the supernatural. This sensibility has been a constant feature of modern intellectual life in France and continues to shape how the French think.[6]

The Heavenly City

Many of the central tenets of French occultism—its belief in man's goodness and capacity for self-mastery, its readiness to embrace different cultures and values, its sense of mystery, its notion of an underlying harmony in the universe and its search for a new form of spirituality—are rooted in Enlightenment thinking. This may sound paradoxical, inasmuch as the dominant ideas of the eighteenth century are typically associated with religious skepticism and the rejection of metaphysical and supernatural beliefs. In *Philosophical and Political History*, Enlightenment thinker Guillame-Thomas Raynal concluded bullishly, "The world is too enlightened to be taken in by incomprehensible propositions which are an affront to reason, or be fooled by the wondrous lies which are common to all religions, and prove none of them."[7]

The same forthright rationalism was expressed in the emblematic compendium of Enlightenment thinking, the *Encyclopédie*. Published in twenty-eight volumes between 1751 and 1772 under the direction of Denis Diderot and Jean Le Rond d'Alembert, this monumental work counted among its contributors the era's most distinguished *philosophes*: Voltaire, Rousseau, Montesquieu, and d'Holbach. The *Encyclopédie* sought to highlight the technical advances of the modern age and the unity of human knowledge as well as its irreducibly secular character. Religion was treated as an inferior form of understanding, barely distinct from superstition: in the tree of knowledge, it was placed on a remote branch, right next to black magic, and the philosopher was celebrated as the provider of specific (as opposed to speculative) knowledge. As the *Encyclopédie* entry put it, "Other men walk in darkness; the philosopher, even in his passions, acts only after reflection; he walks through the night, but preceded by a torch. The philosopher forms his principles on an infinity of particular observations. He does not confuse truth with plausibility; he takes for truth what is true, for forgery what is false, for doubtful what is doubtful, and probable what is probable. The philosophical spirit is thus a spirit of observation and accuracy."[8]

Yet for all its claims to concentrate on experience and to eliminate knowledge based upon faith, conjecture, and fantasy, the *Encyclopédie* itself was not entirely exempt from these tendencies. The entry on the tropical plant *agaty*, for example, claimed that its root had the power to "dissipate tumors" when crushed and mixed with cow urine. In fact, the leading thinkers of the eighteenth century were much more ambivalent about metaphysical questions than their buoyant public statements implied. The case of Voltaire is, in this respect, exemplary. He never wavered in his strident denunciation of monotheistic religions, observing, for example, that Christianity was "assuredly the most ridiculous, the most absurd and the most bloody religion which has ever infected this world." He was equally contemptuous of sorcery, astrology, and alchemy, regretting toward the end of his life that these matters remained an object of intellectual fascination for his compatriots. But, like most of the *philosophes*, Voltaire was also a deist. This was partly a matter of expediency (he loudly assured Pope Benedict XIV of his Christian sentiments in order to facilitate his election to the Académie Française in 1746). But he also seems genuinely to have believed that the structure of the universe was underpinned by a purposive harmony that was proof of the "wisdom and benevolence" of God. As Voltaire put it, "for a very long time people mocked at occult causes. We should rather ridicule those who doubt them. . . . Vegetables, minerals, animals, where is your first principle? It is in his hand who made the sun turn on its axis and clothed it in light." In making such an assertion, Voltaire was giving voice to one of the most important features of the Enlightenment's intellectual revolution: its substitution of natural harmony for divine revelation. This transformation was completed in the writings of Diderot and Rousseau, whose idea of natural religion effectively recycled traditional Christian notions of the Garden of Eden, the myth of a Golden Age and the purification of the soul. Behind its rhetoric of rupture, the Enlightenment's idealization of humanity was thus rooted in Christian theology. As has rightly been observed, "The *philosophes* demolished the Heavenly City of St Augustine only to rebuild it with more up-to-date materials."[9]

It is only against this spiritual backdrop that we can make sense of all the key precepts of the later Enlightenment and their links with occultist thinking: the belief in the Great Chain of Being, a faith in progress and a confidence in man's ability to transform his material and social environment. Above all, this ideal of nature produced a subtle amendment to the Cartesian vision of human reason. There was a growing sense that the essential attribute of rationality was not so much its analytical, mathematical quality as its ability to express man's "internal energy," notably, through such spiritual faculties as feeling, imagination, and enthusiasm. The Abbé de Saint-Pierre defined the *grand homme* as the one who "procured great advantages to society through his actions" thanks to his "particular qualities of mind and heart." For some, like Diderot, the essence of humanity lay in the heart: "The passions always inspire us rightly, for they inspire us only with the desire for happiness. It is the mind that misleads us and makes us take false roads." To find the true standard for knowledge and moral behavior, so Rousseau intimated in *Émile* (1762), man needed to "*rentrer en soi-même*" (look into himself) and consult his "inner light." In his *Esquisse d'un tableau historique des progrès de l'esprit humain* (Sketch for a historical picture of the progress of the human spirit, 1793–1794), Condorcet affirmed that nature had provided all men with a "delicate and generous sensibility" and a capacity for "active and enlightened benevolence"; he explicitly likened the better world that would emerge in the future to an earthly paradise, an "Elysium created by reason."[10]

The Cult of Humanity

The doctrine of Illuminism provides a more specific illustration of how Enlightenment thinking could blend so harmoniously with esoteric and mystical forms of belief. Illuminism spread across Europe in the later decades of the eighteenth century, largely through secret societies such as the Freemasonry.

In his classic polemic against the French Revolution, Abbé Augustin Barruel lambasted Illuminists and Freemasons as the principal agents of the "antisocial conspiracy" that had overthrown the old order in the name of atheism.[11]

Yet Freemasons in France worshiped their own divinity, the "Great Architect of the Universe," who was typically represented in luminous form. Illuminist doctrine was a spiritual creed that asserted the unity of all natural elements and preached a moral resurgence that would eventually lead to man's reintegration into primal being. Its disciples searched for manifestations of the supernatural and practiced sorcery and divination. Louis-Claude de Saint-Martin, the leading French advocate of Illuminism, welcomed the French Revolution as an act of Providence, the first step in "a kind of magic operation" in which the principle of popular sovereignty would be completed by restoring the "spiritual theocracy" between God and man. Replete with references to bright stars and dazzling rays of light, Saint-Martin's writings provide an eclectic mélange of classical philosophical allusions (notably to his heroes Pascal and Rousseau), religious revivalism coupled with anticlericalism, and cryptic references to a primal, cosmological order. That order, he observed, is like a "key"; it is "dual while never ceasing to be one," and it "embraces the entire universe by its general and penetrating activity." The culmination of his philosophical system is the apotheosis of the afterlife: "Among the dead," he observed, "all is living." The numerous admirers of Saint-Martin's thought included the reactionary thinker Joseph de Maistre, who described him as "the most knowledgeable, the wisest, and the most elegant of theosophists"; one of the intellectual founders of modern French liberalism, Germaine de Staël, who celebrated Saint-Martin's "sublime illuminations"; and a literary giant of the nineteenth century, Honoré de Balzac, whose novels (notably, *Histoire des Treize* [*History of the Thirteen*] and the autobiographical *Louis Lambert*) are peppered with occultist references and allusions to Saint-Martin. Under the leadership of the Parisian occultist Gérard Encausse (known by his esoteric name of Papus), the Martinist Order was founded in 1884. This mystical association played an active role in the propagation of Saint-Martin's ideas in the early twentieth century by publishing pamphlets and creating lodges.[12]

Complementing the moral conceptions of Martinism were the physical theories of magnetism popularized by the Viennese physician Franz Mesmer. Mesmerism asserted the existence of an invisible magnetic force, carried by a fluid, which influenced all animated and celestial bodies and could provide (through the proper massaging of the body's "poles") the cure for a range of physical ailments. Adherents of Mesmerism developed a distinct penchant for the occult, and it enjoyed its greatest vogue in France during the 1780s, shaping the views of both moderate and radical figures. Prominent among the former was the hero of the American and French revolutions, Lafayette, who in a letter of 1784 to George Washington described himself as "one of the most enthusiastic" disciples of Mesmer. The revolutionary Jacques-Pierre Brissot was also an ardent Mesmerist, seeing the doctrine—because of its challenge to conventional scientific orthodoxy—as a "way to bring social classes together, to make the rich more humane, to make them into real fathers of the poor." Despite their scientific limitations and their penchant for speaking to ghosts and communicating with distant planets, these forms of "revolutionary mysticism" were later praised by the republican historian Louis Blanc for their contribution to the cause of liberty: "Through this occult philosophy were won over to the camp of equality these two powerful inspirations of human nature, imagination and the love of the unknown; through the miraculous healings attributed to a universal fluid, the physical solidarity of men became the proof and the symbol of their moral solidarity."[13]

This mystical dimension of radical politics remained prominent in the thought and practices of the French revolutionaries in the 1790s. The republicans who swept away the institutions of the old order sought to conceive alternative forms of spirituality to replace the culture of the *ancien régime*. "We must seize the imagination of men and govern it," declared the Jacobin Fabre d'Églantine. In this enterprise, the revolutionaries readily appropriated the language and imagery of religion, designing their civic rituals to bear a close resemblance to those of Catholicism. The festivals of the Revolution generated their own symbolic objects and were accompanied by holy processions and patriotic hymns. The ceremonies were officiated by lay priests and included secular baptisms and burials and even liberty fasts (*carêmes civiques*). The 1789 Declaration of the Rights of Man and of the Citizen was hailed as a holy text and frequently equated to a new "catechism." (Napoleon later adopted this practice to serve his own ends, personally drafting a catechism in which he was worshiped as a god in French schools.) In popular revolutionary representations, the Declaration's articles were likened, in a biblical analogy, to "tablets descending from the holy mountain"; here again, the contrast between light and darkness was a persistent motif. The figure of God was celebrated through the cult of the Supreme Being and often presented in pantheistic terms. The Jacobin priest Bias Parent, having posed the question of whether God existed, replied, "Yes, obviously. And if there is anyone who dares deny his existence, he should cast his eye on the heavens, the earth, the sea, and all the elements which surround us."[14]

Alongside this civil religion the republicans developed a cult of heroes and martyrs, thus beginning a long and at times colorful French fascination with the human remains of national figures. The Panthéon was designated the repository of *grands hommes* by a decree of the National Assembly in 1791, and among the remains transferred to the holy site in the ensuing years were those of Jean-Jacques Rousseau. Already the object of a vibrant literary cult in the decade preceding the Revolution, Rousseau became the defining symbol of the new order. The Genevan philosopher's works were cited in the National Assembly, in the theater, and in the revolutionary press, and his busts were paraded across the country. But as the Revolution grew in fervor, the Rousseau cult assumed an increasingly pious character. Robespierre worshiped what he called "the sacred image of Jean-Jacques," and Rousseau's bust appeared among a cache of religious objects found in the Tuileries after the overthrow of the monarchy. In popular images, Rousseau was deified and frequently represented as a saint. As one devotee put it, Jean-Jacques's entry into the Panthéon in October 1794 marked the dawn of the celebration of the illustrious dead, "the only reasonable cult which might be allowed to exist." Rousseau thus became "the first god who could be taken from the ranks of men."[15]

This deification of the human—or was it a humanization of the divine?—was brought into sharper relief with the cult of revolutionary martyrs that developed at the height of the Terror. When the Jacobin journalist Jean-Paul Marat was assassinated, the painter Jacques-Louis David was commissioned to depict the episode and bring out its revolutionary significance; his *La Mort de Marat* (The Death of Marat, 1793) drew heavily upon classical representations of Christ after he had been taken down from the cross. Marat's heart was preserved as a sacred relic in a vase and left hanging on the ceiling of the popular republican Club des Cordeliers. Numerous brochures compared him to Jesus, and a religious cult developed among his followers: processions were held in his honor in Paris complete with banners, choirs, and symbolic representations of the martyr (including the bathtub in which he was assassinated by Charlotte Corday).

Even more remarkable was the phenomenon of the cult of "patriotic saints" honoring such people as Perrine Dugué, an ardent republican from the *département* of Mayenne who was murdered by royalists in 1796. Shortly after her burial, there were sightings of her "rising to the heavens on tricolor wings," and her tomb became a site of pilgrimage where miraculous cures were observed. Similarly, in the forest of Teillay, on the border between the Loire-Inférieure and the Ille-et-Vilaine, a shrine was erected in honor of Marie Martin, who was killed by antirevolutionary forces for refusing to divulge the whereabouts of local republicans. The tree where she was hanged became a site of pilgrimage, and her tomb was adorned with a cross; she soon became known as Sainte-Pataude and was credited with extraordinary powers to cure disabled children. Families brought their progeny and marched them around the site several times. According to an article in *Ouest-France* in 2007, Sainte-Pataude continues—even though she has not been recognized by the church and her tomb does not feature on any tourist guide—to attract thousands of visitors each year, who come to pray and leave offerings to the republican saint for the healing of their friends and relatives.[16]

The Supernatural Emperor

Ernest Marré's *Comment on parle avec les morts* (How we speak to the dead) was one of the best-selling works in paranormal literature in early twentieth-century France, reaching its fifth edition by 1910. In addition to its handy tips about communicating with the departed ("a little dose of humor may be helpful"), the book contains a number of photographic illustrations, of which the most remarkable is a picture taken at the home of Albert de Rochas in a village in Isère on September 28, 1895. Rochas, a well-known figure in occultist circles, had gathered together a committee to investigate the work of the Italian medium Eusapia Palladino, an internationally renowned spiritualist. As they posed in the garden for the photographer, Rochas remarked that one member of the group, who was standing with his hands in his pockets, was striking a somewhat Napoleonic pose. No sooner did he utter these words than a "fluidic profile resembling Napoleon" appeared above Palladino's head. Witnessed by all those present, the image was captured on camera.[17]

In one sense, there was nothing extraordinary about the appearance of the emperor in this bucolic setting near the French Alps more than six decades after his death. As the critic Philippe Muray put it, "the entire nineteenth century was in a state of delirium around the ghost of Napoleon, to whom a variety of supernatural qualities were attributed." All the beliefs just described—the unity of man with the cosmos, the power of magnetic forces, the establishment of new religions, the cult of the dead and a faith in magical and occult properties—converged in the French collective imagination around his figure. The phenomenon began immediately after his exile to Saint Helena in 1815, when sightings of the emperor were reported across France. Fueled by rumors of his imminent return, these Napoleonic visions were often tinged with a supernatural aura. In rural France, prophetic tales were spread by clairvoyants and fortune-tellers, often through the newly born: in Creuse, "a vision of Bonaparte escorted by angels" appeared to a mother as she gave birth, and in Auxerre it was claimed that an infant left her mother's womb and cried, "Long Live the Emperor!" (three times). Napoleon was everywhere, in the skies and beneath the earth: some peasants in the Ardèche claimed they had seen his portrait in the moon, while others placed their ear to the ground to listen for the "subterranean Army of Bonaparte," which they believed would emerge to reclaim his throne. These rumors celebrated the emperor's Promethean qualities: like the great conquerors, he was believed to be capable of raising colossal armies—200,000 Turks, 500,000 Americans, and (in a nice orientalist touch) "two million Indians marching across the Ganges."[18]

Belief in Napoleon's supernatural qualities was also fanned through his literary cult, which flourished during the Romantic era in the first half of the nineteenth century. In Balzac's *Le Médecin de campagne* (*The Country Doctor*), an imperial veteran evokes the "Red Man," a prophet who is alleged to have first appeared to Napoleon on Mount Sinai and later lived with him in the Tuileries. The emperor's appeal to the imagination was illustrated by one of the first modern fictionalized historical novels, Louis Geoffroy-Chateau's *Napoléon et la conquête du monde* (*Napoleon and the Conquest of the World*). Published in 1836, it provided an alternative story of the emperor's later years, portraying him returning unscathed from Moscow in 1812 and achieving world domination by launching a successful invasion of England, which ends in a crushing French military victory at the Battle of Cambridge in June 1814. (There was, evidently, an element of wishful thinking here.)

The long shadow of the emperor over successive nineteenth-century generations was reflected in a variety of literary tropes. In Stendhal's *Le Rouge et le Noir* (*The Red and the Black*), the destiny of the novel's main character, Julien Sorel, is constantly interwoven with that of his hero, Napoleon. Often the lines between fiction and reality became blurred. The writer Chateaubriand's obsession with Napoleon runs through the entirety of his magnificent *Mémoires d'outre-tombe* (*Memoirs from Beyond the Tomb*), in which he constantly compares his destiny to that of the emperor. The poet Gérard de Nerval believed he was descended from Napoleon's brother Joseph (Giuseppe), and occasionally signed his name as "G Nap." The Lithuanian mystic Andrzej Towiański (who counted among his disciples the Polish poet Adam Mickiewicz) went one step further, claiming that the history of the universe was marked by a perpetual struggle between the forces of light and darkness and that Napoleon had been sent to earth to reignite the "illumination of Christ." Sadly, the emperor's mission had failed, and so Towiański believed it now fell upon him to rekindle this Napoleono-Christic flame. Seeing himself as a purified reincarnation of Bonaparte, he marched into Notre-Dame one Sunday after Mass and announced that he was the savior of humanity.[19]

The French fixation with Napoleon was not just literary; it was also a physical, corporeal phenomenon. The mysterious tales that surrounded the emperor were fueled by his absence from France from 1815 and the burial of his remains in Saint Helena after his death in 1821. Triggered by the emperor's dramatic testamentary declaration that he was being assassinated by poisoning, the controversy about the cause of his death began immediately. Jean-Claude Bésuchet de Saunois, a former surgeon in the Grande Armée, published a short book on the subject, and conspiracy theories were thereafter periodically inflamed by fresh (and increasingly exotic) allegations—such as the claim that Napoleon's body was whisked away by the British in 1828 and secretly buried in Westminster Abbey. Napoleon's phantom served as a magnet for the mentally imbalanced, and identification with the emperor became the most common manifestation of an acute personality disorder called *monomanie orgueilleuse*. Throughout the nineteenth century, the registers of French lunatic asylums revealed a steady influx of patients suffering from Napoleonic delusions, including, most commonly, the belief that they were descended from the emperor. Some believed that they regularly communicated with his ghost, others that they themselves were Napoleon. After the return of the exiled martyr's remains to France in 1840, which was marked by a grandiose ceremony at the Arc de Triomphe and a tidal wave of Napoleonic enthusiasm across the country, fourteen new "emperors" were admitted to the Bicêtre Hospital in Paris. These men all shared the same pathologies: they were authoritarian, short-tempered, brusque, and believed that they were the masters of the universe. The fantasy of unlimited rule—and also the idea that there was a secret, occult dimension to the exercise of political power—lay at the heart of this Napoleonic mystique.[20]

"We have you as our God," wrote Victor Hugo about Napoleon in one of the verses of his 1830 ode to the Vendôme Column, the Parisian monument celebrating the glory of the imperial Grande Armée. If the emperor could defy the laws of nature, inspire prophecies, and speak to the dead, it was but a small step in the train of esoteric reasoning to believe that he was not a mortal figure but an incarnation of divinity itself. This was the sense in which a mystical cult of Napoleon was celebrated by some Freemasons and by many of his former soldiers. The popular belief that Napoleon was not dead was so widespread that the emperor acquired the nickname of "Malmort." In 1848, many peasants voted for Louis Napoléon because they believed he was a reincarnation of the emperor. An Arab poem in honor of the greatest warrior and conqueror of modern times, translated into French in 1829, hailed Napoleon as "a celestial figure who bears the imprint of divinity."[21]

The crown for the most eccentric celebration of the emperor goes to Simon Vanneau. This adept of Illuminism founded Evadism, a new egalitarian cult that looked to a symbolic combination of Adam and Eve to worship a hermaphrodite divinity, the "Mapah." Vanneau addressed an epistle to Pope

Gregory XVI announcing the advent of the new God and serenely inviting him to renounce his pontificate. His Holiness showed reluctance, whereupon Vanneau revised the holy calendar to include June 18 (the anniversary of the Battle of Waterloo), which was to replace the traditional Good Friday of Easter Week. Vanneau marked the return of the emperor's remains to France in 1840 with a magnificently opaque pamphlet that ended with a prophecy of imminent regeneration for humankind: "Death," he claimed, "is not a tomb, but the cradle of an even greater life, of a more infinite love." He then concluded, "Selfishness is the night, unity is the light of Life." Vanneau was later an enthusiastic supporter of the 1848 Revolution, believing it would mark the realization of his vision. His creed was admired by radical republican figures such as George Sand, Alphonse Esquiros, and Félix Pyat. The prophet even offered to anoint Alexandre Dumas, another of his devotees, as the new Mapah; the author of *The Count of Monte Cristo* prudently declined, on the grounds that "the position did not seem sufficiently well defined."[22]

The Spirits of Jersey

On the evening of Sunday, September 11, 1853, Victor Hugo gathered with family and friends for a séance of table-tapping at 3 Marine Terrace, a small house by the sea on the island of Jersey in the English Channel. Led by Delphine de Girardin, an ardent practitioner of the esoteric arts, they had spent several evenings trying to communicate with spirits, to no avail. On this occasion, however, the small mahogany table appeared to respond, and a number of firm knocks were heard. Hugo, who had been skeptical of proceedings up to this point, inquired who was there, and his curiosity was aroused further when this striking reply was deciphered: "dead girl." The whole room gasped as all thoughts converged on the memory of Léopoldine, Hugo's beloved daughter, who had tragically drowned in the Seine almost exactly ten years earlier. Sensing her presence in the room, Hugo asked her where she was. "Light," came the reply. A series of intense exchanges ensued, lasting until the early hours of the morning, during which Léopoldine was interrogated by all the members of her family.[23]

In the two years that followed, Hugo became a committed spiritualist, holding regular late-night sessions in which he and his companions communicated with more than a hundred souls. The spirits rapping on the tables included literary giants (Plato, Molière, and Shakespeare, who dictated the first act of a play), religious and political figures (Jesus, the prophet Muhammad, Martin Luther, Robespierre), abstract entities (Ocean, Death), and legendary animals: one of Hugo's keenest interlocutors was the Aesopian Lion of

Androcles. Some of the exchanges were brief: Walter Scott, with impeccable Caledonian terseness, tapped back that he had nothing to say, as he was dead. And there was more gloom from an emissary from the planet Jupiter, who indicated that the locals were "less happy" than the inhabitants of Earth. In one of the very first séances, the "Shadow of the Sepulchre" informed Hugo that he had been chosen to mediate between the physical universe and the world of spirits: "You hold the key to a door of the enclosed."[24]

Hugo was drawn to spiritualism for a variety of reasons. His grief at the loss of Léopoldine was still immense, and it was reawakened by her dramatic evocation in Jersey. This sense of fragility was compounded by his political isolation: at the end of 1851 he had fled from France because of his implacable opposition to Louis Napoléon's overthrow of the Second Republic and subsequent restoration of the empire. Hugo was all the more receptive to the sirens of spiritualism because some members of his Jersey entourage believed in reincarnation: his republican friend and fellow exile Philippe Faure claimed that, in an earlier life, he had attended the crucifixion of Christ. This was also a period when Hugo was plunging with gusto into occultist literature, which was experiencing a resurgence in mid-nineteenth-century France because of the influence of American spiritualism: in his Jersey library were such works as Jean du Potet de Sennevoy's *La Magie dévoilée, ou La science occulte* (Magic revealed, or the occult science, 1852) and Alcide Morin's *Comment l'esprit vient aux tables* (How the spirit comes to the table, 1853). But the exiled novelist's spiritualism was a conduit for something more fundamental, too: it was both a means of transcending the personal sufferings he had experienced and an exercise in literary affirmation and philosophical creativity. For the spirits of Jersey spoke like Victor Hugo, that is, in a style and language that reflected the apogee of the French Romantic sensibility. Hugo's spiritualism was also aimed at the irreligiosity of French republicans, of which he disapproved; the tables were, for him, "a way for God to express himself and reveal the existence of spirits to the republican party." The poet was thus able to forge a new prophetism that held up the promise of universal emancipation by means of an original synthesis of French revolutionary mysticism and occultism—all served up with a generous dollop of Hugolian narcissism (he frequently asked the spirits, from Jesus to Chateaubriand, whether they were familiar with his *oeuvre*; only Christ had the impertinence to reply that he was not).[25]

It is perhaps surprising, in this egotistical context, that Napoleon did not feature among the cast of spirits at Jersey. There is a brief evocation of the emperor during a longer exchange with Hannibal, who merely observes that Napoleon was as great in victory as he was small in defeat; he then concludes that the *grand capitaine* should have died gloriously in battle rather than face the humiliations of abdication and exile (a point the emperor himself made on a number of occasions in his final years). The days of Hugo's unqualified adulation of the Napoleonic divinity were over. Indeed, the political sensibility of the exchanges with the spirits is resolutely progressive: the republican chant the "Marseillaise," banned by both Napoleon and his nephew, is thus described by Hugo as "the hymn of Light sung in stormy stanzas by the four winds of the future."[26]

Yet this republican horizon appeared overcast. At one session, interventions were heard from a series of figures from the French Revolutionary period. The assassinated Marat announced the imminent return of the "Universal Republic," but then seemed to contradict himself by suggesting that "humanity only advances in slow steps." Asked to evaluate the hapless republicans of 1848 who had seized power before losing it to Louis Napoléon, the Jacobin martyr dismissed them as "bottle-feeding republicans." There was much contrition: the spirits of Robespierre and Marat's assassin Charlotte Corday returned to express regret at the excessive violence that had accompanied the Revolution in its early years; the Incorruptible even agreed to rehabilitate the memory of his rival Danton, whom he had sent to the guillotine in 1794. This historical revisionism paved the way for the poet André Chénier to announce (after dictating his unfinished verses and meticulously describing his own beheading during the Terror) the impending regeneration of the Republic through the "radiant pantheon" of Victor Hugo. The elements of Hugo's new spiritual revolution were spelled out in the latter part of the Marine Terrace corpus during a series of exchanges with Death, Jesus Christ, and the prophet Muhammad. The last announced that all established religions were destined to oblivion: "The bastilles of the shadows will fall and the earth will tremble beneath those who are standing, and the skies will open on those who are kneeling."[27]

Hugo's new creed was influenced by his readings of the *Bhagavad Gita*, parts of which he had read in French translation. He was particularly taken with the classical Hindu doctrine of reincarnation, which helped to shape his own reinvigorated, primitive Christianity, expanded to incorporate the doctrine of metempsychosis (the transmigration of souls among different beings, both human and animal). These spiritualist exchanges crystallized the novelist's belief that an infinite variety of conscious souls inhabited the universe: this chain of being began at the lower end with stones and vegetation, moved on to mollusks, oysters, and fish, and then progressed through birds, cats, dogs, and monkeys to man. Hugo practiced what he preached, applying his ecumenical philosophy to his new friends from the animal kingdom: his garden became a refuge for all sorts of creatures, and he once announced that he had saved a salamander from certain death; he also told his daughter Adèle to release a lobster into the sea. In this egalitarian creed, there was no hell, redemption for one's mortal sins was possible (through reincarnation), and all souls had a vocation for love. The body, from this perspective, was merely a staging post in the soul's onward journey. Death was not the end of life: indeed, as Moses put it during one of the sessions, "Absolute truth appears to man only after death." In the exhortation of Death, the spirits thus invited Hugo to make the creative leap into darkness, now defined not as the opposite of light but as the apotheosis of being: "You have been the day, come and be the night, the shadow, the unknown; come to be the mystery, the infinite."[28]

Spiritualism enjoyed its heyday in France from the mid-nineteenth century up to the World War I era. Its leading light was Hippolyte Léon Rivail, better known by his *nom d'esprit* Allan Kardec, a positivist educationalist who discovered table-tapping in 1854 and developed spiritualism into a major doctrine combining a belief in the immortality of the soul with an egalitarian and scientific outlook. Three years later he founded the Société Parisienne d'Études Spirites and the journal *Revue spirite* (Spiritualist review, which is still being published); his two major treatises—*Le Livre des esprits* (The spirits' book, 1857) and *Le Livre des médiums* (The book on mediums, 1861)—became classics that were continually reprinted in the ensuing decades. Victor Hugo was an admirer of Kardec, even though the latter rejected the idea that human souls could be reincarnated in animals. Among other writers and artists who became ardent spiritualists in the years and decades that followed were George Sand, Victorien Sardou, Théophile Gautier, and Gérard de Nerval. Sardou wrote a play entitled *Spiritisme* (Spiritism), first performed in 1897, in which he celebrated occultist practices and beliefs, and a volume of Maxime Du Camp's *Souvenirs littéraires* (*Recollections of a Literary Life*) contains a fine description of Nerval knocking his head against a bookshelf during an occultist dance. Such beliefs were also widely held among French Freemasons from the second half of the nineteenth century, as well as among large numbers of ordinary men and women across French society. During his tour of provincial France in 1911, Maurice Barrès found local republican schoolteachers who were devotees of spiritualism.[29]

And Hugo himself? Beneath a photograph of him in contemplative pose taken by the poet Auguste Vacquerie in 1853, Hugo wrote this caption: "Victor Hugo listening to God." There was no hint of irony here. From the moment he began his exchanges with the spirits at Jersey, and for the rest of his life, Hugo believed that he had been chosen as a divine interlocutor to reveal the existence of spirits to humanity (or, as the poet André Breton put it more colorfully, "Hugo is surrealist when he is not being stupid"). Fittingly, the Third Republic honored his messianism by committing his body to the Panthéon in 1885 while at the same instant removing the cross that adorned the front of the building. This symbolic substitution confirmed the prophecy of the spirit of Jesus at one of the final séances at Marine Terrace: Christ had declared that the modern age would see the consecration of the "phantom of death."[30]

The Eternity of Life

"I soared under a mysterious sky, lifted by my passionate emotions as if carried by powerful wings." Thus wrote the young Édouard Charton about his membership in the newly established cult of Saint-Simonism in the early 1830s, during which he traveled enthusiastically across France preaching the new religion in ballrooms, theaters, and gambling dens. Charton's encounter with Saint-Simonism was emblematic in many respects, not least for its brevity: he passed through the movement for a year before moving on to a distinguished career in publishing and republican politics (in 1833 he launched the *Magasin pittoresque* [Illustrated magazine], the first of its type in France). But, like many others of his generation, his Saint-Simonian moment left an abiding mark on his moral values and philosophical outlook—notably, on his conception of human perfectibility.[31]

Charton's engagement bore witness to the continuity of the mystical tradition from the Enlightenment through the nineteenth century. Before turning to Saint-Simonism, Charton had been a disciple of Saint-Martin, and in his newfound creed he perceived strong echoes of the core themes of Martinism: the moral perversion of the *ancien régime*, the emancipation of humanity through the creation of a harmonious spiritual order, and the unity of man with the universe. However, the mysticism of the Saint-Simonians was also distinctive in three crucial respects. Celebrating a cult of humanity, adherents sought to improve the conditions of the poor and to create a new kind of political elite that would administer society in the interests of all. They were in this sense among the pioneers of the socialist movement in France—and, by this token, contributed to the esoteric quality of early French socialist doctrine. Saint-Simonians devoted considerable energy to promoting the emancipation of women and idealizing womanhood at a time when the French republican movement showed little interest in the issue. (The first French feminist journal, *La Femme libre* [The free woman], was published by a group of Saint-Simonian women in 1832.) Finally, the Saint-Simonians looked ahead, not backward, and, unlike the romanticism of the Napoleonic cult—to say nothing of the spiritualist visions of Victor Hugo—their movement had a hardheaded, practical edge to it. Among them were the men who later designed the modern French railway system, who transformed the urban layout of Paris, and who engineered the Suez Canal. Saint-Simonian doctrine thus sought to combine occultist beliefs with a resolutely "scientific" outlook—or, to be more precise, though it may sound contradictory—to achieve the aims of science by means of the occult.[32]

All these qualities appear in the life and works of the founder of the movement, Henri de Saint-Simon, a Parisian aristocrat who was a wonderful blend of adventurer, entrepreneur, social reformer, visionary—and eccentric. Imprisoned during the Terror, he was allegedly visited by the ghost of Charlemagne, from whom he claimed descent. His ancestor supposedly declared to him, "Since the world has existed, no family has had the privilege of producing a hero and a philosopher of great eminence: this honor is reserved to my lineage. My son, your success as a philosopher will equal those I obtained as a military and political leader." Armed with this endorsement, Saint-Simon forged ahead, producing a broad synthesis in his system of ideas combining Enlightenment principles, a grand philosophy of history, and plans for a radical reorganization of the temporal and spiritual realms. But while his focus on "industrialism" mostly echoed the concerns of contemporary political economists, Saint-Simon's distinctive contribution (and that of the tradition he founded) lay in his aspiration to found a new, progressive religion. Saint-Simon's final, unfinished work was entitled *The New Christianity*; in it he sought to outline a novel creed that was entirely dedicated to "the amelioration of the moral and physical existence of the poorest class." His followers, who sought to codify his thought, came up with a form of pantheism in which "being" was defined in universal, cosmic terms.[33]

Among Saint-Simon's most fervent disciples was Prosper Enfantin, who transformed the association into a "church" and called himself the "Supreme Father": the title was emblazoned on his tunic. He also wore a symbolic collar adorned with esoteric pendants made of copper and iron, polished only on one side, to symbolize imperfection. Enfantin installed his flock in his property in the Parisian neighborhood of Ménilmontant, where the cult enjoyed a brief but spectacular flourish: a special Saint-Simonian costume was designed by an artist with the felicitous name of Raymond Bonheur (the waistcoat could only be tied from the back, to illustrate the principle of fraternity). Exotic rituals were carried out (marriages, baptisms, conversions, religious chants), and the creed was projected as the instrument of the final reconciliation between the oriental and occidental worlds. Unimpressed by these mystical aspirations, the Cartesian elites of the July Monarchy closed the church down in 1832 and locked the Supreme Father behind bars—whereupon a Saint-Simonian sect named the Compagnons de la Femme (Female Companions) traveled to Constantinople, and then on to Egypt, in search of a wife for Enfantin. Sadly, the Woman Messiah proved elusive.[34]

This kind of mystical universalism naturally led to speculations on the prospect of eternal life, and this became a common theme in the philosophical reflections of progressive thinkers. "Dying is not a death," wrote the historian Jules Michelet, "but the start of a new life." In an 1830 pamphlet, Enfantin wrote, "My life is indefinite; it manifests itself in me, outside of me, and by the union between me and the non-me"; his final work was entitled *La Vie éternelle, passée, présente, future* (Eternal life, past, present, future, 1861). Similarly, Pierre Leroux, the inventor of the concept of socialism (and a former Saint-Simonian), defended the notion of the immortality of the soul. Socialist writer Alphonse Esquiros affirmed that the soul was eternal, achieving greater perfectibility through successive bodily incarnations. And the socialist philosopher Jean Reynaud (another ex-Saint-Simonian) claimed that souls were purified through reincarnation on distant planets.[35]

The most remarkable contributions on this galactic theme came from two men, a mystical republican scientist and a revolutionary atheist. The astronomer Camille Flammarion, one of the best-known science writers of his era, was both a devout republican and a believer in spiritualism (he delivered the eulogy at the funeral of Allan Kardec in 1869). His first major book, *La Pluralité des mondes habités* (The plurality of inhabited worlds, 1862), a bestseller, combined the latest findings of astronomy with a sweeping portrait of the universe. Flammarion asserted that science pointed incontrovertibly to the existence of higher forms of life and that the human soul could aspire to eternity through successive reincarnations in space: the stars, he concluded, were "the future regions of our immortality." In his response, written from his Paris prison cell in 1872, the radical republican atheist Auguste Blanqui qualified this enthusiasm. *L'Éternité par les astres* (Eternity by the stars) argued that, since the universe was boundless but at the same time made up of a finite number of particles, earthly humans were eternally re-created in other universes: "The number of our body doubles is infinite in time and space." There was some scope for variation: our doubles may live slightly different versions of our earthly lives and might accomplish what we have failed to achieve. But, unsettled by the repeated defeats of his insurrectionary political tradition, Blanqui's overall conclusion was melancholic: progress was an illusion, and "eternity plays imperturbably the same representations in infinity."[36]

The Secret Harmony of Things

Planetary alignments shaping the destinies of individuals; cosmic rays of light working to restore concord among humankind; an invisible fluid with miraculous properties; human deities, blessed with supernatural powers, rising to the skies and symbolized by a ubiquitous Corsican ghost; the lasting presence of the dead, whose remains are sacralized and whose spirits engage in poetic conversations with the living; the transmigration of souls across the chain of being; visions of immortality in the infinity of space, in which alien entities float alongside the ethereal remains of earthly beings; hidden codes, whose secrets may reveal the mysteries of the cosmos: these were some of the enchanted creations of the supernatural imagination in France. They reflected the inventive force of Romanticism at its apogee and its particular combination of introspective sentimentality and yearning to change the world—or to find inspiration in the sheer lyricism of the supernatural, as with the pianist Ricardo Viñes, an adept of spiritualism who believed that his artistic performances could be elevated to a "divine plane" through his practice of "the occult sciences"; or André Breton's "Letter to the Clairvoyants," which evoked "a marvellous realm (*champ merveilleux*) which is nothing less than that of absolute possibility." The attraction of occultism for French literary avant-gardes, from Baudelaire and Mallarmé to the surrealists, was also anchored in a rejection of the religious and cultural values of the West.[37]

Occultism was of course not an exclusively French phenomenon: Mesmer was Austrian, spiritualism was an American import (but was given a new lease on life by Kardec), and through her theosophical movement the Russian occultist philosopher Madame Blavatsky aspired to forge a universal humanistic creed by combining Western and Eastern forms of mysticism. But the appeal of the supernatural in France was exceptional for a number of reasons. At a most basic level, its visions overlapped with preexisting features of French thought: the Enlightenment belief in the harmony of the universe, a longing for universality (taken here to literally celestial proportions), an existential fascination with nature, an obsession with mortality and the afterlife, and a capacity for creativity allied with a fondness for cryptic allusions and opaque formulations. But these forms of occultism also persisted over time because they were an integral—if not always acknowledged—part of the French progressive tradition. As such, they were propelled by one simple, overriding impulse from the eighteenth century onward: the search for an underlying principle of unity. This quest for what the geographer and anarchist Elisée Reclus called the "secret comity of things," a leitmotif in all forms of mystical thinking, also inspired the postrevolutionary dream of a more attractive and alternative religion to Roman Catholicism—especially one that avoided the eternal damnation of hell. Thanks to the robustness of their eschatology and their hostility to the irenic dimensions of the occult, Catholics in France generally resisted the appeal of this kind of esotericism, although it is worth noting that the first apparitions at Lourdes in 1858 were contemporaneous with the emergence of French spiritualism; there was much overlap between these seemingly contrasting systems of belief.[38]

Contrary to many Catholics' apocalyptic vision of a fallen and corrupted humanity, however, this form of occultism was essentially humanistic and forward-looking. Grounded in a belief in the potential for human perfectibility, its outlook was hopeful and at times even buoyant, as illustrated in the optimistic title of one of the most widely circulated occultist periodicals in the early twentieth century, *Le Progrès spirite* (Spiritualist progress). It was not uncommon for spiritualist groups to meet for the purpose of cultural elevation—for example, to exchange views with writers, poets, and artists. Others had even bolder ambitions: in the enthusiastic estimate of one convert, the "intelligent communication between incarnated souls and the world of spirits" had the potential to replace conflict with cooperation and rid humanity of ignorance, injustice, poverty, brutality, prostitution, war, and disease. It was in the same spirit that the pharmacist Émile Coué developed the psychotherapeutical method that eventually bore his name, which enjoyed widespread success in Europe and the United States during the first half of the twentieth century. Its basic principle was to invite the subject to repeat the following phrase: "Every day, in every way, I am getting better and better."[39]

Occultism ultimately serves to highlight one of the singularities of French culture in the modern age: the close relationship between the realm of rationalism and that of spirituality. More fundamentally, this symbiosis underscores the limited value of the classic distinction between "reason" and "religion." The proximity between the two spheres in French thought explains why so many disciples of occultism in France were positivists and scientists: hence the wonderful paradox that its devotees stayed committed to a form of rationalism, albeit one which retained strong spiritual moorings. Eugène Pelletan, one of the leading republican intellectuals of the Second Empire, summarized it this way: "We believe that man is a religious being precisely because he is reasonable." The mystic Freemason Charles Fauvety echoed this sentiment: "We will arrive at faith through science." From the early twentieth century there was a further rapprochement between the worlds of rationalism and occultism: after subjecting the visions of the medium Eusapia Palladino to rigorous testing, a number of leading French scientists, including the physics Nobel

Prize winner Pierre Curie, declared themselves to be convinced of the veracity of her claims. Charles Richet, a Nobel Prize winner in medicine, published his *Traité de métapsychique* (*A Treatise on Metapsychics*) in 1922, affirming that "there can be a science of the supernatural and the occult."[40]

What makes these beliefs even more remarkable—and here, too, the French case is distinctive—is that they were not confined to the margins of collective life. They were widely shared in society and among cultural elites as an important strand of late-Enlightenment thought, in associations such as the Freemasonry, and in mainstream French political traditions—the republican, the liberal, and the Napoleonic. Some of these esoteric aspirations—notably their egalitarian and fraternal dimensions—were also embraced by the founding generation of French socialists. They were later vulgarized in radical political thought and in progressive novels, such as Jules Lermina's Monte-Cristo sequels, where the struggle against social oppression is waged against a constant backdrop of death and resurrection. Speaking to a spiritualist congress held at the Grand Orient de France in September 1889, Lermina praised occultism for its capacity to create a sense of "exaltation" among workers, which in turn could liberate "sublime intuitions" among them. In the conclusion to his *Science occulte* (Occult science) he added that the time had come to open the door to the secret mysteries of the universe, advancing nonetheless with caution, "as the light we will face once we cross that threshold is so powerful, so dazzling, so unsettling that its illuminations may blind us." Communicating with his followers through a medium in Rochefort in November 1920 (fifty-one years after his earthly "disincarnation"), Allan Kardec's spirit personally confirmed this cheerful perspective: the liberation of humankind was on the march.[41]

CHAPTER 3

Landscapes of Utopia

Louis-Sébastien Mercier's *L'An deux mille quatre cent quarante* (The year two thousand four hundred and forty), a time-travel story in which the author visits the future and describes his journey across twenty-fifth-century Paris, was one of the runaway literary successes of the late Enlightenment era. First published anonymously toward the end of 1770, the novel went through eleven editions in the ensuing decades and was widely disseminated across Europe, with several pirated editions and translations into Dutch, German, Italian, and English (in the English translation it was given a different title, *Memoirs of the Year Two Thousand Five Hundred*). The work's triumph rested in part on its amiable distillation of the progressive spirit of its times and its easily understood allusions to contemporary thinkers and movements: the rationalism of leading *philosophes* such as Denis Diderot; Montesquieu's notion of balanced government; the Italian philosopher Cesare Beccaria's ideas about humane penal systems; and Rousseau's notion of a community founded on civic virtue. Just as significant was the novel's trenchant critique of the old order: so vehement were its strictures against the "vileness" of the absolute monarchy and the papacy—"an astonishing monument to human credulity"—that the book was promptly banned in France and Spain, but the censorship no doubt added to its cachet.[1]

The authorities were right to be concerned, as Mercier's novel proved uncannily prescient, anticipating the French Revolution even in specific details: the fall of the Bastille, the flight of the king from his palace, the abolition of slavery, the conception of law as the expression of the general will—right down to the prediction that France would become a "Republic." In the 1799 edition of the work, the author proclaimed himself the "true prophet of the Revolution."²

The fundamental reason for the book's success lay in its reinvention of the canons of literary utopia. Instead of locating his social and political system in an imaginary place, as was conventional in the genre—Thomas More's remote island, Tommaso Campanella's sunny city, Francis Godwin's heavens—Mercier set his novel in the future. He thus breathed new life into European idealist thought, in time sealing his reputation as the "father of modern utopia." By setting his ideal community in Paris, Mercier wrote what turned out to be a harbinger of things to come. The French capital crystallized the dreams of all those who imagined that power could be held and exercised in a radically different way—from the patriotic Jacobin and radical egalitarian revolutionaries of the 1790s through the great republican and socialist movements of the nineteenth century and all the way to the students who erected the barricades of May 1968 in the final, ephemeral fling of the French tradition of "utopian communism."³

This utopian disposition in French thought could trace its origins to the Enlightenment; it developed further during the nineteenth century, notably among progressive republican thinkers and in the idealistic writings of Charles Fourier and Étienne Cabet; and continued in French communist conceptions of utopia during the twentieth century. As will become apparent, these different sensibilities were all closely connected—not least in their common intellectual roots in the writings of Rousseau. This connection was paradoxical, as Rousseau's personal belief in the possibility of a better world often seemed frail; he was more likely to find exemplars of civic virtue in the simplicities of Spartan life than in any future society. Yet Rousseau's thinking was quintessentially utopian, because he regarded the imagination as the key human faculty. His entire *oeuvre* was illuminated with visionary elements. His arresting style was integral to his appeal; as his great admirer Mercier observed, "He could not touch a question without captivating people's minds, because he took them off beaten paths."⁴

Rousseau's major works were driven by two complementary impulses: the denunciation of the corrosive effects of society, and the achievement of republicanism through human regeneration. By comparing modern civilization to a form of "happy slavery" in which men "fling garlands of flowers over the chains which weigh them down," his first *Discourse* (1750) encouraged his contemporaries to break free from the "servile and deceptive conformity" induced by modern arts and sciences. His second *Discourse* (1755), which was devoted to an examination of the origins of inequality, was even more radical: it drew a powerful contrast between the peace and serenity enjoyed by primitive man and the "law of the strongest" that prevailed in modern times due to divisions based on wealth and property. Although he did not specifically advocate the overthrow of the existing order, Rousseau concluded that it was "plainly contrary to the law of nature" that "the privileged few should gorge themselves with superfluities, while the starving multitude are in want of the bare necessities of life."[5]

Indeed, the major strength of Rousseau's writings lay in their appeal to a range of utopian aspirations—the libertarian yearning for absolute freedom, the progressive quest for a better world, and the collectivist desire for equality. His ideal of a natural man played into the myth of the "noble savage" and chimed with those who questioned the complacent urbanity of the Enlightenment and denounced the corruption that was consuming French society. His vision of individual moral transformation, as sketched out in *Émile*, highlighted man's capacity for self-mastery, transparency, and virtue by means of an inward journey toward greater perfectibility. His scheme of an idealized body politic in *The Social Contract* (1762), in which democratic citizens rule themselves through laws of their own making, inspired those who sought to design a better society through the establishment of new institutions. Hence the emphasis on civil equality and the reconciliation of individual interests with the collective good ("Whoever refuses to obey the general will shall be compelled to do so by the whole body") and the promotion of a more virtuous conception of human sociability (the *moi commun*) through the definition of shared collective goals. The sheer radicalism of Rousseau's objective shines through in this passage: "He who dares to undertake the making of a people's institutions ought to feel himself capable, so to speak, of changing human nature, of transforming each individual, who is by himself a complete and solitary whole, into part of a greater whole from which he in a manner receives his life and being; of altering man's constitution for the purposes of strengthening it; and of substituting a partial and moral existence for the physical and independent existence nature has conferred on us all."[6]

Many of these themes were reflected not only in Mercier's novel, but also more generally in the political thought of the later Enlightenment, within which, by the time of his death in 1778, Rousseau occupied a preeminent position. References to his works and his principal ideas were frequent in the early years of the French Revolution—notably in the concept of the sovereignty of the people, the idea of the general will as the inalienable foundation of the political order, the sense of a fraternal community united by shared moral ideals, the belief in the human capacity to overcome selfishness and materialism, and the vision of citizenship based on civic equality and moral autonomy. Such was the admiration of revolutionary leader Saint-Just for Rousseau, and, more generally, for the Enlightenment's ideas, that he wrote, "The eighteenth century should be placed in the Panthéon." Yet it would be a mistake to view Rousseau's ideas as a monolithic blueprint that the French revolutionaries sought to implement. Admiration for his *oeuvre* was widespread in all political camps, including among monarchists: it was the one—and only—thing that Marie Antoinette and Robespierre had in common. Furthermore, although the Revolution was utterly devoted to Rousseau, its embrace of his ideas was highly selective. Its successive leaders did not follow him, for example, in his skepticism about formal education, in his contempt for commerce, or in his abhorrence of large disparities in wealth or his rejection of the idea that elected representatives were the bearers of collective sovereignty—all of which were exact opposites of the philosophy of the early French Revolution.[7]

Rousseau's utopianism was thus rich and diverse in its inspirations and in the ways in which it was interpreted by his contemporaries. His work demonstrated how fluid the line between idealism and realism could be, even in the works of the same thinker. This was perhaps Rousseau's most powerful influence on Mercier's novel. In reflecting on the competing impulses of French society in the late Enlightenment, *L'An deux mille quatre cent quarante* wrestled with some of the central dilemmas of modernity: the contrast between urban living and ruralism; individual self-realization and collective constraint; anticlerical sentiment and religiosity; national belonging and universalism. As has rightly been observed, Mercier's novel was the work of a perfectionist, not a utopist. In the early years of the Revolution, Mercier was a supporter of the moderate Girondins, and his views on some issues, such as the role of women, were quite conservative. Or, as one of the men Mercier encounters in the future puts it, in a formula that Rousseau would not have disowned, "We still have a lot of things to improve upon. . . . I fear that the absolute good is not of our world. However, it is by seeking it that we can endeavor to make matters at least passable."[8]

Paris in the Year 2440

As he awakens from his slumber to find himself in twenty-fifth-century Paris, Mercier discovers a city transformed beyond recognition. He is struck by the sense of order: with its spacious public squares and parks, elegantly decorated and properly aligned streets, and absence of discordant sounds (there is no shouting or public fighting), Paris is "animated, but without chaos or confusion." Designed to share the same height, the roofs of all the buildings are adorned with plants and greenery: seen from above, the city thus appears to be "crowned with flowers, fruits and vegetation." Scientific advances have produced many a marvel, from lamps with limitless energy to cures for diseases that proved fatal in the eighteenth century.[9]

But the most profound changes are moral. In the new era, a "sense of natural equality" reigns: the king walks around the city on foot and graciously visits the homes of ordinary citizens. The "horrible disproportion in fortunes" and the "puerile and ruinous luxury" that had so dismayed Rousseau has disappeared: the better-off no longer display their wealth garishly but behave with sobriety and generosity; and nobility is based not on inherited fortune but on public service. Likewise, the clergy have abandoned their opulent lifestyles to lead selfless, exemplary existences: "They do everything for humankind, and nothing for themselves." Citizens do not gorge themselves on "extravagant" victuals but enjoy a frugal diet of healthy and seasonal foods. These idealized Parisians eat no pastries, work fewer hours than the laborers of Mercier's time, pay their taxes voluntarily, and (most wondrous of all) treat one another with politeness and consideration.[10]

This Elysium is not limited to Paris, or, for that matter, France. The harmony in Mercier's new world is pacific and cosmopolitan—and even cosmic: citizens practice a form of civil religion in which they worship a Supreme Being and believe planets to be inhabited by other spirits who welcome human souls in their serene journey toward "perfectibility." They are helped along by a judicious system of metempsychosis that enables the virtuous to advance more rapidly toward higher being than "depraved souls" (a shrewd reconciliation of Mercier's occultism with progressive principles). Not that human wickedness poses any great social menace: capital executions are rare, and the "plague of war" has been extinguished—forever. Large standing armies are banished (Rousseau's influence is apparent, again) and states' borders are limited to their natural frontiers.[11]

Colonies have been emancipated, and the states of Europe form an integrated community that transcends the narrow appeal of patriotism. Fraternity has spread to all parts of the world—immigrants from India and China are welcomed with open arms in France; and old national rivalries have dissipated. The Scots and the Irish cherish their union with England, which in turn has become France's "intimate" ally. But all this internationalism has a reassuringly Gallic flavor. The French language, the instrument of "universal reason," prevails everywhere. French moral and cultural norms have spread across the globe, causing astounding changes in the dispositions of other peoples: French women's charms have notably succeeded in "softening the melancholic character of the English," and, thanks to the diffusion of Montesquieu's *Spirit of the Laws* in the East, there has been a dramatic fall in the national suicide rate in Japan.[12]

In France, the new sense of public-spiritedness is reflected in the Rousseauian qualities of the government: its laws are expressions of the general will, and its spirit is animated by reasonableness, sincerity, and the absence of artifice. Power is divided among an assembly, a senate, and a benign constitutional monarch whose functions are limited to overseeing the proper operation of state institutions. Further constraints on central government are provided by the extensive powers enjoyed by the provinces: the "absolute sovereignty" of the old order is thus abolished. But the driving force behind the regeneration of the French civic spirit—and Mercier here taps into a major theme in Enlightenment thinking—is public education. Every child is issued a copy of the *Encyclopédie*, and the school curriculum focuses on teaching the French language and scientific knowledge. Universities, likewise, concentrate on subjects which are "useful to humanity": in a vivid and ghoulish chapter, Mercier describes his visit to the Sorbonne, where the "miserable rhetoricians" have been driven out, and the university has been entirely given over to the dissection of corpses.[13]

Rousseau's suspicion of the sterile pedagogical practices of his time is strongly felt in these passages, which were directly inspired by *Émile*. The heir to the throne is kept away from Paris until the age of twenty and receives his education by experiencing the activities of ordinary French people and living in their midst. Public spaces are devoted to civic culture: paintings, sculptures, and plays are all geared toward "the perfection of human nature," and the Great Men whose statues adorn the city provide a "public lesson" in the republican virtues: clemency, generosity, devotion to the public good, courage, and contempt for weakness. The most extraordinary monument Mercier observes is a statue of a liberated black slave, the "avenger of the new world," who has cleansed the earth of colonial settlers in the name of humanity. *L'An deux mille quatre cent quarante* here anticipates the slave revolt in Haiti led by Toussaint Louverture in the 1790s.[14]

Mercier's vision of the future thus reflected widespread beliefs and ideals in French society in the late Enlightenment era, notably those dealing with the injustices and inequities of the existing order. However, the novel also underlines the point that the dominant sentiment among intellectual elites prior to the events of 1789 was reformist, not revolutionary. The Rousseauist transformation envisaged by Mercier was gradual in character and was concerned with the acquisition of liberty through self-improvement and collective involvement in the making of laws. This is why there is no hint, in his rationalist utopia, of the repressive state that emerged during the 1790s in France—more evidence, were it needed, that the French Revolution's slide into despotism during the Terror was the product of historical circumstance rather than political theory or philosophical imagination. Mercier's twenty-fifth-century state is in fact quite genial: only a small force is needed to maintain public order, though the police are assisted by municipal "censors," who perform supervisory tasks such as preventing idlers from exploiting the hospitality provided at the common table. This idea, too, was inspired by Rousseau, who advocated a form of "censorship" to uphold agreed norms of conduct and prevent the corruption of public opinion.[15]

Transparency is another key civic principle in Mercier's scheme. Prisoners are held in public view as a deterrent; tax defaulters are punished by having their names published; authors of "immoral" works are forced to wear a mask in public and to hold discussions with two "contradictors" each morning until they change their views. Any work of art that is not socially useful is banned: it is "expressly forbidden" to sculpt subjects that do not "speak to the soul." History, "the shame of humanity," is almost entirely eliminated from schools, and during a visit to the king's library Mercier is informed that millions of books deemed "shameful to reason" have been purged. In this future utopia, a massive bonfire has consumed 600,000 dictionaries, 200,000 volumes of jurisprudence and poems, 1.6 million travel books, and 1 billion novels and dramas as well as entire collections of reviews and newspapers. Most of Voltaire's work, which "lacked depth," has perished; the only author whose entire *oeuvre* has been preserved is Rousseau.[16]

Regenerating Humankind

Between the autumn of 1831 and the spring of 1832, the Saint-Simonian newspaper *Le Globe* received more than 2,000 letters from its readers. Preserved in the archives of the Bibliothèque de l'Arsenal in Paris, this copious correspondence reflects how widely ideas about political and social reform were disseminated in French society. The correspondents engaged with the often contentious ideas put forward by the Saint-Simonians—the abolition of inheritance, the emancipation of women, and the founding of a new progressive religion aimed at alleviating poverty. But the most striking feature of the letters was their historical depth and intellectual diversity. They are steeped in references to Enlightenment philosophers (notably Voltaire and Rousseau), contemporary writings by republican and liberal authors, and the works of other French utopian thinkers. These contributors came from all walks of life: they were students, workers, artists, priests, mayors, members of Parliament, doctors, lawyers, industrialists, and farmers; there was even a customs inspector. These men (and, in some cases, women) talked about ideas not as ethereal forms of thought but as instruments for making better sense of their lives and times and helping the less fortunate members of society. For even though they did not agree on a common vision of the future, these correspondents were united in the diagnosis that France's successive political revolutions, from 1789 through to the final overthrow of the Bourbon monarchy in 1830, had failed to establish a proper sense of community among the French people. As one put it, "men have become strangers to each other."[17]

Although they rejected the political heritage of the Revolution and condemned its descent into violence, nineteenth-century French utopian thinkers took away one decisive idea from the 1790s: that a reformed humanity would not come about spontaneously but required mobilization and collective action. The time for the sedate utopianism of the Enlightenment era, typified by Mercier's gentle writings, was over: postrevolutionary reformers were zealous voluntarists. Saint-Simon and his disciples sought to lead humanity in improving the condition of the most deprived sections of society; and to this end, they proposed a new temporal and spiritual hierarchy in which power was exercised by industrialists and scientists. The earlier belief in the possibility of reforming the political order by means of an improved public morality—the legacy of Rousseau and the *philosophes*, which shone so brightly throughout Mercier's narrative—was replaced by bolder ideas of human cooperation and more self-conscious visionaries. During his first meeting with the liberal philosopher Germaine de Staël, Saint-Simon told his host: "Madam, you are the most extraordinary woman in the world; since I am the most extraordinary man on earth, the two of us would no doubt make an even more extraordinary child."[18]

The greatest visionary of the era, Charles Fourier, was the first to combine all these elements in a new synthesis, a set of ideas breathtaking both in its sweep and in its imaginative creativity. "It is not with moderation that one accomplishes great things," he observed in his seminal work, *The Theory of the Four Movements*. He was true to his maxim. Forging his "social science" on his twin principles of radical skepticism and absolute distance (*écart absolu*), Fourier began with a damning verdict on the bankruptcy of modern civilization. Political and spiritual leadership had collapsed (the French Revolution had been a "catastrophe"), and the "social misery" of humanity was reflected in the greed and inefficiency of commercialism that was typified by English society. This decrepitude was compounded by the sexual misery of marriage, with its enslaved women and adulterous couples. Fourier, a stickler for numerical accuracy, distinguished nine degrees of cuckoldry: his portrait of the genre included the "fatalist," who was resigned to his condition; the "federal," who chooses his wife's lover; and the "mystic," who surrounds his wife with priests and holy men, one of whom seduces her "for the greatest glory of God."[19]

Fourier's insight was that human emancipation required not yet another grand constitutional redesign but a focus on the human senses. Drawing on the tradition of the libertine thinking of the later Enlightenment (notably, the works of Diderot and the Marquis de Sade), he identified twelve passions, from simple sensual experiences to the complex psychological mechanisms governing calculation and the organization of work, and concluded that "true happiness consists in satisfying all the passions." This new harmony would be achieved by regrouping citizens into "phalanxes," self-contained agricultural communities of around 1,600 members each. These groups, by pooling resources, would overcome the limitations of small landholdings and lack of capital. High returns would be guaranteed to all members, thanks to greater productivity and regulated competition among the units. The people would be housed in "phalansteries," buildings taking their architectural cues from the galleries of the Palais-Royal in Paris. These units would provide everything needed for the flowering of human capabilities: pleasurable and varied economic activities commensurate with the preferences of men and women; a comprehensive system of education for all children up to the age of sixteen; and diverse forms of leisure, from spaces for reflective contemplation to ballrooms, operas, and meeting halls. As befitted a sensualist utopia, the phalanstery would provide an abundance of food (five full meals served each day, as well as two hearty snacks). And sex, too, would be in plentiful supply, with conventional marriage replaced by the "progressive household," a system of free love in which women enjoyed complete sexual liberation.[20]

The advances of Fourier's regenerated humanity were prodigious: harnessed by liberated passions, average life expectancy would rise to 144 years, and human beings would grow to seven feet tall (this was an extension of Condorcet's belief that "the perfectibility of the human race must be seen as susceptible to indefinite progress"). Genius would no longer be limited to exceptional individuals, for there would be 37 million Homers and just as many Newtons and Molières, and their greatest scientific and literary achievements would be rewarded by the title "Citizen of the Globe." The Sahara would be transformed into a fertile zone by a volunteer army of agricultural workers, and canals would pierce through the isthmuses of Suez and Panama. The phalansteries of the planet would be linked together by a territorial system of governance, and leaders would be democratically elected—all the way up to the "omniarch," the universal emperor, whose seat would lie at Constantinople. This harmony would be reflected (and enabled) by cosmic changes driven by the pantheistic laws of "universal attraction": as the earth entered a higher phase in its development, its "original moons" would be restored and the tilt of its axis corrected. With the providential help of an aurora borealis, temperatures in the Arctic Circle would rise, causing a melting of the icecaps and a general shift in the global environment—which would in turn allow for the cultivation of lands in northern Canada and Siberia and the transformation of seawater into a form of lemonade called *aigresel*. Although this Elysium was not infinite, humans would be able to take consolation in the promise that their souls would be reincarnated and could spend (Fourier was again precise) an average of 27,000 years on Earth and 54,000 years on other stars.[21]

Settlements inspired by the idea of the phalanstery were attempted in France and the United States, but with disappointing results. The Brook Farm experiment outside Boston, for example, inspired Nathaniel Hawthorne's *Blithedale Romance* (1852). After his death in 1837, Fourier's disciples sought to maintain his intellectual legacy through pamphlets and newspapers and in annual commemorations of his birthday, and their efforts continued until the late nineteenth century. Fourierist groups were particularly active in creating local producer associations, and they participated in peace movements and anticlerical and educational leagues. But the general view was that Fourier's schemes and the philosophy underlying them were hopelessly naïve and impractical. This was the reason why Marx and Engels, while acknowledging Fourier's contribution to the founding of socialist doctrine, dismissed his ideas as too "utopian."[22]

Yet, once his ideas were stripped of their jargon and unconventional formulations, many of them had a lasting impact on radical republican, socialist, and anarchist thinking. They were a powerful harbinger of a libertarian, antiauthoritarian sensibility that has been a consistent presence in modern French progressive thought—notably, in its celebration of the value of associational activity and human diversity, its desire to reconcile private property with social reform, and its intuition that the progress of a society should be measured by its treatment of women. Along with the Saint-Simonians, the disciples of Fourier also made major contributions to the French tradition of the *grand projet*—perhaps none more so than the engineer Charles Bergeron, one of the early designers of that most fanciful of Franco-British schemes, the Channel Tunnel.[23]

Visions of Equality

Although Fourier and Saint-Simon diverged on a number of important issues, their utopian schemes had one significant characteristic in common: they were not overly preoccupied with the question of equality. They paid scant attention to the issue of political representation, which was one of the primary concerns of liberal and republican thinkers during the first half of the nineteenth century. The idea that poverty should be addressed by making humans conform to some common notion of the good life was an affront to Fourier's libertarian sensibility. Similarly, the precept that the possessions of all citizens should be shared equally did not chime with the Saint-Simonians' commitment to industrial expansion and their belief in legitimate social hierarchies.

Powerful republican traditions of egalitarian utopianism did emerge in nineteenth-century France. They took their cue, of course, from the French Revolution, which had heralded the principle of equality as the first article of the Declaration of the Rights of Man and of the Citizen. However, while successive French regimes from 1789 onward had broadly observed the principle of civil equality, few citizens enjoyed full political rights, such as the right to vote; access to property ownership remained limited; and governments did little to ameliorate the conditions of the poorer sections of society. It was against this historical backdrop, and in the face of ongoing conservative efforts to justify existing social hierarchies, that arguments about promoting equality in the ideal republican society were propounded in France from the 1820s.[24]

The mainstream republican view was that political equality was the cardinal principle of a just social order. The republican leader Godefroy Cavaignac, in his blistering challenge to the restricted political rights enjoyed by French citizens under the system of constitutional monarchy, argued that "absolute equality among men" should be the overriding goal of progressive politics. A pamphlet defined this principle as follows: "the equal participation of all citizens in civil and political matters, irrespective of their rank or fortune." Republicans believed that political equality would lead to the formation of a truly democratic government, which through mass enfranchisement would have as its consequence, as a progressive pamphlet put it, the "improvement of the physical and moral condition of the poorest and most numerous classes."

This idealized vision of universal suffrage was given its ultimate definition in the 1860s by Jules Ferry, one of the rising stars of the republican movement: the mass vote was "the honor of multitudes, the guarantee of the disinherited, the reconciliation of classes, and the promise of legality for all." Seen in this light, equality was about opportunity and enablement: as the republican thinker Adolphe Rion put it, it was not "the equal possession of all things but an equal right to acquire all things." The "monstrous disparities" between rich and poor would not be overcome overnight, or through violence, but by means of a system of public assistance, "the first duty of the Republic." Support to the needy would be funded by progressive taxation, which would enable the state to raise general living standards. As they defended this egalitarian ideal against their conservative critics, republicans were nonetheless careful to stress its boundaries; in the words of a pamphlet outlining the ways of tackling poverty: "Sensible people do not push the love of equality to absurd limits."[25]

More radical voices challenged this vision of a republican society based on political equality. For one thing, its "universality" was limited to men, an idea that naturally provoked strong objections by French feminists. Their rejection of the republicans' masculine conception of citizenship was first expressed in the feminist writer Olympe de Gouges's seminal *Declaration of the Rights of Woman and the Female Citizen* (1791), which preceded Mary Wollstonecraft's *Vindication of the Rights of Woman* by a year. Gouges's first article asserted that "women are born free and enjoy equal rights to men." Such a view found limited acceptance among the revolutionaries in France; the only major *philosophe* who supported feminine equality was Condorcet, who declared in a speech in 1790 that the Revolution's exclusion of women from civic life was a "violation of the principle of equality, and a deprivation of the rights of half of the human race." Later writers, such as the socialist feminist Jeanne Deroin, likewise observed that "to split humanity into two unequal groups, to deny women their rights to freedom and equality, is to contradict [revolutionary] principles."[26]

Advocacy of the feminine cause met with staunch opposition from the male establishment (both progressive and conservative). Male writers pointed out that in 1850 half the female population of France was illiterate. Yet powerful voices nevertheless emerged to champion (and embody) the claims of women's empowerment in the course of the nineteenth century: diverse figures such as the socialist writer Flora Tristan, who captured the progressive blind spot for feminine emancipation when she defined women as the "proletariat of the proletariat," and the writer and essayist George Sand, who became an international celebrity during her lifetime, and whose novels offered a subtle but powerful vision of women's self-realization. Sand was a republican socialist who was blessed with a wonderful capacity to empathize even with those whose views were very different from her own, as her letters to Gustave Flaubert demonstrate. With her fierce hostility to violence, her soaring humanity, and her talent for appealing to people's nobler instincts, her life and political thought bring home the nefarious consequences of the exclusion of women from the French political sphere. The most remarkable of these figures was Juliette Adam, whose first feminist pamphlet was published in 1858, and who became one of the great literary figures of the second half of the nineteenth century, as much because of her prolific writings (novels, memoirs, and political commentaries) as through *La Nouvelle Revue*, which she founded in 1879. Her Paris home became the seat of the most influential *salon* of the early Third

Republic and was frequented by key politicians, such as Léon Gambetta and Georges Clemenceau.[27]

Others were critical of republican doctrine because of its limited understanding of the economic sources of inequality. The republican socialist Louis Blanc argued that the only effective way of dealing with the injustices produced by economic competition was through state-sponsored "social workshops," co-operative associations that would guarantee all citizens the right to work. More controversially, the libertarian socialist Pierre-Joseph Proudhon followed Rousseau in asserting that the modern system of property ownership was a violation of man's natural rights; his conclusion became one of the slogans of modern anarchist thought: "Property is theft."[28]

Although Proudhon did not actually propose to abolish property, his ideas resonated with revolutionary republicans who believed that private ownership was the root cause of social inequality. The radical conspirator Philippe Buonarroti argued that the French Revolution had ultimately failed because it had entrenched political rights in property. The solution was to replace this enduring "order of egoism" with the "order of equality." Inspired by his reading of Rousseau and the memory of the revolutionary republican François-Noël (Gracchus) Babeuf's "Conspiracy of the Equals" in 1796, which sought to create a system in which all citizens enjoyed access to property, Buonarroti made the case for a community in which "the acts and properties of each individual were subject to the will of the sovereign people." Advocating "absolute equality" through the negation of private ownership and the establishment of a society based on the principle of "community," this "Babouvist" approach (named after Babeuf) trumpeted its revolutionary utopianism. As Jean-Jacques Pillot, one of its leading intellectual figures, put it, its aim was "totally to change the surface of the earth, and to bring in for all its inhabitants a completely new life, for which there is no precedent in history."[29]

The most elaborate nineteenth-century vision of this utopian community was sketched by Étienne Cabet. A self-styled communist and former member of the conspiratorial underground movement the Carbonari, Cabet did not believe that change could be achieved through violence. He explained that his political views had completely changed after he had become convinced (again, with Rousseau's help) "that inequality was the real, original, and primordial cause of all the vices and miseries of all societies." Like many of the first generation of French socialist thinkers, Cabet embraced a communism that was also shaped by Christian doctrine. He would quote from the Gospel of St. Luke to justify his egalitarianism: "Every valley shall be filled, and every mountain and hill shall be brought low; and the crooked shall be made straight, and the rough ways shall be made smooth."[30]

Cabet described his ideal community at great length in his novel *Voyage en Icarie* (*The Voyage to Icaria*), first published anonymously in 1839. The work was a great popular success: it was republished four times and translated into English, German, and Spanish. In it, Cabet narrates the adventures of an English nobleman, Lord William Carisdall, on the island of Icaria. Here, in a country with the combined population of England and France, the principle of community has been fully achieved by means of a simple device: "the substitution of inequality by equality." Cabet's political philosophy was indisputably collectivist. Thanks to the vision of the revolutionary dictator and founder of the new order, Icar (something of a cross between Jesus Christ and Thomas More), private property, social classes, and money have been abolished; there is also no commerce, as the republic provides all the citizens' necessities—from clothing, accommodation, transportation, and education to food, which is delivered daily to every household by a provisions cart (the utopian anticipation of the supermarket delivery van). As in Mercier's Paris, all problems of urban public hygiene and communication have been scientifically resolved. Buildings and streets are designed according to "perfect proportions"; hospitals are as beautiful as palaces and staffed with armies of highly skilled physicians; and public transport is provided by a network of carriages, trains, and balloons; there are even, for those wishing to explore marine life, "underwater boats."[31]

Power is exercised in this utopian society by a collegial executive and seconded by a network of national, provincial, and local institutions elected by (male) universal suffrage; popular committees also play an active role in civic life. Family life is serene, happy, even joyful, and all citizens enjoy freedom of religious worship, with the majority subscribing to a civil religion with no idols or rituals. Production is organized by the state, which fixes the number of workers needed annually in different sectors of industry and agriculture. Labor is no longer considered onerous, because some demeaning jobs (such as domestic service) have been abolished; working hours are rigorously fixed, and the most difficult tasks are performed by machines.[32]

Cabet's communist society is highly regulated. There are no cafés or gambling houses, and a nightly curfew is observed between 10 p.m. and 5 a.m. Art is controlled by the state and is characterized by chastity and (just like in Mercier's utopia) by social utility. Clothing is likewise designed according to "model plans"; citizens wear different uniforms that correspond to their age and occupation. Food is abundant, with five meals served each day—but it is up to the legislature to decide which vegetables are to be grown, and "nourishment committees" determine the composition of menus as well as the proper ingredients to be used. Monogamy is the norm, and adultery is considered a crime; there is none of Fourier's amorous frolicking, as Icaria is inhabited only by "chaste women, respectful men, and faithful and respected couples." A form of eugenicism is practiced to improve the species, all under the supervision of a "Perfection Commission" (Cabet was fond of committees). Although there is no public justice system (prisons have been abolished and there are no judges or police officers), civic surveillance is pervasive, and any form of deviance from collective customs is reported to local bodies, which have the power to act as tribunals. As in Mercier's Paris, books deemed injurious to public morality are destroyed (but, in an interesting refinement, some are re-written). The number of newspapers is strictly limited, with only one national daily—and nothing can be printed without the "consent of the Republic."[33]

Ideals of Fraternity

O good, strong, just and all-powerful God, grant thy protection and support to all those who are battling for two great and noble causes: the abolition of standing armies and the advent of a general peace, that is to say the end of wars and massacres through the abolition of all monarchies, and the founding of a universal Republic. Thanks to the constitution of a United States of Europe, all peoples who are brothers will be joined together, and will experience a new era of prosperity and progress such as has never been seen since the dawn of time. May all the great citizens of the world behold, with their own eyes, from the banks of the Thames to the verges of the Neva, from the Tiber to the Bosphorus, the glorious three colors and ten stars of the flag of the United States of Europe.[34]

Published in a local republican newspaper at the height of the Franco-Prussian War in 1870, this rousing appeal, complementing the ideas behind the futuristic and collectivist utopias previously described, illustrates one of the resurgent themes in nineteenth-century French idealist thought: the hope for the establishment of a peace-loving universal republic. The egalitarian dreams of social reformers that had resonated so powerfully in the French Romantic imagination in earlier decades were dealt crushing blows by the failure of the 1848 Revolution. The new Republic began auspiciously, with a decree abolishing slavery, but popular aspirations for a "democratic and social" order were rapidly (and violently) suppressed, and the government refused to side with insurrectionary movements launched by European republicans. Insult was added to injury when Louis Napoléon, the democratically elected president, overthrew the regime a few years later in a *coup d'état* and restored the empire (1852). Instead of the affable dictator depicted in Cabet's utopia, French progressives found themselves trapped under the boot of a despotic Caesar. Their cosmopolitan turn was a reflection of their predicament: along with Victor Hugo in Jersey, many republican intellectuals were in exile during the 1850s and 1860s in London, Brussels, and Geneva. The change in attitude was a tacit recognition of the limitations of the egalitarian creed they had espoused during the previous era.

This universalist reverie marked the apogee of that most powerful and elusive of French progressive ideals: fraternity. The idea of securing global harmony through the creation of a confederation of like-minded, peace-loving states was another legacy of Enlightenment thinking, notably in the visionary projects of the Abbé de Saint-Pierre and Immanuel Kant (whose *Perpetual Peace* was translated into French in 1796). The French Revolution added a more combative dimension to *fraternité:* the word was first used by Robespierre in a speech about the National Guard. From this moment on, *fraternité* designated a principle of active revolutionary citizenship that linked membership in the political community to civic duties and rights.[35]

For the more enthusiastic republicans, fraternity also implied solidarity among the peoples of the world who were struggling against tyranny. In this scheme of things, patriotism and internationalism were mutually reinforcing principles. Commenting on the article of the 1793 Jacobin Constitution that declared all men to be brothers, the republican thinker Albert Laponneraye noted, in the early 1830s, "That a man be born at the extremities of the earth, or among us, that his skin be black or white, he is no less of a human being than us; he is our brother, and if he needs our help, we need to assist him; if he is in danger, we need to fly to his rescue." The French republican struggle against the July Monarchy was thus inextricably linked to support for the Polish insurrection against Russian occupation—the great cause of its time in European progressive politics. In the words of the republican leader Armand Marrast, "The principles of morality are not enclosed by frontiers: they are common to all continents, to all humanity. Peoples are brothers, as are men. The law of nations only has as its goal the universal association of peoples. This association is already being imagined and advocated by superior minds, who on our continent are working in concert for a *European republic.*"[36]

A decade later, this idea had almost become a commonplace. In the early, optimistic months of the 1848 Revolution, the titles of some Parisian newspapers bore witness to the heady appeal of fraternal universalism: *Alliance des peuples, Europe républicaine, Fraternité des peuples,* and *Harmonie universelle* (there was also the robust *Fraternité cri de guerre,* and, for those who still had not gotten the message, the even more direct *Guillotine*). Although bound by a common internationalist outlook, these visions were eclectic in their specific formulations. There was inevitably a touch of ethnocentrism, as with Frédéric Sorrieu's allegorical representation *La République universelle démocratique et sociale* (The universal democratic and social Republic, 1848). It depicted the figure of Marianne, the symbol of the Republic, on a chariot, accompanied by four children from different continents; the people heading the procession, however, are clearly French (and the city represented in the background is indisputably Paris).[37]

Likewise, in Victor Hugo's scheme for a "United States of Europe," there is a common currency and free movement of people and goods across borders; here, too, the popularly elected European assembly is located in Paris, the "center of the earth." In the positivist version of the "Occidental Republic" produced by Auguste Comte's disciple Émile Littré, the hierarchy of the putative "European federation" consists of a group of "superior" nations—the Latin, Anglo-Saxon, and Scandinavian peoples—who lead the way to the creation of a "common fatherland" through the eradication of militarism. In fact, aspirations for greater European unity came in all shapes and sizes among republicans: there were minutely detailed schemes imbued with a touch of religious mysticism, such as that presented in Jean-Joseph Brémond's *Plan de la confédération européenne et universelle* (Plan for a European and universal confederation); visions of organizing a central command of progressive parties, notably in the proclamation published in 1855 by leading European democrats from Hungary (Lajos Kossuth), Italy (Giuseppe Mazzini), and France (Alexandre Ledru-Rollin); radically cosmopolitan projects for universal fraternity, such as a group claiming that "the idea of a Humanity superior to all nations is now accepted by all republicans"; and appeals to form an alliance of progressive youth across Europe.[38]

Out of this diverse body of thought one overriding idea began to crystallize: the universal republic of peace and fraternity could emerge only through a concerted collective challenge to the despotism and militarism of monarchical rule. This notion was one of the major underlying factors in the creation of the International Workingmen's Association in 1864; its French components were active in promoting "universal solidarity" among European workers. A wider cross-section of groups—from pacifists and liberals to Saint-Simonians, republicans, and radical revolutionaries—came together to form the Ligue de la Paix et de la Liberté (League of Peace and Freedom) in 1867. Its founding congress was held in Geneva, with 6,000 delegates in attendance, including many leading lights in the French republican party. The final resolution called for the creation of a European confederation of democratic states; edited by

the former Saint-Simonist Charles Lemonnier, the Ligue's paper was entitled
Les États-Unis d'Europe.[39]

The most original contribution to this vision of fraternal internationalism came in Jules Barni's *La Morale dans la démocratie* (Morality in democracy, 1868). One of the cofounders of the Ligue, Barni elaborated a theory
of democratic peace that fortified Kant's liberal vision with elements drawn
from Rousseau and the nineteenth-century republican tradition of war against
monarchical despotism. In particular, he singled out "Caesarism" as the principal obstacle to a more just and humane society and thus restated the classic
republican imperative of combatting tyranny: "It is indeed a right inherent in
every human being to resist any power that wishes to oppress him; but it is
furthermore a duty of the citizen to overcome oppression by all legal means
available, and in the absence of any other means, by the use of force."[40]

From the Communards to the Communists

This expansive and robust vision of a Universal Republic proved short-lived.
It ended after a brief revolutionary episode that would long resonate in the
collective memory of French and European progressives: the Paris Commune.
This revolutionary movement broke away from the French state and briefly
held power in the capital between March and May in 1871, just after the end
of the war that saw France's defeat by Prussia.

The Commune was a patriotic and idealistic movement that reflected the
richness of the French progressive tradition, notably in the democratic way
in which it was organized (its council was elected and it had nine commissions, and so Cabet's work had been admirably digested). It produced remarkable personalities: moderates such as the journalist Charles Delescluze,
intellectuals such as Félix Pyat, self-taught activists such as Eugène Varlin and
Benoît Malon, uncompromising zealots such as the Jacobin police chief Raoul
Rigault, and extraordinary female figures, the most celebrated of whom was
Louise Michel. Despite Marx's subsequent description of the Commune as
an example of the "dictatorship of the proletariat," most of its elected leaders were petty bourgeois and skilled artisans—and, indeed, largely unfamiliar
with Marx's works (the only genuine "Marxist" among the Communards was
the Hungarian communist Léo Frankel).[41]

The Commune's intellectual inspirations were diverse. They ranged from
the radical revolutionism of Auguste Blanqui, which was driven by his dream
of "happiness for humanity in the future," to the federalist republican tradition, which opposed state centralization and celebrated the ideals of municipal self-government and grassroots involvement in public life. Most of the

Communards shared a general commitment to the idea of social reform drawn from classic thinkers such as Rousseau. They also drew from nineteenth-century republican socialists (notably, Louis Blanc and Pierre-Joseph Proudhon). The Commune achieved little in terms of social reform (the only practical measure it adopted was the abolition of night work in Parisian bakeries), but its spirit was utopian, and many of its leading members expressed the ambition to "write a new page in history." More poetically, the Communards had faith in the regenerative force of the people: the principal character in Jules Vallès's novel *L'Insurgé* (*The Insurgent*) exclaims, "It seems no longer to be mine, this heart which has been scorched by so many ugly wounds, and it is the very soul of the crowd which now has filled and swells my breast." After coming into conflict with the Versailles-based French government led by Adolphe Thiers, the Commune was violently suppressed by the French Army in an atrocious bloodbath that lasted a week (*la semaine sanglante*). Thousands of people were killed.[42]

Traumatized by the circumstances of its birth—the massacre of the Commune and the loss of Alsace-Lorraine to Germany—the republican regime that emerged in France after 1871 increasingly veered away from its utopian roots and embraced nationalism. It displayed a marked hostility to all forms of idealist politics from the outset. Rejecting as "metaphysical" his earlier commitments to cosmopolitanism and global harmony, Émile Littré defined the newly established Republic's primary values as pragmatism, accommodation of competing interests, and maintenance of order—it was to be a "regime that best allows time to keep its just preponderance." And although the Third Republic instituted a representative democracy and traced its ideological lineage back to 1789, it reinterpreted the Revolution in an essentially depoliticized way.[43]

A major factor in the conservative drift of the Republic after 1880 was its massive expansion of the French colonial empire. At its height, between 1918 and 1939, the empire covered more than 12 million square kilometers and had a population of nearly 70 million. Particularly in its early years, there were some utopian aspects to French imperialism. In the nineteenth century, many French socialists and Saint-Simonians had advocated expanding the colonial settlements in the name of progressive ideals: Cabet thus welcomed French colonialism as evidence of the "conquest of the ignorant universe by humankind." Under the influence of Social Darwinism and the emerging discipline of anthropology in the later nineteenth century, republican universalism rapidly gave way to a racialized colonial ideology in which notions of heredity and European supremacy played a pivotal role. In 1884, Jules Ferry (who had by now moved on from the idealism of his youth) justified French colonialism in terms of "the right of superior races over inferior races," and republican education minister Paul Bert portrayed the white race as the "most intelligent, the most hard-working and the most courageous." For their part, African, Arab, and Chinese native peoples were represented in colonial literature in depreciative terms; blacks, in particular, were widely viewed as fatalistic, infantile, vain, and lazy. In their consecration of a hierarchical system that distinguished between subjects and citizens and condoned systematic violence against native populations, the elites of the Third Republic thus turned their backs on the universalism of the 1789 Declaration and the classical republican heritage of equality and fraternity.[44]

The flame of internationalist idealism was kept alive during this period by anarchists and radical elements in the French socialist movement and in the myth of the sudden overthrow of the capitalist system, the *grand soir*. The prospect of a radical transformation of European society seemed so distant by the late nineteenth century that the novelist Paul Adam located his communist utopia (inspired by the principles of Fourier, Saint-Simon, Proudhon, and Cabet) on a faraway Malaysian island. The socialist leader Jean Jaurès alluded to the remoteness of this utopian horizon in the first issue of his newspaper *L'Humanité* in 1904, observing, "Humanity does not yet exist, or barely exists." Jaurès challenged the rise of European militarism, offering the alternative of a community bound by the ideals of international solidarity and peace. He was increasingly critical of French colonialism, not so much on grounds of principle, but because of the imposition and maintenance of French rule by force. Writing about the exactions of the French Army in North Africa in March 1912, Jaurès deplored the greed inherent in colonial interests and the short-sightedness of successive republican governments; the image of France in the Arab world had been turned, he said, into that of a "purely destructive power." In a parliamentary debate in the same year, Jaurès defended Islamic civilization, which, he observed, "had made such great contributions in the fields of philosophy, science and art, and which is full of such promise." The assassination of Jaurès at the outbreak of World War I seemed to symbolize the demise of this vision of possible harmony, paving the way for the emergence, after 1920, of the most comprehensive and powerful articulation of modern French utopian thinking: communism.[45]

At a 1939 meeting of the French Communist Party, party leader Maurice Thorez declared that "the path of the Communist International, our path, is that of the struggle to empower the working class, and of the edification of socialism. Communism is not the stuff of chimeras, dreams, or utopias. It represents the happy lives of 180 million Soviet citizens, the happiness of an ardent youth; it will be our life, too, and that of our children. It will be the life of our people, the lives of all peoples who will one day be freed from capitalist slavery."[46] In these lyrical sentences, he summed up the distinctive features of the French communist dream. Like all utopias, it promised the achievement of happiness for humankind. But in this instance the promise was to come through revolutionary ideals: liberating workers from the shackles of capitalism and constructing an egalitarian and fraternal society. The vision was powerfully disseminated by Thorez's own autobiography, *Fils du peuple* (*Son of the People*), one of the best-selling works of the mid-twentieth century. First published in 1937, and revised after World War II, it outlined the promise of communism by narrating the rise through party ranks of a humble worker (Thorez was born in a poor mining community in the Pas-de-Calais). Thorez celebrated the writings of Marx and Engels, both in their analysis of capitalist oppression and in their depiction of the collective virtues of the proletariat: its pride, heroism, virility, patriotism, and sense of solidarity. Communism, the "purest and noblest ideal of humanity," in Thorez's view, was thus presented as a practical goal, a method of pursuing the liberation of man by effectively harnessing the Promethean capacities of reason.

There was an additional twist. The global advent of the communist Elysium was inextricably linked to the fate of the Soviet state created by V. I. Lenin and the Bolsheviks after the 1917 October Revolution. Hence the particular quality of twentieth-century communism, which was genuine in its universalism but at the same time very much attached to the Soviet state. This was one of the paradoxical keys to the enduring appeal of communist doctrine in France: it retained an idyllic, utopian character despite becoming institutionalized in an existing political order. Thorez's account of his first visit to the Soviet Union in 1925 was in this sense exemplary: he found a "new world" inhabited by joyful workers and emancipated intellectuals; there were vast schools, magnificent laboratories, and a "real" democracy.[47]

Such rose-tinted representations were common in reports of Soviet life in French Communist Party publications. In the late 1940s, the Soviet Union was variously depicted in the regional party press in France as a land "where deserts were fertilized"; "bread would soon be free"; "the aspirations of all workers had been realized"; "wheat grew to unimaginable heights"; and, in a striking echo of Fourier's notion of the regeneration of temperate lands, "cherries and strawberries were cultivated in northern territories."[48] The most remarkable contributions to this idealization of the Soviet regime came from non-communist sympathizers who traveled to the Soviet state and found the promised land: men such as the republican leader Édouard Herriot, who visited Ukraine in 1933 (at the height of the famine) and returned to report that he had seen "a garden in full bloom"; and the writer and poet Charles Vildrac, for whom Stalinist Russia appeared as "a great free road on firm soil, toward distant perspectives, along which a whole people audaciously advances."[49]

Communism's extraordinary appeal in France was partly a matter of context, as were earlier patterns of utopian thinking. Although it was conceived earlier, communism's rise came out of World War I, and its apogee in France between the 1930s and the 1960s coincided with one of the most troubled periods in the nation's modern history: in an era of intensified global and colonial conflicts, endemic regime instability, and entrenched class warfare, there was undeniably a bracing quality to an ideology that promised universal happiness and *des lendemains qui chantent* (singing tomorrows). The belief in a future age of happiness played a major role, all the more so in that communism effectively capitalized upon earlier strands of French idealist thinking. The Enlightenment's quest for an educated citizenry and a common secular morality; the Revolution's Rousseauist yearning for the regeneration of man; Fourier's aspiration to eradicate poverty and promote greater social harmony; the Saint-Simonians' cult of perfectibility and unleashing of industrial productivity; Cabet's benign dictatorship and utilitarian conceptions of artistic and cultural life; the Universal Republic's ideals of antimilitarism, peace, and international harmony among peoples—these age-old progressive ideals all found their place in French communist doctrine.[50]

Communism's seductiveness was reinforced by the visual appeal of its propaganda. Thus Pablo Picasso's classic *Dove of Peace* (1949) became a symbol of the progressive aspiration to universal fraternity. Reproductions and trinkets derived from the drawing were proudly displayed in the homes of communist families across France, as attested in the 1953 letter to the artist from nine-year-old François-José Bernard, who asked Picasso whether he could send him a replacement for "Mummy's porcelain dove," which had been broken. The party also revived, in a barely amended form, the religiosity of nineteenth-century French utopianism in its cult of humanity, its distinction between good and evil, and its sense of patriotic sacrifice and martyrdom (notably, during the Resistance, when thousands of communists died fighting the German occupation). For a while there was even a celebration of human providentialism, personified by the Soviet leader Joseph Stalin. His deification reached its zenith during the commemoration of his seventieth birthday in 1949, when the French communist daily *l'Humanité* reproduced messages of adulation from party militants, including this pious wish: "May your benevolent Light reign on the planet for many more years!" Shortly before his death in 1964, Thorez dreamt that he was conversing with Lenin: for communists, too, it seemed, there was a heaven.[51]

Although twentieth-century communism was doctrinally rigid, the utopian visions it inspired were surprisingly elastic. The Soviet Union's allure in France varied over time: in the early years of the communist regime it was the social and cultural advances of Soviet society that drew praise. The French republican politician Anatole de Monzie thus described the Soviet system as a "social Eden," and the surrealists found an echo of their radically subversive conception of the artistic imagination in the Trotskyite ideal of the permanent revolution. In the 1930s, the Soviet Union was celebrated for its imposition of a centralized order, symbolized by Stalin's Five-Year Plans; even the brutal collectivization of the countryside was welcomed in some Western circles as the "accomplishment of a positive utopia." At the height of the Cold War, as French progressives challenged US military and economic hegemony, the Soviet state appeared as a beacon of liberty and toleration. Jean-Paul Sartre returned from his trip there in 1954 to proclaim that "freedom of expression in the Soviet Union is total."[52]

And when the Soviet star began to fade in the 1960s, other ideological experiments captivated the imagination of Parisian intellectuals: notably, the Cuban Revolution, with its heroic figures (Fidel Castro, Che Guevara) and its tropical sensualism ("The Cubans are a rhythmic people, and hatred does not resist rhythm," declared the journalist Jean Daniel in 1963); and the states emerging from anticolonial struggles, notably in Algeria, where thousands of intellectual activists (doctors, teachers, journalists, technicians, and artists) traveled after 1962 in a spirit of fraternal internationalism to help construct a new society. More exotically, there was the Chinese Cultural Revolution, which drew support in Paris by dint of its mysteriousness, its austere egalitarianism, and its puritanism. Although it proved short-lived, French Sinophilia produced some aberrations that surpassed even the most absurd paeans to the glory of the Soviet Union, as when the feminist writer Julia Kristeva argued that the Chinese feudal practice of footbinding was evidence of women's "secret power."[53]

The most telling illustration of the elasticity of French communist doctrine was its capacity seamlessly to absorb the nation's cultural and political past and redeploy it to its own ends. From Descartes and the Enlightenment *philosophes* through the republican eminences of the nineteenth century to the Paris Communards of 1871 and the memory of Jaurès, all found their rightful place in the communist pantheon and were dutifully trotted out to serve political objectives. Thus, in the early 1950s, the poet Louis Aragon argued that Victor Hugo's commitment to peace and European internationalism precisely foreshadowed ongoing French communist campaigns against Western imperialism. The most fruitful of these ideological reappropriations was the French Revolution. As noted earlier, the Russian revolutionaries were themselves obsessed with analogies between 1789 and 1917. From the 1920s, equating Bolshevism with the "Jacobin" phase of the Revolution became a common theme in French thought (notably among progressive historians such as Albert Mathiez and Albert Soboul). The progressive writer Romain Rolland returned from a visit in 1935 to affirm that the Soviet Union had picked up the torch of the French Revolution and was carrying out its program of human renewal. During the 150th anniversary of the French Revolution in 1939, French communists trumped official commemorations by organizing a grand rally in which they celebrated the memory of key revolutionary figures such as Robespierre, Saint-Just, and Marat, asserting that the "Jacobins have as their successors the communists who are struggling under the banner of Marx, Lenin, and Stalin." At a speech in Arras, Thorez added helpfully (and probably accurately, too) that Robespierre would have approved of Stalin's 1936 Constitution; and in 1949, to complete the fetishism, the collection of French communist gifts sent to Moscow for Stalin's birthday comprised numerous revolutionary trinkets, including a fragment of the house where Saint-Just was born. The Soviets later reciprocated by dispatching a ribbon from a Paris Commune banner around the earth's orbit.[54]

The Utopian Imagination

The first two chapters highlighted the appeal of mysticism and philosophical rationalism to French modes of thinking. The strength, variety, and endurance of utopian ideals brings up another fundamental dimension of modern Gallic thought: the prodigious, captivating power of imagination. French utopianism was in this respect a child of Rousseau and his burning revolt against human injustice as well as his ambition to remove the obstacles that prevented humanity from realizing its true nature. His work reflected the richness of French utopianism and its capacity to inspire hope in successive generations of men and women, especially in the darker moments of their nation's history. In the entry for August 13, 1944, in his wartime diary, the writer and future academician Jean Guéhenno noted, "In his annotation of the *Social Contract*, Voltaire said of Rousseau: 'He was mad enough to believe that his books would cause revolutions.' Indeed so; and this is precisely why we are attracted to Rousseau."[55]

The works of Rousseau also captured the conflicting aspirations of French utopian thinking—between the head and the heart, between freedom from material need and intellectual liberation, between personal fulfillment and the practice of democratic self-government. As it developed over time, this utopianism helped to reinforce the wider modes of French thought identified in the Introduction to this book: a penchant for defining the good life around metaphysical ideals; a thirst for novelty and for departing from conventional reasoning; a capacity for producing broad, sweeping visions and a generous embrace of universalistic horizons; a love of paradox and a willingness to develop lines of argument to their furthest possible conclusions; and a passion for extensive and detailed programmatic blueprints.

Abstract in its design, systematic in its form, and radical in its goals, this utopian way of thinking about politics has been one of France's enduring contributions to modern political thought—and undoubtedly its most controversial. From Rousseau's citizen who acquires freedom through collective self-rule to the communist vision of the "new man," these schemes to bring about a transformation in human nature came to be viewed as one of the most dangerous features of French rationalism. Echoing Edmund Burke's denunciation of the French Revolution's "new conquering empire of light and reason," Alexis de Tocqueville noted the "extraordinary and terrible" influence of literary men in the eighteenth century and lamented their disposition to "indulge unreservedly in ethereal and general theories" in order to "rebuild society on some wholly new plan." Starting from a more philosophical premise, the philosopher Michel Foucault's questioning of Enlightenment thought arrived at no less a melancholic conclusion: the liberating sweep of "Reason" effectively cleared the way for new—and more perverse—forms of social and political oppression. To complete this sinister reputation, French utopian thinking was also frequently portrayed as prefiguring the homogenizing despotism of "totalitarianism"—defined by the philosopher Claude Lefort as the temptation to fill the void of modern democratic politics with the imaginary self-identity of the people.[56]

The utopian belief in the perfectibility of the human mind undeniably led at times to perverse forms of thought. This tendency was exacerbated by the cumulative quality of the utopian imagination: an internal dialectic of hope spurred it on and moved it forward. In this sense, twentieth-century communism represented the apogee of this tradition—which only underlines my assertion that, for all its idealization of the Soviet system, French communism remained deeply rooted in the nation's history and political culture. Utopian schemes, however, also represented an attempt to move beyond the individualistic horizon of Cartesian reason toward an ideal that was more collective. If there is a common theme that emerges in the vast literature of memoirs produced by ex-communists in France, it is that communism offered its intellectual adherents a way of experiencing the values of friendship, human solidarity, and fraternity.[57]

Here, too, Rousseau was a strong influence: social criticism was powerfully articulated in his work, and utopianism tapped into it, offering an escape from the narrow horizons of established society and the oppression of social conventions. Evoking the urgency of the revolutionary imperative, the main character in Paul Nizan's *La Conspiration* (*The Conspiracy*) decides that "it was time to end it all, without quite knowing whether it was a matter of covering Paris with barricades, or taking the train to get away from his father and mother for a few weeks." Utopian doctrines fitted comfortably with (and in some sense complemented) republican patterns of thinking: the aspiration to break with the past; the belief in the possibility of a rational organization of society; the desire to restore some form of community among the citizenry based on new spiritual values; the sense that individual liberty could be effectively realized only through participation in a shared collective enterprise; and the thought that not just society, but human nature itself, could be changed by reshaping public institutions. This progressive heritage is still very much part of the imagination of the Left in France. Evoking the distinct "republican horizon" of contemporary French democratic culture, the historian Mona Ozouf described it as "forever carrying the hope that we are not condemned to accept the social order as it is."[58]

The intriguing point here is that these virtuous ideals were generated by the Republic even (and perhaps especially) after it became established as France's dominant regime. Utopia, in this sense, was not merely a remote prospect, something to be achieved in some distant time or location: it was a practical ideal that could be nurtured in a wide range of settings, from the mundane to the creative—in schools, municipal libraries, and holiday camps for children and in novels, films, and on stage. In December 1970, Ariane Mnouchkine's Théâtre du Soleil began a series of performances of a play entitled *1789*; its subtitle was *The Revolution Has to Stop with the Perfection of Human Happiness*. In historical terms, utopia was thus both an acknowledgment of the French Revolution and a recognition of its insufficiency. Or, to say the same thing in political terms, French political radicalism was the last avatar of the revolutionary tradition of 1789. This is why Bolshevism could appeal to so many different intellectual sensibilities in France during the twentieth century—and even serve as an efficient vehicle for celebrating French cultural supremacy. Thus the historian François Furet, writing from a postcommunist perspective in 1995, concluded that it was only through its amalgamation with French Jacobinism that the "primitive" revolution of the Bolsheviks had captured the modern utopian imagination. Honor was safe: the Revolution was over, but French Reason could retain its universality.[59]

CHAPTER 4

The Ideals of Science

In his two-volume *Bibliothèque d'un homme de goût* (Library of a man of taste), published in 1772, the Abbé Louis-Mayeul Chaudon listed the works that he believed should be held in any well-appointed library. He was a devout Christian and a critic of the *philosophes*, so, unsurprisingly, his recommendations included a raft of pious publications along with the books on travel, history, politics, literature, and rhetoric that one might expect. But he also gave special weight to works on subjects such as astronomy, geology, biology, chemistry, and medicine, commenting, "The books that are most agreeable and most useful, without doubt, are those that focus on the sciences."[1]

The later decades of the Enlightenment marked the apogee of French political and cultural influence in Europe, and in few spheres was this dominance more emphatic than in the sciences. It was during this period that Paris became known as one of the principal centers of a European "Republic of Sciences." France's *génie scientifique* was celebrated for its inventiveness as well as for its precision and accuracy: the 182 sheets of the cartography of France completed by successive generations of the Cassini family through the triangulation method, for example, became a model for the rest of Europe. In particular, thanks to the Cassinis, maps became a key instrument of modern statecraft.[2]

From the mid-eighteenth century to the Revolution, France witnessed a prodigious expansion across all sectors of scientific activity: the development of state-sponsored institutions, notably, the Académie des Sciences and the Collège Royal; the proliferation of international networks of collaboration; the growth of learned societies in the provinces; and the emergence of specialized scientific journals, such as the *Journal de physique*, founded by the Abbé

François Rozier in 1771. Diderot and d'Alembert's *Encyclopédie* celebrated the "empire of the sciences and the arts," and leading figures in their respective fields, such as Joseph Louis Lagrange and Gaspard Monge in mathematics, Antoine Lavoisier in chemistry, and Buffon in botany, became celebrities whose renown mirrored that of the *philosophes*—and at times even surpassed it. Daniel Mornet's survey of the catalogs of five hundred private book collections in Paris between 1750 and 1780 found the most widely owned work to be the *Dictionnaire historique et critique* (*Historical and Critical Dictionary*) by Descartes's disciple Pierre Bayle, held in almost three out of every five libraries—putting it well ahead of the literary and philosophical works of Voltaire and Rousseau. Also greatly prized was Buffon's *Histoire naturelle* (*Natural History*), which is estimated to have sold up to 50,000 copies and is extensively cited in the literature of the period.[3]

The Age of Enlightenment was utopian, and it was ever ready to embrace bold schemes and sweeping visions. But it also had a practical, utilitarian side, and part of the appeal of science, in addition to its ability to quench the thirst for knowledge among educated audiences, lay in its perceived benefits to society. Botany was established as a field of research at the Jardin du Roi, and public lectures on the subject began early in the morning, so that people could attend them before going to work. Science was also enjoyed for its aesthetic qualities. The title of another widely read work, Abbé Noël-Antoine Pluche's *Spectacle de la nature* (*Nature Displayed*, 1732), was in this sense revealing: although its pious author's underlying purpose was to show the hand of Providence in the operation of nature, his ostensible aim was to amuse and entertain his readers—a goal he achieved with flourish. There were at least eighteen French editions of the book, and it was translated into English, Italian, Spanish, and German. One of the figures who did the most for the popularization of science was the Abbé Jean-Antoine Nollet, a specialist in electricity who carried out experiments in public: a large gathering in Paris thus watched with wonder as he used a Leyden jar to transmit an electric shock to 180 Royal Guards, making them jump simultaneously. The scientist René de Réaumur became famous for his work on the history of insects, and admirers came from far and wide to gaze at his *cabinet de curiosités*, one of the richest in Europe. The taste for collecting natural relics of all kinds became widespread in the later eighteenth century, further fueling interest in the life sciences. The art dealer Edme-François Gersaint established a thriving business in his Notre-Dame store by selling collections of exotic plants as well as insects and reptiles from the Indies; he initiated the trade in shells, which flourished in subsequent decades.[4]

The prominence of science in French public life had important intellectual dimensions. Fundamental issues of scientific principle were frequently, and often passionately, discussed by the great minds of the age. And, unlike in England, where the Newtonian revolution had become so entrenched that it had turned into an orthodoxy, eighteenth-century French thinkers did not concur on many significant scientific issues—notably, on whether humanity's place in the universe was best seen in physical and mechanistic terms or through the framework of the organic sciences. And even as the latter view gained the upper hand in the later decades of the century, spirited debates continued among interlocutors with Christian, deist, and atheistic conceptions of the natural world. Rousseau, who acquired a late passion for botany, observed, "By the manner in which it is treated, natural history can today be regarded as the most interesting of all the sciences." This fascination was all the more significant in that the thinkers of the late Enlightenment did not consider the physical and natural sciences in isolation from their wider moral and political philosophy. On the contrary, their ideas about the cosmos and nature were closely intertwined with the range of intellectual questions analyzed in this book's previous chapters—the role of reason, the meaning and limits of progress, and the best way to reorganize the nation's political institutions.[5]

Science was thus at the heart of the major issues that dominated cultural life in the later decades of the eighteenth century and eventually culminated in the French Revolution. This incorporation of scientific elements into visions of the good life has been a constant feature of the modern French way of thinking. The concern with science underscores some of the classic traits of Gallic intellectual culture, such as its celebration of men of learning, its propensity to view things on a grand scale, and its fetish for unifying theoretical syntheses and for formulations that are far-reaching, or perhaps outlandish, or sometimes both. But other aspects of the French style of thinking also came to light with the rise of science: its inherently disputatious and polemical character; its fascination with the notions of order, predictability, and linearity (and, paradoxically, its contempt for conformism); its obsession with religious forms and metaphors; its belief that the possession of a high degree of culture provides (in and of itself) an entitlement to rule; its ability to transform private setbacks and personal misfortunes into general philosophical worldviews; and its capacity to swing from energetic optimism to melancholic pessimism.

The Physical and Natural Worlds

Science is typically represented as one of the defining attributes of the Enlightenment era. Although this characterization is undeniably accurate, it has often led to the portrayal of the scientific thinking of the age as an anticipation of "modernity" rather than a reflection of the distinct preoccupations of its own times. While they traveled in a broadly similar direction, the trajectory of the Enlightenment and that of scientific inquiry at times diverged and, on occasion, clashed. There was no necessary conflict between science and religion—the clerical authors already cited illustrate the extent to which scientific ideals were embraced by men and women of faith. And, far from celebrating the value of universalistic explanations—"general laws," in today's parlance—the science of the eighteenth century was often skeptical of what it termed *l'esprit de système*. It was not just Catholic writers who warned about the limits of a purely humanistic science. Voltaire stressed the importance of building a complex picture of the world from simple, observable elements, and he was doubtful about the possibility of medical progress. Diderot's entry on "certainty" in the *Encyclopédie* disparaged the account of the world offered by mathematics; Rousseau, likewise, insisted on the limits of what the physical or mechanical sciences could achieve—a hostility perhaps not unrelated to his being nearly blinded by an explosion in 1737 while experimenting on invisible ink.[6]

The complexities of the Enlightenment's scientific outlook can be illustrated by one of the scandalous classics of the mid-eighteenth century, Julien Offray de La Mettrie's *L'Homme machine* (*Man a Machine*, 1747). Written as a polemic against theological accounts of human nature (notably, Descartes's distinction between mind and body), this book was a triumphant exposition of atheism and scientific materialism. At its heart was the claim that man was a purely mechanical entity whose functions (including the operation of the mind) were organically caused: "The body," La Mettrie affirmed provocatively, "is nothing more than a clock." Rejecting purely rationalist accounts of man (with a passing swipe at "those idlers whom vanity has decorated by the name of *philosophes*"), he asserted that the body was a self-sufficient entity, "a machine which builds its own components." But behind such brazen formulas lurked a more ecumenical vision. By applying Descartes's mechanistic view of animals to humans, La Mettrie was merely taking Cartesianism to its logical conclusion. His emphasis on the sensationist basis of knowledge was directly in line with English empiricism. Far from embracing a strident view of science, La Mettrie was at pains to underscore the limits of knowledge: "In all bodies, as in our own, the first causes are hidden, and will likely remain so for ever." And despite the coldness of his mechanistic metaphors, La Mettrie's vision of man was joyfully, liberatingly hedonistic: instinct, imagination, and eroticism were among the attributes he most cherished in his fellow humans. Fittingly enough for an epicurean who waxed lyrical about the "potent effect of Meals," he died in 1751 after overindulgent consumption of pheasant and truffle paté.[7]

The demarcation between rationalist science and supernatural beliefs was not always clear-cut in the eighteenth century. The powerful cultural impact of Mesmerism in the decade preceding the French Revolution was by no means an isolated occurrence. In his survey of Parisian book collections, Mornet found a considerable number of works on magic and sorcery listed under the rubric of "physics"; among the titles were Longeville Harcourt's *History of People Who Lived for Several Centuries and Who Were Rejuvenated*, L. L. de Vallemont's *Occult Physics; or, Treatise on the Divining Wand;* Daugy's *Treatise on Magic, Sorcery, Possessions, Obsessions and Evil Spells;* and the Abbé de Villars's *The Count of Gabalis; or, Discourse on the Secret Sciences.* The esteemed natural scientist Claude-Nicolas Le Cat, a member of several academies, published a book about animals found alive inside solid objects. In 1773, the *Journal encyclopédique* (Encyclopedic journal) published an article about a woman who gave birth to a girl who, in turn, delivered a baby eight days later. There were also stories about the palingenetic return to life of dead plants and animals, a tale of a man found alive after being immersed under water for seven weeks, and the old favorite: the account of a woman with horns growing on her head.[8]

There were significant divisions in eighteenth-century French scientific thought, notably between mechanistic and organic accounts of the universe. For physical scientists such as Lagrange, Pierre-Simon Laplace, and d'Alembert, and philosophers such as Voltaire and Helvétius, the cosmos was arranged according to a predetermined pattern whose laws could be apprehended through a mathematical type of reasoning; theirs was in many respects a continuation (or radicalization) of the tradition of Descartes and Newton. In opposition to this view emerged a naturalistic conception of the universe, which gained considerable ground in the later decades of the Enlightenment. It was expressed implicitly in the accounts of Buffon, and more robustly in the philosophical writings of Diderot, Montesquieu, and Rousseau: the emphasis here was on flux and change, on the transformation of being through death and rebirth, and on the potential for human goodness through free will and the proper disposition of sensibility. It has been suggested that this sentimentalism was one of the characteristic features of Enlightenment science. What gave an added tension to this clash between the physical and the life sciences was the metaphysical objective they shared. At stake in this dispute was the meaning of the transcendental order that could account for man's purpose and ultimate destiny. So, despite its professed adhesion to the Newtonian ideals of experimentation and observation, the primary purpose of the science of the eighteenth century was to demonstrate the congruence of the universe with the designs of a higher power.[9]

Across the scientific spectrum, writers competed with one another to come up with ever more ingenious arguments to establish this symbiosis. Voltaire expounded the "preformation" theory of the origins of man, which held that God created the embryos of all beings; such a "fixist" view did not allow for evolution. He also believed that Newton's science proved the existence of God, both in terms of first cause (if there was a creation, there had to be a creator) and through the design argument: the principle of gravity was thus believed to have been formulated to enable God's continued supervision of the universe. Natural design was a particular favorite among experimental theologians such as Pluche; another defining work in this tradition was Bernard Nieuwentijt's *The Existence of God Demonstrated by the Wonders of Nature* (1725). Not that such views were the preserve of the clergy: Bernardin de Saint-Pierre's *Harmonies de la nature* (*Harmonies of Nature*, 1815) made similar claims. And although there were no explicit references to the Scriptures in *Histoire naturelle*, Buffon was at pains to stress that his view of nature was consistent with Christian orthodoxy.[10]

Another type of first-cause argument was wielded by the proponents of *ferment* theory, the most notable defenders of which included Montesquieu and Rousseau. Rejecting the fixed view of the preformationists, those taking this approach saw life as the product of *ferment*, an invisible substance created by God and subject to constant change and evolution. Montesquieu's views on climate as the principal determinant of social order and belief in the need for laws to be adapted to different social conditions were direct outgrowths of his vision of nature. Similarly, Rousseau's democratic cult of the natural world and his revolutionary theory of the natural goodness of man were underpinned by his deistic conception of nature: life force existed in matter because it had been placed there by God. His profession of atheism notwithstanding, Diderot's views about humanity's solidarity with nature were entirely metaphysical. It was not only the political thought of the *philosophes* that was grounded in the imagination of the Heavenly City: their natural religion was, too.[11]

Both strands of French scientific thought, the physical and the naturalistic, played their parts in undermining the Christian cosmology of the *ancien régime*, helping to pave the way for the 1789 Revolution. But it was the ascendancy of the life sciences that proved determinant during the second half of the eighteenth century. Their ideals of transformation and regeneration and of inherent human goodness meshed harmoniously with the political thought of the early French Revolution, and, in particular, with the Jacobins' primitive Rousseauism, as did their pursuit of socially useful applications of science and their belief that science could be intuitively accessible. Hence the virulent hostility toward the established scientific academies displayed by figures such as Marat, who likened their work to "the quest to find the most advantageous design for toupées."[12]

Although the Jacobin Committee of Public Safety created a commission of scientists who "specialized in chemistry and mechanics" to assist with national defense, the major institutional landmark of the early revolutionary era was the Jardin du Roi, which was transformed into a democratically run Musée National d'Histoire Naturelle by a decree of the National Convention in June 1793. This change was accompanied a few months later by the abolition of the academies, which most Jacobins saw as symbols of "despotism, aristocratic prejudice and feudalism." In his project on the reform of public instruction, the Revolution-era painter and poet Gabriel Bouquier asserted that "free nations have no need for a caste of speculative scientists, whose minds constantly wander, through obscure paths, to the region of fantasies and chimeras. The purely speculative sciences detach individuals from society and in the long run become a poison that undermines, irritates, and destroys all republics." It is a measure of the extent to which the events of the immediate post-1789 years were misunderstood by their critics—notably, Edmund Burke—that this sentimental naturalism was the exact antithesis of the utopian philosophical universalism they believed to be animating the Revolution. Ironically, for much of the late Enlightenment, it was the English who were regarded (because of their commitment to the Newtonian heritage) as the principal purveyors of speculative thinking: as Montesquieu put it, "The imagination works to invent systems, and in this respect the English have made a greater contribution than any other nation."[13]

Solving the Problem of Life

On July 23, 1823, at noon, an auction of Napoleon's library at Saint Helena was held in London, at Sotheby's on Wellington Street, off the Strand. On offer was a large selection of works on history and geography as well as a sampling of literary classics, from Plutarch to Voltaire; many volumes contained handwritten comments by the emperor. But the most striking books of the collection were the ones devoted to scientific matters: there was a complete set not only of Buffon's *Histoire naturelle*, one of Napoleon's favorite works— but also Bézout's *Cours de mathématiques* (Mathematics course); Bouillon La Grange's *Manuel d'un cours de chimie* (Chemistry manual); Haüy's *Traité de minéralogie* (Treatise on mineralogy); Mentelle's *Géographie mathématique* (Mathematical geography); Delambre's *Astronomie théorique et pratique*

(Theoretical and practical astronomy); Fourcroy's *Système de connaissances chimiques* (System of chemical knowledge); and the Abbé Rozier's *Cours complet d'agriculture* (Complete agricultural course). After listing the nine volumes of Lacroix's *Traité du calcul* (Treatise on calculus), the catalog noted, "At the end of the volume that contains the algebra, there are three pages of calculations by Napoleon."[14]

These inscriptions confirm the observations of Napoleon's secretary, Emmanuel de Las Cases, who noted that the emperor was engrossed in these scientific works at Saint Helena, sometimes spending entire days reading them. And this was no fortuitous occurrence: as the naturalist Geoffroy Saint-Hilaire observed, from his early adolescence Bonaparte had a real passion for the sciences. At the Brienne military academy, and later in Paris, he was noted for his aptitude in mathematics and his general interest in the physical sciences. During the temporary hiatus in his career in early 1795, in the wake of Robespierre's fall, he occupied himself by attending lectures on chemistry and botany in Paris. In December 1797, upon his return from his triumphant Italian campaign, he decided to raise his profile by having himself elected to the Institut de France, the national scientific body established to replace the defunct academies.[15]

There were self-interested calculations on both sides here: Napoleon knew that his affiliation with France's scientific elite would further enhance his prestige, and the scientists, in turn, hoped they would stand to gain by their association with a military hero whose political star was rising. (Both parties turned out to be right.) In the ensuing years, Napoleon actively participated in the scientific life of his section at the Institut: in 1798 he helped draft a report on a steam car invented by Nicolas-Joseph Cugnot, and two days after his seizure of power in the *coup d'état* of the 18th Brumaire in 1799, he attended a session that discussed, among other things, a paper on differential equations by Jean-Baptiste Biot. Napoleon once remarked that from his adolescence he had dreamed of completing the Newtonian revolution by uncovering the secrets of the atom (*le monde des détails*): he regretted not having been able to devote himself to this task, for it would have allowed him to "resolve the problem of life in the universe."[16]

This was a typical display of Napoleon's intellectual ambition, as flamboyant as it was immodest. But it was no accident that he uttered these words in Egypt, during the course of an expedition he had specifically designed both as a colonial conquest and a scientific *grand projet*. More than a hundred scientists, including eminent figures such as the mathematician Gaspard Monge and the chemist Claude Louis Berthollet, accompanied him on his mission; their equipment included astronomical telescopes, compasses, levels, pneumatic machines, barometers, and surgical and medical instruments—as well as a printing press and complete laboratories for doing physics, chemistry, and work in natural history and aeronautics.

The scientific project carried out by the Institut d'Égypte was characteristic of the Napoleonic conception of science: it was a celebration of his glory (and became all the more important when it helped mask the eventual failure of the project to colonize Egypt). But it also represented remarkable advances in learning, notably in the discovery of the Rosetta Stone and Jean-François Champollion's subsequent deciphering of the ancient Egyptian hieroglyphs, and in the publication of the monumental *Description de l'Égypte* (*Description of Egypt*), the final volume of which appeared in 1826. The scientists were simultaneously involved in practical projects such as helping to devise efficient systems to bake bread for French troops, and producing gunpowder from local resources. War and science, in the Napoleonic scheme of things, went hand in hand, and examples of this cross-fertilization appeared in the Institut's publication *La Décade Égyptienne* (The Egyptian decade). Monge's article on mirages, for example, was based on observations gathered during the French Army's march from Alexandria to Cairo.[17]

In a sense, Egypt exemplified Napoleon's attitude toward science throughout his reign. The fact that he militarized the École Polytechnique reflected his primary instinct about the purpose of science. But he also lavished honors on his favorite *savants*, such as Berthollet and Laplace, men who played a key role in the advancement of pioneering scientific research during the empire. More generally, he supported the work of leading scientific institutions with awards of subsidies and prizes. The empire was thus the moment when French science was reorganized on a modern basis.[18]

His most important legacy, however, lay not in his accomplishments but in what he represented: the forging of a synthesis among the different ideas of Enlightenment science. After the upheavals of the early years of the Revolution, Napoleon marked a return to the Newtonian conceptions of the first half of the eighteenth century—that is, to a science based on observation, resting primarily on physics and mathematics. As a man of order, he found the notions of symmetry and linearity congenial. His conception of progress was technical and utilitarian: hence his high esteem for men such as the Montgolfier brothers and Alessandro Volta (known for the invention of the battery), who were awarded prestigious prizes by the Institut. At the same time, there was a powerful naturalist streak in Napoleon. In the spirit of Rousseau's *Émile*, he did not believe that scientific education should be universalized, and he had little faith that science could make for human happiness: "I do not believe that science is indispensable to man and I certainly do not think that, without

Euclid, one cannot experience joy." His lifelong admiration for Buffon has already been noted; he also had great esteem for the work of Georges Cuvier and Bernard-Germain de Lacépède and for naturalist writers such as Bernardin de Saint-Pierre. His support for the Musée d'Histoire Naturelle was exceptionally strong.[19]

This explains why, when contemplating his impending exile in the summer of 1815, Napoleon declared that "only the sciences" could henceforth captivate his spirit. The republican astronomer François Arago was invited to accompany him on a grand exploration of the New World so that they might together examine "all the great physical phenomena of the globe." Fate determined otherwise, but the emperor would no doubt have pursued this path with vigorous determination; one of the works in his Saint Helena collection with the most annotations was Constantin-François Volney's *Voyage en Syrie et en Égypte pendant les années 1783, 1784 et 1785* (Voyage to Syria and Egypt in the years 1783, 1784, and 1785). He combed through it methodically, taking, as the editor of the Sotheby's catalog observed, "notice of the most trifling error." A large number of pages were "entirely covered" with his handwriting.[20]

The Specialist of Generalizations

The philosopher Auguste Comte caused something of a commotion at his wedding by signing his name as "Brutus Bonaparte Comte" on the marriage registry. Like most progressive thinkers of his generation, Comte despised Napoleon's militarism, but he remained fascinated by the emperor's single-minded determination to end the anarchy unleashed by the French Revolution and by his ambition to reshape the world in his own image. Albeit through less bellicose means, Comte was driven by the same aspirations, and he devoted his life to forging an original scientific synthesis that would herald "the definitive stage of human intelligence." He was inspired by Descartes and had been a disciple of Saint-Simon, having worked as an assistant to the latter for seven years until they fell out in 1824. Although he wrote extensively about astronomy, physics, chemistry, biology, and mathematics, Comte was above all a moral and political philosopher; he saw himself (modesty was not his strong suit) as representing the apogee of the Encylopedic tradition of eighteenth-century philosophy. His pursuit of science was not an end in itself, but a means to create a more prosperous, educated, and caring society. Comte invented the term "altruism," and "living for others" was one of his principal mottos.[21]

Comte was one of the most brilliant products of the era of "mechanical romanticism" that emerged during the first half of the nineteenth century, which sought to combine the competing imperatives of technological development and social reform. His major work, which crystallized his reputation among his contemporaries, was his *Cours de philosophie positive* (*The Course in Positive Philosophy*), a systematic exposition of all the major branches of scientific inquiry. Its six volumes, covering the natural sciences (mathematics, astronomy, physics, chemistry, and biology) as well as the new "science of society," were published between 1830 and 1842. One of its central propositions was that human society, and all the forms of knowledge it contained, had proceeded in three historical movements. First had come the era of theology, when all ideals were explained through deistic fictions (hence, for example, the age of fetishism, when inanimate objects were thought to possess a living spirit, or the belief among primitive peoples that natural forces were controlled by different gods). This was followed by the transitional metaphysical stage, which was dominated by the formation of abstractions, such as the belief in "popular sovereignty" in the era of the French Revolution (a construct of the mind, but based on a real social entity). This stage, in turn, paved the way for the positive age, when knowledge was based on scientific observation and theoretical coordination. Comte claimed that this scheme had come to him as a revelation after a night's meditation.[22]

As a method, positivism sought to formulate the theoretical principles common to all the sciences. In an expression that encapsulated one of the essential features of modern French thinking, Comte referred to the positivist philosopher as the "specialist of generalizations." The main purpose of the *Cours*, to which the final three volumes were devoted, was the establishment of a "social physics" (which Comte would later call "sociology," a Comtian invention), which he considered to be "the greatest and most pressing need" of the era. To this end, he proposed a new, "rational" conception of knowledge ordered around humanity and its needs. He hailed mathematics as the first of all sciences on the grounds of its formal and universalizing qualities; he placed the organic and physical sciences lower on the scale of importance in a position that reflected their potential contribution to understanding society. Rejecting the political solutions offered by his contemporaries, Comte also proposed a "spiritual reorganization" that would reconcile the conservative principle of order with the liberal ideal of progress. The ensuing social harmony would flourish through the emergence of a "new class of scientists" that would be represented in the spiritual realm by positive philosophers and in the temporal by a caste of industrial administrators.[23]

In his subsequent works in the 1840s and 1850s, Comte moved away from this "scientific" positivism, placing greater emphasis on morality (which even displaced sociology in his opinion as the most important discipline) and the institution of an elaborate "religion of humanity" complete with its own institutions, cult, festivals, and dogma. From being its antithesis, religion thus now became the culmination of his science. How was this apparent contradiction to be explained? For the Victorian classicist and Master of Balliol College Benjamin Jowett, the answer was simple: Comte "was a great man but also mad." For many of his erstwhile admirers, notably the utilitarian English philosopher John Stuart Mill, Comte's later philosophy was an authoritarian aberration; it was marred, claimed Mill, by the abandonment of his progressive impulses to a "mania for regulation."[24]

More sympathetic commentators have pointed out that the break from his earlier work was less brutal than it seemed, as Comte had from the outset underscored the importance of common ethical and spiritual values in the positivist order. Indeed, Comte's evolution makes better sense if it is appreciated that his conception of science was in no way Promethean. Despite the elevated status he accorded to mathematics, he did not believe it could play a useful role in understanding the complexities of human society, and he thought that there were clear limits to what the physical sciences could explain. More generally, he was suspicious of the specialized pursuits of scientists, and he sought to devise a system of popular scrutiny to prevent their work from becoming too esoteric—an echo of the Jacobin suspicion of the speculative sciences in the early 1790s.[25]

Arguably, the greatest single factor in Comte's philosophical evolution was the personal crisis he experienced in the wake of the illness and death of his beloved Clotilde de Vaux in 1845—an event that, by his own admission, had a profound impact on his thinking. As he put it, in his typically ponderous prose, "Affection must increasingly dominate speculation to lead to a true systematization of human existence." The general prescriptions of his religion of humanity matched his own habits. He believed, for example, in opening up all aspects of one's private life to the public gaze (the *vivre au grand jour* precept). Thanks to this principle of absolute transparency, we know intimate details about Comte's existence, from his mental illnesses and sexual frustrations to his precise daily intake of bread—60 grams—and his occasional bouts of constipation. Also devised from his own experience was the practice of sexual abstinence and the avoidance (in the name of "cerebral hygiene") of stimulants such as coffee and wine; he regarded tobacco as "one of the most striking indices of occidental anarchy." His religious practices also closely mirrored the system of beliefs he devised for Clotilde, and he adhered to them steadfastly until his death. They included saying prayers thrice daily, engaging in rituals of remembrance of the dead through the handling of cherished personal objects, and writing an annual "confession" letter to the deceased, to show his altruism and give a report on his progress in advancing the cause of human regeneration (in this he was inspired by Rousseau). To those who might have doubted that his science had taken a more fatalistic and paradoxical turn, Comte now declared that the dead represented the better part of humankind and that it was their destiny to govern the living.[26]

This necrocracy was complemented by a unifying component in Comte's thought: his obsession with the biological and medical sciences. His sociology was largely organized around a comparison between human and animal organisms. Comte readily appealed to physiological metaphors to characterize the condition of modern society: he spoke of positivism as a philosophy that corresponded to the "laws of nature," and his frequently expressed belief that society had the capacity to "cure" or "heal" itself was an echo of one of the main biological doctrines of his time, the concept that animate bodies were primarily driven by a "vital force."[27]

Comte was a great admirer of the phrenology of the German physician Franz Joseph Gall, who sought to map out the different functions of the central nervous system according to purely materialistic principles. So enthused was he by this schema that Comte later produced his own chart of the eighteen internal functions of the brain. (He named the thirteenth month of the positivist calendar after the French anatomist Xavier Bichat.) It is against this backdrop that Comte's more eccentric (to put it kindly) scientific notions have to be understood, particularly those allowing for the survival of the same brain in several bodies; the mutation of cows and other herbivorous creatures into carnivores; the incorporation of altruistic animals (such as dogs) into humanity; the realization of the ideal of the Virgin Mother through procreation without sex; the eugenic improvement of the human race through collective control of childbearing and childrearing; and the creation of a "biocracy" in which only the species serving "useful" functions would be allowed to survive. Among the entities slated for natural elimination was the male reproductive organ; in his *Système*, Comte celebrated the ideal of chastity, holding up the promise of "eternal widowhood" in a future positivist society—which probably helps explain why no volume sold more than five hundred copies.[28]

The Future of Science

The entry on "science" in Flaubert's *Dictionnaire des idées reçues* (*Dictionary of Received Ideas*) was no doubt composed with Comte in mind. It claimed that "a small dose of science leads away from religion, a large dose brings us right back to it." In this sense, Comte's conception of science marked the conjunction of two traditions we have already encountered: occultism and utopianism. But his heroic attempt to integrate all forms of scientific inquiry into a single overarching philosophical system was also in the Cartesian tradition. The parallel is appropriate inasmuch as Comte has so far been the last major French (and, indeed, European) thinker whose work has aspired to range across the entire spectrum of the natural sciences as well as the social sciences and humanities. By the end of the nineteenth century, the growth of specialization within and across scientific disciplines had rendered this kind of encyclopedism all but impossible.[29]

The comparison with Descartes also captures the richness of Comte's intellectual posterity in France: a wide range of individuals, groups, and institutions acknowledged his influence on their thought. In the main, it was his earlier, "scientific" thought that was celebrated, rather than his more esoteric later views. The exception was the positivist family, which was divided between dissidents such as Émile Littré, who abandoned Comtianism in the wake of its "metaphysical" turn, and orthodox disciples, who stood by the teachings of the founder. Positivist lectures, weddings, pilgrimages, and festivals blossomed under the impetus of Pierre Laffitte, Comte's official (and uncharismatic) successor, who instituted a festival in honor of the prophet Muhammad and was appointed to the first chair in the history of science at the Collège de France.[30]

Another measure of the ecumenism of the Comtian legacy was its influence on the evolution of French social thought. Neopositivist schools in history and economics developed; and sociology emerged as a distinct field of inquiry, with Émile Durkheim underscoring his debt to Comtianism. Even more remarkable was the resonance of his message among radically different political and literary constituencies. During the early 1870s, Comte's humanitarian ideas appealed to the revolutionary republicans of the Paris Commune, whose destruction of the Napoleonic Vendôme column (carried out under the supervision of the painter Gustave Courbet) was inspired by an explicit recommendation in his *Système*. Yet Comte was also admired by the archconservative royalist thinker Charles Maurras, who celebrated his positivist method of reasoning as a scientific instrument for justifying monarchical authority, and by the nationalist writer Maurice Barrès, who believed his cult of the dead could provide an effective basis for cementing social bonds. More recently, Comte's lament at the destruction of social and spiritual bonds by modern individualism, and his yearning for a world based on the values of compassion and altruism, have found powerful echoes in the novels of Michel Houellebecq.[31]

However, Comtian ideals were most comprehensively lauded—and acted upon—by republicans. It was under the positivist banner that Freemasons successfully battled to remove all reference to God from their constitution and to promote the ideal of a progressive, secular society. The republican political leadership that came of age under the Second Empire and early Third Republic was similarly immersed in positivist ideas and values: Léon Gambetta hailed Comte as "the most powerful thinker of the century" (although he, like many others, assimilated his ideas through Littré); and Jules Ferry cited Comte's *Discours sur l'ensemble du positivisme* (translated in English as *A General View of Positivism*) as one of the seminal influences on his political thinking, saying it nurtured his belief in progress, science, and education and provided his generation with a sense of hope and purpose. It was this general spirit of optimism that shaped the republicans' educational reforms in the late nineteenth century. As the republican education minister Paul Bert (a physiologist) declared in 1881, a more thorough scientific education would help wean the French people from beliefs in abrupt, revolutionary changes: "To the idea of *coup d'états*, sudden transformations, of visible destructions and new creations, science has substituted the notions of constant progress, of slow evolution governed by laws, and this as much in the social and political spheres as in the domains of cosmology and geology."[32]

It was thus entirely logical that, in 1902, a statue of Comte was erected at the Sorbonne (monuments were also dedicated by the regime to great republican scientists such as the chemist François-Vincent Raspail and the astronomer François Arago). The Third Republic gave a practical demonstration of its scientific commitment at the 1889 Universal Exposition, with the erection of the Eiffel Tower and the imposing Gallery of Machinery. The Republic's elites included scientists in their ranks—some of them distinguished, such as Marcellin Berthelot, the pioneer of chemical synthesis, and the mathematician Paul Painlevé. The regime's colonial expansion also took place under the rhetoric of the liberating potential of science.[33]

Yet all of this represented only a symbolic, and in some senses Pyrrhic, victory. Indeed, the overall profile of science in French public life declined noticeably from the second half of the nineteenth century. This retrenchment was partly an effect of declining state support: Germany notably invested more resources in scientific research than France, as a meeting of the French Academy of Sciences mournfully observed after the Franco-Prussian War. In 1871 the French chemical biologist Louis Pasteur criticized "half a century of neglect" of the exact sciences, and his arguments were repeated in almost identical terms by Maurice Barrès in the aftermath of World War I. The decline was partly a product of internal sclerosis. Commenting on the teaching at the

École Polytechnique, the physicist and astronomer Biot wrote of it as "descending every day to a state of uniform mediocrity, which engenders neither resistance nor noise." The situation was paradoxical: in the later nineteenth century, science became popular, as attested by publications such as *La Science française* (French science), which celebrated the triumphs of French applied research. At the same time, the very success of positivism among administrative and cultural elites contributed to a less heroic, more prosaic conception of science. Hence the tendency of French *savants* to confine themselves to their limited research pursuits rather than articulating general "metaphysical" visions of the world. Neither the physiologist Claude Bernard nor Louis Pasteur, the two greatest French scientists of the later nineteenth century, developed any wider philosophical conclusions from their work.[34]

These ambiguities in the Comtian heritage, and in wider French thinking about science, were reflected in Ernest Renan's *L'Avenir de la science* (*The Future of Science*). He wrote this book in 1848 during a phase of socialist and republican foment, when an undimmed confidence in France's status as a leading power prevailed. Although critical of Comte for underestimating "the infinite variety of human nature," Renan remained broadly faithful to his conception of science: hence his affirmation that the nineteenth century had been an age of progress; his belief in reason and in the perfectibility of human nature; his view that science was "the first need of humanity" and that its primary purpose was to explain man to himself; and his prediction that, in the long run, through its capacity to provide an experience of beauty and truth, science would become a new "religion." Renan's emulation of Comte even extended to elaborating his own law of three stages, which culminated in a quasi-Comtian platitude: "Life is not absolute unity or multiplicity, but multiplicity in unity, or rather, multiplicity resolving itself in unity." The work was published only in 1890—by which time Renan's worldview had become considerably less sanguine. Although he stood by his contention that the real quality of a civilization lay in the depth of its popular education, Renan no longer believed that this universalistic ideal was achievable, or indeed desirable. Abandoning his commitment to cultural egalitarianism, he conceded that higher forms of knowledge would forever remain the preserve of an elite. More fundamentally, he had now come to the painful realization that science could not provide happiness or absolute truth—it could merely save man from error.[35]

Behind their buoyant façade, the later nineteenth-century novels of Émile Zola, notably the ones in the Rougon-Macquart series, expressed a view of progress that was just as ambivalent. For Zola, scientific notions (drawn from evolutionary biology) revealed the limits of human agency and the implacably destructive role of heredity. An equally powerful sense of ambiguity about science appears in the works of Jules Verne (1828–1905). The prodigious success of his works—he became one of the most translated authors in the world in the twentieth century—played a significant role in the popularization of science. The subjects explored in Verne's novels of scientific imagination included land and sea voyages, geology, air and space travel, chemical and industrial techniques, and urbanization. Although he was not trained as a scientist, he developed an insatiable curiosity for the subject, which was reflected in his membership in around forty learned societies and in his correspondence with many leading thinkers of his age. Politically, Verne was conservative, and he was wary of revolutionary agitation; in a letter to his father late in 1870, he expressed the hope that the new republican government would "shoot the socialists like dogs."[36]

Verne was from the outset conscious of the limits of science and technology. He observed that there was a trend toward positivism in modern society, but that it was not clear whether it would triumph in the face of religion. As is notably apparent in his *Voyage to the Center of the Earth*, Verne's science was fundamentally a celebration of the mystical dimension of nature—or, as the philosopher Michel Serres put it, an attempt to narrate "the totality of the world's legends." He was concerned about the exhaustion of natural resources, the polluting effects of factories, the inhumanity of capitalist industrial organization, the devastating consequences of catastrophes (both natural and man-made), and the dictatorship of experts. Many of his most vivid scientific characters are misanthropes, such as Captain Nemo, or deranged megalomaniacs, like Dr. Ox (or both, like Robur the Conqueror). Although his utopia, Franceville, was presented in a favorable light, there was a chilling quality even to that hygienic vision.[37]

One of Verne's earliest works—refused by his publisher, Hetzel, and published only in 1994—was *Paris au XXe siècle* (*Paris in the Twentieth Century*). Set in the French capital in 1960, which is still under imperial rule, it was the antithesis of Mercier's gentle utopia. It portrayed a grim world dominated by finance and machinery, in which the arts and music have disappeared, and only writings about technology can be found in bookshops (in a pregnant anticipation of socialist realism, Verne imagined works of poetry with titles such as "Electric Harmonies" and "Meditations on Oxygen"). Women have evolved into mindless and cynical careerists. Food supplies are destroyed in the wake of a ferocious winter, and mass famine ensues; the main character, Michel, is pursued by the "Demon of Electricity."[38]

The Science of the State

In March 1963, the French minister of scientific research, Gaston Palewski, delivered a lecture on "Science as the Key to France's Future." The allusion to Renan was an homage to the positivist tradition, to which he paid fulsome tribute. But Palewski's central argument was that science had entered a new age, one in which it both occupied a more pervasive role in everyday life and required a greater level of state support: "Science has now fully entered the sphere of politics." Detailing the revolutionary changes that his generation had seen in areas such as communication, medicine, automation, and atomic energy, the minister offered a lyrical celebration of the material and moral benefits of science to humanity. He argued that scientific activity had helped to nurture some of the greatest human virtues: "intelligence, humility, a sense of cooperation, patience, and fortitude in the face of failure." The greatest benefit of science was its capacity to liberate man from dependence, opening the way to a life of material comfort and spiritual elevation.[39]

Palewski's views reflected the voluntarism of French postwar elites, who shared a faith in the nation's technological capabilities and confidence in humanity's capacity to conquer nature. In the words of one analyst, this was the apogee of "the scientific state" in France. By the 1970s, this Promethean spirit had helped bring about a renewed Gallic self-confidence about the nation's *savoir-faire*, as reflected in a government advertising slogan: "In France, we have no oil but we have ideas." But this sense of scientific assertiveness was short-lived, in large part because it no longer rested on the classic assumption among rationalists that science could provide the basis for absolute human fulfillment. The rise of material prosperity also brought worries that social morality would be replaced by a destructive, alienating ethos in which all human relations would become commodified; in a short book published in 1970, cultural theorist Jean Baudrillard warned that consumerism was becoming the "morality of modernity." The dangers of the overexploitation of natural resources also became a growing preoccupation. Inspired both by May 1968 and the development of environmental politics in the United States, development economists began to argue that Western prosperity was based on a mode of industrialization that was destroying the natural world; among the most active contributors to this new awareness was René Dumont, the father of modern French political ecology.[40]

The potentially devastating costs of nuclear power were brought home to the unfortunate Palewski in the most tragic way: he died of leukemia in 1984, believing that his illness was caused by radiation exposure during a French nuclear test in Algeria in 1962. As the ends of scientific research became increasingly contentious, attention focused back on an older component of the positivist program: the idea of entrusting the administration of the state to a specially trained elite. This was the last stand of the tradition of French scientism, and it combined the classic rationalist faith in logical reasoning with the utopian goal of regenerating humanity. Its roots harked back to the concept of "administrative science" that haunted the nineteenth century, and not just through Comte: under the influence of Saint-Simonist ideas, republicans had created a (short-lived) École Nationale d'Administration (ENA) in 1848, and Napoleon III aspired to found a school to teach the "science of the state." In *L'Avenir de la science*, Renan had imagined the possibility of a "scientific government" in which elites who had been educated in a special academy of moral and political sciences would find effective solutions to the country's problems.[41]

Revived by the political crisis of the 1930s and the onset of World War II, these technocratic ideals flourished anew in the post-Liberation era. It was in this context that the French provisional government established the École Nationale d'Administration in 1945. The school was designed by Michel Debré, a young Gaullist civil servant who later played a key role in drafting the constitution of the Fifth Republic, and who then had served as its first prime minister. His rationale for the school was to provide better training for French higher civil servants, notably in the fields of history and political science, and to harmonize and democratize the state's mode of recruiting them. Debré also sought to forge a new moral ethos among civil servants that would imbue them with such qualities as "strength of character, unity of views, a yearning for rapid execution and the desire to succeed." However, in the decades that followed, the ENA went well beyond its original mission. Under the Fifth Republic, it became (along with the École Polytechnique) one of the leading institutions in the formation of French corporate elites, displacing the École Normale Supérieure and penetrating not only the upper reaches of the civil service but also the ministerial *cabinets* and the political class more broadly.[42]

From the early days of the Gaullist era, this technocratic ideal was contested and satirized—as in Jean-Luc Godard's film *Alphaville* (1965), a dystopic portrait of a computer-governed world in which the rules of logical science have triumphed, and individualism, emotion, and poetry have been banned. Sociologists blamed technocratic thinking for dysfunctional aspects of the French decision-making system, notably its conservatism, its incapacity to innovate, and its propensity to allow special interests to triumph over the common good. In the later twentieth century, the organization and funding of scientific research in France also came in for scathing criticism, particularly with respect to excessive bureaucratization, cultural constraints on innovation, a lack of transparency, and, above all, the siphoning of elites into the Grandes Écoles. Over time, these negative representations were increasingly channeled through the ENA, which became the scapegoat for all the ills of modern France. Some of these criticisms could be attributed to the search for rhetorical effect, such as, for example, the claim that *énarques* (graduates from the ENA) "lacked sexual maturity," or the liberal political leader Alain Madelin's quip during the 1995 election campaign that "Ireland has the IRA, Spain has the ETA, and France has the ENA." One of the less frivolous charges was that the school recruited from a very narrow section of the social elite and thus subverted the republican ideal of meritocracy—a phenomenon common to the principal Grandes Écoles. But the main accusation was that the *énarques* were (paradoxically) poorly equipped to think creatively. This drawback was said to be a consequence of a system of learning that was obsessed with ranking (the famous final *classement*, which successive French governments have failed to abolish) and that rewarded rule-following, superficiality, and formalism. One recent graduate summed up his time at the school as a "prodigious apprenticeship in conformism"; another lamented its "pedagogical sterility." A common view in the French press is that *énarques* "live in a parallel world."[43]

No French negative stereotype would be complete without the myth of secret power and influence, and so it has been for the *énarques*, who have been charged with forming a closed and cynical power-obsessed caste. This theme was revived in the aftermath of the election of François Hollande to the presidency in 2012, as socialist *énarques* flooded the Élysée. The new president picked many of his closest advisers out of the 1980 cohort of ENA graduates from which he was drawn, the *promotion Voltaire*. All of which provided the perfect fodder for Bernard Domeyne's esoteric thriller *Petits meurtres entre énarques* (Minor murders among *énarques*), in which a group of seven ENA-trained technocrats from the finance ministry are successively assassinated. The murderer turns out to be one of their *énarque* colleagues, who has decided that their elimination is warranted on the grounds that "the least competent people are systematically given managerial positions."[44]

CHAPTER 5

To the Left, and to the Right

In April 1870, a group of French republican parliamentarians published a "Manifesto of the Left." In a valiant (but ultimately unsuccessful) effort to prevent the electorate from endorsing a new imperial constitution, the document recalled the past eighteen years of despotic rule by Napoleon III, who had governed France with an iron fist since seizing power in December 1851. Under the guise of introducing a more liberal regime, the manifesto argued, the imperial monarch was retaining his panoply of arbitrary prerogatives: his powers to appoint ministers and civil servants, to oversee the budget and public expenditure, to command the armed forces and declare war, and to control the political process by determining which issues should be subject to a referendum—"a Caesarian privilege" that was nothing but "the permanent threat of a *coup d'état*." The declaration urged French voters to reclaim their rights from the clutches of "one man and his family," and thus to reject the proposed constitution in the name of the Left's cherished principles: "popular sovereignty, social order and democratic freedom."[1]

In the sharp contrast it drew between the authors' values and those of their adversaries, the manifesto symbolized the French passion for schematic divisions and the clear-cut division in the national consciousness between a progressive, republican, and doctrinal Left and a conservative, monarchist, and pragmatic Right (Louis Napoléon famously declared that he was "not of the family of ideologues"). The distinction between Left and Right has often been viewed as yet another expression of the "Cartesian" character of French thought—in particular, of its propensity to cast political ideas in binary terms and to follow lines of reasoning to their extremes. And, in many respects, such a dichotomy accurately conveyed the polarization of French political life in

1870. Republicans categorically rejected the premise on which the imperial regime was based—namely, dynastic rule—while the Bonapartists dismissed the republicans' conception of active citizenship as a recipe for anarchy and social fragmentation.[2]

Yet things were not as simple as this frontal opposition seemed to suggest. Because the divisions grew out of the untidy and always changing realities of politics, there was a certain fluidity to the concepts involved, and the disagreement between political groups on either side of the boundary was far from absolute. Despite their antagonism, republicans and Bonapartists shared a common attachment to the heritage of the 1789 Revolution and the Napoleonic Empire, to the institution of universal suffrage, and to the preeminence of the state over the church. For this reason, Bonapartists were often considered to be on the Left during the first half of the nineteenth century. And, for all its apparent hostility to the Second Empire, the Third Republic borrowed widely from its predecessor regime after 1870, notably in such areas as the organization of civic festivities and its accommodating policies toward the peasantry. Indeed, seen from a broader historical perspective, the underlying principles of the modern French state (administrative centralization, the promotion of the general interest, the dominance of the political sphere, the suspicion of intermediate bodies, and the priority given to uniformity over diversity) are the product of a combined republican and Napoleonic heritage.[3]

Not only was the division between Left and Right less emphatic than it at first appeared, but the internal conflicts on each side could prove intense. The rivalry among Bourbon royalists, Bonapartists, and Orléanists (supporters of the July Monarchy of Louis Philippe), the three main divisions on the Right, was the defining feature of conservative politics for much of the modern age: in southern France under the Second Empire, royalists preferred to vote for republican candidates rather than support the representative of an imperial dynasty they loathed. Nearer our time, few hatreds have proved as enduring as that between the conservative patriots who joined the Resistance and the supporters of the Vichy regime—to say nothing of the chasm that separated Gaullists and the colonialist advocates of Algérie Française. Likewise on the Left: after the Russian Revolution of 1917, the bitter rift between socialists and communists frequently overshadowed the struggle against their common capitalist enemy; it was, after all, the socialist Guy Mollet who first said that communists were not on the Left or the Right, but in the East. The communist rejoinder appeared in a classic pamphlet written by Étienne Fajon in 1975; the title encapsulated the communists' robust conception of political partnership: *L'Union est un combat* (Unity is a struggle).[4]

These examples already point to a very Gallic paradox: the concepts of the Left and Right have served as much to create a loose sense of fellow feeling among disparate and often antagonistic political forces as to forge a common doctrine or elaborate a shared ideal of the future. At the same time, the use and continuing appeal of this kind of language highlights more generic features of the French style of thinking—the occasionally strident and hyperbolic quality of its rhetoric; the tendency to legitimize arguments by appealing to fictionalized pasts; the willingness to attribute complex symbolic meanings to the most mundane of social practices; the capacity to generate eccentric conceptual combinations; the resort to essentialist arguments, notably about what constitutes the "true" France; and the construction of visions of the good life around the idealization (and demonization) of particular social groups.

Revolution and Counterrevolution

Like much of modern French political terminology, the concepts of Left and Right emerged during the French Revolution. In the late summer of 1789, as the Constituent Assembly debated whether the king should be granted a legislative veto, the members of the assembly spontaneously clustered on opposing sides of the chamber in Versailles. The majority, supporting the monarch's prerogative, gathered on the right, and those opposing it went to the left—and so the distinction took root. From 1815, it became common to distinguish the affiliations of parliamentarians in terms of the *côté droit* and the *côté gauche*. However, this terminology was not exclusive. For much of the nineteenth century, for example, groups on the Left used a range of different expressions (democrats, Montagnards, socialists, radicals) to distinguish themselves both from each other and from their adversaries. Even in the parliamentary arena, the dominant group consisted of those who defined themselves not as left or right, but "center."[5]

These early uses of these terms shaped the way the French understood political distinctions in several fundamental ways. First, there was a lingering sense that the concepts provided only a partial approximation of the complexities of French political thought. They were shorthand, then—but important: for more than a century after 1789, the debate between Left and Right took place largely between advocates and opponents of the French Revolution itself. Speaking in the National Assembly in 1891, the republican leader Georges Clemenceau hailed the Revolution as a "bloc from which nothing can be retrenched," adding, "This admirable revolution still continues, we remain its agents, we are today the same men who are faced with the same enemies." A political dictionary published in 1821 did not even bother to give a substantive definition of "Right": it simply provided a cross-reference to "aristocracy" and "*ancien régime* interests." Such was the pivotal character of the Revolution that the dictionary even characterized the "center" as "the immense majority of the French people, equally hostile to the abuses of the old order as to the excesses of the Revolution."[6]

Moreover, as in 1789, the legitimate authority to wield state power remained a key dividing line between the two camps. Albeit under a range of different names—king, monarch, prince-president, emperor, general, chief—the Right consistently argued that power should be vested in the hands of one individual who was uniquely qualified to rule by virtue of his personal attributes (divine right, birth, experience, wisdom, military prowess, and/or charisma). The Left, in contrast, maintained that such an approach was a violation of Rousseau's principle of popular sovereignty: "No individual can by himself exercise sovereign power." In the progressive scheme of things, it was the collective will of the people that should be represented in state institutions, and this left-wing aim could best be achieved through a delegation of power to elected representatives of the nation (even though, as noted earlier, Rousseau himself had emphatically rejected such a delegation).[7]

The Revolution did not merely provide the Left and the Right with historical starting points, however: it also supplied their doctrines and counterdoctrines. Central to the mindset of the Left was a belief in the possibility of redesigning political institutions to create a better, more humane society whose members were freed from material and moral oppression. There was an idealized, Rousseauist dimension to this vision—but it was also a practical philosophy drawn from the experiences of the early revolutionary era. It centered on the concept of universal rights as outlined in the 1789 Declaration of the Rights of Man and of the Citizen; the principles of patriotism and religious neutrality; the provision of universal education; and, above all, the establishment of a republican form of government in which power was exercised by elected representatives in the name of the people.

This identification of the Left with the heritage of 1789 was a leitmotif among republican groups throughout the nineteenth century. In the aftermath of the 1830 Revolution, for example, one of the main republican associations called itself the Société des Droits de l'Homme et du Citoyen (Society of the Rights of Man and of the Citizen). Its most widely disseminated pamphlets included a reprint of the 1789 Declaration, with additional commentary to highlight the document's continuing relevance to present times—and especially to the struggle against all forms of "tyranny" (the code word for "monarchy"). Universal education was seen as "the foundation of society": its purpose was to develop a sense of "public reason" among the citizenry that would fortify patriotic sentiment and a commitment to virtue. Inherent in this vision were two assumptions that became central to left-wing thinking: the integrity of the people—"We love the people because the people are good"—and the idea of progress: "The Republic is not merely an aggregation of citizens who have agreed to live together. It is a community which is handed over from one generation to the next, and which is constantly in search of greater perfectibility." The literary symbol of this popular capacity to find redemption and virtue through the transcendence of "social fatality," or unfavorable life circumstances, was Jean Valjean, the hero of Victor Hugo's *Les Misérables*.[8]

The Right initially rejected this entire philosophy. French counterrevolutionary doctrine was shaped by Edmund Burke's *Reflections on the Revolution in France* (1790), which was immediately translated into French. The book became such an iconic representation of anti-1789 sentiment that revolutionary peasants burned copies of it in bonfires. Burke's measured lament at the destruction of the historical "capital of nations and of ages" was amplified (and radicalized) in the early nineteenth century in the writings of ultraroyalist thinkers such as Joseph de Maistre, who saw the events of the 1790s as a manifestation of divine retribution for decades of French irreligiosity and philosophical skepticism: at the same time, the Revolution was an act of "regeneration through Divine punishment." The doctrine of the universal rights of man was a senseless abstraction, de Maistre observed: "I have seen Frenchmen, Italians, Russians; I even know, thanks to Montesquieu, that there are Persians, but as to man, I have never met one."[9]

For these conservatives, the ideal world lay not in the future but in the nation's royalist past: Chateaubriand thus savaged the Revolution for destroying the genteel and civilized era of the old monarchy, which had lifted man from barbarity and allowed the flourishing of culture and religiosity. Some went even further, associating the *ancien régime* with the myth of a golden age. Louis de Bonald, a prominent early nineteenth-century ultra-royalist thinker, said that French society in the *ancien régime* had acceded to the "strongest, most spiritual, most moral, most perfect state it had ever attained." (It is worth noting—and this was one of the paradoxes of French counterrevolutionary thought—that its vision was just as formally abstract as the one imputed to the revolutionaries.) This ideal condition, partly shrouded in "mystery," rested on the wisdom accumulated by successive generations and transmitted through the monarchy and the institutions of the church. In the words of Bonald: "Remove God from this world, man owes nothing to man, and society is no longer possible."[10]

From this perspective, it was a mistake to believe, as the revolutionaries had, that education should be entrusted to state authorities: only religious orders could provide the wisdom needed to lift humanity from the "infirmity" of childhood. French counterrevolutionary thinking was a mirror of the progressivism of the Left. Indeed, through its rejection of the reformist aspirations of 1789, ultra-royalism helped to give French conservatism a powerful antimodern component that was more pronounced and long-lasting than elsewhere (for all his hostility to the French Revolution, Burke embraced key elements of the Enlightenment). According to the logic of this "rhetoric of reaction," schemes for radical social and political change were undesirable because they could not be implemented (the futility argument), because they endangered the gains already accomplished (the jeopardy claim), or because they were likely to produce consequences opposite to those intended (the perversity thesis). Thus a common conservative line of reasoning against universal suffrage was that it was a dangerous innovation that would overturn the natural order of society, handing over power to "demented utopians" and "beardless tramps"—and it was not clear which was worse.[11]

The most fervent proponents of this rhetoric of reaction in nineteenth-century France were Catholic traditionalists and the more hard-line elements of the legitimist party, the royalist group that supported a restoration of the Bourbon monarchy. The anniversary of the execution of the king in January 1793 was mourned by legitimists, and a clergyman described the fight against the Revolution as "a religious duty of the first magnitude." In a pamphlet published in 1867, the royalist intellectual Gabriel de Belcastel lambasted the Revolution as a threat to the nation's most sacred institutions: the monarchy, private property, the family, and religion. In response to the individualism celebrated by revolutionary doctrine, royalists asserted the primacy of the collective: "A society is not a mere assemblage of heterogeneous parts; all its components are connected and linked to form a whole."[12]

In the royalist scheme of things, the primary task of politics was to cultivate traditional moral values in the citizenry: "courage, hard work, perseverance, economy, temperance, honesty and sincerity, and respect for authority." The revolutionary idea of constructing a new polity based on rationalist principles was thus seen by supporters of the monarchy as a violation of the natural order: "The constitution of a nation such as France does not lie in a page written by man; it is all in its traditions." Similarly, the Rousseauist notion of the natural, inherent goodness of man was a dangerous fallacy that intended to turn society away from the church: "Man is born in evil, and it is the church which restores him to goodness." Indeed, for the more pessimistic conservatives, it was already too late. Far from embracing the greater perfectibility promised by republicans, humanity was plunging inexorably toward decadence. In the words of the Catholic intellectual Louis Veuillot, "Mankind, weakened by sin, inclines gradually toward error, and the road to error leads on to death."[13]

Order and Movement

The notions of Left and Right thus initially drew upon the opposing philosophical assumptions about human nature, society, and the state that grew out of the experiences of the revolutionary era. What gave added relief to these concepts was that they were not mere intellectual abstractions but inscribed in wider social and cultural practices: in celebrations of religious activities, political festivals, and anniversaries; in symbolic gestures, such as the planting of trees, the naming of streets, and the institution of public monuments; and in civic rituals such as marches, processions, and funerals.[14]

Instead of the *salon*, the urbane social gathering of the well-heeled, the social life of ordinary men and women of the Left coalesced around the café, one of the principal arenas of progressive sociability in France from the mid-nineteenth century on. The republican leader Gambetta spent his days as a student in the Latin Quarter moving from Café de Madrid to Café Procope, and then, finally, Café Voltaire. Socialist and revolutionary associations met in cafés across the country under the watchful eye of the police; at Saint-Gilles (Gard) in 1900, local workers groups met at Café Perruchon and, in the words of the local police, "hung a red flag surmounted by a large tricolor cravat at the window." Symbolic colors have a rich political history in France, the tricolor being associated in the century following the Revolution with the progressive cause, and white with royalism; in 1815, after the final defeat of Napoleon, the republican Agricol Perdiguier was roughed up by monarchists for not sporting a white rosette—and then beaten up again by the other camp when he put one on. From the 1830s, the red flag became the symbol of revolutionary politics, inspiring fear among conservatives and a quasi-mystical devotion among radical republicans; at socialist banquets, everything was red: the tablecloth, the napkins, the plates, the wine—right down to the menu of radishes, tomatoes, crayfish, and *filet saignant*.[15]

The progressive and conservative factions could readily be distinguished by their respective vocabularies. The language of the Right was typically about the avoidance of conflict, the defense of hierarchy, the appeal to tradition and religious faith, and (particularly in its literary sensibility) a certain aesthetic disposition centered around a celebration of talent, a cult of friendship, and a yearning for adventure and exoticism. ("My agitation," confessed Maurice Barrès in his diaries, "was never a race toward something, but a flight toward an elsewhere.") In times of crisis—and to many conservatives it seemed crisis was the defining feature of modernity—the Right was predominantly concerned with the preservation (or restoration) of social stability, the battle cry of all conservatives from Napoleon Bonaparte and the "party of order" of the Second Republic through to the Vichy regime. The rhetoric of the Left was universalistic, appealing to general principles and resting on a conscious sense of superiority (a socialist leader once observed that France had the "most stupid Right in the world"). It invoked ideals such as justice and equality; it justified its goals and actions through the notion of the common good; and it sought to build a different kind of society whose members were freed from material and spiritual dependence. To be on the Left was to believe, above all, that popular participation in political life was an essential condition of social progress. As a republican pamphleteer put it shortly after the 1848 Revolution, "The democratic element is emerging in all parts: it will be its destiny to transform the world."[16]

Transformation, renewal, regeneration: the ideal of change sometimes seemed sufficient in itself to sum up the aspirations of the Left—hence the recourse to the imagery of "struggle," one of its enduring metaphors. Whether challenging kings and tyrants, fighting for the dignity and emancipation of workers, rebelling against the cultural establishment, or confronting the agents of global capitalism, those on the Left defined their political commitment as an imperative of "movement." Under the monarchy, observed a radical republican newspaper in 1849, the people are an "inert corpse"; under the Republic, they became a "robust athlete" (so robust that they sometimes left their elites behind—"There go the people," mused the nineteenth-century republican Alexandre Ledru-Rollin as he was overtaken by demonstrators. "I must follow them, for I am their leader").[17]

This sense of movement naturally climaxed in the notion of rupture. From the Paris Commune of 1871 through the syndicalist dream of the general strike all the way through to the communist ideal of world revolution and the radical utopias of May 1968, left-wing thinking in France rested on the belief that political change could be meaningful only if it was comprehensive and cleansing. The refrain of the socialist poet Eugène Pottier's revolutionary anthem, the Internationale, succinctly captured this aspiration: "Of the past let us make a clean slate / The world is about to change its foundation"—or, as a poster from May '68 put it more succinctly: "Let us smash the old systems." This radicalism exercised such a powerful appeal on the progressive imagination that it was embraced even by some of the more moderate strands of the Left: thus, in 1971, the socialist leader François Mitterrand declared that "whoever does not accept a rupture with the established political order, and thus with the capitalist order, has no place in the socialist party."[18]

Yet despite this apparent convergence about the ends of politics, the intellectual history of the French Left has been one of enduring division. The fractures have been due in part to the penchant among French progressives for theoretical debate, which itself came out of something Tocqueville noticed about the revolutionaries: the overrepresentation of the intellectual classes among their ranks. More fundamentally, the divisions reflected France's relatively late industrialization and the absence of a large party representing the aspirations of working people like those in Britain or Germany. Hence the existence of smaller tribes on the Left organized around contrasting philosophical sensibilities: liberals, with their elitist and cerebral outlook, who have championed the ideal of a society based on private property and individualism; Jacobins, who embraced a holistic view of society, promoting state centralization and anticlericalism; collectivists, who have argued for a more egalitarian society, greater state regulation, and a socialization of the means of production; and libertarians, who prioritize freedom above all and advocate the principles of antimilitarism, associational politics, and decentralization. These intellectual divisions help to account for the tendency toward fragmentation in leftist parties. The schism between socialists and communists in 1920, caused by a fundamental disagreement over allegiance to Lenin's revolutionary Third International, cast a shadow over left-wing politics in France for much of the modern era. Yet this divide was also a continuation of older patterns of political disunity among progressives; shortly before a party congress, the French pacifist Aristide Briand joked that his fellow socialists were about to gather "for one of their annual schisms."[19]

So why did these fissiparous groups nonetheless regard themselves as members of a shared community? An important part of the answer is that they had the sense of a common historical ancestry. In many regions of France—in cities such as Paris, Lyon, and Marseille, with their proud revolutionary antecedents, and in parts of both the north and the south (the Midi)—support for the Left was a vibrant local tradition passed on from one generation to the next. This heritage was perhaps most visible in the ways in which the Revolution was remembered. The memory of 1789 (and the ensuing struggle to promote its values) provided a frame of reference for successive generations across the nineteenth century. The Revolution was all the more pivotal in that it provoked sharp disagreements: there were liberal, Jacobin, libertarian, socialist, and Marxist versions of the events, each with its distinct interpretation of its historical significance. This influence was not limited to political elites

and thinkers: the Revolution also left a lasting legacy in French popular culture—notably in literature, theater, and music.[20]

The ability of the past to shape the thinking of the Left can be seen in a
speech given at the Sorbonne in 1948 by the socialist leader Léon Blum to
mark the centenary of the 1848 Revolution. Blum revealed that one of the first
books he had read as an adolescent was Louis-Antoine Garnier-Pagès's classic
Histoire de la Révolution de 1848 (History of the Revolution of 1848), a copy of
which he had discovered in his father's attic. Garnier-Pagès's epic narrative inspired Blum's lifelong commitment to the republican cause and his belief that,
for all its mistakes, the Revolution had been one of the landmarks of modern
French history. But in the events of 1848 the socialist leader also identified
some of the enduring weaknesses in the psychology of the Left, especially a
certain naïveté and a lack of a sense of legitimacy, which manifested itself in a
fragility of spirit—"a fear of causing fear," a reference to the traumatic memory
of the revolutionary Terror.[21]

Blum's insight underlined a critical—if paradoxical—dimension of the progressives' unity: its predominantly defensive character. "Nothing," observed the
nineteenth-century republican Jules Simon, "binds men together more closely
than the hatred of a common enemy." The tradition of a republican front
against the Right was born in the rejection of Louis Napoléon's *coup d'état* in
1851; it enjoyed its heyday in the later nineteenth century, both in the battles
against the monarchist resurgence and in the Dreyfus Affair. In the modern
era, a similarly defensive spirit manifested itself in the antifascist progressivist
alliance of the 1930s, in the Resistance against German occupation, and in the
Left's virulent hostility toward de Gaulle, who was portrayed as a latter-day
Bonapartist. This negative, oppositional dimension of the Left sat awkwardly
with its aspiration to represent the progressive ideals of change, transformation,
and "movement."[22]

Indeed, an ironic consequence of this defensive tradition was that the Left's
rhetoric could often sound strangely conservative. By the turn of the century, once the Third Republic was consolidated, the moderate Left wanted
to preserve the status quo: the Radical Party's manifesto proclaimed the need
to defend peace, property, and local interests against the forces of "reaction."
For all its revolutionism, the French Communist Party was often perceived
as an ally of the state that preferred preservation of its social and institutional
power to challenges against the interests of the ruling "bourgeoisie." In June
1936, as a wave of strikes spread across French factories, party leader Maurice
Thorez famously declared, "One should know how to end a strike." Unsettled
by the tumultuous events of May 1968, the communist intellectual Jean Rony
confessed, "I had only one wish: that order be restored as soon as possible."[23]

Visions of the Nation

The concept of the French nation itself further captures the complexities of the intellectual divide between Left and Right. Initially, the patriotic ideal of nationhood belonged firmly on the Left. Driven by the memory of the Jacobin defense of the Revolution in the early 1790s, and vividly celebrated in the couplets of the Marseillaise and in key elements of republican doctrine (notably, popular sovereignty and fraternity), the Left's classical doctrine of nationhood emphasized a universalistic form of patriotism. It depicted France as a collectivity of citizens molded into a nation with shared values through the Gallic genius for assimilation: as the historian Jules Michelet put it, "The original, French part of France has been able to attract, absorb, and integrate the English, German, and Spanish elements with which she was surrounded." This robust conception of the nation included a commitment to defend the *patrie* against foreign invaders: powerful echoes of the vision were heard both during the republican prosecution of the Franco-Prussian War and in the Paris Commune.[24]

Universalism was also apparent in the widespread belief among progressives that France, because of its Enlightenment heritage, its revolutionary tradition, and its willingness to fight tyranny in all its manifestations, was a beacon to the rest of the world—hence the deliciously Gallocentric formulation of the historian Henri Martin: "If the French patriot is proud of his fatherland, it is because he feels destined to spread the good news across the world, the news of justice and truth. If he wishes his fatherland to be great and glorious, it is for the good of humankind; he loves France in and for humanity." The socialist Paul Lafargue echoed the sentiment: "All socialists have two fatherlands: the place where they happened to be born, and France, their adoptive fatherland." It was this belief in the inherently emancipatory quality of French culture that led twentieth-century progressives consistently to advocate a policy of assimilation in the colonies, turning (with the honorable exception of the communists) a blind eye to the social inequalities and cultural domination that it produced. The socialist Guy Mollet, who rejected all manifestations of colonial nationalism as "reactionary" and "obscurantist," for example, had an uncritical belief in the supremacy of the French *mission civilisatrice*. Presiding over the escalation of violence in the final years of French rule in Algeria in the late 1950s, he epitomized the "bankruptcy" of the French republican Left's approach to colonial matters.[25]

An alternative to this progressive idea of the nation emerged in the late nineteenth century. It was not so much an ideology or a doctrine, however, as an intellectual sensibility shaped by two main factors: a sense of wounded patriotism, triggered by the loss of the province of Alsace-Lorraine in 1871; and the rise of a virulent populist movement against the Republic, which manifested itself in the popularity of General Georges Boulanger in the 1880s and then in the turn-of-the-century Dreyfus Affair. This nationalist sensibility overlapped in some respects with classical French counterrevolutionary doctrine, particularly in its yearning for strong leadership, its belief in tradition, and its rejection of universalism. However, it was a new and more potent synthesis. Its power lay in its ability to pull in new constituencies—indeed, it even appealed to many conservative republicans—as well as in its abandonment of the more metaphysical doctrines of the counterrevolutionaries (such as the divine right of kings) in favor of a more Nietzschean conception of spirituality and heroism. Promoted by some of the greatest literary talents of the age, it contributed to the genesis of fascist doctrine.[26]

One of the enduring tropes of this nationalist narrative is the contrast between the artificial nature of life in the capital, on the one hand, and the authenticity of "true" France, on the other. This opposition was often expressed as a lament against modernity. Jules Barbey d'Aurevilly's novel *L'Ensorcelée* (The witch), set in Normandy at the time of the royalist revolt against the First Republic, for example, opens with a description of the region's rugged landscape and compares it to the "sacred rags that will be blown away by the winds of industrial modernism, and the crude materialism and utilitarianism of our age." Charles Maurras, an ideologue of conservative nationalism, formalized the same dichotomy in his distinction between the *pays légal* (official country) and the *pays réel* (real country). He viewed the official institutions of the republican state as a "grotesque mask" and said the cult of uniformity was systematically destroying the foundations of French collective sentiment. His Action Française movement thus advocated a new political system that would restore the extensive local liberties that had existed in France prior to the 1789 Revolution. Because of their instinctive aversion to universalist thinking and their attachment to France's historical and cultural diversity, authoritarian nationalists were generally reluctant to offer general definitions of the French nation. Even Maurras, their most doctrinaire intellectual, shied away from using the concept of "race," except in the loosest of senses. (His loathing of all things German probably helped here, as biological conceptions of the nation were generally favored across the Rhine.)[27]

The figure of Joan of Arc emerged during the Third Republic as the representative of this more defensive and conservative ideal of French nationhood. The nationalist Édouard Drumont hailed her as a Celtic heroine, and Maurras sought, somewhat improbably, to present her as a resolute defender of the French monarchy. For conservative religious groups, such as one in Poitiers where she had been interrogated in 1429, the national heroine was a guide for all those "seeking to follow without question the path of the lord Jesus Christ." The Republic embraced Joan of Arc as well: at the instigation of Maurice Barrès, the anniversary of her death became an occasion for national commemoration in 1920, a sober reminder of the horrific toll of the Great War on French lives. The paramilitary leagues of the interwar era celebrated Joan as a martial figure; the Vichy regime and its supporters deployed her as a rural Catholic icon and a symbol of "the cruelty of the English government"; and since the late 1980s, the extreme right-wing National Front has turned May 1 into a "Joan of Arc Day," invoking her legend to promote the ideals of French sovereignty and the doctrine of "national preference."[28]

In contrast with the universalism of progressive thinkers, the rhetoric of "real" France thus celebrated a distinct range of social institutions, values, and customs. The first of these institutions was the family, hailed by traditionalists as a pillar of social order and deemed to be threatened by modern individualism and sexual permissiveness. It was no accident that the Vichy regime heralded the family as the primary symbol of its much-vaunted (if incompletely achieved) "national revolution." Another common characteristic among nationalists was their tendency to view provincial life as the repository of the moral and cultural treasures of the nation—including regional dialects, wondrous illustrations of the French "genius" that had been ruthlessly suppressed by the Revolution in the name of national unity. The Action Française's cultural chauvinism extended to the domain of the culinary arts: Marthe Daudet, wife of the editor of the movement's principal newspaper, wrote regular columns promoting the excellence of French regional cuisine. Her response to the feisty redness of progressive food culture was to publish a best-selling cookbook entitled *Les Bons Plats de France* (Delightful French recipes). Marcel Proust hailed it as a "delicious work": among its dishes were Provençal *aigo-boulido* (a garlic and herb soup), *garbure béarnaise* (a stew of ham and vegetables), Lorraine crêpes, Alsatian *kougelhopf* (marble cake), and the *matelote*, a northern stew served piping hot and garnished with fried croutons, boiled eggs, and fish.[29]

All of this came together in the populist imagery of the Poujadist movement in the 1950s. Celebrating his origins "in the old land of France," its leader, Pierre Poujade, championed the cause of all the "little people," the "honest folk" (*braves gens*), such as artisans, shopkeepers, and small producers—the "backbone of the Nation." He supported their cause because their livelihoods were threatened by excessive state taxation and the disproportionate power of the National Assembly, "the biggest brothel in Paris." Poujadist language was notable for its crude and graphic imagery: in the run-up to the 1956 legislative elections, the movement's newspaper, *Fraternité française*, compared France to a "cesspool in which the number of defecations is increasing by the day."[30]

The Myths of the Right

The distinction between Left and Right thus rested on clearly identifiable doctrinal foundations, historical experiences, and social practices. But the concrete factors that exacerbated the divide between the two sides—the 1789 Revolution, the republican political system, the place of religion in public life, and the meaning of Frenchness—subsided in significance over time. A major turning point in this respect was the Vichy period of 1940–1944. Discredited for its racism and political authoritarianism as well as for its collaboration with the Nazi occupiers, the regime fatally undermined the counterrevolutionary tradition and prompted a significant ideological transformation of the Right. This process accelerated with the advent of the Fifth Republic in 1958. Under the impulsion of Gaullism, the Right accepted the Republic and the democratic political system, and social hierarchy and religious ideals began to play a smaller role in its vision of society. In 1995, the neo-Gaullist Jacques Chirac won the presidential election by promising to heal France's "social fracture"—a classic theme in the progressive repertoire. The Left, for its part, began to acknowledge (first silently, and eventually, after the election of François Mitterrand to the presidency in 1981, publicly) that private property and a mixed economy were unmovable features of the French polity. In the late twentieth century, the socialist prime minister Lionel Jospin thus sought to distinguish between a "market economy" (which was necessary and valuable) and a "market society" (where inegalitarianism was socially and morally destructive). These semantic borrowings and transgressions caused confusion on both sides, providing openings for satirists such as Frédéric Beigbeder, whose semi-autobiographical character Oscar Dufresne loses his sense of ideological bearings after finding Jospin dining at the Café du Commerce on the fashionably chic Île de Ré "with a pullover over his shoulders."[31]

Yet despite the erosion of its material foundations, the vision of a country divided into two camps—*la France coupée en deux*—has persisted, in some senses becoming more entrenched. This was partly a natural outcome of French political processes, such as the two-ballot electoral system for parliamentary elections, in which the run-offs have typically produced contests between candidates of the Left and Right, thus constantly repeating patterns of polarization. There was, however, a deeper reason as well. The notions of Left and Right survived because of their enduring symbolic and emotional appeal: their capacity to conjure up not only luminous tropes about youthfulness, heroism, a collective destiny, and the metaphysical unity of the French people, but also darker images involving betrayal, impurity, and the ultimate apocalypse and dissolution of the nation.

The Right has imagined the presence of sinister forces working to unravel the fabric of French society, destructive agents perceived as all the more noxious because they were thought to represent alien interests and values. In his influential work on the French Revolution, first published in 1797–1798, the Abbé Augustin Barruel denounced the Freemasons as an inherently subversive cosmopolitan group with links to secret societies across Europe, all of which were dedicated to the unholy objectives of "waging war against Christ and his cult, and kings and their thrones." In the demonology of the Catholic and nationalist Right, Freemasons and their successor organizations, such as the Carbonari, were a major source of moral corruption in French society. They were accused of seeking to replace the traditional foundations of authority with pernicious theories—the ones underpinning the Left's most fundamental ideas: the rights of man, material progress, social equality, and universal fraternity. In 1941, a Vichyist publication blamed Freemasons for all the internal and external "convulsions" that had torn French society apart, from the 1789 Revolution to the German invasion of 1940. A few years after World War II, the Catholic writer Georges Bernanos warned against the destruction of French civilization by Anglo-Saxon commercial industrialism, which he saw as "a universal conspiracy against any kind of spiritual life."[32]

Equally baleful, from this perspective, were the activities of groups advocating greater social equality. The multiple revolutions of the nineteenth century—notably the 1830–1848–1871 sequence, ending with the Paris Commune—and the political challenge posed by radical republican and socialist groups gave rise to the rhetoric of the "red peril," one of the less savory inventions of French conservative thinking. Deployed with great consistency, this anticommunist terminology associated the figure of the "red" with violence, bestiality, sexual debauchery, and the dissolution of social order: a pamphlet published in 1851 thus warned that France was about to be overrun by "millions of proletarians, indoctrinated by hatred."[33]

In the aftermath of the Russian Revolution and the formation of a Communist Party in France with close material and spiritual ties to Moscow, a further layer was added to this demonology: the threat of Soviet domination. Communist conspiracies, real and (mostly) fabricated, haunted the imagination of *bien-pensant* conservatives. In the 1920s, Minister of the Interior Albert Sarraut referred to the French Communist Party (PCF) as a "universal enterprise of national and social disintegration." By the late 1940s and 1950s, anticommunist propaganda in France had reached the height of its intensity—and paranoia. In May 1952, when Jacques Duclos, one of the leading PCF figures, was arrested after an anti-American demonstration, two pigeons were found in the car in which he was traveling. Although they had been destined for the family dinner, it was immediately assumed they were intended as couriers for some dastardly communist plot. The absurdity of the alleged conspiracy was exposed only when a three-man commission appointed by the French government (which included the president of the National Federation of Carrier-Pigeon Societies) concluded that the two suspected birds were "incapable of flying, let alone completing a mission of communication." The sense of panic was still alive and well among conservatives after Mitterrand's election in 1981, when the presence of communists in government led to fears that private property would be abolished. The right-wing journalist Louis Pauwels told one of his friends, "If you have valuable objects, bury them in your garden"; there were also rumors that Soviet troops would soon be stationed in Paris.[34]

Jews came to be identified as posing the ultimate existential menace to the conservative nationalist ideal of Frenchness. Édouard Drumont's *La France juive* (Jewish France, 1886), one of the best-selling books of its time (two hundred editions had been published by 1914), denounced the penetration of the republican state by Jews, who he claimed had become nothing less than "a state within the state." Drumont's success lay in his effective combination of Christian, anticapitalist, and racialist strands of French anti-Semitism. This toxic atmosphere converged around the Dreyfus Affair, when nationalists asserted that the accused officer's guilt was a function of his race. In Proust's *Du côté de chez Swann* (*Swann's Way*, 1913), this popular strain of anti-Semitism is shown in the portrayal of the Jews during the holiday season at Balbec: with their garish appearance, their refusal to "mix," their affront to Catholic values, and manifestly "Oriental" ways, they are seen as the very incarnation of the "foreigner." Another common perception among French anti-Semites was the inherently conquering nature of the Jew. The Tharaud brothers, prominent conservative intellectuals of the late Third Republic, thus observed, "Like everything that lives in nature, the Jew seeks to persevere in his being and to prosper, and he can do this only at the expense of his surroundings." The notion of "dispossession" was a key accompaniment to these notions. The claim that "true France" had been appropriated by sinister forces was systematized in Charles Maurras's representation of the Republic as the perverted rule of four "confederacies": these were made up of the Jew, the Protestant, the Freemason, and the foreigner (*métèque*). It was in this spirit that the Action Française oath of allegiance began with a vow to rid France of the republican regime, "the rule of the stranger."[35]

The myth of *la France juive* was a constant underpinning of the French nationalist imagination in the twentieth century, providing an additional cultural basis to the Right's hostility toward the Left. (Many left-wing leaders, such as Léon Blum and Pierre Mendès-France, were pilloried on the grounds of their Jewish origins.) This trend culminated in the Vichy regime's statutes of 1940–1941, which deprived French and foreign Jews of their civil and political rights and led to the deportation and murder of thousands of Jews in the German death camps. Under the leadership of Jean-Marie Le Pen in the late twentieth and early twenty-first centuries, the basic components of this rhetoric of exclusion (conspiracy, national decadence, and the marginalization of "native" French citizens by foreigners) were appropriated by the National Front, which added two overlapping elements to the Maurrassian confederacy: immigrants and Islam.[36]

This bleak vision did, however, provide an instrument for its own transcendence, through that most cherished of figures in French right-wing mythology: the providential leader. The dominant strand of this providentialism was initially represented by Bonapartism. Napoleon rose to power in the late 1790s in a context of political anarchy and social disillusionment: his prowess on the battlefield, his commitment to safeguarding the essential principles of the 1789 Revolution, and his talent for leadership enabled him to present himself as the only effective recourse for the nation; as one of his admirers put it, "only such a great man could pull France out of the abyss." His nephew Louis Napoléon later used the same ingredients to propel himself to the presidency in 1848 and restore the authoritarian empire four years later: in the words of the conservative liberal thinker François Guizot, Bonapartism was "all at once a national glory, a revolutionary guarantee, and a principle of authority."[37]

After 1870, another variant of this providentialism arose, symbolized by such conservative figures as Adolphe Thiers, Raymond Poincaré, and Antoine Pinay, civilian leaders who stepped into the breach in times of national crisis to restore confidence (notably, in public finances). Speaking of Thiers, one writer noted, "His name alone was a protection, a moral force." A third strand developed around the cult of military icons, such as General Georges Boulanger in the late nineteenth century, and General Philippe Pétain in the interwar years. Pétain's emergence as France's perceived savior under the Vichy regime was based on his credentials as the victorious general of the Battle of Verdun in 1916; the personal qualities that were attributed to him—modesty, dignity, and especially wisdom—also helped: he was all at once an icon, a chief, and a father figure. A more muscular type of providential heroism flourished in the French colonial setting as well, notably in the figure of Hubert

Lyautey, who was widely acclaimed for his military successes and his belief in "peaceful conquest." Lyautey certainly applied the latter principle broadly, penning homoerotic prose about Africans, Arabs, Greeks, and Ceylonese and taking every opportunity to dress in elaborate Arab garb. His appointment as the resident-general (governor) of Morocco in 1912 was greeted with a wave of patriotic fervor across France: he was elected to the Académie Française and received thousands of letters celebrating his manly virtues; one of his correspondents felt he had "the aura of Bonaparte on the eve of his conquest of Egypt."[38]

Friends and Enemies of the People

Neatly counterpoised to the providentialism of the Right was the Left's primary myth: the collectivity in whose name the 1789 Revolution was carried out and which provided the philosophical legitimacy for its new political order: the people. But although the revolutionaries and their republican successors were united in celebrating Rousseau's principle of popular sovereignty, there was a tension in the way in which the notion was understood. On the one hand, the "people" meant the entire citizenry, as in the third article of the 1789 Declaration of the Rights of Man and of the Citizen, which asserted that "the source of all sovereignty lies essentially in the nation." On the other hand, the term referred to specific groups within the national community that had been singled out by virtue of who they represented (the Abbé Joseph Sieyès's Third Estate); their superior political consciousness (the "people" of the Jacobins, and later the communists); or their economic deprivation (as in the radical republican tradition, in which the Revolution would be completed only when the "wretched of the earth" were delivered from economic servitude). Others defined the "people" in terms of their creativity and emotional intelligence: for Michelet, the people were the principal heroes of the French Revolution and were distinguished, above all, by their "instinct for action." It was precisely this ideal of a collectivity in movement, bold and triumphant and drawing on a multitude of social forces, that was represented in Eugène Delacroix's magnificent portrayal of the 1830 Revolution in his painting *Liberty Leading the People*.[39]

The tension between the ideal of a single, undifferentiated people and an empirical collectivity made up of diverse sensibilities and aspirations that was in some sense separate from the nation remained unresolved on the Left—an ambiguity captured by the common expression *peuple de gauche*. The variations in progressive representations of the people were also a function of contrasting experiences. The iconography of the 1848 Revolution depicted a young, idealistic, generous, and fraternal collectivity transcending all the divides of French society. In the imagery of the Paris Commune of 1871, in contrast, the people were the proud and defiant agents of a "social" Republic, leading the charge against the "sickening bourgeois exploiters." Indeed, for its radical republican and syndicalist heirs, the Commune marked the birth of a new ideal: that of a government in which workers took control of their destinies in order to create a world in which "toilers were liberated of all constraints, all oppression, all forms of exploitation."[40]

With the rise of the Communist Party and its political domination of the Left in the postwar years, the Jacobin ideal of a single "people" returned, this time through the idealization of the working class. The communist worker symbolized all at once the highest form of social morality, the perverseness of capitalist oppression, and the instrument of its revolutionary overthrow. Evoking his first encounter with ordinary people through his association with an antifascist organization in the 1930s, the progressive journalist Jean Daniel described them in these lyrical terms: "These men and women were linked by a fraternity that I envied. I suffered to think that I could not become one of them. There was among them all the different possible qualities of humanity in its most simple, most generous, and undoubtedly most noble facets. These people were poor but not miserable, rebellious but not unhappy, revolutionary at times but never embittered. They were conscious of representing a force and that it was the only one which was legitimate."[41]

To be on the Left, in short, was to be a friend of the people promoting their march toward greater sovereignty: hence the title of Marat's newspaper in the early years of the Revolution, *L'Ami du peuple* (The people's friend). It naturally followed, in the binary logic of French political reasoning, that those who were hostile to the exercise of this sovereignty were its "enemies." The expression *ennemi du peuple* appeared during the Jacobin era to stigmatize those who were opposed to the Revolution—either by conspiring against it, at the behest of royalists and aristrocrats, or by working against its interests in smaller ways, as were hoarders, rumormongers, separatists, and defeatists. The proposed treatment of these hostile elements was harsh: as Robespierre put it, "the people are led by reason, and the enemies of the people by Terror." But although the primary method of dealing with these adversaries—through decapitation—was short-lived, the distinction between friends and enemies was destined to have a promising future in the Left's political imagination. In the typology of the Left that followed, pride of place was occupied by the figure of the tyrant, who was reviled by progressive intellectuals throughout the modern era for confiscating power from the people and wielding it instead in the interests of a small minority. This representation underpinned republican struggles against monarchical rule throughout the nineteenth century and all the way up to de Gaulle, whose reign in the early years of the Fifth Republic was likened by the socialist leader, François Mitterrand, to a "permanent *coup d'état.*"[42]

Equally odious to many progressives were the activities of the clergy, which were seen as a threat to the people's moral sovereignty; in fact, this anticlericalism has been one of the most distinctive features of the French Left. The roots of the conflict harked back to the revolutionary era and the opposition of parts of the church to the new political order. The clash was exacerbated during the nineteenth century, when the Catholic clergy generally sided with the royalists against the republicans. The poet Pierre-Jean de Béranger thus railed against the "men in black" who "crawl out from underground"; the socialist republican Louis Blanc completed the spatial metaphor when he asserted that "between clericalism and freedom there is an unbridgeable chasm." Much of classical anticlerical demonology became concentrated in the noxious role of congregations: the myth of the Jesuit conspiracy was a powerful theme in republican writings in the decades following the Restoration, culminating in Gambetta's denunciation of "clericalism" as the "enemy of the Republic" in 1877. This militant spirit survived well into the late twentieth century in certain sections of the left-wing press, notably the satirical *Charlie Hebdo.* (In 1976, after the revelation that Pope Paul VI had had a homosexual experience in his youth, *Charlie Hebdo* came up with the delicate headline "I Buggered the Pope.")[43]

The group that eventually overtook tyrants and priests as the emblem of popular enmity was the bourgeoisie. This special position was partly a reflection of the insidious power attributed to this social class: in the radical republican and socialist traditions, members of the bourgeoisie were often presented as idlers who had appropriated the revolutionary heritage in order to defend their values of individualism and greed. In the philosopher Roland Barthes's *Mythologies,* an influential exposition of the cultural power of modern capitalism, the "principal enemy" is described as the "bourgeois Norm." Bourgeois elites were also viewed as the primary instruments (and beneficiaries) of capitalist exploitation—hence the enduring appeal of the myth of the privileged few on the Left, from the Popular Front's "two hundred families" to the nationalization of "dominant capitalist groups" promised by the 1972 Common Program of Government. This representation of the bourgeoisie as a parasitic force was still widespread in French progressive circles in the late twentieth century. "The bourgeoisie," declared François Mitterrand toward the end of his life, "always chooses its self-interest, or what it believes to be its self-interest. Its patriotism is merely conditional." The historian François

Furet concluded that one of the distinctive features of the modern French democratic imagination was that its passion for equality expressed itself through a hatred of the bourgeoisie.[44]

A Living Legacy

In 2012, shortly before his death, Pierre Mauroy published *Ce jour-là* (On that day), a memoir narrating his experiences in the Socialist International, as the mayor of the great northern industrial city of Lille, and as Mitterrand's first prime minister. Mauroy was one of the leading figures of the French socialist movement during the second half of the twentieth century, and his account is striking for its emotional homage to the traditions of the Left: one section is entitled "A Heart on the Left." Mauroy's attachment to his *camp* (a term that appears repeatedly in the book) was tribal. Yet his core political beliefs had little to do with the ideological conflicts examined earlier in this chapter—the struggles between Republic and monarchy, state and church, bourgeois and worker, town and country, and democracy and authoritarianism. The driving forces behind his commitment to the Left were instead sentimental (his childhood memories of the Popular Front) and personal (his friendship with and loyalty to Mitterrand). In many respects, his principal adversary in his political life was not the Right (indeed, he always admired de Gaulle) but the Communist Party. And many of the values he ascribed to the Left—such as a belief in humility, a sense of toleration and respect for others, and a contempt for materialism—were essentially manifestations of his personal ethical creed.[45]

It was no accident that Mauroy's celebration of his life on the Left dwelled so little on ideological considerations. By the time he became prime minister in 1981, the division between Left and Right was already beginning to decline. As noted earlier, the Right moved away from its republican rejectionism during the first half of the twentieth century; the Left completed the movement in the 1980s by abandoning the universalist abstractions that underpinned progressive thought: the belief in human perfectibility and the sense that history had a purpose and that capitalist society could be radically overhauled. These shifts facilitated a convergence among mainstream parties around the institutions of the Fifth Republic, which was symbolized by the three experiences of shared government (*cohabitation*) between Left and Right during the 1980s and 1990s. Unsurprisingly, opinion polls revealed that the French were becoming increasingly skeptical of the importance of the notions of Left and Right. By the early twenty-first century, even the representations of the past seemed to be getting blurred, with the canonical heroes of Right and Left ceasing to be the exclusive property of their respective tribes: Charles de Gaulle was invited into the progressive pantheon, and celebrated with gusto by leading figures of the Left, while the spirit of Jaurès was fervently (if selectively) invoked by the National Front; when the National Front mayor of Hénin-Beaumont, Steeve Briois, was elected, he brought a bust of the socialist leader into his office.[46]

However, it would be a mistake to conclude that the Left-Right divide is no longer relevant to the way the French think. As we have seen, the division between the two camps had as much to do with political symbolism and idealized representations as with material and programmatic concerns. And closer inspection shows that these (mainly negative) mythological elements are still very much present in French political debate. During the 2012 elections, the Left's campaign against Nicolas Sarkozy's style of governance offered an uncanny parallel with the 1870 manifesto discussed at the beginning of this chapter. Sarkozy was pilloried for his authoritarian style, his lack of democratic accountability, and his tendency to govern by dividing rather than uniting the people—all classic elements in the progressive rhetorical repertoire. And even though the mainstream Left has quietly buried the revolutionaries' ambition to create a new type of social order, its frame of reference continues to be defined by the dualism between friends and enemies. This attitude is reflected, among other things, by suspicion of the state, demonization of the market, and widespread aversion to "liberalism" among most shades of progressive opinion. It also shows up in the common stereotypical contrast between "French" and "Anglo-Saxon" societies. As *Le Monde* put it in an editorial in 2005, "the 'Anglo-Saxon model' is based on social inequalities accepted by the British but which would seem intolerable here. . . . [O]ne cannot expect a people that made a revolution, guillotined its king and hung aristocrats on lamp-posts to have the same conception of social relations as a monarchy where one of the chambers of parliament is composed exclusively of lords."[47]

These are not idle words: they have the power to mobilize. France's rejection of the European constitutional treaty in 2005 was largely predicated on the Left's successful campaign against a "liberal" Europe, which opponents represented as the embodiment of authoritarianism, individualism, and capitalist exploitation. In the same vein, François Hollande declared in the run-up to the 2012 presidential elections that money had become the "measure of all things." The populist radical Jean-Luc Mélenchon struck an even more emphatic chord with the *peuple de gauche* with his call to "sweep the nation clean" of "the bosses, the sorcerers of finance who transform everything human into a commodity, the fiscal exiles, the financiers whose exorbitant demands are decimating French businesses." Anticapitalism thus still provides the emotional anchor for the Left's promise of a more fraternal world. This was the principal reason for the runaway success of Resistance veteran Stéphane Hessel's pamphlet *Indignez-vous!* (*Time for outrage!*), which sold more than a million copies in France after its publication in 2010; as he put it, "the power of money [. . .] has never been as great and selfish and shameless as it is now, with its servants in the very highest circles of government." As a specialist in the history of occultist beliefs in France has observed, part of contemporary French society remains attached to a vision of history dominated by mythologies, and in particular by the idea of conspiracy. In an editorial published shortly after the January 2015 shootings in Paris at the offices of *Charlie Hebdo* and other sites, the daily *Libération* noted the many outlandish stories about the attacks, attributing their conception and widespread dissemination to murky "subterranean forces." The piece concluded: "We are all, to some extent, susceptible to these conspiracy theories."[48]

The appeal to negative abstractions remains just as pervasive on the Right, if not more so. Nicolas Sarkozy's entire career, from his decisive leadership as minister of the interior to his "hyperpresidency," unfolded under the sign of conservative providentialism—notably, in his strong attack on the values of May 1968, which he equated with corruption and immoralism; in his repeated efforts to manipulate his compatriots' fears and anxieties; and in his stigmatization of particular groups (such as Islamic women and the Roma) for failing to conform to the canons of "Frenchness." Even when he campaigned for reelection in 2012, he repeatedly donned the mantle of the "protector," arguing that his robust handling of the euro crisis had saved France from disaster. Since his defeat, the former president has returned to front-line politics, recapturing the leadership of his party, the Union for a Popular Movement (UMP). He thus tweeted that it would be "a form of abandonment to remain a spectator of the situation in which France finds herself." His wife, the singer Carla Bruni, has relayed this providentialist message in her own inimitable style by declaring, in a television interview, "Il est tellement cool" (He is so cool). And if local talent was deemed unsuitable, some were prepared to look further afield. Lamenting the absence of decisive leadership from President Hollande, and the "collapse of patriotic values" across society, the conservative nationalist Philippe de Villiers affirmed, in 2014, that "France needs a Vladimir Putin."[49]

The apocalypse of national disintegration is even more central to the rhetoric and imagery of the National Front. Despite claims that she has "normalized" her party since taking over its leadership from her father, for example, Marine Le Pen is still firmly wedded to the demonology of French conservative nationalism: hence the constant references in her public utterances to degradation and decadence, and her obsessive warnings about the impending death of the French nation (themes extensively canvassed in her book for the 2012 campaign, *Pour que vive la France* [So that France may live]). Hence, also, the barrage of Frontist conspiracy theories about the abandonment of French national interests by technocrats, bankers, and European federalists, accompanied by denunciations of the dispossession of the French nation by immigrants and Gulf sheiks. In December 2010, Marine Le Pen compared the Islamic street prayers being held in France to the Nazi occupation, and in November 2013 she blamed the poor results of the French football team on a lack of national pride among the players and an excess of foreigners in the French league—a perverse consequence of "ultra-liberalism." This was no doubt the kind of thing Pierre-Joseph Proudhon had in mind when he remarked that "doing politics is like washing one's hands in shit."[50]

CHAPTER 6

The Sum of Their Parts

On August 15, 1866, the 1,100 inhabitants of the village of Foix (in the *département* of Nord) assembled to celebrate the Saint-Napoléon. The fifteenth of August was the birthday of Napoleon I, and it was commemorated as France's national day under the Second Empire; it coincides with the Catholic Feast of the Assumption. In Foix, as in thousands of other towns and cities across the country, the day's events followed a well-established pattern: distribution of food to the poorer members of the community in the morning; a civic procession of local officials to the church; and then, after the religious service, where the congregation prayed for Napoleon III's health, public games and refreshments for all, offered up by the municipality.

However, there was an additional twist to the celebrations at Foix on this occasion. At precisely six in the evening the rejoicings ceased: the church bells rang again, announcing the funeral of a veteran of Napoleon's Grande Armée, a man by the name of Saumin, who had died on the previous day at the age of eighty-four. Saumin was one of the leaders of the imperial veterans association, and among the village's most beloved elders, and the population turned out en masse for his burial. They accompanied his coffin to the church, and then to the cemetery, where they heard one of his comrades recall the epic and tragic experiences of the Napoleonic Wars. Summing up the event, the mayor of Foix described the gathering as a tribute to the "qualities of the soldier and citizen that made Saumin a brave soldier and an honorable and honored man." Noting the emotion of the mourners around him, the official later wrote, "The festivity ended amid an imposing calm that gave rise to the most serious reflections about the duties of the citizen toward his homeland."[1]

It was an article of faith among nineteenth-century elites, both on the Left and on the Right, that the experiences of the postrevolutionary decades in France had "reduced society to dust," in the expression of the liberal intellectual Paul Royer-Collard. This theme of a despotic modern state "draining the citizenry of all common passion, of all mutual need, all necessity of acting in concert, all occasion of common agency," was central to the work of Alexis de Tocqueville, and in particular to the negative contrast he drew between France and America. Such views implied that the French people were (at best) constrained from exercising their collective intellectual faculties by the state, or (at worst) lacking in the aptitude for any independent, let alone meaningful, social thought.[2]

Yet the festive displays of the citizens of Foix in 1866 suggest a more complex and captivating story—one in which the French showed a capacity for participating in collective expression through local rituals, for tracing audacious connections with the past, and for bringing ideas and sentiments together in ingenious combinations: joyful celebration and solemn remembrance, loyalty to the sovereign and a sense of civic equality, local pride and identification with national achievements. This bucolic patriotism uncannily anticipated the conception of the nation developed by the philosopher and historian Ernest Renan. In a lecture delivered in 1882, Renan argued that the idea of Frenchness was based neither on metaphysical abstractions nor on shared ethnic features such as race, language, or religion: it was a "spiritual principle," based on emotion, shared experiences of suffering, and a collective will to accomplish great things together. The nation, in his felicitous expression, was a "daily plebiscite": a coming together of collective endeavors and popular aspirations expressed through common rituals and memories of the past. How was this synthesis constructed, and how does it continue to shape the way the French see themselves to this day?[3]

Local Sentiment, National Belonging

The difficulty in translating Renan's notion of shared experience into a sense of collective belonging is that postrevolutionary France was deeply divided—not just on ideological grounds, as we saw in the previous chapter, but also across social, cultural, and geographical lines. There was a wealth of mutual animosity between the bourgeoisie and the workers, town dwellers and *campagnards*, devout Catholics and secular-minded citizens, to say nothing of the abyss separating the inhabitants of the capital from the rest of France; if anything, the Parisian revolutions of the nineteenth century further exacerbated these rifts. Reflecting on the succession of radical political changes his generation had witnessed in the French capital (where he lived for most of his life), and the destruction of the traditionalist customs he cherished, the Catholic intellectual Louis Veuillot mused, "We find ourselves as in a foreign country."[4]

Nowhere was this sense of estrangement more powerfully felt than in territorial attachments. Although the 1789 Revolution abolished the provinces of the *ancien régime* and replaced them with *départements*, older forms of attachment to place endured, and in many parts of France, the *pays* (loosely defined to mean anything from the village to the region) remained the primary source of intellectual and emotional identification. After a visit to the eastern Pyrenees in 1837, the economist Michel Chevalier noted not just the remoteness of the region from the rest of France, but the isolation of local communities from each other: "Each valley is still a little world which differs from the neighbouring world as Mercury does from Uranus. Each village is a clan, a kind of state with its own form of patriotism. There are different types and characters at every step, different opinions, prejudices and customs." Lengthy absence from one's locality could induce severe, and possibly fatal, pathologies: in the early decades of the French colonization of Algeria, a virulent strain of homesickness known as *nostalgie* was deemed to be one of the principal causes of mortality among French soldiers. In metropolitan France, this seemingly entrenched localism was often symbolized by parochialism and petty conflicts—the famous *querelles de clocher*. Hence the enduring skepticism among national elites as to the capacity of inhabitants on the periphery to nurture a civic sense. This, for example, is what an exasperated administrator sent from Paris had to say about the natives in his southern *département* in the mid-nineteenth century:

> The population of the Var is not very enlightened: it generally lacks elevation in its ideas and sentiments. These people are susceptible and vindictive, and a sense of tribalism and local animosities are pervasive. They stay among themselves and only ever band together to inflict harm upon their enemies. This adversary is not killed here, as in Corsica, but he is denounced and discredited by any means available. There are Italian and Arab influences in the character of the populations of this part of Provence, where several races have been mingled, and where war has been longer than elsewhere the normal state of affairs.[5]

Such derogatory statements were compounded by the provincials' lack of mastery of the French language and the profusion of local dialects that were spoken across the country. To those in one region, dialects from elsewhere often seemed to make use of strange dissonances: the poet Prosper Mérimée compared the sound of the Breton "c'h" to the chewing and spitting out of a raw olive. Indeed, the Parisian stereotype of "provincialism" as a narrow, enclosed sentiment that was incapable of generating the ethical universalism of the kind that Renan had in mind was one of the enduring myths of French culture from the Enlightenment onward. In one form or another, such disparaging representations were often shared by courtly aristocrats, Jacobin republicans, and the literary and cultural elites of Paris. Madame de Sévigné contemptuously referred to the inhabitants of the provinces as "people from another world"; the publicist Charles Dupont-White glorified Paris as the nation's "dazzling and electrifying capital" and summed up rural France as a "land of mountains and idiots." Traveling through the provinces in the mid-nineteenth century, the historian Hippolyte Taine likewise found "a sort of moral inertia" on the expressions of the inhabitants: "A society is like a garden, it can be arranged so that it produces peaches and oranges, or carrots and cabbages. Our society produces only carrots and cabbages." Articles on Breton folkloric dances in the Parisian press in the early 1840s stressed the "clumsiness" and "heaviness" of the gestures and the "vulgarity" of the performers. Parisian sarcasm reached its apogee in Eugène Guinot's *Physiologie du provincial à Paris* (Physiology of the provincial visitor in Paris) where a rural visitor's experience of the capital is likened to the loss of virginity: "Once he treads the soil of Paris, the provincial loses his primitive character, his regional naïveté; contact with us has deflowered him." This spirit was still visible in the twentieth century—in, for example, Gabriel Chevallier's satirical novel *Clochemerle* (1934), a mocking portrait of the parochialism of life in a village in Burgundy.[6]

Yet such stereotypes in many ways concealed the real story. Just as these representations were becoming entrenched in some circles, more buoyant views of the provinces were beginning to take shape in others. Travel writing about the regions of France evoked a malleable, impressionist, and poetic space of picturesque landscapes and romantic memories. Michelet's narrative of French history cleverly presented the temperaments of different areas as a harmonious whole that perfectly balanced negative and positive features: "the eloquent and vinous Burgundy between the ironic naïveté of Champagne and the critical, polemical, warlike toughness of Franche-Comté and Lorraine; the fanaticism of the Languedoc between the levity of Provence and the indifference of Gascony; the ambitious and conquering spirit of Normandy contained by the resistant Brittany and the massive opacity of Flanders." Provincial life was associated especially with the virtues of gentility: for aristocrats such as the Duchess of Dino, the countryside was a haven of "calm, meditation, and contemplation"; the Comte de Falloux similarly celebrated pastoral life for offering its inhabitants the possibility of "perfectibility": "One can read there with greater concentration, discuss matters with greater intimacy, and also make lasting friendships." From the opposite side of the political spectrum—and his native region of Franche-Comté—Proudhon celebrated the ideal of a federal France that was happily divided into a multitude of local self-governing communities to provide a decisive means of "cultivating intelligences and fortifying consciences."[7]

These visions were completed by the idealist philosopher Émile Boutroux:

> There is a good reason why our country is called, and will continue to be called, *la douce France*. We are a patriotic people, and we rally whenever it is necessary to defend the honor and the existence of our country. But this union is not imposed from outside upon heterogeneous entities, which merely complement each other. The principle of union is in the very soul of the French people, in their common nature, in a common sentiment of fidelity and love for the ideal and eternal France, of which our history provides such beautiful images. And our sentiment of Frenchness is indissociably bound in a love of the diverse traditions and tendencies that collectively make up the French spirit.[8]

There were new patterns of thought, too, about revitalizing regional life through the cultivation of local heritages, the strengthening of representative institutions, and the creation of civic and cultural associations. The contribution of these ideas and practices to the modern sense of nationhood in France is often overlooked, largely because they were not directed by one central institution or philosophical movement. A key element in this ensemble is what the historian Stéphane Gerson has termed "a new pedagogy of place." Its intellectual inspiration came—here again—from Rousseau, whose towering *oeuvre* had created a new "language of the heart" equating authenticity of feeling with a retreat from the artificial agitations of city life: at the end of *Émile*, Rousseau celebrated rural life as "the most peaceful, the most natural, and the most attractive to the uncorrupted heart"; he also believed in the use of public rituals to generate feelings of "fraternity" among the citizenry. From the 1820s, these regionalist ideals began to be canvassed across France by pamphleteers and other writers of all persuasions, and they were notably reflected in the voluminous production of local monographs. More than 18,000 book-length works on local history were published between 1825 and 1877, and local *mémoires* became the leading subgenre of French history.[9]

This flurry of research and memorializing, spurred by the development of provincial learned societies throughout France, yielded an imposing output: collections of historical documents, studies of monuments and traditional folklore, topographical surveys and local chronicles, biographies of illustrious figures, and histories of towns and villages. And although the focus of these works was often very specific, their underlying assumption was that local regions, towns, and villages were an essential vehicle for nurturing an authentic sense of national belonging. In his preface to the history of the village of Balneolum, one teacher asserted that "the locality does not cast a shadow over the nation: on the contrary, it makes us love it even more." This incipient local patriotism was reinforced by the organization of civic rituals, such as historical pageants in provincial towns, often coinciding with traditional festivals. In the *département* of Nord, such spectacles sought to combine education and entertainment: with the help of floats, costumes, hymns, and banners, they lavishly dramatized the histories of local towns from the Middle Ages and celebrated the virtues and achievements of local citizens. The public turnout attested to the popular echoes of these exercises in municipal patriotism: 70,000 spectators in Douai in 1839; 63,000 in Rouen in the late 1850s; 100,000 in Valenciennes in 1866.[10]

This drive to celebrate the heritage of French regions and other localities was accompanied—and reinforced—by a collective recognition of the need for greater local self-government. The question of decentralization was one of the pivotal debates in France during the mid-nineteenth century, and thousands of books, pamphlets, and articles were devoted to the subject. By the 1860s, all the major political forces agreed that the weight of Paris on the rest of France was overwhelming, and that the *départements* and municipal institutions should be given greater say in the management of their own affairs. Even Napoleon III agreed with this view, complaining that state centralization produced "an excess of regulation."[11]

There were inevitable disagreements over the scope of this liberty: schemes went from modest increases in democratic control to the restoration of *ancien régime* provinces and full-blown federalism, which would have granted substantial self-governing powers to the regions. Yet there was a consensus around Rousseau's intuitive thought that greater local patriotism would enhance the sense of collective belonging among the citizenry. In the estimation of the Bonapartist Ernest Pinard, "patriotic sentiment" rested on "rootedness in the native soil": "One loves one's great motherland only insofar as one remains attached to one's place of origin." The liberal view was scarcely different: "The zeal of the citizen for the interests of his commune is the sign and guarantee of his devotion to the general interest of the country." The royalist Charles

Muller made essentially the same point, but with a religious twist: "We live among men to whom we are attached by common bonds of memory, affection, and experience; the church where we kneel with them to pray to the Lord, the cemetery where our fathers rest next to theirs. It is in the commune that the fatherland has its roots." Inspired by the writings of Proudhon, federalist republicans pleaded with their fellow Jacobins, saying that republican sentiment could thrive only under a regime of absolute local freedom: "The aggregation of parts, based on adhesion, voluntary alliance and contractual commitment, is much more solid and generates a much more energetic form of patriotism than a system that is simply the product of coercion."[12]

French collective sentiment was also fortified by the growth of associations—which flourished across the nineteenth century, contrary to Tocquevillian conventional wisdom: there was a host of circles, clubs, and sociable organizations, including musical ensembles, sporting associations, and gymnastic societies, whose histories are only now beginning to emerge from the dust of regional archives through the patient research of local scholars. When the mayor of the small town of Bondues in the Nord (2,500 inhabitants) was installed under the Second Empire, the ceremony was attended by representatives of societies of cock-fighters, military veterans, archers, *boules* players, and musicians, as well as 262 members of the town's mutual aid association. The cultivation of patriotic sentiment was often specifically identified as the primary goal of sporting groups, especially after France's defeat by Prussia in 1871. And many of these associations formed links across localities, which encouraged a sense of commonality among Frenchmen both within and across regions. In Doubs, for example, musical associations from small villages traveled to larger regional towns, where competitions were held, and even across the border into Switzerland. Describing the festivals in which his band participated, one musician noted, "These friendly competitions have allowed the humblest of us to become familiar with the geography of France. Travelling to competitions has fused the various parts of the nation . . . Bretons, Gascons, Burgundians and Normans have become French thanks to the village band."[13]

This sense of commonality was further encouraged through associations such as the Freemasonry. While the Parisian elites of the Grand Orient de France often focused on broad social and political issues, the ethos of the organization in provincial towns was somewhat different. Its active lodges promoted a sense of public-spiritedness, emphasizing the ideals of honor, sobriety, hard work, honesty, and philanthropy—the values of the provincial bourgeoisie, whose members were prominently represented in the organization. In 1870 the Masons elected Léonide Babaud-Laribière as their grand master; in his victory speech, he went out of his way to stress that he was "a humble journalist from the provinces." Associations such as the Grand Orient thus acted as a gateway between Paris and the rest of France, in particular through the dissemination of the ideal that Masons shared with all progressives: public education. "Freedom," as one Masonic pamphleteer put it, "lies in the ability to develop our physical, intellectual and moral faculties." There were close links between the Masonry and Jean Macé's Ligue de l'Enseignement, and provincial lodges sponsored public conferences, popular libraries, and adult literacy courses in towns such as Lyon, Marseille, Aix, Nîmes, Bordeaux, Toulouse, Nantes, Grenoble, and Amiens. Through such endeavors, the local sphere thus also became a conduit for a more robust ideal of patriotism animated by democratic and fraternal values, while some Freemasons pursued even more radical goals "of interest to the whole of humanity," in the words of the Masonic intellectual André Rousselle: international peace among nations, greater equality between men and women, and the reconciliation of class antagonisms.[14]

Feelings of Frenchness thus emerged through the contributions of a wide array of local forces whose representatives expressed a sense of belonging that combined universal ideals with buoyant celebrations of particular heritages, traditions, and values. This was the full implication of Renan's vision of the nation as a "daily plebiscite," and he made the point explicitly: "The bond that ties us to France, to humanity, does not diminish the strength and tenderness of our individual and local sentiments."[15]

The Cult of the *Petite Patrie*

The French long believed that the modern sense of the collective French self emerged through the combined effects of a republican political culture, which provided French society with a coherent vision of the world, and a centralized educational system, which rested on a unitary conception of the national community. This vision of a cohesive national spirit forged by the institutions of the revolutionary and Napoleonic state is now increasingly disputed—not least because of the lack of inclusivity of the Third Republic's conception of citizenship: to varying degrees, women, workers, Catholics, immigrants, and colonial subjects were not invited to partake in the Republic's national banquet.[16]

But, just as importantly, Frenchness was not defined in opposition to local sentiment, as has long been thought, but as a complement to it. Indeed, this dual sense of belonging was so widely diffused by the late nineteenth century that the Republic drew heavily upon it to shape its nascent political culture while at the same time seeking to adapt it to its own needs. The cult of regional memories was given a fresh impetus from the 1880s. New historical and geographical societies in the regions were part of this process. Streets were named after local historical figures, and a new type of museum, the *musée cantonal*, was created. The inventor of the *musée cantonal*, the republican lawyer and historian Edmond Groult, saw it as a means of teaching the inhabitants of the countryside to "elevate their grateful thoughts to the Fatherland." This placid vision was something of a comedown from the robust ideal the republicans had championed before 1870, in which the physically and morally empowered citizen "resolutely marched toward the conquest of the universe." The Third Republic's municipal doctrine further reflected this retreat. Although mayors were elected by universal suffrage, the office was designed for the rising notables of the towns and cities, the *couches sociales nouvelles* of lawyers, doctors, and small entrepreneurs. As the republican thinker Eugène Pelletan put it, "one does not create a mayor, a mayor already exists." Municipal institutions were presented as practical bodies that would eschew political passions and dedicate themselves to improving roads, building schools, maintaining public gardens, and preserving the health and sanitation of neighborhoods.[17]

The central theme was that the Republic could keep the municipalities in "good order." In a message directed at the peasantry, pamphleteers went so far as to celebrate the end of the Paris Commune in 1871. Although French population figures in the countryside were shrinking, a sizable proportion of the rural population was still engaged in agriculture in the later decades of the nineteenth century. Republican thinkers did their best to appeal to the peasants' socially conservative values, which they had previously derided. Léon Gambetta argued that France's "reserve and force of the future" lay in its "agricultural and rural populations," and Jules Ferry celebrated the peasants' "ancient love of the land," which he said inoculated them against "social revolutions." A republican minister of agriculture went even further: "We peasants do not pretend to be among those who will change society by waving a magic wand, or who believe that a community that has lasted for centuries can suddenly be transformed into a new society."[18]

In the educational sphere, the same spirit of synthesis was promoted through a reaffirmation of the cult of the *petite patrie*, which saw teachers embracing local idioms and school textbooks celebrating a regional sense of belonging as an underpinning of citizenship. As a school inspector declared in 1906, "there is no phase in our national history that cannot be illuminated through an account of local history." This folkloric provincialism reached its apex in Augustine Fouillée's *Tour de la France par deux enfants* (Tour of France by two children), a schoolbook that enjoyed a prodigious success (by 1901 it had sold 6 million copies). Set in the aftermath of the Franco-Prussian War, it describes the discovery of French regions by two orphans, André and Julien Volden. The book offers vivid descriptions of the French climate and geography, as well as the produce of the various regions, while constantly evoking a sense of national pride in the different areas (the subtitle of the work was *Devoir et patrie* [Duty and Fatherland]). The values celebrated in this representation of Frenchness were self-confidence, industriousness, integrity, respect for others, and, above all, a sense of the rightful order of things: "conscience" was deemed important not for its intellectually enabling properties but for its capacity to illuminate "the laws of moral obligation." Julien's uncle insists that he approach all matters with "order and method"; during his visit to Lyon, the young boy is told, "Order in one's occupations and in our work is even more beautiful than order in our clothes and in our appearance." The mystical ideal of *la France profonde*, a celebration of ancestral memories, the family home, and the peasantry—"the bedrock of the nation"—was thus seamlessly incorporated into the mythology of republican patriotism.[19]

In their efforts to cultivate this image of a cohesive nation, the elites of the Third Republic assigned an especially important role to remembrance rituals such as commemorations and festivals. They heeded the historian Taine's description of the French as "a race that was not moral, but sociable and gentle, not profoundly reflective but capable of understanding ideas, all manner of ideas, even the most elevated, through wit and gaiety." This was especially visible in the establishment of July 14 as France's national holiday in 1880. While the reference to the Revolution was intended to underscore the regime's progressive historical lineage, the festival was designed as a joyful, depoliticized gathering—as reflected in the very choice of this date, which was the product of extensive deliberations among republican elites. Other dates that resonated in the progressive collective memory of the Revolution, such as August 4 (the abolition of feudalism in 1789), September 22 (the founding of the First Republic in 1792), or even January 21 (the execution of the king in 1793), were ruled out because of their potentially subversive connotations, as was the anniversary of the founding of the Second Republic in 1848 (February 24). The regime's overriding aim was to erase any association of republicanism with its own insurrectionary traditions—not just the Paris Commune of 1871 and the revolt of June 1848, but also the popular resistance in Paris and in the provinces to the *coup d'état* of 1851. Thus, events that had decisively shaped the consciousness of earlier generations were deliberately buried after 1880—an edifying instance of Renan's observation that "forgetting and historical misrepresentation are essential factors in the creation of a nation."[20]

The advantage of July 14 was that it was doubly symbolic: it harked back not only to the capture of the Bastille but also to the Fête de la Fédération a year later, that fleeting moment of revolutionary concord that preceded the violent storms of the 1790s. The memory of the Revolution was thus both idealized and reinvented. Its aspiration to fraternity was recast as a quest for "national unity," and, in a striking reinterpretation of the past, the Republic was celebrated not as a rupture, or a new dawn, but as the culmination of centuries of nation-building by royalism—as one senator put it, the Republic was "the consecration of what the ancient monarchy had prepared." Napoleonic-style military parades were brought in to underscore the regime's patriotic and martial credentials and to celebrate the values of "respect for authority and sense of duty," as President Jules Grévy put it somewhat sternly in 1881. Any reminder—even symbolic—of the Republic's more robust revolutionary past was frowned upon: on July 14, 1880, the Parisian police removed a red Phrygian cap (one of the iconic symbols of revolutionary fervor) that had been pinned to a tricolor flag hanging from a window on Rue des Épinettes.[21]

But the main point of the July 14 holiday was to create a sense of collective merriment. The Republic's idyllic patriotic narrative was played out in the celebrations held in French provincial towns and villages. In rural communities, in the absence of a sufficiently large public hall, the evening banquet was sometimes held in barns or wheat sheds, or even in the open air. The festivities were blanketed with the regime's symbols of Frenchness: tricolor flags and banners; images of Marianne, the allegorical representation of the Republic since the Revolution; and performances of the Marseillaise, which was sung after the mayor's speech, at the openings and closings of balls, at the end of fireworks displays, and in the vicinity of trees of liberty, planted all over France to symbolize the ideals of progress, hope, and regeneration. In their speeches to the assembled citizenry, local officials dwelled on the unity of the French people: as a mayor in Charente-Maritime put it, this was a moment to celebrate "the greatness of a nation that can inscribe Liberty-Equality-Fraternity on its banner." These concepts were consistently cleansed of any radical implications—and at times reinterpreted as their opposite. After evoking the Republic's holy trinity, a mayor from Cher hailed these values for promoting a "sense of respect for order, family, and property."[22]

Festive Contestations

The July 14 festivities were undoubtedly successful in attracting large numbers of French citizens into the Republic's orbit, at least in the early decades of the regime. But across the nation, and to a much larger degree than has been appreciated, the celebrations were also often contested, in keeping with the lively French traditions of dissent, contrarianism, and impertinence. These challenges provide interesting glimpses of the types of resistance encountered by the Republic's patriotic narratives and the ways in which they were adapted and reappropriated. Outright opponents of the regime saw the holiday as an affront to their own values. Rejecting a political order that in his view symbolized godlessness and moral depravity, the local priest in the village of d'Ormes-le-Voulzies, for example, tore down the tricolor flag from the church tower on the national day in 1884.[23]

Five years later, anarchist groups condemned the day as a symbol of an oppressive capitalist order. One pamphlet stated: "Others may choose to decorate and illuminate their windows; as for us, we follow the only just, the only logical, path: to declare a social war against those who seek to enslave us." Many antimilitarist critics of the Republic objected to the concept of "patriotism" that was at the heart of the celebrations. Another pamphlet, from 1913, claimed the people of Brittany had more in common with their brethren across the Channel than with the inhabitants of other French regions; the primary purpose of this "patriotic mystification," it added prophetically, was to prepare the French people for war.[24]

Adversaries of the Republic sought to subvert the occasion by transforming it into an "anti-*fête*," a commemoration of their own political traditions. From the 1880s, royalists (particularly in their strongholds, such as the Vendée) marked July 14 as a day of remembrance for the martyrs of the revolutionary era. A similarly defiant spirit was displayed by the Breton nationalist Yann Sohier, who, to the consternation of local authorities, celebrated France's national day by flying the black-and-white flag of Brittany above his home. In Paris, socialist students sometimes abstained from participating in the rejoicing and urged their compatriots to boycott as well. Some dressed provocatively in a challenge to the police, while others hoisted red flags on public buildings on the night preceding the national day.[25]

The most creative challenges came from progressives who sought to reclaim the day by celebrating alternative strands of the republican tradition. In Lyon, for example, radical groups used the day for counter-commemorations in which they honored those aspects of the revolutionary era that had been "forgotten" by the Third Republic—notably, the execution of the king. Even socialist municipalities officially marking the anniversary of the Third Republic sought to give the festivities a distinct coloring—by providing more charitable aid to the poor, by dwelling on the need for greater social reforms, and even by performing the Internationale alongside the Marseillaise—a musical rendering of the point that patriotism and internationalism were complementary values.[26]

Most progressive critics of the Republic challenged the festivities of July 14 not because they rejected patriotism, but in the name of a more robust and inclusive conception of the ideal. The principle of fraternity was again of central importance. For many socialists, the Revolution's sincere aspiration to forge a new sense of collective belonging had been perverted by the Republic, both by its emptying of the concept of any substantive significance and by its pursuit of objectives that contradicted its spirit, such as the cult of the army, the adoption of extreme nationalist rhetoric, and the expansion of the French colonial empire. Others saw the official rituals themselves as inconsistent with the ideal of fraternity. For the socialist Jules Delmorès, the ceremonies of July 14 betrayed the Rousseauist ideals of equality, transparency, and natural human goodness, and were based instead on artifice: the "vain speeches" and "pretense of felicity," he said, were a disguise for the appropriation of public space by the bourgeoisie and the exclusion of poorer sections of the community; and the displays of glamor and luxury and the decorations handed out to dignitaries of the regime were evidence of "human and social corruption."[27]

This criticism of the degradation of a once-noble ideal was widespread and often came up in references to the Marseillaise: according to an anarchist newspaper, the French now sang this glorious anthem of liberation only when they were inebriated. The same point about the perversion of French morals found an echo in the common observation that July 14 was not a celebration of genuine collective sentiment but a routine ceremony with little resonance among popular classes. A trade unionist observed in 1930, "The fourteenth of July is merely an official festivity, a conformist celebration of an event that successive governments of the Third Republic have sanctified and that has accordingly taken its place in the sequence of archaic and indolent anniversaries that are offered up for the celebrations of an alienated populace."[28]

Progressives challenged the idealized ecumenism of July 14 by pointing to more combative interpretations of the ideals of equality and fraternity in French revolutionary history. This "counter-memory" centered primarily on the Paris Commune. From the early 1880s, annual demonstrations at the Père-Lachaise Cemetery in Paris marked the anniversary of the *semaine sanglante* in May 1871, the crushing of the Commune by the French Army. A monument to the Commune was inaugurated there in 1908, and it became a site of pilgrimage for radical republicans, socialists, and anarchists. This "socialist Easter," in the fervent evocation of one socialist thinker, prompted different and at times conflicting visions of what the Commune had stood for. In the early years of the Third Republic, the Blanquists, a radical group that espoused the ideas of the revolutionary republican leader Louis-Auguste Blanqui, were the principal standard-bearers of the Commune's legacy. Their particular vision of the events of 1871 fitted into a more general historical mythology of Jacobin republicanism that emphasized the cult of heroism and revolutionary virtues, dividing the world into sharply drawn camps of good and evil. In the Blanquist narrative, the Commune symbolized all the values lacking in the official rituals of July 14: not only radicalism and atheism, but also a truly revolutionary sense of fraternity based on a cult of the will and the defense of *la patrie en danger*.[29]

Libertarians, in contrast, commemorated the Commune as a "cry of social revolt": rather than the French Revolution, its historical antecedents had been the workers' revolts in Lyon in the early 1830s and the insurrection in Paris in June 1848. A common theme here, particularly among anarchists, was the appeal to the ideal of spontaneity—the mirror opposite of the values of order and unity underpinning the patriotism of the "one and indivisible Republic." Anarchists argued that the Commune had occurred without any organization, and that "when organization was brought to it, the Commune was killed." Libertarians thus idealized the Communalist movement (including its provincial episodes) because they perceived it as the first serious effort by French revolutionaries to replace authority with freedom in all aspects of social life—in the family, in the workplace, and, of course, in the state itself, which was eventually to be replaced by a confederal system of freely associated communes. In the two decades preceding World War I, this Proudhonist ideal was picked up by revolutionary syndicalists, who portrayed themselves as the "legitimate heirs" of the Commune because of their comprehensive opposition to the "bourgeois centralized state."[30]

French socialists also marked the anniversary of the Commune, although they were more conflicted than the libertarians about its significance. They portrayed the Commune as the real historical precedent of the revolutionary principle, an example of the "intense struggle, for a moment victorious, of the proletariat"—in contrast with the "bourgeois" moment of 1789. Echoing Marx's (extravagant) claim, the socialist leader Jules Guesde asserted that most of the Commune's leaders had come from the proletariat, and that its program had been explicitly socialist. But the Commune's political authoritarianism clashed with the legalistic instincts of most of the socialist leadership, particularly their profound abhorrence of violence. Jean Jaurès thus explicitly stated that, for all its heroism, the Commune could in no way provide a tactical or strategic model for socialists. The socialists resolved the dilemma between these two conflicting views in an uncannily similar way to the Third Republic's consensual gloss on the French Revolution—by refusing to dwell on the Commune's more contentious policies (such as its anticlericalism) and concentrating instead on its aspirations to promote greater social harmony.[31]

The municipal campaigns of Guesde's Parti Ouvrier (Workers Party) illustrate how the reinvention took place. By 1900, the party had already established itself in such localities as Lille, Montluçon, Roubaix, and Marseille. Its electoral propaganda dwelled on its social policies—increasing financial help to the poor, providing school lunches for children, limiting the working day for municipal employees, and reducing taxes for workers. This "municipal socialism" was portrayed as a direct continuation of the tradition of the Paris Commune—a progressive adaptation of the ideal of the *petite patrie*.[32]

By the early twentieth century, the Commune thus became the principal alternative focus of France's revolutionary past in the progressive imagination. This counter-memory was underpinned by a powerful sense of the ties that bound the French people together, although these ideals were markedly different from the "official" patriotism of July 14. In contrast to the rhetoric of the Communards themselves, who were steeped in revolutionary culture, these celebrations of their memory contained very few references to 1789, or even to the radicalization of the French Revolution from 1793: their primary purpose was to look ahead to the advent of a more egalitarian and fraternal *République sociale*. The Commune's survivors emphasized this message. The emblematic figure here was the "red virgin," Louise Michel, the socialist feminist whose personification of the spirit of 1871 led to her deportation and then her imprisonment for several years in the 1880s, followed by another spell in exile. When she returned to France in 1895, she became the Commune's most potent living symbol. Close to radical republicans and socialists in the early 1880s, she eventually moved over to the anarchist camp. Until her death in 1905 she traveled tirelessly across France extolling the memory of the Commune and reminding her provincial audiences that the Republic would be secure only when it fully lived up to its ideals of equality and fraternity.[33]

Varieties of Patriotism

French collective sentiment was inherently elastic and malleable. Frenchness was a matter of constant negotiation in the varied interactions among champions of universalist ideals and upholders of localism, Parisian elites and civic and political associations, and advocates of the "one and indivisible Republic" and their critics. The results of these encounters were dynamic and often gave rise to hybrid senses of belonging, combining attachments to the local town or city, the region, and the nation—as well as, on occasion, the greater family of humanity beyond France. Jaurès was perhaps the noblest advocate of the cosmopolitan belief in the elasticity of humankind: he was deeply immersed in French and European culture, and his writings are laced with poetic hymns to provincial France (and especially his beloved Midi). He was also capable of addressing his constituents in the Tarn in the local *patois*.[34]

This hybrid effect was very much apparent in French regional sentiment. It was a delicate issue, because of the legacy of the revolutionary era: at the height of the Terror, the revolutionaries' attempts to impose political unity had led to brutal repression of provincial republicans, who were (spuriously) accused of separatism. The centralizing movement was accompanied by drastic moves toward cultural uniformity, with regional languages being perceived as threatening the integrity of the nation. In his report on idioms to the Committee of Public Safety in January 1794, the Jacobin Bertrand Barère observed, "Federalism and superstition speak Lower Breton, emigration and hatred of the Republic speak German, counter-Revolution speaks Italian and fanaticism speaks Basque." Lest there be any misunderstanding, he added, "Let us destroy these damaging and mistaken instruments." A century later, it seemed that little had changed: the anticlerical leader Émile Combes declared that the Bretons would become republican only when they spoke French. The specter of separatism was often invoked to counter any aspiration to greater provincial autonomy; this negative myth was exacerbated by the experience of the Paris Commune and the loss of Alsace-Lorraine in 1871.[35]

Yet, away from the inflated rhetoric, things were considerably more nuanced. The republican intellectual Alphonse de Lamartine rehabilitated the memory of the regionalist Girondist movement of the early revolutionary era, and with it the idea that federalism was compatible with patriotic sentiment. A form of provincial radicalism flourished in parts of southern France in the decades following the 1848 Revolution, and later reemerged during the Franco-Prussian War in the form of the Ligue du Midi, a patriotic republican association seeking to rally southern *départements* to the cause of national defense. More fundamentally, the Third Republic was in many respects dominated by the subcultures of the Midi and the East, as symbolized by provincial eminences such as Adolphe Thiers, Léon Gambetta, Raymond Poincaré, and Édouard Daladier; 60 percent of the regime's ministerial elites had been born in rural communities and small towns.[36]

Even in the former bastions of the "counter-revolution," local loyalties could take a host of different forms. In nineteenth-century Brittany, for example, regionalist sentiment was suffused with aristocratic and religious values. Its manifestations were mainly linguistic and cultural. Collections of songs and popular folktales, such as Hersart de la Villemarqué's *Barzaz Breiz* (Ballads of Brittany, 1839), for example, were published. In 1870, a petition calling for regional languages to be taught was sent to the French government by a group of Breton notables, including one Charles de Gaulle, the uncle of the future leader of the Free French; it presented the teaching of dialects as a way of strengthening national unity. In stark contrast, the manifesto of the first Breton nationalist party in 1911 asserted that it recognized Brittany as its only fatherland and rejected all cultural symbols of Frenchness, including the tricolor and the Marseillaise. Breton regionalism could, however, also take forms that brought disparate ideas into harmony, as illustrated by the emergence of social Catholicism in lower Brittany in the late nineteenth century—a movement that successfully synthesized regionalist ideas, republican values such as democracy, and a more progressive conception of Catholic faith. In this instance, it was the periphery that gave new meaning to the ideal of Frenchness and projected it back toward the center.[37]

French "Jacobinism" was thus flexible, and there were many ways in which regionalist sentiment and the cultural demands of the Republican state could find common ground. A case in point was Frédéric Mistral's Félibrige movement, which orchestrated a major revival of the language and poetry of Provence in the second half of the nineteenth century. Although Mistral's conception of territoriality extended beyond the horizon of the nation-state (he dwelled on the roots of the Provence region in classical Latin culture), his vision of southern culture was essentially romantic; in this respect, it overlapped with the Republic's folkloric provincial mythology. Disillusioned by the failure of the Second Republic, which he had at first greeted with enthusiasm, Mistral consistently refused to engage publicly with the "bitter irritations of politics." He affirmed in 1904, "I am a monarchist but I could not care less about the form of government"—which was, of course, a tacit endorsement of the Third Republic. He asserted that the flowering of regional cultures would fortify French national unity—a common theme among the *félibristes*.[38]

This creative ambiguity allowed many progressive thinkers to sympathize with the Félibrige cause. Among the most notable of these "red *félibristes*" was Louis-Xavier de Ricard, who edited an almanac in Provençal in Montpellier and created *L'Alliance latine* (The Latin alliance), a journal devoted to promoting the federalist ideal among Latin peoples. There was also Clovis Hugues, one of the leading figures in revolutionary Marseille in 1871, who later became a socialist parliamentarian and the author of well-known republican verses in French. Hugues was an ardent defender of regional languages and wrote around forty poems in Provençal (including "La Sociala," an ode to the Commune)—which did not prevent his election in 1898 to the position of *majoral* in the Félibrige movement.[39]

In contrast with the sunny and optimistic regionalism of the Félibrige movement, with its colorful celebrations, poetic evocations of troubadours, and (occasional) embrace of radical ideals, Maurice Barrès offered a more somber provincialism that was rooted in the cult of ancestors and those who had fallen for France: *la terre et les morts*. From his native Lorraine, Barrès rejected the Parisian Jacobinism that he believed was suffocating French towns and cities and flirted with federalism: in 1895, he endorsed the establishment of regional assemblies. Yet one of the main purposes of Barrès's provincialism was to "restore vitality to the nation"; it is arguable that his project of strengthening collective sentiment throughout France was primarily driven by a national (and nationalist) agenda, and especially the desire to cultivate greater French resistance to Germanic influences.[40]

Mistral's disciple Jean Charles-Brun combined republicanism and regionalist sentiment, developing an approach that incorporated influences from both progressive and conservative thinkers (notably, Proudhon, Comte, and Barrès); in his scheme, the concentric communities of the local area, the province, and the nation were mutually reinforcing. Although this reformist brand of regionalism became an important element in national republican politics before 1914, it was latently conservative in its empiricism, mysticism, and hostility to parties. This disposition became more overt in the interwar years, when Charles-Brun's regionalism took on a folkloric character. That such rapprochements between regionalism and republicanism should have occurred under the Third Republic was not coincidental: as we have just seen, the cult of the *petite patrie* was integral to the regime's frame of mind, and its elites were largely drawn from outside Paris. In 1913, this *entente cordiale* was symbolically sealed when Poincaré, inaugurating his presidency with a trip to southern France, stopped for lunch with Mistral in his village of Maillane.[41]

These eclectic combinations among political cultures, as well as a sense of belonging, were also evident in the emergence of new political rituals, such as the celebration of May 1. This "counter-festival" was initially intended to support the proposal for an eight-hour working day, but in the mind of its creator, Jules Guesde, it also had a more ambitious purpose: to show that working men and women were an integral part of France's national heritage. The first "Festival of Labour" (Fête du Travail)—which involved public demonstrations by working men and women across France—took place in 1890. The significance of the day was affirmed by the violent opposition it provoked from the Republican state. The first demonstrations took place in an atmosphere of fear and intimidation, and a year later the police opened fire on a crowd in Fourmies (Nord), killing ten demonstrators and injuring many more. The "massacre of Fourmies" became an integral part of progressive memory during the Third Republic, as it was perceived as a true measure of the regime's disposition toward the working people. It was consistently cited in French Labor Day speeches in subsequent decades.[42]

This violence gave rise to spirited discussions about the nature of the celebrations and demonstrations. Socialists saw the Fête du Travail as an inclusive ritual and a peaceful demonstration of socialism's redemptive potential; their members of Parliament even proposed that the day be declared a national holiday, as a complementary celebration of the republican ideal of "fraternity." (Ironically, it would be under Vichy that May 1 would become an official celebration.) Many trade unionists, who sought to use May 1 to express their separateness from other social groups and to promote the ideals of the "general strike" and social revolution, contested such consensualism. Some even rejected the designation of the day as a "festivity." As an anarchist placard put it, scathingly, "A festival! As if Labour, crushed by the parasitic forces of capitalism, could be made to celebrate its slavery!" Over time, however, it was the more inclusive ideal that won the day, especially in small and mid-sized towns, where the May anniversary was marked by public meetings, peaceful marches, and the presentation of lists of economic grievances by union representatives to local authorities. In Bordeaux in 1899, for example, local groups organized six different festive and commemorative events, and all passed off without incident. This ecumenical spirit was best illustrated by the socialists at Lorient, who celebrated May 1 under a tricolor banner on which was inscribed the First International's slogan: "Workers of all countries, unite!"[43]

The real character of this annual festivity lay in the multiple manifestations of fraternal sociability it engendered among progressive groups. In many areas, May 1 became a (secular) remembrance day in which the members of political associations and trade unions assembled in local cemeteries to pay homage to fellow workers who had died in the course of the previous year. These rituals unfailingly brought back memories of past tragedies, such as the massacre of Fourmies, especially in the Nord. Workers also expressed their solidarity with those who had pursued earlier forms of working-class militancy: in the Rhône, the May anniversary of 1891 took place around the tomb of the Canuts, who had revolted against the July Monarchy in 1834. Explicit links were noted between the repressiveness of monarchical and republican governments toward French workers (and, as if to prove the demonstrators right, this particular expression of working-class memory was violently broken up by the Lyon police).[44]

But this "remembrance" dimension was only one aspect of the celebration of May 1, and its solemn character in no way set the tone for the entire day. On the contrary, the general mood was festive, especially in provincial France. This was fraternity at its most playful, celebratory, and sociable. In contrast with the July 14 celebrations, which were increasingly nationalistic in tone, on May 1 foreign workers were invited to participate; the Italian members of a socialist association in Grenoble did so in 1900, for example. The demonstrators took the opportunity to taunt local authorities: a group of fourteen socialists who assembled in the Café du Midi in Cahors (Lot) in May 1898, for instance, exasperated the local police inspector by hanging "three red lanterns over the windows of the first floor" of the café. Like the July 14 events, the May 1 rituals also often assumed a pastoral and bucolic character. In the commune of Thizy (Rhône), the May 1 celebrations of 1891 ended with 3,500 local inhabitants marching to the summit of a mountain, armed with provisions and music; the ensuing revelry went on until the late evening, in front of a "large red banner." In Besançon in 1898, the Workers' Federation marked May 1 with a family-oriented festival in the woods of Chailliez; the 2,000 participants (accompanied by a police official, who took detailed notes of the proceedings and who was clearly fraternizing with the enemy) traveled there on foot "preceded by three buglers and six trumpeters."[45]

An entire collection of songs emerged around the subject of May 1. In these songs, republican, Communard, and internationalist motifs were blended together in cacophonic harmony: there were performances of revolutionary tunes such as "Les Fils de '93" (The children of '93), sung by the Socialist Choral Society at Nevers; Étienne Pedron's "Chanson des huit heures" (Song for the eight hours), which became a classic in the progressive repertoire; Jean-Baptiste Clément's Communard hymn "Le Temps des cerises" (The time for cherries); and robustly antimilitarist songs such as "Il faut supprimer les patries" (We must eliminate the fatherlands). At the same time, there were appropriations of traditional republican hymns: in the Nord, for example, locals developed a Marseillaise *fourmisienne*, which used the celebrated republican anthem to lambast the Third Republic's acts of violence against workers.[46]

The Identity of France

Reflecting on the essential characteristics of France, the historian Fernand Braudel observed that the nation had come into being through a slow and cumulative process: Frenchness was "a residue, an amalgam, a thing of additions and mixtures." It could be recognized in "certain stock images, certain passwords known to the initiated, in a thousand touchstones, beliefs, ways of speech, excuses, in an unbounded subconscious, in the flowing together of many obscure currents, in a shared ideology, shared myths, shared fantasies." Braudel intended to devote four volumes to illustrating the complex ways in which this process of national formation occurred in France, but only completed two of them before his death.[47]

Although I subscribe wholeheartedly to Braudel's idea of the nation as a gradual and collective construct, my aim here has been much more modest: to show how, by the early decades of the twentieth century, a certain convergence around the ideal of Frenchness had become apparent, both among members of the elite classes and in broader sections of society. In this vision, France was a resilient nation that had survived the vicissitudes of history with its essence unscathed. Its endurance, as Renan pointed out, had been strengthened through the experience of common suffering and by the people's collective capacity to overcome adversity. Frenchness was defined by a certain stoicism, a refusal to accept domination—an almost magical, spiritual power. This common trait infused not only the republicans' championing of individual moral autonomy, but also the socialists' struggle for the defense of workers, and the nationalists' exaltation of French virility. This was the spirit in which the nationalist poet and essayist Charles Péguy, whose thought combined elements of all three value systems, hailed the "glory of war." This self-image was also shared by regional groups: celebrating the patriotism of the populations of Provence, a schoolteacher from Digne asserted that "the resistance to oppression" had been a characteristic of the peoples of his region over the centuries.[48]

Above all, there was a general agreement that France was an exemplary nation whose mission it was to serve as a guide to humanity, as much through its effective leadership as through its cultural and scientific creativity. This vision was shared by conservatives and progressives alike. The reactionary royalist Joseph de Maistre asserted that France had survived the Revolution only because it was destined by Providence for a mission of universal salvation, and the republican thinker Edgar Quinet noted that it was France's calling to "consume herself for the glory of the world, for others as much as for herself, for an ideal which is yet to be attained of humanity and world civilization." Describing his country as a "supreme creation of intelligence and human will," the republican leader Léon Gambetta claimed that France possessed the finest treasures of human civilization: "research in the arts, perfection in crafts, superiority in the sciences, sublimity in philosophical conceptions, integrity in public conduct, clarity in intelligence, enlightenment and justice everywhere, in sum, and for all the world, the highest expression of the human spirit." The only missing element in this encomium was the past, and it was supplied in magnificently hyperbolic fashion by Renan, who claimed that all the great principles of modernity (the abolition of slavery, the rights of man, equality and freedom) had "been first spoken in French, [were] coined in French, and [had] made their worldly appearance in French." This sense of self-satisfaction also prevailed in the general public. In 1906, the newspaper *Le Parisien* asked its readers to name the Frenchmen who had contributed the most to the nation's greatness over the previous hundred years. Fifteen million replies were received, from all over the country, and the answers revealed a judicious sense of balance in the collective psyche: Louis Pasteur, the glory of French science, came first, just ahead of Victor Hugo, the icon of the Republic of letters; third was Gambetta himself, the hero of French defensive patriotism, and fourth, Napoleon, the symbol of expansive imperialism.[49]

The other great theme in this national synthesis was the pursuit of unity. Labeled in different ways (patriotism, concord, peace, fraternity), this ideal symbolized the aspirational side of Renan's concept of the "daily plebiscite." In this regard, the idea of the complementarity of France's different territorial components was one of the most important intellectual breakthroughs of the second half of the nineteenth century: as we have seen, it became a leitmotif across all strains of French thought. Symbolized by the cult of the *petite patrie*, the historic compromise between center and periphery was consecrated by a harmonious distribution of roles. Paris was the guarantor of national unity, the provider of a unifying collective memory and counter-memory (for the Commune was, conveniently, part of the capital's heritage, too), and the upholder of progressive values such as secularism and universal education. The provinces, for their part, became the privileged incubators of patriotic sentiment, thanks to their hearty municipal traditions, the beauty of their landscapes, the richness of their folklore, and the resilience of their collective spirit, all of which reflected the willingness of their inhabitants to sacrifice themselves for the greater good.

World War I was in this respect a major landmark, as it witnessed not only a further dissemination of the concept of the *petite patrie* but also its explicit entrenchment in a neo-ruralist nationalist ideology; fittingly, the ceremony honoring the unknown soldier in November 1920 was also a celebration of a "return to the land." There was a massive increase in the number of war memorials across the country: more than 36,000 public monuments were built within five years of the end of the conflict. Religious motifs also made their appearance. Speaking in July 1919 at a Mass in honor of the sons of the village who had been killed in battle, the priest of the parish of Marchampt (Rhône) celebrated the primary inspiration of their patriotism as "the Christian education they received" in the village. The proclaimed aim of the *Petite Patrie*, a monthly Catholic publication from Bayeux, was to "lead the struggle against religious indifference." Indeed, although it occupied an ostensibly subordinate position in the greater chain of patriotic being, the periphery emerged as the site of the authentic France, a haven of truth and simplicity where the values of heroism, constancy, and industriousness were upheld along with a proper sense of perspective on life—and notably, all of this was achieved through the cultivation of the soil. In the interwar years, this idealization of the provincial spirit became pervasive. It was clear across a range of writings, from the historian and essayist Daniel Halévy's celebration of the ingeniousness of the peasantry in central France to the works of literature published depicting the flowering of the theme of region (Henri Pourrat for the Auvergne, Marcel Aymé for the Jura, and Jean Giono for the Basses-Alpes). As the writer François Mauriac put it in his *La Province* (The province, 1926), "The greatest piece of good fortune which may befall a novelist is to be born in the provinces, from a provincial lineage."[50]

Even the communists, the self-styled inheritors of the Jacobin tradition, enthusiastically added their voices to this provincial chorus. During its Ninth Congress at Arles in 1937, the French Communist Party organized an exhibition celebrating the accomplishments of French workers, peasants, and artisans; there was an unmistakable regionalist flavor to the exhibits, which included costumes and pottery from Quimper, dairy products from Normandy, porcelain from Limoges, gloves from Saint-Junien, soap from Marseille, oysters from the Gironde, truffles from Périgord and the Lot, knives from Thiers, and wine and liqueurs from Cassis and Calvados. The Third Republic also extended the *petite patrie* analogy to the empire: the 1931 Colonial Exposition marked the apotheosis of this vision of a French dominion that was universal in its geographical scope but constructed around a multitude of small homelands. This vision of the countryside as a fulcrum of national virtue reached its zenith in Vichy's regionalist and pastoral rhetoric; in a December 1940 speech, Pétain asserted that "the attachment to the *petite patrie* not only removes nothing from the love of the fatherland, but contributes to its strengthening."[51]

This "provincialization" (for want of a better term) of France's sense of its collective self is still alive and well. Its traces can be found in the celebration of French culinary art, an ideal judiciously combining national and local traditions of excellence in the field, and in the prominence of regional towns in the national landscape—notably, in French cinema (for example, the films of Eric Rohmer and Claude Chabrol). The provincial ethos also shines through in the popularity of French mayors, who administer the nation's immense web of villages and small towns; these local officials remain the most trusted elected figures in the country through their possession of those once-derided values of familiarity and proximity.[52]

For all its portrayal as the epitome of the distant centralism of the Jacobin tradition, the French presidency has also imbibed some of this territorial symbolism. From Charles de Gaulle's beloved village of Colombey-les-Deux-Églises through François Mitterrand's *force tranquille* to the Corrèzian fiefs of Jacques Chirac and François Hollande, successive presidents of the Republic have constructed their legitimacy around their rootedness in *la France profonde*. The only exception, Nicolas Sarkozy, confirmed the rule (Hungary was too exotic, and Neuilly too suburban and posh, to provide the required symbolic capital). As one seasoned observer noted, "The ideal France still resides in the countryside."[53]

And as the nation finally exorcized its fear of dismemberment in the late twentieth century by granting substantive devolved powers to its subnational levels of government, who better to represent the patriotic reconciliation of center and periphery than the comic-strip warrior Astérix the Gaul, the hero of the feisty Breton village resisting Roman occupation? Embodying all at once the national incorporation of regional folklore, the Rousseauist utopia of communal sociability, the tradition of local resistance to foreign invasion, and the ideal of an unchanging France, forever insulated from the ravages of modernization, the Astérix stories marked the ultimate triumph of the *petite patrie* in the French collective imagination.[54]

New Paths to the Present

In the years that followed the liberation of France from Nazi occupation in 1944, the French began to see themselves and the world in new ways: a new vision of Frenchness emerged in the wake of Charles de Gaulle's success and the entrenchment of Marxist ideas among the intelligentsia. In Jean-Paul Sartre's formula, Marxism became the "unsurpassable horizon of the times." The transformation bore witness to the robustness of the traditions discussed in preceding chapters: rationalism, mysticism, utopianism, scientific idealism, nationalism, and the production of overarching ideological visions. But it also underlined the extent to which ideas are driven by decisive historical moments. In this respect, both Gaullism and Marxism demonstrated the pivotal role of the experiences of the 1940–1944 period in shaping the French self-image in the modern era.

De Gaulle did not emerge from the ranks of the traditional republican political or intellectual elite. He was a general in the French Army and, although he published a few books, he was largely unknown to the French public before World War II. His destiny changed after France's military collapse in 1940 and the Third Republic's humiliating capitulation to Hitler, which de Gaulle refused to accept. As noted earlier, his most famous speech called on his compatriots to continue the fight against the German invaders: "Whatever happens," he concluded, "the flame of French resistance must not be extinguished and will not be extinguished." Disavowed by the official Vichy government for his insubordination, de Gaulle was sentenced to death in absentia. Exiled and isolated in his London offices in Carlton Gardens, he was initially entirely dependent on the support of Winston Churchill, who appreciated his intellectual rigor, his determination, and his lack of verbosity—qualities the prime minister mockingly described as "un-French" (Franklin D. Roosevelt, who never took much of a shine to the French Resistance leader, called him "Lady de Gaulle"). The general eventually became the leader of the French Resistance, forging a large coalition around his Free French movement to unite all the groups (from monarchists to communists) who rejected the Vichy regime's collaboration with the Nazis. When France was liberated in 1944, de Gaulle was hailed as a national hero: he became the latest incarnation of the savior figure, or, as one pamphlet put it, "the man sent by providence."[1]

The general's political thought drew heavily upon the sensibility of the French Right: its disdain for materialism, its fear of collectivism, its obsession with death, and its fascination with decisive individual leadership. But behind his stiff demeanor, de Gaulle was also a pragmatist. He had none of his reactionary predecessors' nostalgia for the golden age of the French monarchy; nor did he share their misty-eyed romanticization of French provincialism—to say nothing of their contempt for democracy. In fact, even though he liked to find refuge in his village of Colombey, de Gaulle's philosophy of the state was unapologetically Jacobin. He did not hesitate to discard key elements of the heritage of the French Right, especially its hostility to republicanism and its xenophobic, racialist, and anti-egalitarian tendencies. Over time, he modernized French conservative thought by incorporating more fraternal ideals into its scheme of values—notably, by granting voting rights to women and ending French colonial rule in Algeria. He was able to carry the French people with him not only because of his personal charisma but also because of his idealistic vision of the country's calling, which chimed with their collective aspirations: "France," he claimed, "cannot be France without grandeur."[2]

In order to recapture this national greatness, de Gaulle campaigned for the creation of a strong centralized executive, and it was in this spirit that he established the Fifth Republic in 1958 and served as its first president until his resignation in 1969. He was full of paradoxes: inaccessible and yet utterly transparent, he was a man of order who became a rebel, a Bonapartist who disliked war, a republican whose style of rule was monarchical, a radical reformer who appealed to conservatives, a melancholic spirit who constantly trumpeted his optimism, and a statesman who would have loved to be a writer. (After surviving one of the many attempts on his life, he joked that he was, in all French literary history, the author who had been most shot at.) Especially in his later years, his leadership was strongly contested, and the monarchical trappings of his presidency were mocked. His death in November 1970 elicited this headline from the satirical French weekly *Hara-kiri* (the predecessor of *Charlie Hebdo*): "TRAGIC BALL AT COLOMBEY: 1 DEAD." But, precisely because of his capacity to draw together and reconcile opposing ideals, de Gaulle's *certaine idée de la France* became an enduring source of inspiration to his compatriots.[3]

Marxism, too, was a relatively unknown quantity in France before 1940. Efforts to disseminate the doctrine had produced meager results, partly because of the strength of home-grown socialist ideas (particularly those of Proudhon) in the French labor movement before 1914, and partly because the principal French socialist theoreticians, such as Jules Guesde and Paul Lafargue, had only a superficial acquaintance with the *oeuvre* of Marx and Engels. After reading one of Lafargue's works, Engels wrote sternly to Lafargue, "I believe you should go back and properly read *Capital* from one end to the other." Marxist ideas also struggled to gain ground in elite academic institutions, especially in the social sciences, due to the appeal of France's humanist and positivist traditions.[4]

The Russian Revolution in many ways compounded the problem. Because of the "bolshevization" of the French Communist Party from the mid-1920s, Marxist doctrine received less attention within the party organization than Leninist classics such as *What Is to Be Done?* and *The State and Revolution*, which celebrated the role of the party as a "vanguard of the proletariat." This tendency was accentuated in the aftermath of the Liberation, when the French Communist Party (PCF) became the dominant progressive force on the Left, thanks to its key role in the internal resistance. The party exploited its position to disseminate Marx's central ideas about the inequities of capitalism through the publication of canonical texts and pamphlets and its vast network of newspapers and periodicals. But this doctrinal French communist version of Marxism remained largely Leninist in inspiration—a tendency fortified by the party's complete identification with the strategic objectives of the Soviet Union during the Stalinist era.[5]

Alongside the rise of the PCF, French Marxism was nurtured and disseminated in the postwar era at the École Normale Supérieure, where a quarter of all students were party members, and where it was fashionable for men to sport a Stalin moustache. As the philosopher Régis Debray later remembered, these were times when Marxist intellectuals in France "marched to the tune of the rationalist canonball." Heterodoxy, or even dissent, was tracked down and purged: in the Manichaean reasoning of the times, it was "better to be wrong with the party, in the party, than to be right outside the party, and against it"; until 1976, the PCF remained committed to instituting a "dictatorship of the proletariat" in France. Fittingly, the major Marxist thinker to emerge during the postwar era was Louis Althusser, a communist philosopher who taught at the École Normale. He was prodigiously learned, curious about new ideas and genres, and full of emotional intelligence and sensitivity to the beauties of the world, and generations of *normaliens* remembered him for his kindness and generosity. His private correspondence reveals a yearning, from his "deepest inner self," for a total form of natural freedom rejecting all manner of artifice and convention and expressing itself in "an extravagance of inventiveness, of gesture, of movement, of head and of heart."[6]

Yet Althusser was a tormented figure who symbolized the contradictory place of Marxism in French intellectual culture. None of his personal qualities were ever manifested in his Marxism, which was schematic in the extreme. Althusser rejected any interpretation of the doctrine that was grounded in moral conceptions of human nature, purporting instead to find Marx's "scientific" essence in his theory of history and in his view of the determination of social relations by economic structures. Althusser's notion of the role of intellectuals was reductionist: he claimed that "the philosophy professor is a petit-bourgeois. When he opens his mouth, it is petit-bourgeois ideology that expresses itself. . . . On the whole, intellectuals are irredeemably petit-bourgeois in their ideology." This abstruse Marxism, dogmatic and almost theological in its implications about the sinfulness of thought (Althusser never entirely shook off his Catholic heritage), paradoxically left little room for human agency. Nevertheless, Althusser's rigidity was integral to the seductiveness of his philosophy: as a former admirer put it, his work offered an appealing "philosophy of order"; another disciple noted that he "made us proud to be communist." And the philosopher-cleric was even at hand to receive the confessions of those of his students who doubted the faith and to steer them gently back to the path of orthodoxy; the ritual became so common at the École Normale that it earned its own special expression: *se faire althusser*.[7]

This was what gave the French Marxism of the postwar decades its spiritual homogeneity: whether inside or outside the PCF, and whether they labeled themselves communists, Trotskyists, humanists, existentialists, structuralists, critical Marxists, or situationists, progressive intellectuals devoted much of their theoretical energy to salvaging or rescuing the doctrine from potential forms of "deviation" (or simply from unfortunate events, such as the denunciation of Stalin's crimes by Nikita Khrushchev at the Twentieth Congress of the Soviet Communist Party in 1956). Hence their concern not with the concrete economic and political dimensions of Marxism but with philosophical abstractions of a particular kind—the justification of the role of the Communist Party, the idealization of the working class, the rationalization of political violence, and the moral imperative of bringing about a new political order through revolutionary struggle. And, if all else failed, there was always the ultimate idealist argument that Marxism had to be true simply because any alternative hypothesis was inconceivable: as the philosopher Maurice

Merleau-Ponty put it, "it is very possible that no proletariat will emerge to perform the role of the ruling class that is assigned to it by Marxism, but no other class can replace it in that function, and so the failure of Marxism would be the failure of the philosophy of history." This was the kind of reasoning that prompted the liberal essayist Raymond Aron's cruel but not inaccurate description of French Marxism as "the opium of the intellectuals."[8]

In their schematic visions of the world after World War II, and in their bitter opposition to each other, Gaullists and Marxists symbolized the capacity for intellectual polarization among the French and their apparent relish for endlessly reproducing the older divisions created by the Revolution. When de Gaulle visited the École Normale in February 1959, less than a year after returning to power, Althusser's communist students refused to greet him, claiming that they could not bring themselves to "shake the hand of a dictator." Yet the styles of thought of the two camps had more in common than they believed—or cared to acknowledge. As the bearers of exclusive truths, and faithful inheritors of the Cartesian tradition, Gaullists and Marxists offered their respective constituencies that most prized and most elusive of intellectual commodities: certainty. Such was their belief in their singularity that they even claimed to have devised a formally original type of organization (the communists asserted that, because of the scientific nature of their Marxist doctrine, theirs was a party "not like the others"; the Gaullists maintained that their movement was "above parties"). Both regarded their respective causes as a form of religiosity. (Marxist doctrine was treated as a catechism by communists, and André Malraux likened de Gaulle to the leader of a religious order, because everything he accomplished was based on an act of faith in France.) Both shared a contempt for capitalism and Anglo-American mercantilism: de Gaulle asserted that his principal adversary throughout his political career had been "money," and a large part of the Gaullist mystique in the developing world stemmed from his iconic speech in Phnom Penh in 1966, when he denounced the American war in Vietnam.[9]

Both provided a narrative of hope that was rooted in historical visions while entertaining a complex and often duplicitous relationship with the past. Gaullists and communists exaggerated their respective roles—notably, in the history of the Resistance—while downplaying historical episodes that did not fit into their heroic narratives. The communists were particularly masterly here, denying events that had occurred, and fabricating episodes in their own past that never took place (such as a proclamation inviting the French people to resist the German occupation, which the party spuriously claimed to have issued in July 1940). But de Gaulle was impressive, too; he rewrote—or, to be more precise, doctored—some of the historical documents about the Free French that he included in the appendix of his *War Memoirs*.[10]

Above all—and this was a direct consequence of the experiences of the period between 1940 and 1944—both viewed collective sovereignty and liberation from subjugation as central to the ideals of Frenchness. For de Gaulle, everything was ultimately explained and justified in terms of the need to preserve the integrity of *la France*—a gloriously idealized community, carefully distinguished in his mind from the irritatingly anarchic *français*. Likewise, for the different strands of the French Marxist family, the touchstone of any political action or thought was the extent to which it served the interests of a "transcendent" proletariat. The French passion for grand theorizing and for engaging in metaphysical and holistic argument was alive and well, as we shall see in the second half of this book.[11]

CHAPTER 7

Freedom and Domination

The major cultural landmark of the year 1955 was the publication of the anthropologist Claude Lévi-Strauss's *Tristes Tropiques* (Sad tropics), a memoir detailing his ethnological experiences among the Amerindian tribes of Brazil between 1935 and 1939. So exquisite were the book's poetic and literary qualities that the Goncourt Academy issued a communiqué regretting that, because it was not a work of fiction, it could not be awarded the academy's prestigious annual prize. An article in the women's magazine *Elle* described the author as "the most intelligent man in France"—a tribute to Lévi-Strauss's formidable eclecticism, reflected in his creative borrowings from linguistic theory, Freudian psychoanalysis, the field of geology, Enlightenment thought, Marxism, and music (an operatic version of the book was performed in Strasburg in September 1996).[1]

Yet few could have anticipated such acclaim for a work written in four months, whose primary subject matter was as remote as could be imagined from the preoccupations of French public life at the time. Moreover, its author was almost completely unknown and, indeed, something of an outsider: because of his Jewish origins, the Vichy regime had deprived him of his teaching post, forcing him into exile during World War II. After the resumption of his academic career in his native country, he failed to secure election to the Collège de France in both 1949 and 1950. And, even later, when Lévi-Strauss became famous, his name's homonymy with the famous brand of American garments provoked confusion: throughout his life he received letters asking for supplies of blue jeans.[2]

Although *Tristes Tropiques* was fiercely critical of the modern desire for exoticism, it also traded on it; it even won a prize in 1956 for best travel book. It captured the public imagination with its contrast between the Western world's grinding, monolithic drive toward uniformity and the fleeting glimpse of the natural freedom enjoyed by the Amerindian communities, which preserved "an era where the human species was comfortable in its universe." This theme of loss was all the more resonant in the mid-1950s because France was still deeply scarred by the memories of war, divided by economic and ideological conflict, and in the midst of an ever-deepening crisis of the Algerian War. But *Tristes Tropiques* conjured an unexpected antidote to this disenchanted mood. Out of its heterogeneous subject matter of facial paintings, graphic art, religious rituals, and kinship arrangements, it offered a miraculous vision of the fundamental universality of human thinking. Lévi-Strauss's account was based on the simple idea that all social thought was underpinned by certain shared symbolic patterns, or myths. The inventory of this hidden, unconscious order was the cornerstone of the "structuralist" approach that Lévi-Strauss systematized in his subsequent works, which helped revolutionize the French intellectual landscape. This was French thinking at its boldest and most innovative, drawing on external experiences and outside ideas to challenge entrenched patterns of thought. *Tristes Tropiques* traded discrete Cartesian analysis for a holistic conception of knowledge, the rationalist search for certainty for an open-ended conception of meaning, the positivist yearning for clarity and stability for the inversions and dissonances of myths, and the comforting dogma of science for a sense of wonder at the mysteries of the universe.[3]

Lévi-Strauss's perspective seemed to be dominated by an abiding sense of pessimism about modernity—in the words of a later commentator, his was "a world without destiny, without ultimate aim, a world of remnants." There is an inescapable poignancy about *Tristes Tropiques*, from its condemnation of the destruction of indigenous communities by European colonialism to its melancholic observations about the overexploitation of the world's natural resources, the oppressiveness of Islam, and the caste system in India—to say nothing of the incontrovertible finality of the book's last sentence: "The world started without man and will end without him." Yet to dwell on these negative aspects alone would be to misunderstand the arc of Lévi-Strauss's philosophical narrative. His purpose was not to turn away from the concept of progress, but to specify its singular character within each culture while providing an account of the common bonds uniting humanity—bonds that went beyond Marx's universalist ideal of the proletariat.[4]

This was where Rousseau's inspiration was critical. Saluting Rousseau as "our master and our brother," and as "the most ethnographic of philosophers," Lévi-Strauss conceived *Tristes Tropiques* as a resolute affirmation of Rousseau's sensibility and philosophical anthropology. He thus found confirmation of Rousseau's conception of natural man in the embraces of the Nambikwara tribe: "One feels among them an immense kindness, a profound cheerfulness, a naïve and charming sense of animal satisfaction, and, uniting these different sentiments, something like the most touching and truthful expression of human tenderness." The relationship of solidarity between the members of the tribe and their chief that Lévi-Strauss observed vindicated Rousseau's contention that human sociability was founded on contractual exchange and consent rather than patriarchy. The underlying purpose of Lévi-Strauss's ethnographic structuralism was in complete alignment with Rousseau's social philosophy: to recover the genuine ideal of "fraternity" by separating what was artificial from what was natural in human society. And to underscore the point, Lévi-Strauss affirmed that there was still time to turn things around: "Nothing is settled, we can start afresh."[5]

The work's dramatic impact rested on its capacity to unsettle the dominant intellectual representations of Western thought since the Enlightenment: the belief in the superiority of European civilization and acceptance of the nation-state as the ultimate form of government; the progressive faith in the pursuit of mastery over nature; the Marxist idea that history was teleologically driven by material forces; and the existentialist postulate that human liberation could be realized through the autonomous choices of rational, self-conscious individuals—a "metaphysics for shop girls," as Lévi-Strauss observed derisively. In all of these respects, *Tristes Tropiques* paved the way for new patterns of French thinking in the postwar decades that stressed that human emancipation was much more fraught (and much less assured) than had been implied by conventional rationalist doctrines, and that its true accomplishment could come about only through the neutralization of deep-seated forms of intellectual, political, and cultural domination.[6]

Liberation from Colonial Rule

In 1961, six years after the publication of *Tristes Tropiques*, its call for an intellectual revolution was repeated in even more arresting terms in Frantz Fanon's anticolonial work *The Wretched of the Earth*: "For Europe, for ourselves, and for humanity, comrades, we must make a radical break, develop a new way of thinking, try to construct a new man." Lévi-Strauss was one of Fanon's intellectual inspirations, all the more so in that *Tristes Tropiques* denounced the sordid arbitrariness of the colonial order in Fanon's native island of Martinique, through which the French philosopher had traveled during his escape from Vichy in 1941. But while Lévi-Strauss's search for a new universalism took him back to Rousseau, Fanon's indictment of colonialism ended in a seemingly comprehensive rejection of "the European model," the "negation of humanity."[7]

Published at the height of the Algerian war of independence against France, in which Fanon had taken an active role, and at a moment when the struggle against Western domination was intensifying, Fanon's words resonated across the Third World; his book was translated into more than a dozen languages. The appeal of Fanon's universalism rested on its radicalization of the aesthetic sensibility of *négritude* developed by Francophone writers such as Léopold Sédar Senghor and Aimé Césaire: hence his burning sense of mission and his belief that emancipation from colonial domination could be accomplished only through a general, collective struggle by the oppressed. *The Wretched of the Earth* directly influenced the political strategies of anticolonial and national liberation movements in Africa and the Middle East in the 1960s, from South Africa to Palestine. Fanon's emancipatory concepts also shaped the thinking of progressives in the Americas, from the political philosophy of Che Guevara to the black liberation movement in the United States; Eldridge Cleaver observed that his fellow African American activists referred to *The Wretched of the Earth* as "the Bible."[8]

Fanon had been trained as a psychiatrist in France in the early 1950s and went on to practice in Algeria, directly witnessing the psychological alienation produced by colonialism and the atrocities of war; he discussed a number of clinical cases reflecting these issues in *The Wretched of the Earth*. But just as determinant a factor in his rejection of European humanism was his earlier experience as a combatant during World War II. Enlisting into the Free French forces because of his disgust with the racist behavior of the Vichy military in Martinique and his ideological opposition to Nazism, Fanon rapidly became disillusioned as he encountered the painful reality of racial prejudice against soldiers from the colonies during the campaign for the liberation of France in 1944 and 1945. Even though he received the Croix de Guerre, he came out of the war convinced of the hollowness of the French claim that their struggle against German occupation was based on universal values of liberty and equality.[9]

This gap between principle and reality took on an even more extreme form in the colonial setting. *The Wretched of the Earth* highlighted the polarized nature of this universe, which was based not only on physical separation, coercion, and exploitation but also on the representation of the colonized individual as a dehumanized being, "the quintessence of evil." Expanding on the insights developed in his earlier work on the psychology of racial domination, Fanon showed that the ultimate force of the colonial system lay in its creation of a dominant culture constructed around the ideals and values of the settler.

The colonizer and colonized were thus locked in a mutually destructive relationship; indigenous populations were condemned to passivity and self-hatred while at the same time being driven to aspire to the impossible dream of substituting themselves for their masters.[10]

Jean-Paul Sartre made a major contribution to the international resonance of *The Wretched of the Earth* by writing the preface to the original French edition. The two men met in Rome in 1961, and Sartre was swept away by Fanon's passion, his sense of urgency, and his belief in the possibility of forging a new form of human fraternity through collective struggle. Fanon's global horizon also offered a way out for Sartre's philosophy of existentialism, which had reached an impasse in France. Yet while Sartre's preface captured the revolutionary quality of Fanon's thought, his treatment of the question of violence somewhat denatured it—notably, when he wrote: "To shoot a European is to kill two birds with one stone, eliminating an oppressor and an oppressed; what remains is a dead man and a free man."[11]

Violence did indeed play a formative role in Fanon's ethic of liberation, but in a collective, organized form that was directed toward specific political ends—not the personal, purifying act that Sartre seemed to be celebrating. This distortion no doubt reflected the Sartrian predilection for reductive formulas. But it was also symptomatic of the paradoxical fate of Fanon's ideas as they traveled across time and space after his death in 1961. Fanon's life and thought stood, above all, for internationalism and the universalistic belief that all human beings were equal and entitled to the same social and political rights. He vigorously opposed a folkloric and essentialized conception of black culture, was wary of the appropriation of nationalism by bourgeois elites, and was especially contemptuous of communitarianism and all forms of political tribalism. It was therefore ironic that he later became something of an icon among the postcolonial advocates of "identity politics."

Fanon's universalism was also spurned by the elites of the newly independent Algeria, notably after the regime's symbolic embrace of Islam in 1965; in subsequent decades, his role in the liberation struggle was minimized. Too "French" for the Algerians, Fanon was also seen as too Algerian by the French—the accursed symbol of a "war without name" that they did their best to forget, and a colonial project whose practices blatantly contradicted the lofty ideals of French republicanism. Yet this was perhaps the most peculiar twist in what became Fanon's intellectual posterity: for his embrace of French culture ran much deeper, and lasted much longer, than is conventionally believed.[12]

Even toward the end of his life, when he identified completely with the cause of Algerian self-determination, his thinking remained rooted in the postwar traditions of French philosophical radicalism. The work that most shaped the vision of *The Wretched of the Earth* was Sartre's *Critique of Dialectical Reason*, with its powerfully bleak vision of the alienating effects of capitalism. In its passion, its hatred of tyranny, and its belief in the universality of freedom and the redemptive virtues of collective action, Fanon's thought was classically republican. In his substantive views as much as in his style, he was a throwback to Louis-Sébastien Mercier's "avenger of the new world" (who was discussed in Chapter 3), and to the first generation of French Jacobin revolutionaries. In this sense, he, too, like Lévi-Strauss, found his way back to Jean-Jacques Rousseau—so much so that the *New York Review of Books* hailed him as "the Black Rousseau."[13]

The Structures Speak

In July 1967, a cartoon in the literary review *La Quinzaine littéraire* (Literary bimonthly) depicted four men conversing intensely in a tropical setting, dressed in grass skirts and anklets. Represented in this *déjeuner structuraliste* were Claude Lévi-Strauss, who had by now become very distinguished, particularly with the publication of his *Anthropologie structurale* (*Structural Anthropology*) and his election to the Collège de France; the philosopher Michel Foucault, whose work on the history of madness and the transformation of modern scientific discourse had caused a sensation; the psychoanalyst Jacques Lacan, who had revived interest in Freudian thought and investigated the disruptive impulses of the subconscious; and the literary theorist Roland Barthes, whose writings explored the symbolic power of language and mass culture. Structuralism was at the apogee of its influence and intellectual prestige in France in the mid-1960s. One devotee later humorously compared his embrace of this mode of thought to a disease: "I could not shake off the fever but I wallowed in this plague, and refrained from seeking any cure for it." Such was the vogue for all things structural that the term was equated with the highest form of intelligence and credited with miraculous properties: the French national soccer coach announced that he would carry out a "structural reorganization" to improve the team's performance.[14]

In some respects, the generic use of this label was misleading. Structuralism was not a movement offering an overarching theory of political action, like Sartre's existentialism or Fanon's revolutionary anticolonialism, and only Lévi-Strauss used the term more or less systematically. The liberation it offered was not from material deprivation but from cultural domination, moral complacency, and intellectual confusion—although there was no shortage of verbiage in structuralist writing itself, as we shall see. Its relative cohesion lay primarily in certain assumptions it made about human understanding. These assumptions, which were shared by a diverse group of thinkers, included a belief in the pivotal nature of language and symbols; an affirmation of the contingency of history and its nonlinear character; and a contestation of the fixed nature of meaning—as Barthes put it, there was "no immutable character to mythical concepts: they can be constructed, change, be altered, disappear completely." This sense of the fluidity, the changeability, of things nourished the structuralist intuition that the truly significant forms of knowledge lay in the interstices, at the margins or beneath the surface: in an interview in 1975, Foucault likened himself to a scavenger of the deep seas. Structuralism was thus perfectly positioned to offer new illustrations of the French intellectual's love of the paradox, as when Lacan asserted the primacy of the unconscious by neatly standing the Cartesian formula on its head: "I think where I am not, therefore I am where I do not think."[15]

Structuralist thinkers repeatedly questioned the philosophical concept of the autonomous self, the cornerstone of Cartesian and Enlightenment rationalism. The strongest challenge to this schema came from the work of Foucault, undoubtedly the most prolific, creative, and influential French thinker of the later twentieth century. Ranging freely across the disciplines of philosophy, history, sociology, and literary theory, his writings opened up new and often fruitful avenues of research in these areas. Foucault's *oeuvre* explored the ways in which modern societies subjected their citizens to various forms of intellectual and physical control, ranging from state power and dominant modes of thought to medical and sexual practices. His writings defied simple categorization, partly because he saw his works as pioneering rather than conclusive (he described himself as "an experimenter, not a theorist"), and partly because he took a coquettish pride in his own intellectual plasticity. (He once wrote, "Do not ask who I am and do not ask me to remain the same.") His work was challenging and at times cluttered with jargon, and some of his central concepts (such as "discourse" and "governmentality") remained frustratingly imprecise. But these limitations were compensated for by his prodigious, encyclopedic learning—and by a certain nonchalance, as when he described his historical works as "fictions" (a view endorsed by many of his critics, who took him to task for his cavalier treatment of historical sources; as Lévi-Strauss put it, delicately, Foucault "took some liberties with chronology").[16]

One of Foucault's consistent aims as a historian was to uncover the darker sides of the Western conception of human rationality. In *Madness and Civilization*, he showed how mental illness came to be seen from the seventeenth century onward as an aberration of thought. This was notably the case for Descartes, for whom madness and reason were antithetical notions. Insanity was also perceived as a form of social deviance, as reflected in the increasingly repressive treatment of the mad by means of moral censure, the medicalization of their condition, and their physical confinement in asylums. Foucault believed this imperative of social control to be at the heart of the Enlightenment's ideal of "reason": it was thus less concerned with liberating and empowering the mind than with imposing a bourgeois order of "pure morality and ethical uniformity."[17]

It was no coincidence that Foucault's work on madness was published at the height of the Algerian War—and, indeed, a few months before Fanon's book. In very different ways, they both highlighted the extent to which the emancipatory ideals of Western societies were not only contradicted by their practices but, in a deeper sense, corrupted from within. Foucault took this paradoxical thought to its logical extreme. One of his central ideas was that domination was in some respect inherent in all ideologies and modes of thought—even those claiming to be "progressive." Naturally, such a view had serious implications for the ways in which the possibility of an alternative (and better) world could be discussed and imagined. Foucault addressed this issue through the development of a new "archaeological" framework in which he systematically confronted conventional conceptions of intellectual history. He particularly questioned what he claimed were its assumptions of universal truth, continuity, and progress and the "coercive illusion" of its underlying notion of a "knowing subject."[18]

Political change was therefore possible, but only if its goals were framed modestly and adjusted in keeping with an understanding of historical circumstances and the limits of possibility. (Foucault, who was particularly fond of metaphors, likened this posture to "being at the frontiers.") Utopian projects that had sought to refashion human nature in the name of "global or radical" ideals had to be discarded: "In fact, we know from experience that the claim to escape from the system of contemporary reality so as to produce the overall programmes of another society, of another way of thinking, another culture, another vision of the world, has only led to the return of the most dangerous traditions."[19] For this reason, Foucault was especially wary of offering strategic directions and grand visions of the future:

> My position is that it is not up to us [intellectuals] to propose. As soon as one "proposes"—one proposes a vocabulary, an ideology, which can only have effects of domination. What we have to present are instruments and tools that people might find useful. But if the intellectual starts playing once again the role that he has played for a hundred and fifty years—that of prophet in relation to "what must be," to "what

must take place"—these effects of domination will return, and we shall have other ideologies, functioning in the same way.[20]

The fact that Foucault was nonetheless proposing a vocabulary of his own—and, indeed, something approaching an intellectual system—obviously begged the question of the status of his own thought. His refusal to challenge the existing order directly also made him vulnerable to the accusation of tacitly condoning it. But his aversion to intellectual leadership resonated with one of the leitmotifs of French structuralist writers: the rejection of the very idea of a literary canon. Lévi-Strauss asserted that myths "have no author," a claim echoed in Barthes's seminal essay "The Death of the Author," which argued that writing constituted a "multidimensional space" that could not be "deciphered," only "disentangled." This point was given a historical illustration in Foucault's claim that modern man was a creation of nineteenth-century biologists, political economists, and philologists: as he put it, in his characteristically provocative way, it was "an invention of recent date, and one perhaps nearing its end." He ended *The Order of Things* with the striking image of man's erasure, "like a face drawn in sand at the edge of the sea."[21]

There were also biographical dimensions to the structuralists' reluctance to intervene publicly in the grand ideological controversies of their time. Structuralism's principal thinkers were typically outsiders who did not readily fit within traditional disciplinary and institutional boundaries, and they were often scarred by personal traumas (Foucault's attempted suicide being the most extreme example). This retreat from the public sphere was not unproblematic, most notably during the events of May 1968, which were widely seen as a challenge to the structuralists' skepticism about political action. The proposition that "structures do not take to the streets" became a popular slogan among the student protesters, and a play by Roger Crémant cruelly satirized the main structuralist thinkers, lamenting their aloofness and verbosity, the conservatism lurking behind their professions of radicalism, and their "interpretative delirium."[22]

The latter remark was aimed at the philosopher Jacques Derrida, the *enfant terrible* of French structuralism. He took its concerns about the centrality of language, the dissolution of the thinking self, and the hidden aspects of rationality to their most systematic (and extreme) conclusions, ultimately challenging the very concept of philosophical certainty. His output during a career spanning more than four decades was colossal, with over forty books and hundreds of essays published. He was a polarizing figure, admired to the point of adulation by his fans but denounced as a charlatan by his adversaries, who accused him (among other things) of lacking substance and being paralyzingly

obsessed with questions of method. His philosophical colleagues often cen-
sured him for his obsession with the Western literary tradition (among his
favorite authors were James Joyce, Samuel Beckett, Stéphane Mallarmé, and
Paul Celan) and his frivolity (he was especially fond of puns, free associations,
and rhymes). His utterances were distinctive for their florid, reflexive, and di-
gressive nature and their resistance to any form of closure or finality; this style
partly came from his tormented personality. (I remember attending a lecture
he gave at the Sheldonian Theatre in Oxford in 1992, when he stressed the
virtue of being in a state of constant "anxiety" about the world.) His writing combined an emphatic style—he had a manic habit of putting words
in italics and quotation marks—with an unerring capacity for mystification:
thus *Postcards from Socrates* opened with love letters addressed to no particular
person. Indeed, Derrida's singular mode of expression was a key part of what
made him the most controversial French thinker of his generation. He once
explained that unsettling his audience was a deliberate strategy: "What I try
to do through the neutralization of communication, theses and stability of
content, through a microstructure of signification, is to provoke, not only in
the reader but also in oneself, a new tremor or a new shock of the body that
opens a new space of experience."[23]

Disruptions and displacements were in no short supply in Derrida's own
life. From his early days in French Algeria, where he was expelled from school
in 1942 because of his Jewish origins, then as a *pied-noir* in France and as
a skeptic of the Stalinist culture of French communism during the 1950s,
Derrida always remained something of an outsider. Although his intellectual
formation at the École Normale was fairly orthodox, the magic circle always
eluded him: unlike Lévi-Strauss, Barthes, Foucault, and Lacan, who all eventually obtained prestigious institutional affiliations in Paris, Derrida was regarded with suspicion by the French philosophical establishment and denied
the ultimate accolade of an election to the Collège de France. How far this
sense of marginality shaped his philosophical concern with the problem of
"absence," as has been claimed by his main biographer, is open to debate.[24]

Derrida believed that the meaning of a concept could only be properly elu-
cidated through its relationship with other, related concepts and the ways in
which they were deployed in different contexts. This notion of *différance* [sic]
lay at the heart of the new method of textual interpretation he championed,
which came to be known as "deconstruction." For Derrida, the writings of
all the major Western philosophers were structured around binary oppositions (inside and outside, man and woman, reason and madness, freedom and
domination), one element of which was generally suppressed. These polarities
gave texts a semblance of meaning, yet, once identified, they undermined it

and ultimately destroyed its very possibility. As a Derrida scholar explained, "The guiding insight of deconstruction is that every structure—be it literary, psychological, social, economic, political or religious—that organizes our experience is constituted and maintained through acts of exclusion."[25]

Derrida applied his method not only to the writings of Plato, Rousseau, and Hegel but also to his fellow structuralists, arguing that even their works were trapped in the "logocentric" assumptions from which they sought to escape. He thus took Foucault to task for not completely abandoning the Cartesian notion of the thinking subject, and Lévi-Strauss for his appeal to Rousseau, which seemingly contradicted his opposition to ethnocentrism. He also suggested that Lacan's work was undermined by its unquestioned attachment to a scientific epistemology. Aware that his *oeuvre* was largely perceived as lacking an affirmative, positive dimension, his later works engaged more directly with moral and political questions, broaching such issues as death, violence, friendship, cosmopolitanism, and justice. However, as with Foucault, it was hard to see how any substantive views he might offer on these matters could be reconciled with his rejection of value certainty—to say nothing of his radical skepticism about the possibility of meaning. He characteristically avoided confronting these problems directly, taking refuge in counterintuitive moves and elliptical propositions.[26]

For example, his discussion of friendship argued that modern democracies were inherently flawed because they were grounded in ideals of community that were, by their very nature, dominating. The homogenizing ideal of "fraternity" could be realized only through the creation of oppressive hierarchies (between brothers and sisters, citizens and foreigners, and, ultimately, friends and enemies). This was a classic piece of deconstructionism, and it manifestly contained an element of truth. But could democracy ever move beyond these polarizing divisions and provide a meaningful horizon for the liberation of humankind? Even allowing for the difficulties of translation, Derrida's answer was gloriously perplexing: "For democracy remains to come; this is its essence in so far as it remains: not only will it remain indefinitely perfectible, hence always insufficient and future, but belonging to the time of the promise, it will always remain, in each of its future times, to come: even when there is democracy, it never exists, it is never present, it remains the theme of a non-presentable concept."[27]

Likewise, Derrida chose an eccentric moment to return to Marx—in the wake of the collapse of communism in Europe in the early 1990s, precisely at the time when he was being unceremoniously jettisoned by progressives across the Western world. Derrida's "spectral" reading of Marx was in part a critical deconstruction of his philosophy, which concluded (predictably) that his writings could not entirely escape from the metaphysical ghosts of German idealism. At the same time, Derrida asserted that Marx's "emancipatory promise" of a better world continued to haunt the modern era and still offered a moral impetus for those seeking an alternative to capitalism and neoliberalism: "I believe in Revolution, that is to say in an interruption, in a radical break in the ordinary course of History. There is indeed no ethical responsibility, no decision which is worthy of its name which is not, in its essence, revolutionary, which is not in rupture with the system of dominant norms, or even with the very idea of normativity itself."[28]

But the intellectual basis for this ethical imperative was unclear, to say the least. Characterizing Marx's legacy as a "hauntology" (a typical wordplay on the term "ontology"), Derrida thus noted, "After the end of history, the spirit comes by *coming back*, it figures *both* a dead man who comes back and a ghost whose expected return repeats itself, again and again." This conclusion was an appropriate metaphor for deconstruction itself. It had little to say about how emancipatory ideas could be constructively channeled, and seemed able to offer nothing except a promise to change the world through interpretation—which was itself doomed, because no stable meaning could be elicited from any body of writing. At the dizzying heights of deconstructionism, Derrida had famously declared that there was "nothing outside the text." By the end, in France at least, it was far from clear whether anything was left inside it.[29]

Letters from America

A possibility of salvation for the structuralist project opened up from without. From the late 1960s there was an increasing dissemination of the works of contemporary French thinkers outside their native land. Just as their influence was peaking in France, Foucault's writings about power, knowledge, and sexuality, and Derrida's work on deconstruction, found new international audiences.

"French theory" transformed the internal configuration in a range of disciplines in the humanities and social sciences across the Western world, from philosophy to film studies, and helped to generate new fields, such as postcolonialism and ethnic and gender studies. With the proliferation of terms such as "episteme," "discourse," "archaeology," "absence," and "(phal)logocentricism," and the support of a fresh wave of theorists—notably, Julia Kristeva, Jean Baudrillard, and Gilles Deleuze—the disembodied ghost of Western reason was subjected to a further round of battering. By the turn of the century, concern with disordered taxonomies, collapsed hierarchies, enunciative modalities, and privatized truths had become so pervasive in the American intellectual sphere that they were lampooned in Andrew Boyd's *Life's Little Deconstruction Book*, which summed up the new age of the fractured self with such delicious maxims as "Scrutinize power," "Lose the centre," and "Fashion reason, and reason about fashion."[30]

For reasons that will become clear, it was in the United States that this diffusion of French theorizing had its most sustained impact. The most important single characteristic in this transplantation of French philosophy across to the New World was its literary reappropriation: more than half of the articles devoted to Barthes, Lacan, and Foucault in the United States during the 1980s were in the field of literature. Derrida's work had an even more catalytic effect, contributing to the transformation of many university literature departments (notably, at Yale) into bastions of deconstructionism. This structuralist momentum was fueled by the zeal of Derrida's American supporters, by the philosopher's frequent lecturing tours in the United States, and by his appointment in 1986 to a professorship in the Humanities at the University of California, Irvine.[31]

Derrida added to the mystique with suitably cryptic interventions, as when he claimed in 1985 that deconstruction was synonymous with America—before withdrawing the assertion. A taste of this mystification can be savored in the following rendering of this seminal episode by a Derridian devotee a decade later: "The image discarded—America as a geopolitical enterprise—does not qualify the 'toponomy' of *America* for deconstruction, that is America as deconstruction's hypothetical 'residence' at a specific moment, a moment whose historicality might be most appropriately captured by calling it *in* deconstruction. Deconstruction may be America to the extent that America *is in* deconstruction."[32]

This migration of French ideas was made possible by the increasing frequency with which structuralist philosophers were invited across the Atlantic from the mid-1960s on as well as by a propitious institutional and editorial context in the United States. As their works were translated into English, these thinkers helped to provide younger academics with the conceptual instruments needed to unsettle the conservative traditions dominating the humanities and social sciences in American universities. The literary theorist Edward Said thus described the inspiring effects of the works of Barthes, Lacan, Foucault, and Derrida on his generation, which he attributed not only to the novelty and radicalism of their ideas, but also to their playfulness and irreverence.[33]

Said's later work bore witness to this rich and multilayered influence—notably, in *Orientalism* (1978), in which he acknowledged his debt to Foucault: "My contention is that without examining Orientalism as a discourse one cannot possibly understand the enormously systematic discipline by which European culture was able to manage—and even produce—the Orient politically, sociologically, militarily, ideologically, scientifically and imaginatively during the post-Enlightenment period." *Orientalism* has been described as one of the "major mediators of Foucault's thought into the American academy." Another example in the same vein was Foucault's conception of sexuality as an instrument of social control of the body, which had a decisive impact on the works of American feminists such as Judith Butler and Joan Scott—although other feminist writers warned against "the charming and dangerous seduction of French theory."[34]

The main reason for the appeal of French theory was that it became enmeshed in America's "culture wars" between progressives and traditionalists during the 1980s. Across the humanities (with the exception of philosophy), Foucault and Derrida were perceived as natural allies in the emerging battlegrounds of identity politics, particularly among thinkers who both celebrated difference and "implicitly understood how cultural phenomena and institutions contrived to suppress the voices of minorities, women and gays." This was a somewhat generous view of their work. Foucault paid relatively little attention to female subjugation in *The History of Sexuality*; if one of his biographers is to be believed, the question of domination mattered to him principally in his own practice of sadomasochistic sex.[35]

Indeed, the transplanting of French theory to the other side of the Atlantic offered much potential for intellectual distortions and cultural misunderstandings. The philosophical context in which structuralism emerged in France—notably, its challenge to Marxism and existentialism—was largely ignored, all the more readily as neither of these two doctrines enjoyed much appeal in the United States. Most importantly, a tradition of writing that was tentative and predominantly critical of existing hierarchies of knowledge was systematized, and thus turned into the very object whose limits it sought to confront. Lamenting the uncritical adoption of French theory by "foggy humanists" who lacked the historical sophistication to criticize the works they were reading, the American feminist Camille Paglia concluded that Lacan, Derrida, and Foucault were "the perfect prophets for the weak, anxious academic personality, trapped in verbal formulas and perennially defeated by circumstance." She added, cruelly, "They offer a self-exculpating cosmic explanation for the normal professorial state of resentment, alienation, dithery passivity and inaction."[36]

The success of French theory in the Anglo-American world was thus accompanied by multiple paradoxes. According to a survey of citations from academic journals around the world published in 2009, Foucault was the most-quoted author in the humanities (Derrida was third). Yet the decontextualization of the original French works and the cult status accorded their leading authors flew in the face of the epistemological premises of their thought. It also contributed to a growing bifurcation in interpretations and approaches on either side of the Atlantic. There was a particularly notable gap between the historicism and methodological skepticism of the French thinkers and the way their work was represented and used by their American counterparts, who portrayed them as bearers of certainties: the political scientist Wendy Brown understood Foucault as a critic of the "political rationality" of Western neoliberalism, and Gayatri Chakravorty Spivak enlisted Derridian deconstruction in the battle to form a coalition of oppressed groups. Yet American-style "identity politics" rested on a notion of the continuity of the subject whose coherence and, indeed, very possibility Derrida emphatically denied.[37]

At the same time, the combination of French and American theorizing generated a body of literature whose overriding characteristic was its obscurity: in the words of one critic, this opaqueness was an attempt to cover the theories' analytical limitations by "creating a feeling that something extraordinary and unusual was going on." The ultimate hollowness of this production was exposed in 1996, when Alan Sokal, a physics professor at New York University, submitted a spoof article on the philosophical implications of quantum gravity to the journal *Social Text*, accompanied by real citations from the works of French and American writers. Unaware of the subterfuge, the journal published the article. The ensuing controversy laid bare the scientistic pretensions of postmodern writings and highlighted the moral and political dangers of a mode of philosophizing that rejected truth in favor of relativism. By this time, structuralism had fallen out of favor in France—so much so that when Woody Allen's film *Deconstructing Harry* (1997) was screened in France, the title had to be rendered as *Harry dans tous ses états* (Harry in all his states): like the character played by Robin Williams in the movie, who appears out of focus on the screen, the Derridian concept had become a blur.[38]

Jean Monnet Channels Barthes and Foucault

The French emancipatory project was thus in difficulty as the second half of the twentieth century advanced. Its *tiers-mondiste* revolutionary variant, symbolized by Fanon's generous and egalitarian vision, came to grief as newly independent states of the Third World continued to be racked by poverty, debt, and economic destabilization. Despite its international success, the structuralist enterprise fared no better. Its ambition to uncover a new archaeology of human understanding was distorted by its transplantation to the New World, and then engulfed by the black hole of Derridian postmodernism.

But the French Promethean spirit still had one more visionary ideal up its sleeve, albeit one more tentatively framed and geographically circum-scribed: the creation of a European confederation. After a long hiatus, feder-alist schemes for a "United States of Europe" swung back into fashion in the 1940s, both in France and throughout Europe. The figure who became its most forceful champion was Jean Monnet, a French diplomat and grandee. Monnet believed that the nation-state was an unproductive and parochial in-stitution that was potentially menacing to human freedom and world peace, and he devoted his career to building a European confederation that would release its citizens from these shackles. His appreciation of the virtues of po-litical cooperation had been crystallized in the early moments of World War II: in June 1940, as Nazi troops overran French defenses, he devised a plan for the fusion of Britain and France. The proposal was approved by the British cabinet and by de Gaulle, but the French capitulation to Germany prevented its implementation. Monnet later opened his memoirs with this dramatic in-cident, from which he inferred that national sovereignty, the cornerstone of the modern state system, was "an obstacle" to the realization of human free-dom. In 1943 he floated the idea that states should form a "European entity" that would make them "a single unit," and he doggedly pursued this objective from the early 1950s onward. Monnet was the architect of the European Coal and Steel Community and served as the first president of its High Authority from 1952 to 1955. By the time of his death in 1979, he was widely hailed as one of the principal founders of Europe, and it was in this spirit that his remains were transferred to the Panthéon in 1988.[39]

Monnet saw Europe as a "laboratory for the new type of man." His ideal of freedom was that of a well-heeled cosmopolitan who regarded national af-filiations as outdated and somewhat irritating burdens on his international lifestyle. He was a genuine European, but also a committed Atlanticist, at times seeming more comfortable in London and Washington than in Paris. In the early years of World War II, he worked for Churchill, and then Roo-sevelt, even doing his best to fuel American resentments against de Gaulle; in 1943, he presented the latter as "an enemy of the French people" who had to be "destroyed." His style was the very opposite of that of the French *grand intellectuel*. He had little interest in high culture (he left school at the age of sixteen) and was instinctively distrustful of abstract systems of thought. He always claimed to approach problems empirically, in an "Anglo-Saxon" man-ner. (As he put it, "I am wary of general ideas and never let them carry me far away from reality.")[40]

Monnet's approach was deliberately unheroic: his prose was flat and work-manlike, and he had a manifest preference for operating behind the scenes, "in the shadows." In his speech at the Panthéon ceremony in 1988, President Mitterrand described Monnet as "a man of silence for whom every word is a deed." Monnet's ideas were something of a bricolage, in his case a singular combination of functionalist beliefs about the virtues of integration, liberal and Saint-Simonian economic intuitions about interdependence, technocratic ideals of pragmatism and efficiency, and sound Charentais common sense: his father was a brandy merchant in Cognac, and Jean himself had begun his career as a representative of the family business. He consistently portrayed himself as an enabler rather than a leader, and a practical statesman rather than a utopian. He put his trust not in those who spoke in "the language of imagination," but in those "whose first rule was not to err": "bankers, indus-trialists, lawyers and journalists."[41]

Yet Monnet's conception of Europe was far-sighted. Its strength lay in its simplicity and its lack of specific detail, which made it adaptable to changing circumstances—and creative reinventions in later decades. Monnet eagerly embraced the classic liberal internationalist belief that greater human freedom and progress could be brought about through cooperation among people of goodwill. Rejecting the conventional wisdom that international relations were an arena of violence and self-interest, he asserted that states could be moralized through participation in institutions that would gradually change their expec-tations and, in the long run, their very nature. He also maintained—taking a very unconventional view in international relations of the twentieth cen-tury—that the general interest was always greater than the national interest of any one state. Hence his conviction that the more states worked together, the more readily they would see the benefits of sharing sovereignty and appreciate the wider advantages of cooperation. Against those philosophical realists who retorted that the will to dominate was entrenched in human nature, or who were tempted by Marxian notions of class conflict, Monnet cited his practical successes as a European functionary—notably, the exemplary collaboration that had been achieved by representatives of workers and producers in the Coal and Steel Community. This proved to him "that significant psycholog-ical transformations, which some seek to achieve through violent revolutions, can be brought about very peacefully if the minds of men are oriented toward the point where their interests converge. This point always exists, it is simply a matter of persevering to find it."[42]

Charles de Gaulle was a consistent critic of Monnet's supranationalist ap-proach; for the general, the only viable Europe was the one that was devised and sustained by governments—all else, as he declared dismissively in 1962, was "myths, fictions and parades." Yet de Gaulle, the arch-illusionist, should have been the first to appreciate that myths could sometimes prove more powerful than reality. Monnet came to occupy a pivotal place in the history of European integration through his elaboration of a coherent idealized narrative. This narrative was disseminated through his own writings, through the writings of his associates, and through the work of the lobbying organization he founded, the Comité d'Action pour les États-Unis d'Europe (Action Committee for the United States of Europe). This vision became the dominant representation of Europe among French elites during the final decades of the twentieth century.[43]

Monnet himself referred to his ideas as possessing "intellectual power," and there was a certain Foucauldian quality to his European "discourse," which legitimized certain patterns of thinking while sidelining others. For example, he associated European institutions with the preservation of peace, while nation-states were seen as bearers of atavistic and potentially dangerous values. He stressed that Europe was a political space where "equality among countries and peoples" was the norm—even though the reality was that some states, most notably France and Germany, were more equal than others. He asserted that European integration was a guarantee of growth and economic prosperity, at the same time likening this ideal of Europe to the accomplishment of a natural teleology and the realization of a self-evident prophecy.[44]

Monnet's patient, covert style—"an approach of small steps," in the words of his disciple Jacques Delors—was transformed into a "communitarian method" for advancing European integration through incremental means. The father of Europe had to be not only a visionary but also a sage, and so a school manual produced in his native Charente credited Monnet with influencing "all the advances in the construction of Europe," thanks in part to the wisdom he had learned from the brandy-makers of Cognac: "The only way to make a good product is through concentration and the absence of haste." Even the criticisms leveled against Monnet indirectly reinforced the myth of his omnipotence. The socialist euroskeptic Jean-Pierre Chevènement credited Monnet's ideas with providing the "founding matrix" for all the major developments in European integration during the second half of the twentieth century, from the creation of the Council of Europe and the establishment of the European Monetary System to the agreement on the single market and the 1992 Maastricht Treaty leading to the creation of the European Union and the European single currency. Writing in the early twenty-first century, at a time when the French public had become much warier of Europe, Chevènement thus brought home the limits of Monnet's vision—notably, its overreliance on technocratic rule and its complete absence of any democratic or republican dimensions. In effect, the freedom promised by Monnet was illusory: what he was offering was foreign domination. De Gaulle summed up this view more concisely when he observed to his aides that Monnet was "America's man"—a claim later repeated by François Duchêne (who had served as Monnet's collaborator), for whom Monnet's main function had been to facilitate the penetration of US political and economic influence in postwar Europe. Hence Duchêne's conclusion that "consciously or not, Monnet was an agent of the American empire"—a point established beyond reasonable doubt when one of his American biographers revealed that Monnet had boxes full of Boston baked beans stored in his cellar.[45]

Dollars, Metal, and Cooked Meats

The contractions of French universalism during the second half of the twentieth century overlapped with (and was partly an effect of) the robust projection of American power in postwar Europe—a collision of messianisms that could not fail to produce some sparks, and much aggravation, on both sides of the Atlantic. At a lecture delivered at Princeton in 1954, Hannah Arendt argued that anti-Americanism was in some sense a necessary catalyst for the emergence of a shared consciousness among Europeans. But the deeper reason for this animosity toward the United States, she suggested, was that friendship required equality, and the disparity of wealth between the American and European states was too great to make equality possible. She thus concluded, "It has always been the misfortune of rich people to be alternatively flattered and abused—and still remain unpopular, no matter how generous they are."[46]

The attitudes of French political elites (notably, de Gaulle) in the postwar decades certainly supported this assertion to a considerable extent, and it was in the post-1945 era that anti-Americanism became a defining criterion of French political and intellectual life. Yet there was much more to French anti-Americanism than a sense of ingratitude toward a selfless benefactor, or a manifestation of what the intellectual Jean-François Revel termed an enduring "French hatred for liberal society." What is striking about the phenomenon is that its central components were forged from the earliest days of the American Republic, and had developed into a coherent whole by the early twentieth century—well before the rise of America as a global power.[47]

With the notable exception of Tocqueville (whose *oeuvre* was largely forgotten in France by the late nineteenth century), French writings consistently represented American society as alienated, violent, and materialist, dominated by eccentric beliefs, and possessing an absolute incapacity for cultural elevation. Charles Maurras could find nothing in America except "a pyramid of dollars, metal and cooked meats." Yet—myths do not have to be coherent—this void was also portrayed as a menace. Launching a campaign against American movies in postwar France, communist leader Maurice Thorez asserted that Hollywood was "an enterprise of disaggregation of the French nation, of moral corruption and perversion of our young men and women, where eroticism competes with bigotry, where the gangster is king; these movies are not meant to prepare a generation of citizens conscious of their duties towards France, but rather a troop of slaves."[48]

This kind of language confirms the intuition that modern French anti-Americanism is essentially a civilizational construct whose underlying force lies in its evocation (through its negation of America) of an idealized France. It stressed remaining resistant to foreign cultural influences and steadfastly attached to France's home-grown values—the "French way of life," which was defined by a sense of sociability, an attachment to local traditions, and a belief in social justice and morality. Not surprisingly, the most vehement manifestations of anti-Americanism were articulated around America's perceived challenges to the French lifestyle, and particularly its cuisine. The conservative antimodernist Georges Duhamel described American food as "leaving an aftertaste of industrial waste," and in the postwar years, the communists led a spirited campaign against the "Coca-colonization" of France. And while it failed to prevent the introduction of the drink to France, this cultural mobilization succeeded in winning over many sympathizers to the cause, including the Catholic newspaper *Témoignage chrétien* (Christian witness), which presented Coke as "the vanguard of a movement of economic colonization."[49]

In the 1990s and early 2000s, similar arguments were deployed in campaigns by French environmental groups against McDonald's restaurants, symbols of economic imperialism and genetically modified foods, according to the peasant trade-union leader José Bové. In 1999, a group of activists led by Bové dismantled a McDonald's franchise under construction in Millau (Aveyron), a gesture that brought international attention to the cause—and widespread comparisons of Bové with Astérix the Gaul. In an uncharacteristically French postmodern refinement, the environmental advocate Paul Ariès saw the fast-food chain as evidence that America itself had become a victim of globalization: "McDo is American because the Americans have in fact ceased to be real Americans." At the end of an exhaustive catalog of America's dysfunctions (drugs, gun and sexual violence, poverty, and the production of hormonally enhanced meat), the authors of *Non merci, Oncle Sam!* (No thank you, Uncle Sam!) concluded that the struggle against the "sterile uniformity" of American power was, above all, about preserving French culture and its "universally recognized art of living."[50]

The message was received loud and clear by a doctor in Grenoble, who, in the summer of 2003, put up a poster in his office warning against the dangers of obesity; its title was "The Anglo-Saxon Diet Is Undermining the Health of Your Children." The populist Jean-Luc Mélenchon found a way of associating McDonald's products with the destruction of the thinking self: the consumption of this "fodder of the *pensée unique*," or intellectual orthodoxy, he affirmed, would lead to "annihilated men without identity." The most creative offering came from the philosopher Yves Roucaute, who used a sustained comparison between the blandness of the fast-food hamburger and the authenticity of the French *sandwich jambon-beurre* to conclude that McDonald's products were "absolutely not French," not only because of their content but also on account of the functional and dehumanized setting in which they were served. This opened the way to a lyrical evocation of the liberating virtues of the French café, a veritable cocoon of republican sociability: "Remarkable school of equality, the French café symbolizes equal dignity. Extraordinary school of liberty, the French café opens its doors to all and allows true choice. Prodigious school of fraternity, by this apparently simple act of buying a sandwich is created a communion around regional products. So with butter, bread and pork, without knowing it, you declaim these three words: 'liberty,' 'equality,' and 'fraternity.'"[51]

The Language of the Poor

With Americanization perceived by its detractors as the primary threat to French civilization, it was only a matter of time before it came to be seen as an existential menace to the French language, too. The proliferation of English words in the language of Molière was denounced by the essayist René Étiemble in a ferocious book, *Parlez-vous franglais?*, which was met with acclaim when first published in 1964. The author, a fervent Gaullist, presented alien verbal imports as an attempt to impose the "American way of life" in France; he invited his compatriots to resist this insidious form of "Yankee colonization."[52]

In the ensuing decades, successive French governments reacted to this clarion call with a veritable flurry of linguistic activism; commissions with grand titles were formed, weighty guidelines issued, and imperious edicts enacted about the mandatory use of the French language in public settings: work, education, research, the media, and advertising. This wave culminated in the Toubon Law of August 1994, which, among other things, included provisions for fining individuals and institutions that failed to abide by this kind of cultural patriotism. (In 2006, General Electric Medical Systems was sentenced to pay 580,000 euro for not translating documents used by its technicians.) But the law was widely flouted by French public institutions, and in any event it proved powerless to stop the invasion of Anglicisms. By the late twentieth century, it was thus estimated that more than 8,000 words of English origin were in regular use in written and conversational French—not only direct transpositions, such as *best-seller, discount,* and (the much-resented) *fast-food,* but also barbarous neologisms, such as the noun *tennisman,* the verbs *booster* and *stopper,* and the adjective *surbooké* (which means "overbooked"). Since 2011 the website of the Académie Française has had a section dedicated to weeding out "neologisms and Anglicisms" from the French language; among the expressions singled out for censure during the first half of 2014 were *conf call, off record, donner son go* (authorize), *chambre single, news, faire du running,* and *replay.*[53]

Arguments for the preservation of the integrity of the French language came in many forms. Derrida weighed in with a characteristically oblique perspective in *Monolinguism of the Other* (1992), where he recognized that his intolerance of any use of English words in the French language was "shameful." He explained his adherence to the ideal of a "pure" language as a "compulsive demand" that came from deep inside him, an imperative "to 'listen' to the domineering murmur of an order which someone in me flatters himself to understand."[54]

Others were less subtle, and the campaign for the defense of the French language produced a new breed of cultural warriors. They were distinctive for the violence of their rhetoric, with the deployment of gruesome metaphors about conflict, occupation, and mutilation, and the characterization of the use of English words as a form of mental dispossession. For the writer Dominique Noguez, there were "only two parties: the colonized and the defenders of universalism"; in his satirical book *Comment rater complètement sa vie en onze leçons* (How to completely screw up your life in eleven lessons), he listed "learning the English language" as one of the main ways of achieving this goal. For Jean Dutourd, a member of the Académie Française, many of whose members played a leading role in the campaign, the French language was "under siege," and what was at stake was nothing less than "the soul of the nation." Dutourd likened those who adopted Anglo-American words to "deserters" who "had passed to the enemy" and were "aspiring to the condition of colonized." (The silent homage to Fanon's psychology of racial alienation was worthy of note, and was echoed by the neo-Gaullist parliamentarian Jacques Myard, who called his struggle for the French language that of a "white negro.")[55]

But the most common analogy was with the World War II era. A former French ambassador explicitly compared the Anglicization of France to the German defeat of the Third Republic in June 1940; his compatriots who used English terms were represented as "collaborators" who were "agents of the American empire." The philosopher Michel Serres, also from the Académie Française, observed even more dramatically, in 2010, that the use of Anglo-American expressions had penetrated French advertising to such an extent that there were now more English words on the walls of Paris than there were German terms during the Nazi occupation. And in case the apocalyptic message was somehow missed, another campaigner for the defense of the French language observed (at the height of the George W. Bush years, admittedly) that the United States "had only ever had one enemy, France"; he then likened the cultural battle between France and America to a civilizational fault-line: "Two visions of history are pitted against each other, two universalisms, two irreconcilable Western ideals: this is the real clash of civilizations."[56]

How this grim state of affairs had come to pass was a source of much soul-searching among these hardy crusaders. For some, this "change of civilization" had occurred seamlessly and silently: "We have integrated American cultural codes without really noticing them at any given moment in time." The process was, however, assisted by a certain French psychological disposition toward slavishness, compounded by the widespread belief that English was a more precise and powerful language than French. Others saw the rise of "Globish" as a by-product of capitalism, an expression of the "unbridled globalization of Anglo-Saxon financial forces that seek to destroy world languages." The linguist Claude Hagège offered a further twist, observing that European bureaucrats had constantly pushed for the promotion of English as the sole language of the European Union, as it was "the language of neoliberal markets"—a frustration experienced by President Jacques Chirac in 2006. Chirac had marched out of a European Union session with his ministers when the (French) head of a European employers' group had the temerity to address the assembled delegates in English, on the grounds that it was "the language of business." There were also some fine conspiracy theories: one pamphleteer argued that the messianic belief in Anglo-Saxon destiny was an inherent feature of Americanism; she also claimed that in 1997 the Central Intelligence Agency had come up with a plan to impose English as the global language within five years.[57]

Yet, for many, the real culprits were the feckless French ruling classes, who had capitulated to Anglo-Saxon hegemony from the end of the Gaullian era. In a lecture in 1981, Étiemble ruefully observed that the ones who were truly responsible for the "betrayal" of the French language were the nation's politicians, broadcasters, and advertisers. This message was also driven home by cultural lobbying groups such as Défense de la Langue Française (Defense of the French Language) and Avenir de la Langue Française (Future of the French Language); in 1999, they founded the Prix de la Carpette Anglaise (The English Doormat Prize), awarded each year to a member of the French elite who showed particular zeal in promoting the English language. The first award went to the managing director of the car manufacturer Renault, Louis Schweitzer; subsequent recipients have included leading French journalists and industrialists as well as politicians of the Left and Right, such as Martine Aubry, Christine Lagarde, and Jean-François Copé—Copé for his belief that French children should be taught English starting in kindergarten, and for writing an article entitled "*Les Français* Must Speak English" (which, along with his shady financial dealings, perhaps helps to explain why Copé is one of the most unpopular politicians in France today). When the town of Loches came up with the catchy slogan "I Loches You" to enhance its attractiveness to tourists, the local branch of Défense de la Langue Française complained noisily: according to its president, Christian Massé, English was the "language of money and commerce."[58]

Of course, behind these lamentations lurked something much more profound: a sense of nostalgia for the golden age of French universalism and the belief in the absolute supremacy of the French language. It was deliciously ironic that the case for the "French exception" was made in the name of cultural diversity by elites who stridently rejected the application of this principle within France itself. It was no accident that in 2001 the historian and essayist Marc Fumaroli published *Quand l'Europe parlait français* (When Europe spoke French). In this brilliantly erudite evocation of the apogee of French culture in the Enlightenment era, Fumaroli recognized that English had taken over from French as the universal idiom. But defeat was not conceded gracefully: he bemoaned the lack of style in the English language, adding (perhaps a touch hyperbolically) that it "required no commitment from its speakers either in the manner or in the substance of their speech."[59]

And so, for the pessimists, the game was over: the Gallic addiction to English had turned the French into a folkloric community of exotic "Frenchies"—or, worse still, in the estimation of the novelist and member of the Académie Française Jean Dutourd, a nation of zombies, "a vapid, esoteric, hermetic people, speaking in slogans." (In an exquisitely cruel confirmation of Dutourd's worst fears, the Académie Française elected the poet Michael Edwards as his successor in February 2013—the first ever English-born *immortel*.) Linguistic and gastronomic decadence went hand in hand: traveling on Air

France, Noguez was dismayed to be served salted butter, contrary to Gallic conventions; insult was added to injury when he observed that the wrapping was labeled in English. The murderous consequences of Anglo-Saxonism were further driven home when *Avenir de la Langue Française* reported that a hospital in Épinal had caused the deaths of five cancer patients by inflicting lethal doses of radiation on them: the local operators had not understood the machine's instruction manual, which was in English.[60]

This sense of doom was further accentuated in May 2013, when the socialist majority in the National Assembly passed a law allowing French universities to provide courses in the English language—despite a barrage of criticism from the Académie Française, Francophone associations, and hardy resistants such as Claude Hagège, who declared in an op-ed in *Le Monde*, "We are at war." The extreme Left noisily joined in: a petition in *L'Humanité* by the Collectif Unitaire pour la Résistance, l'Initiative et l'Émancipation Linguistique (Joint Association for Linguistic Resistance, Initiative, and Emancipation) warned that the nation's elites were presiding over a "silent assassination" of French, which was being submerged by the "language of business"; it urged the people to "speak up so as not to lose their tongue." This inspired the ever-creative philosopher Michel Serres to call for a "strike against the English language," notably, by boycotting all shops selling commercial products not labeled in French, and the products themselves. Invoking the spirit of Fanon, and placing himself at the vanguard of the new wretched of the earth, the academician concluded, "Dominant elites now speak English, and French has become the language of the poor, and so I defend the language of the poor."[61]

CHAPTER 8

Writing for Everybody

On April 19, 1980, Jean-Paul Sartre was buried in Paris. He had become one of the most renowned figures of his age through his novels and plays, his highly publicized political writings, and his philosophical synthesis of Marxism and existentialism, which combined a belief that collective values were shaped by human choice with a commitment to revolution, "the seizure of power by violent class struggle." More than 50,000 people followed his funeral procession—making it the greatest public turnout for a man of letters since Victor Hugo's burial in 1885.[1]

Sartre's tumultuous trajectory during the postwar decades was rooted in the cardinal tenets of French thought discussed in earlier chapters: he embodied the progressive tradition's yearning for human perfectibility, the *normalien*'s compendious and abstruse philosophical spirit, the unsatisfied but persistent radical quest for new utopias, and the ideologue's Manichaean vision of a world in which the categories of good and evil were intuitively self-evident. Sartre was so perfectly emblematic of the main categories of French thought that, toward the end of his life, under the influence of his personal secretary Benny Lévy, he also seemed to be drawn into the occultist orbit. In an interview published in *Le Nouvel Observateur* shortly before his death, he claimed to be fascinated by Judaism's mystical vision of the "resurrection of the dead." Perhaps hoping to see the concept enacted, one of the mourners plunged into his grave at Montparnasse Cemetery.[2]

Above all, Sartre had been a flamboyant personification of the French "intellectual." The term was first coined in the late nineteenth century to designate public figures such as Émile Zola, who campaigned for a revision of the Dreyfus case in the name of the universal ideal of justice. But this type of intervention was merely an extension of cultural practices dating as far back as the Enlightenment era, when the great literary figures of the age denounced arbitrary power. Voltaire, for example, campaigned for the exoneration of Jean Calas, a Protestant merchant who was executed after being falsely accused of murdering his son to prevent his conversion to Catholicism; his ensuing *Treatise on Tolerance* (1763) was an eloquent plea for greater religious concord and the rejection of dogma. French intellectualism was thus forged in the postrevolutionary age as a distinct form of secular authority that rivaled and eventually superseded that of the church. Long before the advent of figures such as Sartre, this "consecration of the writer" had become one of the distinct characteristics of the nation's cultural life, turning novelists and poets into spiritual guides of society. Although the rise of intellectuals in the wake of the Dreyfus Affair was celebrated as a victory of republican reason over nationalist and racial prejudice, the reality was considerably more complex. Indeed, during the interwar era intellectuals distinguished themselves by the passion with which they embraced a wide range of causes, from royalism and nationalism to pacifism and communism: this militancy was denounced in the writer Julien Benda's celebrated work *La Trahison des clercs* (Treason of the intellectuals, 1927).[3]

Sartre entered the fray in the aftermath of World War II, arguing that human beings could escape the contingency of existence by seizing control of their destiny, and that the writer had a duty to speak for those who had no voice. He brought these two notions together in the figure of the *intellectuel engagé*, of which he became the archetype. *Engagement* was a vocation that gave the author a responsibility to "compose for the whole collectivity"—a function that made him a critical social intermediary: "He is writing for everybody and with everybody because the problem which he is trying to solve by means of his own talents is everybody's problem." The Sartrian intellectual's duties were defined in extensive terms: "to interfere in matters that do not directly concern him, to question established truths, and to champion the cause of the oppressed." *Engagement* was thus inseparable from Marxian revolutionary practice: its purpose was "to get to know the world in order to change it."[4]

Sartre's presence on the French intellectual scene during the postwar decades was magnetic: from his lair in Café Flore in Saint-Germain-des-Près he occupied the cultural terrain, defined the terms of discussion, and shaped social attitudes and practices, notably through his bohemian lifestyle and his contempt for the conventions of "bourgeois" existence. (In this respect, there was a compelling parallel with Rousseau's rejection of "civilization.") He developed a specific voice through his review *Les Temps modernes* (Modern times), founded with his companion, Simone de Beauvoir, in 1945, and through his organization of public petitions and manifestos, of which he became the absolute champion in the postwar decades. At the height of the Algerian War, when Sartre's name appeared in a manifesto urging French soldiers to desert the ranks, criminal proceedings against him by the government were halted by de Gaulle, who declared, "One does not imprison Voltaire."[5]

Sartre's towering position in French public life in the postwar years was thus a product of several factors: his powerful status as a philosopher (he represented the apogee of the humanist culture of the École Normale); his successful definition, and subsequent modeling, of a new form of intellectual practice that combined idealism and militancy; and his ability to express his ideas in a variety of genres, including fiction, drama, criticism, and biography, and (through his privileged relationship with his publisher, Gallimard) to disseminate his work through prestigious outlets. His style was an important asset, too. His philosophical writings were turgid, and yet his political and journalistic prose was elegant and fluid and wore its learning lightly. Although his formulas were at times too sweeping, he excelled in using unexpected contrasts to achieve a devastating effect, as when he described the conservative writer Pierre Drieu la Rochelle as "wishing for the fascist revolution in the same way as some wish for war, because they dare not break with their mistress." In his pugnacious approach, everything was viewed from the perspective of an ongoing political and ideological battle. In contrast with the mercurial subtleties of the structuralists, and their labyrinthine world of archaeologies and genealogies, Sartre's world was divided into easy categories—bourgeoisie and proletariat, socialists and imperialists, revolutionary heroes and *salauds*. Any form of wavering was subjected to instant moral censure: for example, the writer is "complicit with the oppressors unless he is the natural ally of all the oppressed." His contempt for those who did not share his way of thinking was legendary: "An anticommunist," he once declared, "is a dog."[6]

Sartre was a powerful polemicist, and his uncompromising conception of political and literary activism naturally provoked repeated clashes with his fellow intellectuals. He was often attacked by the communists, but the most emblematic and revealing of his conflicts was his split with the novelist Albert Camus. The two men first met in June 1943, after Sartre published an enthusiastic twenty-page review of *L'Étranger* (*The Stranger*); their personal friendship was cemented during the early postwar years, when they became the celebrated symbols of "existentialism." Yet although Camus shared Sartre's progressive outlook, his individual sensibility was very different. He was a moralist as opposed to an ideologue, and more of an individualist than a believer in group affiliations and collective causes. Unlike Sartre, whose vision of human nature was rather bleak, Camus's instinct toward his fellow humans was one of sympathy, seeking "to find what is valuable in every man." Camus was also much less inclined to view the world through ideological abstractions: for example, partly because he grew up in a working-class district of Algiers, he did not idealize the proletariat in the way Sartre and the postwar generation of Marxist intellectuals did.[7]

Although there was undoubtedly an element of personal rivalry in the break between the two men (both were vying for literary preeminence in the 1950s), its direct cause was their contrasting view of political violence: a necessary evil for Camus (who had been active in the Resistance), a necessary good for Sartre (who had not). As with all questions, Sartre approached the matter theoretically, embracing the Marxian postulate that social change was possible only through collective force; violence was in this sense part of the logic of history. Camus's abhorrence of bloodshed was as much grounded in experience as in a humanitarian instinct, which inspired his opposition to the death penalty and the use of nuclear weapons, and his dismay at the killing of enemies during political conflicts.

This tension came to a head in *L'Homme révolté* (*The Rebel*, 1951), where Camus criticized the different forms of rebellion in modern society and denounced the modern progressive cult of violence with a tirade manifestly aimed at Sartrian reasoning: "Those who throw themselves into history by preaching its absolute rationality end up with servitude and terror." The book was duly savaged in *Les Temps modernes* the following year; to add insult to injury, the review concentrated on the author's stylistic deficiencies and was written not by Sartre but by one of his collaborators. Responding to a letter of complaint from Camus, Sartre penned a blistering—and public—reply, which sealed their break. Sartre accused his erstwhile comrade of "philosophical incompetence," "hastily compiled information," and (the ultimate insult) "a dislike of intellectual complexity."[8]

In his dealings with Camus, and in his intellectual style more generally, Sartre embodied the penchant in French thought for considering matters in their total or absolute dimensions, and in their essence rather than in their contingent forms. These qualities allowed him to pose extraordinarily ambitious questions, as in his *Critique de la raison dialectique* (*Critique of Dialectical Reason*, 1960), where he sought to establish "whether there is any such thing as a Truth of humanity as a whole" (unsurprisingly, the book remained unfinished). This holism also enabled him to retain his faith in the purity of the revolutionary cause, irrespective of the state of mind of the proletariat or actual events in France or the Soviet Union. Sartre's frequent excursions across Marxist philosophical terrain in the postwar decades, such as the theory of the proletariat and the role of the revolutionary party, performed a critical function: he provided a "plausible and engaging" account of Marxism that could justify the positions of the Communist Party and explain Stalinism away as an unfortunate aberration. In *Les communistes et la paix* (*The Communists and Peace*), a series of articles published between 1952 and 1954, Sartre thus credited the communists with representing the essential interests of the working class and the nation as a whole: the party was the only force that was "teeming with life," while all else was "teeming with worms." (Metaphors of decay and putrefaction were a particular Sartrian favorite.)[9]

Sartre's influence on French thought was as remarkable as it was varied. His version of existentialism provided his countrymen with a means of coming to terms with the trauma and humiliation of the war years, notably by stressing the collective heroism of the French people and the individual's capacity to make a clean break with the past. During the late 1950s and early 1960s, his support for the cause of Algerian self-determination offered a form of intellectual leadership that contrasted with the depraved cynicism and opportunistic prudence of most French political elites. Even in his later years, as his faculties waned, he lent his prestige to a wide assortment of groups, including Basque and Breton nationalists, French Maoists, Portuguese revolutionaries, Soviet dissidents, and Vietnamese refugees. Yet underlying these variations lay a consistent commitment to fighting for the weak and a no less resolute rejection of all forms of official or dominant power—hence his rejection of the Nobel Prize for Literature in 1964, and his refusal to become dependent upon the powerful institutions of his era, whether it be the Parisian university elite, the "bourgeois" state, or the Communist Party; as he once put it, he was always a "traitor."[10]

This permanent posture of dissent explained the colorful coalition of men and women who spontaneously assembled to accompany him to his final resting place in April 1980—students and trade unionists, *gauchistes* and ex-communists, movie stars and postmen, European social democrats and Iranian revolutionary Islamists, African anticolonialists and Latin American revolutionaries. The turnout was a testimony not just to Sartre's global peregrinations but also to the universalism of a certain French humanist tradition. Régis Debray spoke for all its devotees when he observed that "from Buenos Aires to Beirut, all the intellectuals of our era have belonged at some time in their lives to the 'Sartre family,' and even in their enmity his adversaries have shared a profound intimacy with him."[11]

Sartrian Legacies

It was clear that the substance of French intellectual life would change fundamentally after the death of Sartre. This was not only because he had been such an extraordinary figure, but because the ideals that were at the heart of his redemptive conception of politics—communism, the revolution, the proletariat—lost much of their symbolic resonance in the 1980s. Marxism ceased to be the "unsurpassable horizon" of French intellectual life as the nation elected a reformist socialist as its president, the Communist Party declined, the working class withered away, and the Cold War drew to an end. The sense of loss was compounded by the disappearance, within a few years of Sartre's death, of many of the other great philosophical giants of the postwar decades. Structuralism was decapitated with the demise of Roland Barthes in 1980, then of Jacques Lacan a year later and Michel Foucault in 1984. Louis Althusser was also removed from the scene—but in a very unexpected way: he strangled his wife, Hélène, in 1980. (His critics unkindly observed that he was finally able to give practical expression to his theoretical antihumanism.) By the summer of 1983, *Le Monde* was concluding that left-wing intellectuals had become "silent." The deeper cause of this placidity was said to be the incoherence of the ideological universalism that had nurtured previous generations of radical thinkers. In the words of Jean-François Lyotard, Sartre's quest to determine his stances from the "point of view of the oppressed" had "perverted his thinking."[12]

What died with Sartre was not only a certain type of radical universalism but also the domination of the French intellectual scene by literary figures. Yet many aspects of the mode and style of French thinking during the Sartrian era continued to flourish in the ensuing decades: the transience of intellectual fashions (just as existentialism and structuralism had enjoyed their triumphs, liberalism would soon enjoy its moment in the sun); the belief that the possession of a certain cultural capital entitled writers and thinkers to intervene in public debates and to provide answers to the problems faced by French society; the preference for abstract argument over concrete, evidence-based discussion; the conversion of personal animosities into theoretical feuds; and the transformation of contentious social and cultural issues (such as the integration of ethnic minorities) into general ideological battlegrounds.

These elements of continuity were facilitated by the concentration of intellectual life in Paris. In many respects, the late twentieth century marked the apogee of this phenomenon. In 1981, Hervé Hamon and Patrick Rotman's *Les Intellocrates* offered a vivid ethnography of the capital's key cultural decision-makers, revealing an incestuous world based almost exclusively within Paris's sixth arrondissement—with its centers of power in elite academic institutions such as the École des Hautes Études and the Collège de France; publishing houses such as Gallimard, Seuil, and Grasset; and newspapers and reviews such as *Le Monde*, *Le Nouvel Observateur*, and *L'Express*. Hamon and Rotman revealed a world where power was held by a small intellectual oligarchy, the members of which occupied strategic positions across these institutions, and who were not shy to use the media to promote their works and their worldviews—notably, by appearing on Bernard Pivot's literary program *Apostrophes*, one of the most popular cultural television shows of the era. Seen from this vantage point, the French intellectual realm was less concerned with the intrinsic value of ideas than with strategies of advancement, marketing techniques, and social networks—the prime example being the emergence of the "new philosophers" in the later 1970s, an operation brilliantly orchestrated by Bernard-Henri Lévy and his circle.[13]

Sartre's intellectual legacy continued to be a source of critical discussion and inspiration. This was a manifestation of an enduring feature of French thought: the construction of a "tradition" around a major figure or intellectual moment. So just as the ideal of the "Dreyfusard" intellectual haunted French republican politics during the first half of the twentieth century, the Sartrian heritage became the focus of lively exchanges, polemical arguments, and creative reappropriations. There was, as might be expected, a wealth of testimonies from Sartre's entourage in the years following his death. Simone de Beauvoir's *La Cérémonie des adieux* (The farewell ceremony) was a poignant evocation of the final decade of his life and an affirmation of her love for the man at whose side she had been a steadfast presence since 1929. His former secretary Benny Lévy, for his part, offered a singular "dialogue" with Sartre in *Le Nom de l'homme* (The name of the man), a dense and passably eccentric blend of Sartrian existentialism and Judaic philosophy. Written from a sympathetic but critical standpoint, Olivier Todd's *Un fils rebelle* (A rebellious son) tried to identify the "honorable" causes Sartre had championed, singling out his neutralism and anticolonialism during the Cold War, his support for the student movement in May 1968, and his defense of immigrants. However, his overall conclusion was that posterity would remember Sartre principally for his plays and novels, not for his politics.[14]

This refuge in the more neutral territory of Sartre's literary *oeuvre* was a typical move aimed at diverting attention from his political heritage. (French republicans had done the same with Rousseau in the nineteenth and early twentieth centuries, using his literary eminence to cloak the awkwardness of his political appropriation by the Robespierrists.) It was all the more convenient as Sartre's work as a writer had always been impeccably classical in form and style. This was the overriding theme in the testimonies published in *Les Temps modernes* on the tenth anniversary of his death. (Such temporal landmarks became an increasing feature of the French publishing landscape.)

The novelist Claude Roy observed that the "essential point to remember is that Sartre is a writer—a great writer"; this untainted literary glory allowed him to maintain a strong link with the humanist tradition of Voltaire and Victor Hugo. Some intriguing insights into Sartre's mode of reflection were offered by one of his former secretaries, Jean Cau, who indicated that, when Sartre was thinking, his right shoulder and arm would instinctively take the posture of a boxer. Yet Cau also affirmed, somewhat disturbingly, that this pugilist had little real interest in the causes he supported: his real passion was for literature, and he found politics "dead boring." Why then did he put his name to so many petitions? The answer was an inventive but paradoxical defense of Sartrian intellectualism: he had, according to Cau, become a prisoner of the public figure he had created. It thus came as little surprise when the magazine *Le Point* summarized Sartre's politics as "a passion for error"—or, as the Cartesian philosopher Denis Moreau put it only slightly more subtly, "I am fond of Sartre, but even fonder of the truth."[15]

Yet framing the question in these terms underlined an even greater paradox: Sartrian intellectualism may have become a thing of the past, but its spirit continued to haunt French thought. As a field of academic research in France, the history of intellectuals experienced a substantial growth in the final decades of the twentieth century, as reflected in the publication of a compendious and widely commented upon *Dictionnaire des intellectuels français* (Dictionary of French intellectuals). Sartre featured prominently in these productions—even though the evaluation of his contribution to French intellectual life was often severe. For the historian Jean-François Sirinelli, Sartre's political analysis had missed the boat of history, being completely flawed on such fundamental questions as the redemptive role of the Third World revolutions and the transformative politics of the extreme left in Europe.[16]

The reassessments of the Vichy regime and Soviet-style communism after the end of the Cold War also impacted negatively on Sartre: his reluctance to break fundamentally with the Leninist system was castigated as a manifestation of moral blindness, and his postwar political militancy was ascribed to his bad faith for failing to engage meaningfully with the Resistance (and, some alleged, his less than honorable dealings with Vichy authorities). The most vehement charge was laid by Tony Judt, for whom the philosopher of *engagement* symbolized the egregious flaws of French progressive thought from the 1930s through to the late 1970s: a fetish for abstraction; a hatred of the bourgeoisie, which concealed a form of guilt and self-loathing; a cult of violence, reinforced by a contempt for liberal democracy; and a moral amnesia, expressed in an incapacity to recognize publicly the crimes committed in the name of freedom, merely to avoid providing ammunition to the adversaries of one's own cause.[17]

But this polemical anti-Sartrianism was short-lived, and the pendulum soon began to swing in the opposite direction. As France sank into a growing political and economic crisis in the 1990s, the radical Left experienced an intellectual resurgence—and a more muted, but distinctly recognizable, version of *engagement* made a comeback in the figure of the sociologist Pierre Bourdieu (like Sartre, a product of the École Normale Supérieure). Relatively withdrawn from the political arena, and indeed openly critical of the Sartrian formula of the "total" intellectual during its heyday, Bourdieu became convinced in the 1990s that direct political action on the part of intellectuals was imperative in order to break the stranglehold of globalization and economic liberalization—or, as he put it in his somewhat wooden prose, "it is possible to use knowledge of the logic of the functioning of the fields of cultural production to draw up a realistic programme for the collective action of intellectuals." During the strikes against the "Juppé Plan" to reform the French social security system in the winter of 1995, Bourdieu entered the fray, delivering a speech "against the destruction of civilization" at the Gare de Lyon. In its apocalyptic tone, it was a return to the rhetorical dichotomies of the ideological era (and a conscious imitation of Sartre's iconic address to the striking workers at Billancourt in 1970). A few years later, after Bourdieu had engaged in a whole series of political activities, in the form of signing petitions, participating in demonstrations, writing newspaper editorials, and making television appearances, the *Magazine littéraire* posed a question with powerful Sartrian undertones: Had Bourdieu now become France's "dominant intellectual"?[18]

The twentieth anniversary of Sartre's death in 2000 confirmed this resurrection of the great intellectual's thought and his remarkable capacity for reinvention. Despite his hostility to Sartre's politics, Pierre Grémion described him as "a writer and philosopher, bohemian and man of letters, anarchist and ultra-bolshevist—an uncommon genius, capable of holding a great variety of roles." Confirmation of this plasticity came in Bernard Fauconnier's novel *L'Être et le géant* (Being and the giant), an imaginary dialogue between Sartre and de Gaulle, which was one of the literary successes of the anniversary year. But the book that stole the limelight was Bernard-Henri Lévy's *Siècle de Sartre*, a passionate defense of the man and his *oeuvre*. As one of the scourges of French radical thought in the 1970s and 1980s, Lévy was an even less likely advocate of the Sartrian cause than Bourdieu: in *La Barbarie à visage humain* (Barbarity with a human face, 1977), he had argued that all progressive utopias had been "catastrophes": "Our dreams go far back but they always turn into bloodbaths." Intellectuals therefore had to abandon the Sartrian conceit that they should "serve the oppressed." A decade later, although more nuanced in his appreciation of the record of intellectual *engagement*, Lévy maintained that any kind of return to Sartre would be "ridiculous." But this was hardly a serious obstacle for Lévy, and *Le Siècle de Sartre* (The century of Sartre) duly celebrated his hero's literary and philosophical creativity as well as his "planetary moral authority."[19]

The book glossed over Sartre's errors, offering a calorie-free repackaging of his politics as a "defense of liberty." Indeed, a close reading of the text suggested that this Sartre was something of an idealized version of Lévy himself—notably, in his intellectual brilliance (Lévy, too, was a *normalien*), his capacity for love, his playfulness and generosity, his insatiable curiosity, and the visceral hatred he provoked among certain sections of the intelligentsia. A few years later, the film *Les Amants du Flore* (The Lovers of the Flore, 2006) completed Sartre's posthumous reinvention as the figure that Lévy himself now perfectly embodied: the frivolous Saint-Germain-des-Prés dandy and literary celebrity.

The Liberal Renaissance

Among the many public figures who attended Sartre's funeral in 1980 was Raymond Aron. The two men had been close friends when they entered the École Normale in 1924, but had followed opposing paths in the postwar decades, only briefly renewing contact in June 1979 to plead the cause of Vietnamese refugees. Aron had become a fierce critic of the Sartrian ideal of the committed intellectual, rejecting its revolutionary utopianism in the name of the ideals of toleration and skepticism. Yet behind the difference in substance there was an uncanny similarity in form. For Aron, as for Sartre, Marx had been a privileged intellectual interlocutor. Despite his self-description as an isolated figure, Aron had been an "intellocrat"—a powerful presence on the Parisian scene, who had used his cultural capital as an academic and columnist for the conservative daily *Le Figaro* to promote his views vigorously: he thus became one of France's leading critics of the Left and an advocate of constitutional liberalism, the rule of law, and Atlanticism. And, like Sartre, who was at times violently attacked by the communists, Aron took stances that were not always appreciated by his own camp. (De Gaulle once described him as a "journalist at the Collège de France and a professor at the *Figaro*.")[20]

When Aron died in 1983 at the height of his literary fame (his *Mémoires* had just been greeted with acclaim), the ground was being laid for a revival of liberal thought in France. For a brief moment, the French seemed to embrace liberalism with the same uncritical fervor they had shown toward Sartre's revolutionism. Invited to lecture in Paris in 1984, Friedrich Hayek was pleasantly surprised by the new mood, announcing that "even in France, classical liberalism has become the new orthodoxy"; the Gaullist leader Jacques Chirac duly decorated him with the Grande Médaille de Vermeil of the city of Paris. It was a measure of the changing times that the economic programs of Ronald Reagan and Margaret Thatcher were greeted with critical interest in France, both by rising political stars such as Alain Madelin and economists such as Guy Sorman. Two years later, this neoliberal flurry culminated in the Chirac government's privatization and deregulation policies, with long-standing believers in French *dirigisme*, such as Édouard Balladur, pledging their undying allegiance to the principle of economic liberalism.[21]

In the intellectual realm, a more philosophical version of this liberal creed began to coalesce around long-established reviews such as *Esprit* as well as around new publications such as the center-right *Commentaire* (founded by Aron's disciple Jean-Claude Casanova) and the center-left *Le Débat*. Many of the leading contributors to these publications were Parisian academics, and the new vision of intellectual practice they sought to formulate was an idealization of the scholarly virtues: in the words of Marcel Gauchet, the time had come for "the promotion of real values against false ones, analysis against clichés, reasoning rather than sloganeering, the sense of difficulty against the dictatorship of facility."[22]

In the first issue of *Le Débat*, the historian Pierre Nora pronounced the demise of the Sartrian revolutionary tradition: "The era of the intellectual-oracle is behind us." This was accurate in one sense, but also somewhat disingenuous. For this rising generation of liberal and progressive "intellocrats" was clearly seeking to lay claim to the terrain occupied by their radical forebears. It was in this spirit that the historian François Furet, the single most influential figure in this renaissance of French liberalism, founded the Raymond Aron Centre at the École des Hautes Études en Sciences Sociales in 1982. Many of its affiliated researchers delved into the history of French liberal thought, producing a raft of original and often brilliant works on classic thinkers, and reexamining key themes such as individualism, human rights, and democracy. Pierre Manent referred to this combination of interests as a "liberal political science of democracy," and the view of modern France that emerged from it was strongly colored by nineteenth-century conceptions—and, in particular, by a Tocquevillian ambivalence about democratic modernity. When Manent concluded his book on Tocqueville with the assertion "to love democracy well, we must love it moderately," he was expressing the characteristic liberal unease with the ideal of popular sovereignty while also echoing widespread fears about the redistributive policies of the recently elected socialist government.[23]

Another widely canvassed Tocquevillian theme was the celebration of political consensus. In *La République du centre* (The Republic of the center), written after Mitterrand's reelection to the presidency in 1988, François Furet, Jacques Julliard, and Pierre Rosanvallon welcomed the advent of the post-ideological age in France: "The idea of the Left, the idea of socialism, the idea of the Republic have all perished at the same time." Given that most voters were "somewhere between the center right and the center left," Furet claimed that France was now ready to join the ranks of democratic normality. Julliard, for his part, welcomed the "convergence of all social groups to limit the role of passions in public life." But these hopes were overoptimistic, especially as the consensus that had emerged was negative rather than positive: quoting Tocqueville's *Souvenirs* (*Recollections*) Rosanvallon drew a parallel between France in the 1980s and the atmosphere in the final years of the July Monarchy, which were characterized, he said, by "languor, incapacity, immobility, boredom." The post-ideological age had thus paradoxically stifled intellectual debate—hence the authors' conclusion that the most urgent task was the promotion of "democratic deliberation" through "the production of ideas, the elaboration of projects, and the formulation of diagnoses."[24]

Furet and Rosanvallon were the driving forces behind one of the more interesting products of this post-Sartrian quest to revive French thought: the Saint-Simon Foundation. Established in the autumn of 1982, this think tank sought to provide a nonpartisan forum for reflection on France's political, economic, and social problems—a more collective version of the Sartrian intellectual formula. Based in the Rue du Cherche-Midi in Paris, the foundation attempted to reconstitute the coalition of "industrialists" identified by Saint-Simon in the nineteenth century: thinkers, academics, political and administrative elites, trade unionists, and entrepreneurs. (There is, alas, no evidence that it also revived the more colorful hedonistic rituals of the Saint-Simonians.) Although the circle of participants was restricted (attendance was by invitation only), the proceedings were disseminated in little green booklets, the *Notes de la Fondation Saint-Simon*, which became a quasi-monthly publication from 1990.[25]

While the range of subjects treated was broad, the pamphlets formed a coherent series because of their shared intellectual tone (generally of a moderate, reformist, technocratic sensibility) and their common objective: to tackle

French problems from a European and comparative perspective. (The economist Thomas Piketty authored one pamphlet, which compared job creation in France and the United States.) The writers thus investigated the dysfunctions of the French political and economic system with the hope that the solutions offered would form the basis of a modernized version of French liberalism: the devolution of a greater role to intermediate groups and associations; a move toward a more streamlined and less partisan state; and a recognition of the value of European integration.[26]

This "Tocquevillian moment" symbolically ended in 1997 with the death of François Furet. What difference did it make to French intellectual life? The liberal intellocrats were largely successful in their ambition to seize control of public space. Perhaps the best single example was the bicentenary of the French Revolution in 1989, which was dominated by Furet's anti-Jacobin perspective, effectively relayed by a supportive network of publishers, reviews, and journals. And they were not shy to celebrate their triumph: in 1990, in an anticipation of Francis Fukuyama, *Le Débat* announced that its ideals— the pursuit of dispassionate analysis, the development of practical knowledge, and the search for political consensus—had become "the spirit of the times." At a more specialized level, institutions such as the Saint-Simon Foundation also helped give a more pragmatic orientation to debates about public policy (notably, on economic issues), moving away from the grand theorizing of the pre-1981 era.[27]

But this French reconciliation with the market was fragile—all the more so because, as noted earlier with the case of Bourdieu, there remained in France a strong underlying hostility toward capitalism, which manifested itself with growing confidence from the mid-1990s. The liberals did not see this coming—partly because they suffered from a certain Parisian insularity, the characteristic defect of French intellectualism, and partly because they bought too readily into the vision of a world dominated by rational, self-interested individualism. They did not sufficiently appreciate that politics (especially in France) was also about imagination, mythology, and passion. In 1995, reviewing their earlier aspirations in the light of subsequent events, the authors of *La République du centre* recognized that their diagnosis of the end of ideological conflict in France had been premature. Furet admitted that the division between Left and Right had not only survived, but would long remain the essential matrix of national political culture. Raymond Aron's warning suddenly appeared especially relevant: "The essence of history is not to resolve problems. And when, by good fortune, history resolves a problem, it immediately creates others."[28]

The Introspective Turn

The turn of the century brought back another characteristic feature of French intellectual life: the controversy, or *polémique*. The passing of the liberal moment was dissected at considerable length, and with melancholic anxiety, in two bulky issues of *Esprit*. But the more abrasive tone was set by the publication of Daniel Lindenberg's *Le Rappel à l'ordre* (The call to order) in 2002, in which the author (a regular contributor to *Esprit*) identified the outlines of a new form of French "reactionary" thought. Among the themes detected in this rising tide of neoconservatism were a quest for order, a revival of cultural elitism, a contestation of the heritage of May 1968, a critique of equality, and (in the wake of the 9/11 attacks in the United States) a scapegoating of multiculturalism and, especially, Islam. The devotees of this new creed, according to the author, included the novelist Michel Houellebecq; the philosophers Alain Finkielkraut, Pierre Manent, and Marcel Gauchet; and the historian Pierre Nora.[29]

Among French intellectuals, too, the personal is political, and this controversy was, in large part, the result of a falling-out among the barons of the Aron Centre: Lindenberg's key targets included the more conservative members of the group, and his book was published in a collection edited by the more progressive Rosanvallon. At the same time, *Le Rappel à l'ordre*'s main thesis was undeniable: a certain disorientation had set in within the liberal intellocratic microcosm as the constellation of "anti-totalitarian" forces that had held center stage in the 1980s and 1990s began to implode. His pamphlet was uncannily prophetic, anticipating the conservative turn of French thought in the Sarkozy era.[30]

Lindenberg was not the only observer to notice this rightward (and downward) shift in Gallic thinking. Some ascribed the trend to the decline of French universities and the rise of the broadcast media, while others noted that the failure of the liberal intellocrats of the 1990s to cement a consensus around their values echoed the defeats of previous generations of reformists. The historian Perry Anderson's short book *La Pensée tiède* (The tepid mode of thought) was even more damning in its conclusion, contrasting the vitality of French political and intellectual life in the Sartrian era with the "decadence" he perceived in the early twenty-first century. Arguing from a more politically radical premise than Lindenberg, he launched a devastating broadside against the corruption and parochialism of the French intellectual class. He particularly singled out the penetration of the mainstream political elite by technocratic higher civil servants; the depoliticized consensus between Left and Right; the declining standards of the "quality" press (notably, *Le Monde*);

the celebrity status of Bernard-Henri Lévy; and the ideological realignment achieved by the liberal intellocrats, whose real ambition, Anderson claimed, had been to embalm French radical traditions in a patriotic neorepublican nostalgia.[31]

What was to be made of this new zeitgeist? Rather than Lindenberg's term, "reactionary," the new mood could better be described as "reactive," or re-treating—the beginning of a slide back toward the national horizon, accompanied by a less universalist and more defensive and pessimistic demeanor as well as a revival of old myths about national cohesion and the threat to the French collective self (a syndrome to be further dissected in the final chapter of this book). One of the most immediate (and spectacular) manifestations of the phenomenon was the victory of the "no" vote in the May 2005 referendum on the European Constitution. At one level, the rejection of the proposed constitution might simply be seen as a commonsensical public reaction against a weak official campaign and a lengthy, poorly drafted, and jargon-ridden document (the principal author of which was none other than former president Valéry Giscard d'Estaing, freshly elected to the Académie Française). But it was also noteworthy that, with a few exceptions, intellectuals did not intervene publicly in the campaign, and when they did so, they showed little enthusiasm. The disorientation of the pro-European camp after its defeat was reflected in a somewhat contemptuous editorial in *Esprit*, which spoke of a "misleading" vote: "The people have spoken, but they do not know who they are speaking to." *Le Débat* dwelled on the weight of cultural factors, such as the Jacobin heritage and the depth of French hostility toward liberalism, which were often equated with the destructive individualism of the "Anglo-Saxon model."[32]

What was most striking about the victorious "no" vote was its effective aggregation of negatives. Upon the classic euroskeptic fear of loss of sovereignty was grafted a toxic combination of populisms: a xenophobic rejection of European enlargement, a progressive anxiety about the dilution of French social rights (represented by the figure of the cut-price "Polish plumber," willing to provide his services for a fraction of the cost of his French counterpart), and a neo-Poujadist rejection of Parisian elites by grass-roots campaigners. As Jean Monnet's star began to wane, the unlikely hero of the moment was Étienne Chouard, an economics and management schoolteacher who mounted a widely consulted campaign against the constitution on his website. *Libération* hailed him as the "Internet champion" of the opposition campaign, and *Le Monde* devoted an article to the "Don Quixote of the 'no' vote." It was a measure of the impotence of the Parisian intellocracy (but also, conversely, of the growing power of the new horizontal age of Internet communication) that the European project, the brainchild of Jean Monnet and one of the most distinguished creations of Gallic thought, was thus effectively pushed to one side by a blogger from Marseille.[33]

Among the more intriguing manifestations of this introspective, self-referential turn in French thought was the rising prominence of Jean Baudrillard. His work combined a structuralist skepticism about the possibility of objective meaning with his concepts of "simulation" and "hyper-reality," which suggested that reality in contemporary societies had been replaced by symbols and signs, especially through the virtual representations of the mass media. This notion was in many respects a bleaker version of Barthes's mythologies, set against a backdrop of the shattering of the grand historical narratives of Marxism and liberalism. Baudrillard's penchant for provocative paradoxes led him to claim that the First Gulf War (1991) "did not happen"—by which he meant both that the conflict was so one-sided that it was not a real "war," and that it was planned and produced as a media event.[34]

His insistence on the primacy of the symbolic over the real—a parodic world of "ghost-events"—turned Baudrillard into something of a celebrity, not only in France but also in the United States, where he was seen as something of an amusing complement to Derrida. He was one of the philosophical inspirations behind the cult movie *The Matrix* (1999), which featured a scene showing a (fake) copy of his book *Simulacra and Simulation* (1981). However, the Americans were far less amused by Baudrillard's interpretation of the 9/11 attacks, in the wake of which he asserted that the "arrogance" of American power had made the event possible and necessary, before offering this mysterious conclusion, which showed that the French intellectual's love of paradox was still thriving: "The collapse of the towers of the World Trade Center is unimaginable, but that is not enough to make it a real event. If it seems so, it is because reality has absorbed the energy of fiction, and become fiction itself." (Baudrillard's death in 2007 prompted his more mischievous obituarists to question what he had meant by this act.)[35]

Another controversy that came to a head during this period—one that took a sharper tone and had more wide-ranging consequences than the *polémique* about the new reactionaries—was the debate about the integration of ethnic minorities, especially those from the nation's former North African colonies. Multiculturalism was hardly an issue confronting the French alone, but the way French elites approached it bore witness to their enduring capacity to engage with social and political issues through essentialist and dogmatic arguments. Even though a substantial degree of territorial devolution had been introduced since the 1980s, and France officially recognized regional languages in the 2008 constitutional reform, any attempt to extend this cultural pluralism to religious minorities was staunchly resisted. To compound the problem, the French debate was not informed by precise data and statistics. These would have been hard to come by: in the name of the republican principle that all citizens are equal, and the normative ideals of fostering unity and social cohesion, gathering official information about ethnicity and religion is illegal.[36]

So the discussion focused instead on the peripheral question of whether wearing the Islamic veil should be allowed in French schools. This debate turned the issue of integration—a complex but concrete matter, with specific social, political, and economic ramifications—into an abstruse philosophical controversy concerning how to safeguard the republican principle of *laïcité* (secularism), which since the 1905 separation of church and state had kept religion firmly in the private sphere. Beginning in 1989, with the expulsion of three veiled students from a school in Creil (Oise), the discussion rumbled on through the 1990s, with successive governments seeking to find a compromise on the issue. The debate was finally concluded with the report of the Stasi Commission, appointed by President Chirac in 2003, which recommended instituting a ban on all ostensible religious signs and symbols in French schools; in March 2004, the National Assembly adopted a bill to this effect.[37]

Various writers made thoughtful contributions to this debate. The sociologist Dominique Schnapper, for example, sought to reaffirm the universality of republican values while recognizing the need for constructive dialogue among different communities. A few commentators even tried to make the case for a French version of multiculturalism. But these voices of reason were drowned out by the emergence of a strident "national-communitarian" republicanism, which gained the ascendency and eventually carried the day. In the words of the political scientist Sophie Heine, this strand of thought perceived the veil issue as a means of "defending French identity against a perceived growing cultural affirmation by Muslim citizens."[38]

On this line of reasoning, priority was to be given to the preservation of collective cohesion and public order, and the existence of minority cultures (especially Islam) was viewed as a threat to the integrity of the nation. In addition to demonizing immigrants, those arguing for this perspective drew upon an essentialized conception of the national self—a sense of Frenchness that was fixed and enduring, and yet (paradoxically) liable to unravel if subjected to any meaningful interaction with Islamic culture. They also showed a consistent tendency toward hyperbole—exactly like the linguistic crusaders we encountered in the previous chapter. Attempts to reach a pragmatic compromise on the veil in the late 1980s were likened by Régis Debray, Alain Finkielkraut, and Élisabeth Badinter to "a Munich of the republican school." Finkielkraut equated advocacy of multiculturalism with support for the exclusive nationalist ideas of Maurice Barrès, and Christian Jelen equated it with complicity in honor killings. After the National Front's unprecedentedly strong showing in the presidential elections of 2002, Pierre Manent argued that French society had become "dispossessed" by Islamic immigration.[39]

The figure who came to symbolize this conservative rearguardism was Régis Debray. After a brief spell as adviser to François Mitterrand at the Élysée, the former companion of Che Guevara reinvented himself as a champion of the ideal of "archaic modernity," adding his name to a petition demanding more discipline in the classroom and a greater sense of responsibility in young people. After distinguishing himself by his opposition to the First Gulf War in 1991 in the name of anticolonialism, and during the Kosovo conflict by defending the democratic credentials of the Serbian ethnic-cleanser Slobodan Milošević, Debray later served as one of the members of the Stasi Commission, where he provided a fillip to its national-communitarian orientation by calling for greater "respect" for schools and suggesting that educational institutions should be shielded from "group effects." Although he argued against a legislative ban of the veil, thus preserving his "progressive" reputation, he provided those pushing for it with their key arguments: the need to act against the (undemonstrated) unraveling of the French social fabric, the (unproven) incompatibility of religious belief with republican citizenship, and the imperative of forging an ill-defined "community of destiny" through the education system. These philosophical ramblings culminated in Debray's *Le Moment fraternité* (The fraternity moment), in which, bizarrely, he claimed that the overturning of *laïcité* would be the prelude to "the delegitimation of contraception." Little wonder that France's leading academic expert on the history of secularism concluded that the real fundamentalists were now in the republican camp.[40]

Progressive Voices: Rosanvallon and Badiou

The drift of important sections of the French elite toward a parochial and neoconservative republicanism in the first decade of the twenty-first century drew some responses from progressive thinkers. In a series of new works, Pierre Rosanvallon offered a searching analysis of the crisis of French democracy: rejecting the conventional view that citizens were becoming apathetic and turning away from politics, he attempted to show that new forms of collective "defiance" toward authority (notably, in social movements and through the use of the Internet) carried the potential for civic regeneration. He thus made the case for a "renationalization" of French collective life based on greater participatory democracy and a more robust pursuit of equality through redistribution.[41]

Rosanvallon's work was widely praised (although not always carefully read), and his approach was especially noteworthy because he sought, through his position at the Collège de France and his organization of the web platform "La Vie des Idées," to move beyond the dichotomy between Sartrian utopianism and Aronian skepticism that had dominated French intellectual life for much of the twentieth century. However, even though his activities (books, pamphlets, articles and reviews, and workshops) have shed interesting light on the evolution of contemporary French society, and helped to identify new patterns of social and economic exclusion, Rosanvallon's aspiration to reshape the collective understanding of French democracy has remained largely unfulfilled.[42]

There have been a number of reasons for this limited success. The most important, arguably, is stylistic rather than substantive: Rosanvallon's professorial and rather austere prose lacks the playfulness and the rhetorical elegance of his mentor Furet, to say nothing of the captivating quality of the French intellectual tradition in its golden age. (He could do with Sartre's great rhetorical gift: the ability to make his reader feel he is participating in a collective conversation.) Furthermore, his involvement in politics has been relatively circumscribed (he was largely absent from the presidential debate in 2012). His work has sought to integrate concepts borrowed from Anglo-American political science that are little understood in France. Finally, his understanding of democracy operates within a broadly reformist framework. The subtleties of such a position have not always been grasped by others, and indeed such a position runs counter to the Sartrian ideal of the intellectual as a dissenter and a radical critic of French democracy—a point made by those on the Left who contest Rosanvallon's moderation and incrementalism and his refusal to question the fundamental premises of the global political and economic order.[43]

One of the most emblematic figures here was the neo-Marxist philosopher Alain Badiou, whose vigorous challenges to mainstream French political thinking were often more successful than Rosanvallon's at capturing the public imagination. A (critical) disciple of Sartre and former professor at the École Normale Supérieure, Badiou in many ways took up the space left vacant by Bourdieu's death in 2002. His short, colorfully polemical book *De quoi Sarkozy est-il le nom?* (*The meaning of Sarkozy*) was one of the literary successes of 2007. Here, he presented Sarkozy's conquest of power as a consequence of his desire to integrate France into the networks of international finance capitalism and his effective use of fear (of terrorists, of immigrants, of crime and insecurity). But Badiou's core beliefs—particularly those focusing on the greatness of the Maoist Cultural Revolution, the viability of the communist ideal, and the reawakening of "History" in the light of the Arab Spring—have not struck much of a chord with the French public. His authority rests instead on those features of his thought that have always appealed to French progressives: his universalism and contempt for all forms of extreme nationalism; his belief in the limits of "bourgeois" democracy; his anti-Americanism (along with hostility toward Israeli expansionism); his denunciation of the immorality of capitalism; and his willingness to expose the vacuousness of "republican" rhetoric. The article he published in *Le Monde* following the passage of the French law banning the veil was characteristically pithy, highlighting the numerous contradictions of republican communitarian thinking and pointing to its real underlying motivation: fear of the "barbarian."[44]

Camus Strikes Back

Every French intellectual moment needs its (dead) philosophical figurehead: after the Sartrian hegemony of the post-Liberation era, followed by Tocqueville's belated acclaim in the late twentieth century, the man who emerged to claim his posthumous place in the sun was Sartre's old nemesis, Albert Camus. The writer who was once dismissed as a high-school philosopher surged back into the limelight because his handsome looks and signature trench coat were perfectly suited to the age of advertising—and because his novels had remained popular: *The Stranger* is one of the best-selling French paperbacks of all time (over 6.7 million copies in France). Just as importantly, Camus was well suited to the needs of the age of French intellectual retrenchment: Was he not, after all, the embodiment of the ideal of skepticism rather than dogma, the man who had refused to countenance a French withdrawal from Algeria, and famously said that, if forced to choose between justice and his mother, he would opt for his mother? This dubious legal philosophy was mightily appealing to Nicolas Sarkozy, who was embroiled in various financial scandals during his presidency and fittingly became Camus's great champion. Sarkozy even tried—unsuccessfully in the end—to have Camus's remains reinterred in the Panthéon (although the president had obviously not read his cherished author closely enough to remember his first name: at a meeting at Avignon in 2012, he referred to him as "Stéphane Camus").[45]

Yet this Camusian revival was also, in a way, another backhanded tribute to Sartre, reflecting the continuing French yearning for a symbolic intellectual leader who could capture the spirit of the times—for was not the fact that Camus was a kind of anti-Sartre the real point? This message was made explicit in Olivier Todd's monumental biography of Camus, in which he tried to argue that Camus was superior to Sartre in terms of a number of ways, including his authenticity, his honesty, his humanity, his rejection of violence, and his recognition of the limits of intellectual engagement. This was a somewhat optimistic rendering, as Camus's appeal rested, above all, on his infinite adaptability. Whereas Sartre had symbolized universalism, depth of learning, and constancy (even to the point of error), Camus was an intellectual for all seasons. Celebrated as the "moral conscience of the twenty-first century" by *Le Nouvel Observateur*, he was appropriated to serve a range of causes. For the philosopher André Comte-Sponville, he represented "the urgency and the improvisation of life"; for Alain Finkielkraut, an ethic of humanism; for the philosopher Jean Sarocchi, a tempered ideal of justice; for the essayist Michel Onfray, a philosophy of libertarianism; for the literary historian Stéphane Giocanti, "the pure and noble intellectual"; for critics of colonial repentance, such as Jean-Louis Saint-Ygnan, the memory of French settlers in Algeria; for the rapper Abd al Malik, who devoted a musical show to Camus in Aix-en-Provence, "a big brother from the estate (*cité*)"; for François Hollande, the republican aspiration to equality through education. No new intellectual fad would be complete without its adoption by Bernard-Henri Lévy, and so it was that the unfortunate Camus also found himself hailed as the source of the ideals of the "melancholic Left," including a hopeful pessimism and a skeptical commitment to making a better world. A few years later, in his supremely narcissistic account of the 2011 Libyan war, Lévy portrayed himself as being at the forefront of the French intervention to bring democracy to the hapless Arabs and, in a scene suffused with Camusian orientalism, the intellectual architect of Libyan tribal unity.[46]

From Vanguard to Rearguard?

That there have been considerable changes to the French intellectual landscape since the 1980s is beyond dispute. Figures of the stature of Sartre, Foucault, or Aron have disappeared, and along with them the strident, confrontational tone that marked French public life for much of the twentieth century. Saint-Germain-des-Prés has become a haven of high-fashion boutiques, with fading memories of its past artistic and literary glory: as one disillusioned French writer noted, "the time will soon come when we will be reduced to selling little statues of Sartre made in China."[47]

Also gone is the championing of general political causes by the Parisian cultural elite. As the sociologist Bruno Latour observed humorously, "it has been a long time since intellectuals were in the vanguard. Indeed, it has been a long time since the very notion of the avant-garde—the proletariat, the artistic—passed away, pushed aside by other forces, moved to the rearguard, or maybe lumped with the baggage train." One of the notable features of the 2012 French presidential election campaign was the almost complete absence of public support for either of the main candidates by thinkers, literary eminences, or artistic celebrities—although the ever-resourceful Nicolas Sarkozy did manage to field Gérard Depardieu at one of his meetings (since the election of Hollande, the actor is no longer domiciled in France). Parties still call upon academics and experts to help them draft manifestos and programs, but these interactions are limited and driven by short-term rather than strategic considerations. On the rare occasions when intellectuals do become involved in some form of activism, their contributions are more specific and narrowly focused than in the past—as, for example, when the Nobel Prize–winning writer J. M. G. Le Clézio eloquently denounced the treatment of the Chagos Islanders by the international community.[48]

Yet the extent of these changes should not be exaggerated. Even though the substance of French intellectual life changed in the post-Sartrian era, there remained significant continuities in terms of style and approach. The smugness of the French liberals' belief in the 1990s that their historical moment had come mirrored the confident eschatology of Sartre and the French Marxists in their heyday. The fantasies were very different, of course, but they both represented a very Gallic form of universalism, and the capacity for self-delusion in both cases came from an identical source: a particularly Parisian form of cloistered reasoning, exacerbated by a certain distance from (and contempt for) the actual beliefs of ordinary people. This phenomenon also explained the spectacular defeat of the "yes" camp in the 2005 referendum. Although neither man was of the stature of Sartre, the significant audiences enjoyed by Bourdieu and Badiou—not coincidentally, both products of the École Normale—demonstrated that Sartre's belief in the social and political value of dissent was still alive and well, as was the *intellectuel engagé*'s contention that there was something inherently corrupting about "power." In this key respect, even though they had opposing conceptions of the role of the intellectual, the legacies of Sartre and Foucault were in complete alignment. The discussion of multiculturalism illustrated the continuing attachment of French cultural elites to holistic theorizing and hyperbole and their deeply ingrained resistance to evidence-based reasoning.

But not all of these continuities are negative. The old ideal of the intellectual as a mediator between the thinking elite and the ordinary citizen is still cherished, as can be seen in the creative project launched by Pierre Rosanvallon in 2014, "Raconter la Vie" (Narrating lives). It seeks to provide (through a dedicated website and a book collection, published by Éditions du Seuil) a platform to allow French men and women from all walks of life to tell their stories directly, without professional intermediaries. The Sartrian intellectual aspiration to write for everybody is thus turned on its head: everybody can aspire to write. The broader aim of this "Parliament of the Invisible" is to give voice to the voiceless, and to "forge the elements of a positive reconstruction of a common world, recognized in its diversity and its reality." The series has generally been well received. Among the most acclaimed testimonies are Christophe Petot's *Ligne 11* (Line 11), which relates the life of a driver in the Paris Métro; Nadia Daam's *La Fiche de renseignements* (Fact sheet), recounting the author's experience of working in the black economy; and Anaelle Sorignet's wonderfully entitled *Je suis l'ombre fatiguée qui nettoie vos merdes en silence* (I am the tired shadow who cleans up your crap in silence), a sobering account of a worker in a fast-food restaurant.[49]

Yet however successful such projects of democratic intellectual empowerment turn out to be, they cannot hide or compensate for the more general retrenchment of writers and academics from the public sphere since the Sartrian era. The detrimental consequences of this phenomenon are easy enough to demonstrate. Even if they sometimes fell short of their ambitions, successive generations of French intellectuals in the twentieth century could at least be counted on to alert the public to specific causes (such as the rise of fascism), to broaden the horizons of the nation's leaders (for example, on the issue of decolonization), and to denounce the most egregious shortcomings of French political elites (their vanity and cynicism, their self-centered focus on their own interests, and sometimes their corruption). In the latter context, there has perhaps been no greater failure over the past decade than the collective inability of the intellectual class to confront the rise of the National Front and the growing dissemination of its ideas among the French people—a silence all the more remarkable as, throughout their history, and notably during the Dreyfus Affair, French intellectuals were at the forefront of the battle against racism and xenophobia. It is a measure of the disorientation of the nation's intellectual and cultural elites on this issue that some progressive figures now openly admit their fascination with Jean-Marie Le Pen.[50]

Their abandonment of the public sphere has also facilitated the occupation of the terrain by second-order writers and essayists. In 2010, a poll for the weekly magazine *Marianne* found that the best-known intellectual in France was Bernard-Henri Lévy: he was familiar to 82 percent of the respondents. In terms of influence, he was preceded by the feminist author Élisabeth Badinter and the economist Jacques Attali—figures whose works are mainly derivative and are little known beyond French borders. Little wonder that, in the thirtieth-anniversary issue of *Le Débat*, the historian Pierre Nora concluded that Gallic intellectual life had taken a severe downward turn: France had now become a land of the "shrinking of horizons, the atomization of the life of the mind, [and] national provincialism." Next we turn to the vicissitudes of French thinking in the contemporary era, beginning with the place of history in the national culture and political imagination.[51]

CHAPTER 9

The End of History

On the evening of February 22, 1825, Paul-François Dubois, one of the founders of the progressive review *Le Globe*, welcomed guests to his Parisian home. They had come to hear a reading of a new play by Charles de Rémusat, a young intellectual who had recently joined the *Globe*'s staff. Set on a sugarcane plantation in one of France's most prosperous colonial possessions, *L'Habitation de Saint-Domingue, ou L'Insurrection* (*The Saint-Domingue Plantation; Or, The Insurrection*) was a dramatization of the August 1791 slave revolt that eventually led to the island's independence.[1]

Rémusat painted a powerful portrait of French colonial society in the late eighteenth century and the passions that tore it apart in the aftermath of the French Revolution: greed, fear, lust, hatred, and vengeance. He dwelled on the selfishness of the white settler elite, represented by the plantation owner Boistier de Valombre; the physical exploitation and sexual domination of the slaves, abetted by the complicity of the local clergy and the colored population; and the bravery of the rebels, symbolized by their charismatic leader, Timur, who rallies the slaves to overthrow their oppressors and reclaim their freedom. Yet, despite Rémusat's sympathy for the slaves, there was little indulgence here in the romantic myth of the black Promethean. Although the revolt succeeds, its denouement is tragic: in the final act the liberated slaves challenge Timur's authority and reject his injunction to show mercy to their white captives, the priest and Valombre's son and daughter. Their deaths provoke the disenchantment of the rebel leader, who tells his troops, "Since you have become free, you are no better than your former white masters."[2]

L'Habitation de Saint-Domingue was one of the earliest examples of a genre destined to a great literary future in France: historical fiction. Prompted by the acclaim that greeted the *oeuvres* of Walter Scott and Fenimore Cooper, French writers sought to give greater realism and dramatic depth to their characters by placing them in authentic historical settings: among the prototypes were Ludovic Vitet's *Les Barricades* (The barricades, 1826), a play about a popular rebellion in Paris in May 1588 during the Wars of Religion; Alfred de Vigny's *Cinq Mars* (March fifth, 1828), the tragic story of an idealistic seventeenth-century nobleman caught in the cynicism of the *ancien régime*; Honoré de Balzac's *Les Chouans* (*The Chouans*, 1829), a love story set against the backdrop of the royalist uprising in Brittany in 1799; and Victor Hugo's epic *Notre-Dame de Paris* (*Notre-Dame of Paris*, 1831), a rambunctious evocation of life in fifteenth-century Paris.

The novelty of these works lay in their meticulous attention to detail, their avoidance of classical rhetorical conventions, their engagement with general interests and collective passions rather than introspective emotions, and their projection of current concerns and values into the past. Rémusat's drama was particularly significant in the last respect, for behind his portrayal of the slave revolt of 1791 lurked the wider theme of the French Revolution. The play underscored the capacity of revolution to shape the destinies of different social groups, subliminally and extravagantly (even the plantation owners in the play admire Rousseau, so much so that they name one of their slaves Jean-Jacques). Rémusat also highlighted the Revolution's creative and destructive force—the slaves' revolt against Timur was an obvious allegory of the radicalization of events in France after 1792. And behind all of this lay a stark message pointedly aimed at the nation's ultra-royalist rulers: the failure to introduce timely reforms would inevitably lead to violent revolutions. History, in short, was at least as much concerned with reshaping the present as with recapturing the events of the past.

Steeped in History

The Restoration era, which began in 1815 with the return of the Bourbon monarchy after Napoleon's defeat at the Battle of Waterloo, was obsessed with the past. Observing the proliferation of historical works of all kinds in the 1820s, Augustin Thierry prophesied that "history would constitute the mark of the nineteenth century, as philosophy had been that of the eighteenth." Commenting on this wave of collective enthusiasm a few years later, François-René de Chateaubriand observed, "The times we live in are so steeped in history that they leave an abiding imprint on every kind of intellectual activity. Everything today takes a historical form: polemics, theater, novels, poetry." This fervor was not limited to the artistic world. Newspapers and reviews commented extensively on historical matters, and history found a more prominent place than previously in the education curriculum, with the appearance of the first history textbooks. François Guizot gathered and published new documentary sources on the Middle Ages, and his lecture series on the history of French civilization at the Sorbonne in the late 1820s was one of the major intellectual landmarks of the time, attracting a large and enthusiastic audience that frequently interrupted the orator with thunderous applause.[3]

There were two related reasons for this explosion of historical activity. Common to the political traditions coming out of the post-1789 maelstrom was a sense of loss: all at once a memory of the destructive impact of these experiences, a nostalgia for an earlier era of greatness (whether monarchical, republican, or imperial), and a belief that the links between past and present had been irreversibly fractured. The embrace of history was not only a response to this disorder but also an attempt to heal it, and the cure, it was thought, lay in forging a national narrative that could "gather together the links in that chain of time, which never allows itself to be entirely broken, however violent may be the assaults made upon it," as Guizot put it. This view highlighted one of the striking characteristics of French historical writing from the outset: the historian was seen as a healer and an oracle whose function was to reveal the origins and essential continuity of the French nation as well as its ultimate destiny.[4]

What gave particular coherence to this exercise in divination was the Restoration historians' shared attachment to a tempered liberalism, which informed both their philosophical understanding of the past and their commitment to help steer France toward a constitutional monarchy ruled by enlightened elites. The first priority was to shift the focus away from monarchs, diplomatic treaties, and battles—the traditional subjects of royalist historiography. In the words of Augustin Thierry, "The history of France, such as it has been written by modern authors, is not the true history of the country, the national, the popular history. . . . [W]e still lack a history of citizens, a history of subjects, a history of the people." In a suggestive article published in 1820, Thierry sketched out this alternative narrative through the figure of "Jacques Bonhomme," the archetypal French peasant, whose quest for freedom and property ownership has been consistently frustrated by foreign invasions and state spoliation. Thierry insisted on the importance of race as a driving force in history, celebrating the Gauls as the founders of the French nation; he also held that from the Romans and Franks, through the old monarchy, and all the way to the Republic and the Empire, France's political institutions had adhered to one unswerving principle: "absolute power."[5]

A key challenge for this new narrative was to provide a satisfactory account of the French Revolution in terms of explaining its causes, justifying its course, and locating it within the broader framework of national history. François Mignet's *Histoire de la Révolution française* (*History of the French Revolution*, 1824) portrayed the overthrow of the old order through the prism of class struggles and introduced the seminal distinction between "two Revolutions": that of the middle class against the nobility between 1789 and 1791, and the popular revolution against the bourgeoisie in 1792–1795. Mignet drew heavily on the notion of necessity: the Revolution was not a fortuitous event, but an "inevitable" product of the disintegration of the *ancien régime*. By referring to the "irresistible power" of its successive phases, and observing that "when a society is shaken in its foundations, it is the boldest men who triumph," he provoked heated debates across all shades of opinion for decades to come about the Terror.[6]

The apogee of this new historical school was achieved in the writings of François Guizot. In his series of works on European and French civilization published in the 1820s, Guizot refined Mignet's vision by singling out the distinctive features of the French national tradition: freedom of thought, rationalism, and moral individualism—principles he traced back to Descartes. He added, for good measure, that all the great ideals of European civilization had come through France:

> France has been the centre, the focus of European civilization. . . . And not only has this been the peculiar fortune of France, but we have seen that when the civilizing ideas and institutions which have taken their rise in other lands have sought to extend their sphere, to become fertile and general, to operate for the common benefit of European civilization, they have been necessitated to undergo, to a certain extent, a new preparation in France; and it has been from France, as from a second native country, that they have gone forth to the conquest of Europe. There is scarcely any great idea, any great principle of civilization which, prior to its diffusion, has not passed in this way through France.[7]

Most fundamentally, Guizot identified the bourgeoisie as the driving force of social progress and national unification, as much for its capacity for hard work as for its secular struggle against feudalism. The full meaning of 1789 was thus brought to light: the overthrow of the old order was the conclusion of a "terrible but legitimate struggle between right and privilege, between freedom and despotism." Guizot thus concluded that, in its final incarnation as the Third Estate, the bourgeoisie had been the "most active and most decisive agent of French civilization."[8]

After the downfall of the Bourbon royalists in the 1830 Revolution, which he compared to England's Glorious Revolution of 1688, Guizot became one of the dominant figures in Louis Philippe's constitutional monarchy, serving as minister of education, foreign minister, and, eventually, prime minister. However, his confident faith in the liberal ideal of the sovereignty of reason proved short-lived. By the time his beloved regime was overthrown in 1848, everyone had turned against him—and not just his fellow humans: when insurgents burst into the Tuileries Palace, they found a parrot that was chanting, "Down with Guizot!" The prophetic liberal narrative therefore needed to be adjusted, not least to explain why the irresistible élan of the Revolution had failed to produce a stable bourgeois order.[9]

In his twenty-volume *Histoire du consulat et de l'Empire* (*History of the Consulate, and Empire of Napoleon*), Adolphe Thiers underlined the significance of the Napoleonic era. He offered a compelling portrait of the dualism in the emperor's reign: on the one hand, Napoleon was a pacifier and reforming civilian ruler whose providential leadership helped rescue the Revolution from itself and establish solid foundations for the modern French state; on the other, he was a warrior and despot who "took no note either of men or of nature," and eventually led France into a cycle of destructive wars with the rest of Europe. Yet, for Thiers, these conflicting impulses between civil equality and despotism were merely reflections of the contradictions of 1789: "It was the French Revolution that was delirious in Napoleon, in his vast genius."[10]

An even more pessimistic hypothesis was floated in Alexis de Tocqueville's *L'Ancien Régime et la Révolution* (*The Ancien Regime and the Revolution*). Tocqueville argued that in the two centuries preceding 1789, the old order set in train two contradictory processes that finally led to its downfall: first, the accentuation of political inequality among social groups (notably, between the nobility and the bourgeoisie, and between the peasantry and all other classes); and, second, the replacement of the diversity of provincial juridical orders with a uniform administrative-hierarchy under the absolute monarchy. The singular characteristic of the late *ancien régime* was thus the emergence of an all-powerful state bureaucracy, which paved the way for the centralized despotism of the Revolution and Empire. Through this continuity argument, Tocqueville blurred the antithesis between the pre- and post-1789 eras while at the same time ascribing France's subsequent constitutional instability to the political culture created by the revolutionaries—a deadly combination of egalitarian passion and a cult of authority.[11]

From its very inception, historical writing in France typified many of the wider characteristics of French thought: a penchant for grand theorizing (this was the hallmark of Guizot's work, as well as Tocqueville's); the idealization of a particular group perceived to represent the highest expression of French culture (here, the bourgeoisie); and a style that was both cerebral and literary, and which, at its best, could reach out to substantial audiences. (Thiers's *Histoire* sold more than a million copies, earning the author the unofficial, but all the more prestigious, designation as France's "national historian.") Also notable was the sense of intellectual ambition. The liberal historical school's primary objectives were to integrate France's revolutionary past with the eras that preceded it and to initiate the search for a new national narrative.[12]

And these historians did not simply engage in storytelling: they immersed themselves in archival sources. Tocqueville honed his argument about centralization by drawing on reports of *ancien régime* provincial functionaries in the National Archives; Thiers, likewise, consulted archives, such as the 30,000 files that made up the Napoleonic records. At the same time, the school's intellectual cohesion was facilitated by the fact that its leading figures were affiliated with the Académie Française, the bastion of conservative liberalism in nineteenth-century France: Thiers was elected in 1833, Guizot in 1836, Tocqueville in 1841, and Rémusat in 1846. These historians were all actively involved in promoting various shades of the liberal cause, and they sought to provide an account of modern French history that was congruent with their ideals and their prejudices—notably, against the idea of popular sovereignty. Their most lasting contribution in the latter respect was their representation of the French people as a "vile multitude" (Thiers): an irrational and fickle collectivity prone to despotism. Hence this portrait of his compatriots by Tocqueville, in which his exasperation is compounded by a sense of aristocratic resentment against the lower orders: "insubordinate by temperament, and always readier to accept the arbitrary and even violent empire of a prince than the free and orderly government of its leading citizens; today the declared enemy of all obedience, tomorrow attached to servitude with a kind of passion that the nations best endowed for servitude cannot match; led on a string so long as no one resists, but ungovernable as long as the example of resistance appears somewhere."[13]

Republican Visions

In April 1832, the case of a thirty-four-year-old Robespierrist schoolteacher named Albert Laponneraye was brought to trial in Paris. He had been arrested a few months earlier and detained at the prison of Sainte-Pélagie. His crime, according to the state prosecutor, was to have organized a course of free public lectures on modern French history for workers, during which he preached "subversive" doctrines against the nation's monarchical rulers and "hatred" of the bourgeoisie. Following his arrest, the authorities had closed down the building where the lectures were held, seized all his course handouts, and withdrawn his certification as a teacher. Speaking in his own defense, Laponneraye declared that his principal motivation was his "love" of his compatriots and his desire to "improve the condition of the working class through education." The primary purpose of his "popular chair" was to demonstrate that, since the French Revolution, all societies were moving toward the "destruction of the monarchical principle" and the "achievement of popular sovereignty." Laponneraye concluded that his lectures opened the door to a new type of history: one that was not merely a recitation of events and dates, but "a reasoned history, a moral history, a philosophical history."[14]

Laponneraye's defiant words symbolized the beginnings of a new tradition in French historical writing that was inspired by republican ideals. While sharing the liberal school's aim to integrate the events of 1789 into the wider framework of national history, it had a much more robust appreciation of the Revolution's nature and trajectory, as well as its implications for France's sense of its collective self. Above all, it believed that, beyond his remit to understand and make intelligible the past, the historian had a particular vocation: to educate the citizenry.

The man who became the supreme model of this pedagogical conception of history was Jules Michelet, France's greatest modern historian. Michelet had much in common with Laponneraye: he, too, came from a modest background (his father was a master printer), and he also later lost his official positions (notably, his chair at the Collège de France) for refusing to abjure his republican creed. What gave particular force to Michelet's vision was a belief in his singular mission: to be "the link between past and present." Even by the standards of his age, Michelet's output was staggering: his collected works ran to forty volumes, which included seventeen tomes on the history of France and seven on the Revolution.[15]

But his major contribution lay in his transformation of the very horizon of the past. Michelet believed that the historian was a giver of life and that it was his duty to resurrect the past in all its dimensions—individual and collective, material and spiritual, human and natural. The range of subjects he covered was remarkable: he wrote about Vico and Luther, about medieval codes of justice and love, Jesuits and sorcery, insects and mountains, the Roman republics and the martyrdom of Poland. In this relentless search for the *pensée commune* of previous epochs, he was the first historian to dwell on the symbolic dimension of collective life (according to Heinrich Heine, he was known during his lifetime as "Monsieur Symbole"). He stressed the importance of understanding societies not only through their "rational" forms of consciousness but also through their anthropology—their beliefs, rituals, and myths. In *La Sorcière* (*The Sorceress*, 1862), his pioneering book on medieval witchcraft, Michelet thus presented medieval sorcery as a popular rebellion against the oppressive order of feudalism and the Catholic Church.[16]

The leitmotif in Michelet's *oeuvre* was his quest to demonstrate that the principal actor in French history had been the "people": from the Crusades through the Reformation to the Revolution, the masses had critically determined the nation's fate. The medieval greatness of the Catholic Church corresponded to the moment when it was at its most democratic; its subsequent decline was the product of its drift toward despotism. The French monarchy likewise rested on the masses—in this case, their acceptance of the king as the embodiment of "national identity" (an anachronism Michelet assumed with aplomb); even the survival of the worst rulers, such as Charles VI, was possible only because of the people's sympathy for their deranged king. Michelet rejected Thierry's emphasis on race, as well as the "fatalism" of the Guizot school. His concept of the French people was essentially spiritual, in the Rousseauist tradition: the French were a living, self-conscious collectivity animated by sociability, compassion, and love.[17]

This representation of the collective ideals of the French people culminated in Michelet's portrayal of the French Revolution. The accounts of his fellow republicans glorified particular aspects of the phenomenon (its Girondist leadership, its Jacobin virtues, or its egalitarian or Christian inspirations, for example), but Michelet identified the true greatness of 1789 in the humanism of the people and their creative and often spontaneous involvement in public life. The heroic figures of the Revolution, such as Jean-Paul Marat, Georges Danton, and Camille Desmoulins, stood out because they spoke for the people, as had Joan of Arc centuries earlier. The major political and administrative reforms enacted in the aftermath of 1789 reflected collective popular aspirations for equality and justice; similarly, the coming together of provincial federations on July 14, 1790, into one collective entity, united by a commitment to the common good, symbolized the French people's sense of community. This was "the epoch of unanimity, the holy epoch when the whole nation, free from distinctions of party and scarcely knowing opposition between classes, marched together under the flag of fraternity." And although this national unity was short-lived, Michelet affirmed that it would remain "the ideal toward which we shall always tend."[18]

Michelet's influence on French historical writing was pervasive, particularly among progressives. His belief that knowledge of the past could be a force for positive change inspired a more robust form of historical writing. A century before Sartre articulated his notion of *engagement*, republican intellectuals produced histories of their epochs that sought to challenge the legitimacy of France's monarchical rulers. Louis Blanc's *Histoire de dix ans* (*The History of Ten Years*, 1841–1844), Victor Hugo's *Napoléon le petit* (*Napoleon the Little*, 1852), and Taxile Delord's *Histoire du Second Empire* (*History of the Second Empire*, 1869), for example, all aimed to show that monarchical regimes were contrary to the nation's collective ideals. In the concluding pages of *Histoire de dix ans*, Blanc condemned the "bourgeois" rulers of the July Monarchy for their narrow and self-interested conception of politics, before adding, "The bourgeoisie could integrate into the nation by acquiring from the people the virtues it lacks: a sense of energy, the strength of male instincts, the taste for grandeur and an aptitude for public-spiritedness." After describing the events leading to Louis Napoléon's overthrow of the Second Republic in 1851, Hugo concluded defiantly, "This century proclaims the sovereignty of the citizen and the inviolability of life: it has crowned the collectivity and consecrated humanity." Delord's first volume was published in 1869; in it he began with the observation that he had fought the restoration of the empire, and he hoped his work would inspire the continuing popular struggle against its institutions. Mankind, as Michelet had affirmed, was its own Prometheus.[19]

Republican writers also followed Michelet's lead in writing "popular" histories that gave pride of place to the perspectives of the common people. Louis-Antoine Garnier-Pagès's authoritative account of the 1848 Revolution was based on more than a thousand testimonies from direct participants in the events, including members of the National Guard, workers, and ordinary citizens. Writing "popular" history also involved denouncing the past injustices against supporters of the Republic, such as the White Terror of 1815; recounting tales of individual heroism, as during the Revolution of 1830; and identifying the civilian victims of the murderous repression that followed Louis Napoléon's 1851 *coup d'état* in Paris—among them ordinary women such as Françoise Noël, a seamstress; a Mademoiselle Grellier, a housekeeper; and a Mademoiselle Simas, a shop attendant.[20]

It was imperative, in keeping with the principles of republican pedagogy, that such narratives be made accessible to as broad an audience as possible: hence, as noted by the historian Prosper Lissagaray, the need to produce "short and elementary treatises that are as complete and concise as possible, easy to understand, easy to memorize"; he likened these works to a "civic catechism destined for our brothers in towns and in the countryside." This proselytizing conception of history was reflected in the 1870s in the output of the Société d'Instruction Républicaine (Society for Republican Education), whose pamphlets were aimed at destroying the luster of royalism and imperialism and fortifying the appeal of the Republic among rural voters. The figure of Jacques Bonhomme was thus resurrected to remind the French peasant of his oppression under the *ancien régime* and his cynical manipulation by the Napoleonic empires. Fortunately, change was on its way: as a republican pamphleteer put it, Jacques Bonhomme "had now resolved not to accept dictatorships, *coup d'états*, insurrections, revolutions or restorations. . . . [H]e is beginning to embrace the Republic." Republican history, in this respect, was no less ideological than the liberal tradition that had preceded it.[21]

This pedagogical narrative of the past reached its zenith during the second half of the nineteenth century. Following the lead of Napoleon III, who commissioned a statue of Vercingétorix (the ancient tribal leader who had led the revolt against Rome) at the site of the Battle of Alesia in 52 BC (with the chieftain's features bearing an uncanny resemblance to the emperor in his youth), the Third Republic celebrated the Gauls as the founders of the French nation with a wave of monuments across the country. They also made frequent use of the expression *nos ancêtres les gaulois* (our ancestors the Gauls). The principal advantage of these hardy tribesmen, at a time of growing hostility toward Germany, was that their origins were not Teutonic.[22]

In most respects, this era marked a triumph of Michelet's vision of the French collectivity: such was its breadth that it was embraced across a wide spectrum of republicans, from conservatives to socialists. Renan's definition of the nation as a "spiritual principle" in his 1882 lecture was directly inspired by Michelet, whose lectures he had faithfully attended three decades earlier. The choice, in 1880, of July 14 as France's national holiday was a tribute to Michelet's insistence on the importance of mythology in shaping collective consciousness and his depiction of the celebration of the 1790 festival of the Federation as the defining ideal of republican national unity. Socialists, too, viewed the essence of the French spirit through their readings of Michelet: alongside Plutarch and Marx, the republican pedagogue was the inspiration behind Jaurès's socialist history of the French Revolution (1901–1907), which celebrated the proletariat as the modern fulfillment of its true ideals.[23]

As a mode of thought, republican history shared a number of features with its liberal predecessors. It had a similar sense of mission (but expressed it somewhat more forcefully), and the same underlying claim to be speaking in the name of a wider community (in this case, the "people"). At the same time, its intellectual horizons were undeniably broader. In its sheer scale and ambition, Michelet's grand theorizing surpassed the works produced by even the most innovative liberals, both in terms of the prodigious range of its subject matter and its conception of the historian's vocation as a national educator. Through his emphasis on the role of imagination and mythology and his powerful rhetorical style, Michelet carried the literary quality of French history to new heights.

Republican history also brought forward—and brought to fruition—the task of elaborating a cohesive national narrative. This synthesizing process had advantages, but also drawbacks, as evidenced by the works of Ernest Lavisse. Under the Third Republic, his school manuals propagated an ecumenical and sanitized vision of the *roman national*: they represented the French as a patriotic collectivity forged by the best of the monarchical and revolutionary traditions, united in its cult of great popular heroes such as Joan of Arc, capable of great scientific achievements, and inspiring the world through its ideals of progress. Lavisse did not dwell on awkward episodes such as slavery, and passed over abolition in silence; in keeping with the reorientation of republican ideology under the Third Republic, he also celebrated France's colonial expansion in glowing terms, praising the feats of the military and the "benevolence and generosity of the French for the people they have subjugated."[24]

A More Scientific History

One of the best-selling—and most controversial—works of the early 1860s was Ernest Renan's *Vie de Jésus* (*Life of Jesus*). A year after its publication, it had reached its thirteenth edition, and it sold over 100,000 copies. The book's success stemmed from the author's willingness to venture onto terrain normally occupied by theologians rather than historians, and for his denial of any supernatural quality to the life of Christ. For this was not an edifying tale of miracles, revelations, or divine interventions, but a biography of an extraordinary person, narrated from a purely historical standpoint. Renan's Jesus was a man who became disillusioned with his Jewish faith, and whose remarkably idealistic and selfless life had attained such sublimity that it fostered a religious creed that permanently changed the face of the world. To the dismay of the Catholic Church, Renan affirmed that Christ was not a sage, a moralist, or a saint, but a charismatic, inspirational figure—a leader of men, not the Son of God.[25]

In its secularization of one of the most sacred figures in human history, Renan's approach marked the beginnings of a transition in the role of the historian: after the prophet and pedagogue, now beckoned the age of the scientist. As we saw in Chapter 4, Renan's assertion that only science could provide the real foundations of human knowledge reflected the dominant thinking of his positivist generation. Science was the highest form of praise: appointed to the first chair in the history of the French Revolution, which was established at the Sorbonne in 1885, the historian Alphonse Aulard was credited by one of his admirers (with some exaggeration) with creating "a scientific and impartial history of the Revolution." One of the prominent figures of the so-called *école méthodique*, Gabriel Monod, affirmed in the opening issue of the *Revue historique* that "our journal will be a compendium of positive science." Under the influence of Charles-Victor Langlois and Charles Seignobos, history at this time became the privileged domain of a specialized profession that was based in universities, with distinct methodological rules and practical codes that covered the publication of journals, the careful use of sources, the avoidance of rhetoric, and the nominal pursuit of "objectivity."[26]

This positivist historiography paid lip service to the ideal of a history cleansed of "metaphysics," but it did not represent a complete intellectual or methodological break from tradition—not least because its vision of the past continued to be influenced by ideological considerations, and because it remained wedded to the republican belief that history should help educate the citizenry and foster a sense of collective identity. (A notable example was the *Introduction aux études historiques* [*Introduction to the Study of History*], published by Seignobos and Langlois in 1897.) The most significant attempt at rupture in both respects came in 1929, when Marc Bloch and Lucien Febvre created a review that launched a new school of historical writing that would dominate the field for the next three generations: the *Annales*.[27]

The founders of the Annales movement rejected the pedagogical and nation-oriented narrative histories that had become dominant in French university circles and that found expression in the works of the positivist tradition. With the bluntness of the revisionist leading the charge against bastions of orthodoxy, Febvre opined that "a history that serves is a servile history." The quest to trace the "origins" of France was likewise rejected as anachronistic and for being based on the false underlying assumption of an "immutable" national psychology. The general objectives of the Annalists included focusing on economic and social problems rather than narratives; producing a "total" history that treated the whole range of human activities, rather than just political or elite history; and breaking down disciplinary barriers by locating historical research in the wider framework of the social sciences.[28]

The *Annales* marked a significant reorientation in the focus of French historians. Indeed, France itself ceased to be the privileged focus of analysis. Fernand Braudel's colossal three-volume work on the Mediterranean in the sixteenth century sought to depict the material culture of southern European life across nations, economic systems, and class structures: its strength lay in its panoramic view, its focus away from individuals and political institutions, and its attempt to uncover the deep structures that influenced historical change, such as geography, climate, trade, and migration. (Perhaps the most remarkable aspect of the book was that it was drafted during Braudel's internment in a German prisoner-of-war camp; although he was able to use a local library, he worked mostly from memory.) Between 1965 and 1984, fewer than a third of the articles published in the *Annales* were concerned with France. Braudel also innovated by introducing different notions of time: individual (short run), social (medium term), and geographical—with geographical time operating over what he would later define as the *longue durée*. In keeping with its scientific ambitions, *Annales* history became increasingly quantitative, notably in the works of Ernest Labrousse, whose studies on the history of prices in the eighteenth century shed new light on the economic origins of the French Revolution.[29]

In its creativity, its refreshing departure from the blandness and conformism of republican approaches, and its theoretical sophistication, as illustrated by its bold search for a "total" account of human history, the Annales movement typified the capacity for innovation in French thought—and its yearning for universality. Yet there was something wonderfully paradoxical, too, about the enterprise: its refusal to treat elite or institutional history seriously meant that it had little to say about the vicissitudes of modern French politics in the nineteenth and twentieth centuries or its penchant for ideological upheaval and regime change. This blind spot underscored the importance of a French phenomenon that the Annalists consistently undervalued: the relative autonomy of the political sphere. And yet the "dust" of events that Marc Bloch and Lucien Febvre so derided came back to haunt them tragically during World War II. The attachment to the nation, and the practical implications of citizenship, confronted both men dramatically. In his memoir, written after the defeat of France in 1940, Bloch insisted on his "cult of patriotic traditions" and the resolute attachment to France of successive generations of his Jewish-Alsatian family from the late eighteenth century onward: "France," he wrote, "will remain the fatherland which will never be uprooted from my heart."[30]

This affirmation was a response to the Vichy regime's anti-Semitism, further manifested in its "Aryanization" policy, which provoked a painful disagreement between Bloch and Febvre: in order to continue the publication of their journal, Febvre was prepared to remove Bloch's name as one of the journal's editors. Bloch joined the Resistance, and he was eventually captured and executed by the Germans in June 1944. Although Febvre did not play an active role in the Resistance—and perhaps because of this—his wartime lectures at the Collège de France (on Michelet and the Renaissance) were peppered with contemporary allusions to patriotism. He defined freedom, for example, as "not a law that is imposed from outside: the truly free man carries it within him." In the years after the Liberation, he gave two lecture series on *Honneur et patrie*.[31]

In the postwar decades, these contradictions became even more glaring. A movement that rejected the importance of individuals—"history makes men and shapes their destiny," affirmed Braudel imperiously at his inaugural lecture at the Collège de France in 1950—rapidly became dominated by a small group of forceful figures, including Febvre (who died in 1956) and Braudel himself. An approach that sought to open history to wider intellectual influences became increasingly insular, hampered by its "scientific" jargon and its proclivity to see religious and sexual metaphors everywhere. (François Furet and Denis Richet, for example, thought they had made a triumphant discovery when they identified the typical weapon of the revolutionary *sans-culottes*, the pike, as "an old symbol of sexual origins.")[32]

The laudable ambition of bringing back a "critical" dimension to history was progressively superseded by the professional imperatives of institution-building. As the Annales school established itself as a hegemonic force in the École Pratique in Paris, and then, from 1975, in the École des Hautes Études en Sciences Sociales, it paradoxically became something of an orthodoxy—and as such, it became increasingly vulnerable to sclerosis. In the euphemistic analysis of Pierre Bourdieu, "The gap began to grow between the level of aspiration and the level of accomplishment." The preoccupation with the nation was also more than subliminally apparent in the Annalists' concentration on the history of the "common man"—they exhibited a populist ideological preference that reflected their founders' encounter with fascism as well as their engagement with Marxist theory. The idea of the nation informed the particular rural bias of the Annalists as well. The articles on France in the journal emphasized historical geography and the culture of the peasantry. It was no coincidence that this exhumation of the splendors of Gallic rural life occurred precisely at the moment when France was undergoing a process of rapid industrialization, which was accompanied by depopulation of the countryside. The journal was thus in a very real sense an exercise in national nostalgia, an expression of the "heartbreak" many of the French were feeling over the loss of rural traditions and traits, such as stoicism, wisdom, and rootedness, that had been shaken by France's "Thirty Glorious Years" of growth and economic prosperity.[33]

This trend continued with later generations of Annales historians, who produced studies of collective beliefs, or *mentalités*. The genre began in 1924 with Marc Bloch's study of *The Royal Touch* (about the popular belief in the magical healing powers of the king) and was revived in the 1970s with the writings of the "new historians." It culminated in Emmanuel Le Roy Ladurie's *Montaillou* (1975), a captivating study of a village in Ariège in the Middle

Ages. Drawing on the register of interrogations of the local inquisitor Jacques Fournier, Le Roy Ladurie vividly reconstructed the lives of the heretic villagers—their religious practices and social rituals, their joys and sorrows, their conceptions of death and the afterlife, and their notions of love and sexuality. *Montaillou* became an instant best-seller, not least because of its memorable cast of characters, including the smiling shepherd Pierre Maury, the sensuous noblewoman Béatrice de Planissoles, and the libidinous priest Pierre Clergue with his plethora of mistresses. The archives of the Inquisition thus confirmed Renan's hunch: charisma was central to Christianity.[34]

The Return of the Agent

The year 1958 was marked by two apparently unconnected events: the publication of Louis Aragon's monumental *La Semaine sainte* (*Holy Week*), one of the classic historical novels of modern French literature, and the return to power of General de Gaulle; the first two volumes of his *Mémoires de guerre* (*War Memoirs*) had been triumphantly received a few years earlier. Yet despite their political differences—the communist Aragon was vehemently opposed to de Gaulle's attempt to create a new presidential Republic—both men vigorously pushed back against the Braudelian view of history as a complex structure that was ultimately unintelligible to individuals and impervious to their designs.

Aragon's epic novel was set over a seven-day period in late March 1815, as news of Napoleon's return from Elba reached France, and King Louis XVIII fled to Belgium with his entourage. Although the main character was the painter Théodore Géricault, who rallied to the monarch and joined the military staff of the Maison du Roi, the real heroes of the novel were the multitudes who made up the French nation—the soldiers, peasants, village girls, and bourgeois conspirators who struggled to make sense of events and yet all participated in "making history." In this magnificent fresco of a society torn apart by the chaos of war (echoes of the 1940 debacle resonated throughout the narrative), Aragon evoked the extremes to which people could be driven by their love for their country (Marshal Berthier commits suicide) as well as the challenges of loyalty and betrayal. There is no real political conclusion to the novel; Aragon's central message was instead a reaffirmation of his humanist creed, which asserted that there was no fatalism in history, and that destinies could be decisively shaped by individual choices: "Men and women are not only the bearers of the past, the inheritors of a world, they are also the seeds of the future." The novel thus ends with Géricault's decision to abandon the monarchist camp and devote himself to his true calling—his vocation as an artist.[35]

The novel captured the first great fissure in the French communist intellectuals' vision of history in the era of de-Stalinization. Just as *La Semaine sainte* was published, many of the men and women who would later become the leading historians of their generation—Emmanuel Le Roy Ladurie, Mona Ozouf, François Furet—were abandoning the Communist Party and assuming the risk of living outside of "history." Fortunately, the French faith in the intelligibility of the world was reaffirmed by Charles de Gaulle's *Mémoires de guerre*, which emphatically rejected Braudel's claim that history was not made by individuals. De Gaulle narrated the epic tale of his leadership of the French Resistance, from the devastating defeat of 1940 to the Liberation in 1944. The general assumed the mission of "taking responsibility for France," which extended to shaping his compatriots' *mentalités*; it was his goal "to lead the French by the imagination."[36]

The publication of the first two volumes was the defining literary event of the mid-1950s and played a substantial role in bringing the general back to power in 1958. But the intellectual significance of the *Mémoires de guerre* ran far deeper. By sketching out his *certaine idée de la France* and presenting himself as the sole incarnation of its political legitimacy, de Gaulle reclaimed the *roman national* that had been cast aside by the Annalists, and in so doing brought the focus of historical thought back to what he believed was its rightful place: France (and himself). The Gaullian vision of Frenchness was all at once a heroic representation of the recent past, a restatement of the historical continuity of *la France éternelle*, and a program of national regeneration for the future.

The transformative power of de Gaulle's vision of the past rested on its fusion of two genres: the war memoir, which was one of the principal ways in which the experiences of the two world wars were conveyed to the French public, and "state memoirs," which, from Louis XIV through Napoleon, celebrated successive "epiphanies of the nation" in the modern age, from the absolute monarchy to the revolutionary heritage and the advent of the democratic and republican state. What was remarkable about de Gaulle was his claim to represent the fusion, in his person, of all these elements: he was, in the manner of the old kings, the symbol of "something primordial, permanent and necessary"; he single-handedly represented the authority of the state and was capable of restoring it by virtue of his presence. And despite the cackling of all those around him (notably, the communists) who claimed to embody the revolutionary ideal, it was he, de Gaulle, who was the real bearer of radical change: "I asked myself if, among all those who were speaking of revolution, I was not the true revolutionary," he wrote.[37]

The republican moment came in the emotional climax of the *Mémoires*, at the end of the second volume, with the description of de Gaulle's triumphant march down the Champs-Élysées in August 1944. After invoking the past heroes of France, from Jeanne d'Arc and *ancien régime* monarchs to Napoleon and Clemenceau, de Gaulle likened the spectacle of the 2 million men and women assembled to celebrate the Liberation to a "miracle of national conscience," before concluding, "In this community, which is just one thought, one drive, one expression, differences are eliminated, individuals disappear." In its lyrical vision of the spontaneous coming together of the French people and its sense of foreboding about the ephemeral quality of this unity, this passage harked back to Michelet's depiction of the 1790 festival of the Federation. It also underscored the Gaullian ideal of democracy: unanimous agreement with de Gaulle's views.[38]

The *Mémoires* were also the centrepiece in the emergence of a dominant French narrative about the events of the 1940–1944 period, which revolved around what the historian Henry Rousso described as the "myth of resistantialism." De Gaulle was not its sole architect: it was embraced and propagated by all the components of the resistance in the postwar decades, from conservatives to communists. But it was de Gaulle who, through his words and deeds, gave this myth its most powerful rendering. The main elements of this narrative were, first, the marginalization of the Vichy episode (in the *Mémoires*, de Gaulle observed—speciously—that the regime had had no legal basis); second, the celebration of "the Resistance" as a unified activity, with its specific sites, martyrs, and heroic episodes (the most significant of which, in de Gaulle's eyes, was his Appeal of June 18, 1940, which he describes as a moment of rebirth); and, last but not least, the assimilation of the Resistance by the whole of the nation. This reinvention of the French as a "nation of resisters" was de Gaulle's most enduring legacy. It transformed the Lavissian ideal of French greatness (a satisfied, status-quo colonial power) into a new myth of Gaullian *grandeur* depicting France as a proud, resourceful, and generous nation. It had once again succeeded in defining itself on its own terms through struggle against injustice and oppression, following a pattern that had begun with Vercingétorix (whom de Gaulle called "the first resistant of our race"). Showing the impressive breadth of his metaphorical repertoire, de Gaulle also compared himself, toward the end of his life, to the comic-strip hero Tintin, remarking, "We are the small folk who do not let ourselves be bullied by the big guys."[39]

The Age of Memory

De Gaulle's greatest fear, which he devoted his life to exorcising, was that the French nation's historical destiny would be extinguished. And suddenly, from the late 1980s, the nightmare seemed to become a terrifying reality. The ideological retrenchment of the Left in France, followed by the collapse of communism across Europe, marked the end of the long cycle of historical optimism initiated in the 1820s—a dream that had been successively carried by progressive prophets, republican pedagogues, and Marxist eschatologists. The celebration of the bicentenary of the French Revolution in 1989 was a grandiose farewell to the "revolutionary catechism" that had captured the imagination of so many generations of French men and women. Referring explicitly to the 1880s, but no doubt looking ahead to the new age of consensus he hoped for, François Furet concluded that the Revolution had reached its final berth.[40]

More or less at the same moment, the Gaullo-communist heroic narrative of the "nation of resisters" imploded. Through the combined effects of new historical research, led by the American historian Robert Paxton's groundbreaking work, prosecutions of Vichy henchmen for "crimes against humanity," and revelations about the Vichyist sympathies of leading public figures (notably, François Mitterrand), the French took on the full measure of the sordid realities of collaboration and the complexity of the history of the Resistance. Shortly after his election to the presidency in 1995, Jacques Chirac publicly apologized for the French state's active participation in the deportation of thousands of Jews to Nazi death camps. The dismay this realization brought about soon spread to the historical profession: ground down by the sheer weight (and incoherence) of its ambitions, and punctured by sharp attacks that had been leveled against its scientistic pretensions, the remaining members of the Annales school readily acknowledged their "disorientation." With no radiant future to contemplate, and offering as its sole perspective an "eternal present," history in France was officially in "crisis."[41]

In some respects, this moment of uncertainty was a blessing; it opened new avenues for research on subjects hitherto neglected or marginalized in the academy: the Vichy era and the Second Empire, the experiences of French colonialism (for example, in Algeria), and the history of women. The political sphere, which Annalist and Marxist historiographers had long treated with barely disguised epiphenomenal contempt, regained some ground, and there was a reprise of classic objects of inquiry, such as biographies. Among the most distinguished works to emerge were Eric Roussel's life of Jean Monnet,

Grégoire Kauffmann's work on Édouard Drumont, and Annette Wieviorka's study of Maurice and Jeannette Thorez.[42]

Yet the cunning of history again revealed itself: with its almost exclusive focus on France, this reinvigorated political history marked a triumphant return of the national narrative. The concern with French singularity was thus at the heart of the historical work of Pierre Rosanvallon (whose contributions as a public intellectual were discussed in the previous chapter). Through his academic research on the "conceptual history of the political," Rosanvallon sought to isolate the distinct characteristics of the "French political model" of strong centralized governance inherited from the revolutionary era: the Rousseauist emphasis on collective sovereignty and equality, the domination of society by politics, and the suspicion of pluralism and associational activity as potential obstacles to the principle of unity. Rosanvallon's *oeuvre* thus stood as a subtle corrective to Furet's assertion that the shadow of the Revolution had receded: for Rosanvallon, the Jacobin "political culture of generality," far from being dead, remained the defining feature of the modern French polity.[43]

The decades after 1980 saw the development of cultural history, a rich and sprawling field of inquiry that emerged as the principal successor to the Annales movement. The key concept here was "representation": a displacement of the analysis away from the grand hermeneutics of "total history" toward the construction of social reality in cultural objects, symbolic codes, and collective mindsets. Alain Corbin, one of the most creative historians in this field, thus explored the history of emotional "sensibilities" across the nineteenth century, revealing a world shaped not by class affiliations, grain prices, and mortality rates, but by emotions, sounds, smells, landscapes, and rumors. Yet even though much of this cultural history was not concerned with political questions, an underlying preoccupation with the modern republican tradition was nonetheless evident. Its research on intellectuals was dominated by the Dreyfusard framework; its history of political rituals focused primarily on republican commemorations, from the revolutionary festivals to the invention of July 14 by the Third Republic; and its history of symbolism was dominated by Maurice Agulhon's imposing trilogy on Marianne, symbol of the Republic. The French cultural turn, in short, was also something of a republican one, and nowhere was this symbiosis more apparent than in the work of Pierre Nora, whose seven-volume compendium *Lieux de mémoire* (*Realms of Memory*) reshaped the French historical landscape of the 1980s and early 1990s.[44]

Nora conceived his scheme as a retrieval of a lost heritage: the rehabilitation of France's sense of collective self, which, according to him, had been shattered by the emergence of sectional loyalties based on regional, religious, or ethnic criteria. As he explained, "What in France is now called 'the national memory' is nothing other than the transformation of historic memory which has been invaded, subverted and flooded by group memories." Monumental in its range and breadth, as well as its ambition, Nora's inventory of these realms of remembrance sought to offer nothing less than a vast reordering of France's relationship with its past. Assembled with contributions from leading historians, the collection's most outstanding pieces were the chapters on canonical French symbols, such as the Marseillaise (Michel Vovelle), the Panthéon (Mona Ozouf), and the tricolor (Raoul Girardet). Some of the chapters by Nora himself are particularly brilliant, especially his portrayal of Lavisse's role as national pedagogue and his subtle evocation of the conflictual partnership between Gaullists and communists. The collection offered a dazzling kaleidoscope of French history—the commemorations of its triumphs and tragedies; its national heroes and local emblems; its classic treatises and obscure pedagogical manuals; its landscapes and museums; its cafés and monasteries; its street names and holidays; and its territorial diversity and unifying institutions, from the state and the municipality to the Tour de France.[45]

In response to the criticism that the first two volumes had neglected the conflictual aspects of French memory, one of the later volumes was entirely devoted to the *guerres franco-françaises* that had divided the country (always, Cartesianism *oblige*, into two camps): Francs and Gauls, French and foreigners, Parisians and provincials. Yet, despite its appearance of eclecticism, there was a powerful ideological undertone to Nora's collection. Through its marginalization of alternative national narratives (radical republican, Bonapartist), its sidelining of awkward historical episodes (such as colonialism), and its overrepresentation of a particular strand of the republican tradition—the one that founded the Third Republic—*Les Lieux de mémoire* offered a new teleology to the nation: the celebration of the Republic as the unsurpassable horizon of the present, or, as the historian Perry Anderson put it, cruelly but not inaccurately, a "*union sucrée* in which the divisions and discords of French society would melt away in the fond rituals of postmodern remembrance."[46]

Notwithstanding its limitations, Nora's project to anchor memory at the heart of history was evidence, yet again, of the French capacity for intellectual originality, as well as France's insatiable love of holistic frameworks in which all the discrete elements can only be understood as part of an overarching totality (which has all the more of a *je ne sais quoi* in that Nora never really gives the reader a proper definition of "memory"). Even its critics were drawn to Nora's *oeuvre* because of its monumentalism and its sheer exuberance and panache, and it was all at once a personal, an intellectual, and a professional triumph for the author. He was elected to the Académie Française in 2001, and celebrated as the nation's "public historian." The commemoration of the past became a national obsession, chaperoned by the Ministry of Culture. Thanks to its official adoption, the concept of the *lieu de mémoire* led to the protection of more than 250 heritage sites across France. Yet this success proved to be double-edged. As one historian observed, "The wave of remembrance has invaded and submerged the terrain of history."[47]

The attempted sanctification of national memory did provoke controversy, not least in the emergence of the notion of *devoir de mémoire* (duty to remember), and the French state's repeated and often clumsy interventions in that arena. From 1990 onward, successive governments passed a series of *lois mémorielles*, criminalizing denial of the Holocaust, deploring the Armenian genocide and the slave trade, and noting the "positive" character of French colonialism. This latter edict—a throwback to the Lavissian era—produced an outcry and had to be withdrawn, but the nostalgic genie was out of the bottle. Memories of the good old days of French colonial rule were revived, notably, in Claire Denis's film *Chocolat* (1988) and Régis Wargnier's *Indochine* (1992), as well as in novels such as Annie Cohen's *Le Marabout de Blida* (1996). And if the purpose of memory was to rekindle patriotic sentiment, surely it was appropriate for the state to play a commanding role in the process. This was the thinking behind Nicolas Sarkozy's project to create a "Maison de l'Histoire de France"—a new national museum tasked with promoting patriotism and national cohesion. In December 2012, the Hollande administration finally abandoned the project, after encountering vehement opposition among the confraternity of French historians—including Nora himself.[48]

A Distinct Style

Since the early nineteenth century, French historical writing has undergone major transformations: the age of liberal prophecy gave way to that of republican pedagogy, which was itself displaced by the "scientific" concerns of the Annales movement from the mid-twentieth century onward. The movement's untidy implosion cleared the path for the consecration of the memorialist. Yet a time traveler from the 1820s and 1830s would find the preoccupations of present-day French historians disarmingly familiar. They still emphasize the nature of French collective sentiment and are just as disoriented by the absence of a meaningful horizon for the future (and the vogue for historical novels is as strong as ever, as reflected in the fact that the 2013 Goncourt Prize went to Pierre Lemaitre for his Great War saga, *Au revoir là-haut* [Farewell up there]).

The discontinuities among these different traditions, while real, should not be overstated. Liberals and republicans shared a sense that history was driven by social conflict and had an underlying progressive purpose; republicans and Annalists embraced the ideal of a history that celebrated the meaningful involvement of the masses (it was not by chance that the Annalists' favorite author was Michelet); the anthropological dimensions of contemporary cultural history were principally derived from the Annalists' concept of *mentalité*. The *Lieux de mémoire* project was a synthesis of the essential features of its predecessors, and it was forged in the spirit of the liberal and republican ambitions of the nineteenth century: to reconnect the French with their fractured past, and to revive their collective self-confidence. With the unconstrained breadth of its subject matter, it was also, *sotto voce*, an extension of the Annalists' aspiration to produce a comprehensive history that took into account the whole range of human experience. (Its scope was of course limited to France, but then this constraint, too, was a throwback to the good old days of the ideal of the *nation universelle*.) And, thanks to the ingenuity of its principal architect, *Les Lieux de mémoire* even managed to find in the nation a fitting substitute for the metaphysical entities underpinning the visions of previous historical schools: the bourgeoisie, the people, the "totality." In this sense, from the early historical novels through Michelet, the republicans right up to Pierre Nora's *oeuvre*, French history has been a continuous morality tale in which the people achieve their collective destiny by overcoming what de Gaulle called their "enduring propensity to fragment into verbose tendencies."[49]

These overlaps and commonalities of purpose are not accidental. Historical "schools" in France have been produced throughout the modern era by intellectually cohesive coteries drawn from a small cluster of Parisian elite institutions: the University of Paris, the Collège de France, the École Normale Supérieure, the Académie Française, and, more recently, the École des Hautes Études, the Maison des Sciences de l'Homme, and the Institut des Études Politiques. The close proximity of these elites to the seat of national political power influenced the horizons of historical research, both implicitly and overtly. The liberal historians' fixation with a new national narrative was driven by their quest to legitimize the post-1815 constitutional monarchies with which they directly associated. The republicans' pedagogic history, likewise, sought to translate Rousseau's axiom of popular sovereignty into history, and later to represent the post-1870 republican order as the regime that marked the culmination of the historical process. The Annales movement's concern with measurement and quantification mirrored the technocratic ambitions of the post-Liberation French state to bring "scientific" solutions to the nation's problems. As for de Gaulle, he did not even try to disguise the fact that he was writing a teleological history. The republican nostalgia that suffused *Les Lieux de mémoire* was a specific expression of a broader revival of neorepublicanism in post-1980s France. Lucien Febvre's jibe at positivist history—"a deification of the present with the help of the past"—could in this sense be applied to all the dominant strands in modern French historical writing. This intellectual connivance between historical and political elites partly explains the passion of French political figures for publishing historical works under their names—and, on occasion, even going to the trouble of writing the books themselves.[50]

All the more so as the other common feature shared by modern French historical writing is its fascination with the national self. This Gallocentric tendency was manifested in the choice of subjects treated by historians (France's origins, its physical and territorial dynamics, its external and internal wars, its cultural and spiritual characteristics, its destiny) and in the fact that, despite some significant advances in the past decade, notably in the fields of colonial and war histories, global, transnational, and comparative approaches have yet to make significant inroads into the study of French national history. But this Gallocentricity also shines through in something more fundamental, and arguably distinctly French: the idea that the past is a key ingredient in forging a sense of collective identity.[51]

This pedagogical national narrative—a logical derivation of the republican "civic" model—was provided by historians and later updated by Gaullist mythology. A recent French novel paid tribute to the general's literary talent, expressed in the construction "by the force of his verb, piece by piece, [of] everything we needed to inhabit the twentieth century. He gave us, because he invented them, our reasons to live together and be proud of ourselves." Even the Annales historians, who tried so hard to escape from the emotional logic of the *roman national,* came around to it in the end. The opening sentence of Braudel's *L'Identité de la France* (*The Identity of France*) reads as follows: "Let me start by saying once and for all that I love France with the same demanding and complicated passion as did Jules Michelet."[52]

The resilience of this patriotic theme can be explained by one overarching factor: the experience of war. For nineteenth-century historians, war and revolution were decisive moments: to take the single example of Michelet, it was in the wake of the 1830 Revolution's "huge illumination" that the great historian "caught sight of France." Braudel dated the origins of his quest to map out the French "heartland" to the French military debacle of 1940, when he was struck by the contrast between the nation's institutions, which were in danger, and the "true France, the nation in waiting behind us, which would survive." (The Gaullian undertones of this text are striking, right down to the magic date of 1940.)[53]

The same formative influence of war appears, in multiple textures, in the collection of "ego-historical" essays published by leading practitioners of the discipline in the late twentieth century—from Pierre Chaunu and Raoul Girardet, who wrote about their childhood memories of the Great War, to Georges Duby, explicating his passion for the Spanish Civil War, and Jacques Le Goff, providing an account of his sober and disabused participation in the Resistance. Even Maurice Agulhon's maternal grandmother was a devotee of Napoleon. Ahead of the centenary of the Great War, the historian Stéphane Audoin-Rouzeau, one of France's leading historians of the 1914–1918 conflict, published a remarkable memoir that combined family history (focusing on the devastating impacts of the war on the combatants), literary evocation (of the surrealist milieu frequented by his father), and historiographical reflection (on the unbridgeable gulf between his scholarly interpretation of the patriotic motivations of the combatants and the disenchanted views of his father and grandfather). The tension between Audoin-Rouzeau's yearning to reconnect the affective links with his father (and thus to continue to grieve his loss) and his concluding wish to bid "farewell" to the conflict remained unresolved.[54]

Yet it is an open question how long this inward-looking and introspective historiographical style can survive in an age when France is a less significant actor on the world stage, and where the English language has become the international medium of communication in the humanities and social sciences. Comparing the major trends in world history between the 1950s and the early twenty-first century, Jean-François Sirinelli glumly observed that the global influence of French historians has declined steadily, and that the new generations of researchers in the United States and Latin America are far less likely to read French than they were in earlier eras. To compound the problem, Sirinelli noted, the French historical confraternity is threatened by a "demographic" crisis because of the lack of availability of new posts and the crisis in funding for higher education in France. French history, he dramatically concluded, is faced with the prospect of "necrosis." As we shall observe in Chapter 10, this sense of anxiety about the future of a particularly French mode of thinking is by no means confined to the historical profession.[55]

CHAPTER 10

The Closing of the French Mind

A t the approach of the summer of 2013, a tidal wave of negativity swept across France. Opinion surveys showed that the French had become the "European champions of pessimism," with an overwhelmingly bleaker collective outlook about the future than any of their neighbors; polls consistently showed that more than two out of every three French men and women believed that their country was "in decline." Summing up the sense of dejection, an editorial in the conservative daily *Le Figaro* declared that France was "shipwrecked," with a general sense of despondency; an economy that was falling behind both relative to other European countries and in absolute terms; and a "cold civil war" developing as the authority of the state was contested by a range of groups, from opponents of gay marriage to fiscal dissidents. For an editorialist at *Les Echos*, the perceived decline was essentially a manifestation of nostalgia for the golden postwar era of growth and Gaullist power: "Decline is all we have left."[1]

Throughout the preceding decade, the issue of French malaise had become the focus of discussion among intellectual and cultural elites. There were attempts to explain away the phenomenon as an illustration of the Gallic penchant for the paradoxical, as when a specialist in personal development suggested that French unhappiness might be caused by "too much thinking." The *mal de vivre*—an untranslatable expression—even found its historian, who ingenuously noted that the condition was an essential component of modernity, because "the progress of thought is inseparable from the development of a sense of despair." Yet what was distinctive about the Gallic doom of the late Sarkozy and Hollande eras was the utter absence of redemption on its horizons. Declinism became a fixation among political elites, with former prime minister François Fillon asserting that France was "losing its substance"—a claim all the more alarming because it was not precisely clear what it meant. The Socialist Party came up with a characteristic response to the crisis: it organized a seminar. Yet many progressives conceded that there was a real sense of "moral panic" in society, and a "veering of the French collective imagination to the right."[2]

Images of desolation came from all sectors of activity and all parts of the country. An editorial in *Le Monde* warned of France's "continuing industrial decline," and *L'Usine nouvelle* lamented the "inexorable decline of the French car manufacturing industry"; the piano manufacturer Pleyel, once celebrated by Chopin, announced that it was closing by the end of 2013. The economic decay accompanying the change in mood had important territorial dimensions, with many provincial towns, such as Caen, becoming depopulated, and parts of the north and east experiencing chronic deindustrialization. Rural France was in no better shape, according to a widely acclaimed study of life in a village in Provence: far from the genial representations of the British author Peter Mayle, who has written several best-selling books about life in Provence, the new study showed the traditions of communal solidarity dying out, with local inhabitants living separate existences, alienated from one another and from modernity. As one of them put it, "Our world is dying and I don't know what will take its place." This sense of emptiness provided the inspiration for Michel Houellebecq's dystopic novel *La Carte et le territoire* (*The Map and the Territory*), in which rural France becomes a haven for global tourism, with "nothing to sell except charming hotels, perfumes and potted meat."[3]

Even the commemorative calendar, which could normally be relied on to provide some light relief, seemed to be colluding in the funereal atmosphere. The year 2013 was marked by preparations for the anniversary of the beginning of World War I, an event that, according to Pierre Nora, evoked "a collective realization of the decline of France in the twentieth century" (and things were hardly set to improve in 2015, with the bicentenary of the Battle of Waterloo). Adding to the sense of doom was the hundredth anniversary of the birth of Albert Camus, bringing forth another raft of works parsing the novelist's uplifting themes of self-doubt and alienation. A literary historian concluded that pessimism, formerly the preserve of French cultural elites, had now spread to all sections of society: "Even idiots have now stopped being happy." Unsurprisingly, the only political movement that seemed to be thriving was the National Front, which has become one of France's largest parties since 2012, both in membership and electoral support. Referring to the *"marinisation* of French thinking," the editor in chief of *Le Point*, Franz-Olivier Giesbert, argued that the pessimistic national mood was partly a reflection of the party's revived appeal under Marine Le Pen's leadership and its ability to capitalize on any problem, from immigration, insecurity, unemployment, and corruption to the failings of industry and agriculture. Yet, Giesbert added, the National Front was merely tapping into a deeply felt sense of collective anxiety: "There is effectively something metaphysical in the sentiment of decline that is engulfing the old world in general, and France in particular."[4]

What was happening in France was indeed part of a wider European malaise, even though it seemed to be experienced much more acutely by the French than by other Europeans. This was partly the case because, as noted in the previous chapter, French elites have regularly been afflicted by a sense of anxiety about the future ever since the postrevolutionary era, and "antimodernism" is a constituent component of French thought. Progressive despair, too, has a long history, mainly fueled by repeated experiences of defeat at the hands of conservative forces. Pierre-Joseph Proudhon wrote in 1863, at the height of the imperial rule of Napoleon III, "I believe we are fully in decadence, and the more I recognize that I have deluded myself through excessive generosity, the less confidence I have in the vitality of my nation. I have faith neither in the future, nor in any humanitarian mission of the French people; the sooner we disappear from the scene, the better it will be for civilization and the human race."[5]

The last time such bleak sentiments were in the air was in the 1930s, when a sense of civilizational crisis extended worldwide. In this sense, Giesbert's claim mirrored the view in Robert Aron and Arnaud Dandieu's book *Décadence de la nation française* (Decadence of the French nation), which asserted that France's malaise was symptomatic of a "metaphysical and spiritual agony." In 2013 there were many parallels drawn between the two eras in the press, with colorful titles such as *Au secours, les années 30 sont de retour!* (Help, the thirties are back!). Inevitably, attention turned to the failure of the nation's traditional oracles—the intellectuals—to provide any meaningful alternatives to these visions of despair. The communist daily *L'Humanité* thus deplored the "smell of philosophical decadence" that had pervaded French intellectual life in recent times, and the populist weekly *Marianne* lamented the absence of "global visions that could fill the absolute void in current French thought." Hence the heretical suggestion by the philosopher Gaspard Koenig that if rationalism, Marxism, structuralism, and postmodernism were all dead, perhaps it was time for the French to finally embrace liberalism.[6]

A National Disease

What sense are we to make of these increasingly dismal visions of the nation's condition and future prospects—a syndrome the historian Michel Winock described as "a French national disease"? That the phenomenon should be diagnosed as a pathology by one of France's most distinguished historians is in itself revealing. It reflected a tendency among French intellectual elites to treat the issue of decline in psychological terms, and therefore to view it ultimately as a subjective condition, rather than a matter that could be analyzed empirically by appealing to facts and statistics. Indeed, even though there were references to particular trends, moments, or turning points (such as the presidential election of 2002 or the financial crisis of 2008), one of the paradoxical features of French declinist literature was its paucity of references to hard evidence. In keeping with the holistic style of French reasoning, the phenomenon itself was typically taken as given, and then explained by appealing to more general conceptual frameworks about human nature, history, economics, culture, or race.[7]

In other ways, too, this was a classically French discussion. It underscored a fascination with loss, alienation, and death that has deep roots in the nation's culture. At the same time, particular treatises were often a translation of individual frustrations and disappointments into general philosophical worldviews: a sense of radical disillusionment with former beliefs was often the shared characteristic of the various contributors, whether they came from conservative, liberal, or progressive backgrounds. The literature was also schematic in the extreme, with repeated invocations of rhetorical oppositions between good and evil, civilization and barbarity, and progress and decadence. Hence the high level of hyperbole, with some of the most apocalyptic statements (for example, about the lack of integration of immigrants or the loss of a French sense of collective identity) coming from people who rarely ventured out of the central districts of Paris and who had little understanding of how most ordinary men and women lived. There was much dabbling in conspiracy theorizing (another favorite in the repertoire), with blame being directed not only at French elites, but also at entities that were all the more unsettling because they could not be precisely defined ("neoliberalism" or "Islamism," for example). The discussion was also characteristic of a certain way of French thinking in that, for the most part, it had little to offer by way of concrete solutions and practical plans of action, suggesting instead that the most important change needed was mental or attitudinal. For the seasoned observer of French intellectual life, there was a familiar other-worldliness about these exchanges, especially in their preference for dwelling on sentiments of negativity, their appeal to vague or unrealizable ideals (such as the transformation of the French nation into a racially homogeneous community), and their predilection for taking propositions and lines of reasoning to their furthest possible extremes.

The most comprehensive version of this philosophical pessimism was articulated by the Romanian-born essayist Emil Cioran, who settled in the Latin Quarter in the aftermath of World War II. He first made his mark with his *Précis de décomposition* (Précis of decomposition, 1949), a collection of aphorisms hailed as an existentialist masterpiece, not least for its absolute rejection of the possibility that life could have meaning: "Our illuminations are exceptional, our decadence is the rule. Life is that which decomposes at every moment; it is a monotonous loss of light, an insipid dissolution, without sceptres, without glories, without haloes." The major themes in his work were solitude, boredom, and, of course, death: "the great affirmation." This focus was a direct echo of the occultist tradition, but completely shorn of its optimistic underpinnings. He took his negative fixation to its logical conclusion in *De l'inconvénient d'être né* (*The Trouble with Being Born*, 1973), which portrayed the whole of existence as a (futile) reaction to the tragedy of creation: "We do not rush toward death, we flee the catastrophe of birth, we thrash around, like survivors trying to forget. The fear of death is only the projection into the future of a pathology that harks back to our first instant."[8]

As French thought plunged toward darkness at the approach of the millennium, Cioran's Middle European gloom was given a new lease on life: his collected works were published in Gallimard's prestigious Pléiade collection in 2011, a decade and a half after his death. His most significant contribution to the collective reflections on French decline was made in *De la France* (On France), an essay first written in 1941 during the German occupation and published posthumously in 2009. In this remarkable anticipation of the French mood of the early twenty-first century, Cioran argued that the French spirit was essentially provincial and hedonistic, and (through Descartes's influence) turned toward "narrow perfectionism"—a preference for stylistic elegance and formal clarity over philosophical profundity. France's intellectual greatness had stemmed from its capacity to construct the "rationalist mythologies" that had dominated European thinking in the modern age. But Cioran believed that the French were no longer capable of believing in such ideals: "The wells of the spirit have dried up, and they now wake up in the desert, hands crossed, and terrified of the future." Among Cioran's devotees was the philosopher Frédéric Schiffter, a self-styled "petit-bourgeois nihilist" whose writings railed against the *ennui* of modernity, the futility of ethics, and the uselessness of Foucault (whose work he refused to read because Foucault "wore polo-neck sweaters").[9]

In contrast with Cioran's philosophical and aesthetic sensibility, Alain Pey-refitte's pessimism was expressed through an (appropriately grand) historical framework—even though his overall conclusions were no less melancholic. First published in 1976, *Le Mal français* (*The Trouble with France*) was a composite work, partly an autobiographical reflection on the theme of French "ungovernability" by a disillusioned former Gaullist minister, and partly an attempt to explain the flaws in the nation's political culture in the modern era. Peyrefitte's central argument was that France was different from other advanced industrial societies because it was trapped in an "accursed" confrontation between an alienated citizenry and an invasive state.[10]

Peyrefitte followed Tocqueville in regarding French overcentralization as a product of the absolute monarchy, later reinforced by the Revolution and successive republics. Over time, the French had thus become a nation of "rebellious conservatives" and fallen prey to a particular disease, "convulsionary immobilism" (*immobilisme convulsionnaire*). This illness manifested itself in an idolatry of tradition ("In the quarrel between the ancients and the moderns, it is generally the ancients who gain the upper hand"); a worship of absolute power combined with a love of periodic crises ("spasmophilia"); a universalist obsession with equality and a refusal of difference; a fetish for the unreal ("In France, the logical spirit has been displaced by the magical spirit"); and a penchant to divide issues into simple dichotomies, such as "liberty" versus "authority," and "order" versus "movement." Peyrefitte concluded, laconically, "We are not a people which is at ease with itself."[11]

Although Peyrefitte claimed to believe that the French were capable of accomplishing the "mental revolution" they needed to transform themselves, the sheer weight of Peyrefitte's demonstration, and its quasi-anthropological character, seemed to suggest otherwise. He explicitly assumed this pessimism in his preface to the 1996 edition of the book, noting that, despite the decentralization reforms introduced by the socialists during the 1980s, France still remained in the firm grip of the Colbertian tradition of state interventionism. In this ominous coda, Peyrefitte typified the undercurrent of despondency that was inherent in the Gaullist tradition, however much it was masked by voluntarism and grandiloquence.[12]

An even more virulent strand of French pessimism, associated with the nationalist Right, also reemerged in the 1980s. Its central theme was that France was in "decadence," an irreversible, ontological form of decline that manifested itself in the absolute decomposition of the existing order. This bleak vision drew its ideological inspiration from the antirevolutionary and antimodernist writings of such figures as Veuillot, Drumont, Barrès, and Drieu La Rochelle. It perceived present society to be trapped in a form of moral and spiritual corruption in which rationalist individualism has triumphed over any sense of collective belonging; man is alienated from his true (religious) self, taking refuge in "a vulgar materialism, a product of the monstrous union of lazy thinking and the desire for comfort."[13]

Another distinct theme in this pessimistic narrative is the racial degeneration of the French nation—hence the insistence by the nationalist Right on the threat posed by immigration. This menace of national dispossession by "Islamism" (a vague concept that insidiously conflates the practice of the Islamic faith with extreme religious views) has been at the heart of the National Front's message since the 1980s. It was coupled with a condemnation of the ruinous effects of the permissive society: sexual license, drugs, violence, family breakdowns, and lack of discipline in the classroom—all of which culminated in the fear of national extinction: in a 1994 speech, Jean-Marie Le Pen declared, "France has continued to regress and, following in the path of the Western and Northern world generally, has fallen into such a grave crisis that, at the economic, social, political, but also the cultural and moral levels, her very existence, and with it that of the French people as a whole, finds itself threatened with death."[14]

Manifestations of Decline

Declinist strands of thought were thus already well entrenched by the final decades of the twentieth century, and they provided the matrices for the subsequent widening and deepening of these pessimistic French sensibilities. The next phase came with the theme of the decline of "high" culture—a familiar refrain among conservative nationalist "decadentists," but now appropriated with gusto by Parisian cultural elites. One of the early classics of this new genre was Alain Finkielkraut's *La Défaite de la pensée* (*The Defeat of the Mind*, 1987), a somber essay that warned against the impending destruction of the Enlightenment's heritage by a ragtag assortment of Third Worldists, moral relativists, and popular entertainers. Finkielkraut here developed some of the ideas that would later make him one of France's foremost neorepublican polemicists and a champion of secularism against the perceived threat of multiculturalism. He claimed to be particularly concerned that the celebration of "cultural difference" would delegitimize the intellectual qualities that had enabled the liberation of modern man—skepticism, irony, and rational individualism. From this premise he deduced (somewhat hyperbolically) that civilization was threatened by a new age of barbarity: "Life and thought are slowly yielding to the terrible and derisory confrontation of the fanatic and the zombie." Finkielkraut's intuition that something was fundamentally broken in the

French cultural realm was shared by others—notably, the antimodernist writer and critic Philippe Muray—and was also expressed in Jean-François Mattéi's *La Barbarie intérieure* (Barbarity from within, 1999), a scathing philosophical diatribe against the corruption of civilization by mass culture.[15]

As the debate about decline entered the cultural terrain, it was inevitable that the state of French literature would also come under its purview. In 1995, the former editor of *Esprit*, Jean-Marie Domenach, published an alarmist account of contemporary French fiction. He lambasted the absence of a genuine tradition of literary criticism, as manifested in Britain and the United States by such publications as the *Times Literary Supplement* and the *New York Review of Books*, and railed against the "sinister" quality of most French novels, with their absence of effective characterization, their divorce from social reality, and their celebration of abnormality. In a long piece on the "death of the novel" in France in 2001, the weekly *L'Express* echoed Domenach's dismal view, noting with dismay the emergence of a new form of introverted writing that expressed a subjectivity that was "hysterical, irritable, miserable, and megalomaniac, both extraordinarily puritan and pornographic." More than a decade later the novelist Patrick Besson gave an equally gloomy overview of contemporary French literature in an article provocatively entitled "Is French Literature Dead?" Such observations resonated with the widespread view in the Anglophone world that contemporary French literature had lost its way, had become too inward-looking, overly obsessed with abstraction, and no longer possessed the capacity of its great forebears for narrative storytelling.[16]

Yet there was, in this respect, a French paradox (another one): with more than 2,000 book prizes, including prestigious awards such as the Goncourt, the Renaudot, the Femina, and the Médicis, and the excitement that continues to build up every autumn around the *rentrée littéraire*, French literary culture appeared to be flourishing. But the real measure of the problem was international. While the likes of Flaubert, Dumas, Proust, and Camus have become part of the global literary heritage, their best-selling (or award-winning) contemporary successors—the likes of Katherine Pancol, Guillaume Musso, Anna Gavalda, Emmanuel Carrère, Amélie Nothomb, Marie Darrieussecq, and Christophe Ono-dit-Biot—struggle to attract sizable Anglophone readerships. Even Nobel Prize winners such as J. M. G. Le Clézio and Patrick Modiano remain virtually unknown in the English-speaking world.

It is true that in the United States more novels are translated from French than from any other language. But the numbers are relatively small (sixty-two in 2012, and seventy-seven in 2013), and most tend to be published by smaller imprints, with only a handful of titles ever reaching American bestseller lists. If anything, the successes tend to confirm native stereotypes about the French: their overpoweringly cerebral nature (symbolized by Renée, the cultured concierge in Muriel Barbery's *The Elegance of the Hedgehog*); their capacity for frivolousness and levity, even in the most gruesome of settings (Laurent Binet's *HHhH*, where the author's personal musings are woven into the story of the assassination of the Nazi security chief Reinhard Heydrich); their enduring anti-Semitism (Irène Némirovsky's *Suite française*, a posthumously published work of fiction about World War II, whose author died in Auschwitz); and, of course, their sexual perversion (Michel Houellebecq's entire *oeuvre*).[17]

In the early twenty-first century, France's growing economic malaise became a privileged terrain for theorists of decline. The seminal work here was Nicolas Baverez's *La France qui tombe* (France in decline, 2003), a short but influential book that sought to provide a more focused version of Peyrefitte's diagnosis, drawing upon Raymond Aron's conservative liberalism. Baverez's main argument was that France's decline was a product of policies deliberately pursued by its elites from the late nineteenth century. This resulted in a "French model" of a large public sector, an expanded role for the state in economic and social affairs (especially in the realm of health and welfare), and a constant preference for internal social stability over dynamic change (an echo of the American political scientist Stanley Hoffmann's classic notion of a "stalemate society").[18]

According to Baverez, the French response to the changing post–Cold War world had followed this historical pattern: as other nations modernized their economies by reducing the size of the public sector and promoting greater innovation and competitiveness, successive governments of the Left and Right had simply reaffirmed the traditional "French model," thus allowing the national debt to escalate and inward investment to fall steeply. Although more than a third of France's gross domestic product (GDP) was spent on welfare and public-sector employment, only 2.5 percent was devoted to long-term investment in public infrastructure. In Baverez's estimation, the result of this "political autism" (we note again the pathological term) was an "immobilism which was political, economic and social, as well as intellectual and moral"; its ineluctable consequence, the author averred, had been "to plunge France into decline."[19]

A somewhat more nuanced vision was offered in the late Jacques Marseille's *Du bon usage de la guerre civile en France* (How to make good use of French civil wars), written in the immediate aftermath of the 2005 referendum on the proposed new European constitution. Drawing on a range of historical examples, Marseille argued that there was no fatalism to French decline, and indeed, that France's political crises could sometimes provide an impetus for change. This effect could be seen, for example, in de Gaulle's return to power in 1958. In the early twenty-first century, however, such a positive eventuality was unlikely. French society was racked by new divisions—between the employed and the unemployed, between the optimists and the pessimists, and between those sectors which benefited from state protection and those exposed to globalization. He concluded that the French elites would most likely make a "squeamish withdrawal into their shell."[20]

This prophecy of stasis was made again in the runup to the 2012 presidential elections in Christian Saint-Etienne's *L'Incohérence française* (French incoherence), which blamed the country's continuing economic woes on the "intellectual cowardice" of French elites. Philippe Manière's *Le Pays où la vie est plus dure* (The country where life is hardest) was a variation on the same theme, although it lacked the catastrophic finality of Simone Wapler's *Pourquoi la France va faire faillite* (Why France will become bankrupt). In a 2012 pamphlet, Baverez twisted the knife in the wound, mournfully observing that his pleas had not been heard even by those in his own ideological camp: despite his promises to reform the French system, Nicolas Sarkozy had presided over an extension of public spending and borrowing, aggravating the country's decline. Little would change, Baverez concluded, until France's rulers moved away from their statist and antiliberal economic bias.[21]

The theme of decline-as-state-failure spawned a large body of literature that combined hard-nosed analysis of the "crisis" in different sectors with (at times) judicious proposals for reform. But the language used to diagnose the problems was often overinflated, particularly in discussions of the French educational system. In the estimation of teacher Marc Le Bris, French public schools were responsible for nothing less than a "cultural catastrophe." The country was suffering from serious shortfalls in basic literacy and numeracy, a general lack of discipline, and a collapse of authority and an abandonment of classical culture. He concluded his "cry of alarm" with the observation that the very ideal of the republican school as a transmitter of the nation's cultural heritage had been compromised.[22]

In an equally hard-hitting pamphlet, teacher Jean-Paul Brighelli denounced a process of "fabricating cretins," largely blamed on the education philosophy of the post-1968 era, which had replaced the traditional notion of pedagogy with the pernicious concepts of student "competence" and individual autonomy. In the sham egalitarianism of this newspeak, students were no longer described as "pupils" (élèves), but as "learners" (*apprenants*), highlighting a less hierarchical relationship between teacher and student. A particularly perverse consequence of this system, Brighelli claimed, was the widening of the cultural gap between bourgeois social elites and the "decerebrated" underclass.

Introduced in the early 1980s, the attempt to create "priority education zones" (ZEPs) in "difficult" neighborhoods had been a complete failure. This two-tiered system ultimately flew in the face of the fundamental mission of the republican educational system, which was to promote greater equality of opportunity.[23]

Even though the cultural gap in relative attainments that it identified was real, this vision of educational decline blamed the problem not on the absence of resources or on institutional failings, but on ideology—a characteristic style of French intellectualist reasoning. Thus, one of the aggravating factors that Brighelli identified was the influence of "neoliberalism" in French education (a code word for Anglo-American thinking): its pedagogical philosophy, he claimed, was to create an individual "without past, without history, without attachments," a docile servant of the interests of global capitalism. This complaint was echoed by Alain Planche, a progressive academic from Bordeaux, who argued that the republican educational system had been successfully penetrated by "neoliberal ideology."[24]

Conservative declinists concurred even more emphatically. In his final speech as leader of the National Front in 2011, in which he said that French elites had been leading the nation toward "decadence" since the end of World War I, Jean-Marie Le Pen charged that the national educational system had been taken over by "utopian dreamers, Marxist pedagogues and ultra-liberal materialists" (a broad cast of villains, admittedly, but all proponents of modes of thinking for which Le Pen had such contempt). Le Pen agreed that French schools were producing alienation and lamented the loss of the nation's heritage. He complained, in particular, that students were no longer taught "the love of France, or the beauty of its past." Indeed, instead of focusing on France's glorious achievements (its monarchical and Napoleonic triumphs, and the benefits of its colonial empire, for example), the history curriculum sought, in his view, to foster a sense of "guilt" among pupils by dwelling on such "ignoble" episodes as slavery and collaboration. This was a typical piece of Le Pen rhetoric, identifying a real phenomenon (the shrinking place of French history in the school syllabus and the curriculum's greater engagement with the world), but exaggerating its consequences in order to make a dubious (and extreme) political claim: the alleged conspiracy among educators to demoralize the nation by stifling French patriotic sentiment.[25]

The emphasis on moral failure was also the leitmotif of the British expatriate Peter Gumbel's *On achève bien les écoliers* (Finishing off the schoolchildren, 2010), which claimed that the principal inadequacy of the French school system was its creation of a "culture of mediocrity" (*nullité*), which generated widespread fear and anxiety among students. Surveys showed that, faced with intimidating teachers and a difficult grading system (the top mark of twenty was almost never awarded, whereas a zero grade was common), French students graduated so lacking in self-confidence that they were more worried about failure than their counterparts in other advanced industrial societies. Political sociologist Anne Muxel agreed: "Compared to other European countries, France has a real problem with the integration of its youth." In a characteristic Gallic move from the particular to the universal, some professed to see a link between the declining standards in schools and France's troubled collective self. The economist Claudia Senik hypothesized that the main cause of French *mal de vivre* was its educational system, which instilled among students "a cultural disposition toward unhappiness." Her colleagues Yann Algan, Pierre Cahuc, and André Zylberberg made an even more audacious claim, suggesting that the French had distinguished themselves by their sense of "social defiance." Their incapacity to develop cooperative and reciprocal behavior was a direct product of France's vertical educational culture, which instilled values of "hierarchy and elitism."[26]

Progressive Pessimism Returns

With its extension to the cultural, economic, and educational spheres, the French declinist sensibility gained considerable intellectual ground on the Left. One of the first to observe (and express) this progressive pessimism was the socialist Michel Charzat, who opened his *La France et le déclin* (France and decline, 1988) with a dramatic declaration: "Nous sommes tous malades" (We are all sick); his compatriots, he suggested, had a particular fondness for defeatism and masochism. Although he did not accept that national decadence was fatal, Charzat recognized that it represented a psychological reality, like "a mirror that illuminates our malaise." The return of declinist narratives in the 1980s, he believed, revealed a France increasingly engulfed in an era of "postmodern nihilism," with a loss of a sense of collective destiny and an unhealthy "retromania" that manifested itself in a fetish for national commemorations and a nostalgia for golden ages. The main danger with this new pessimism, he concluded, was that it would push the French toward an "egoistic closure."[27]

Charzat had good reason to be apprehensive. One of the first to catch the disease was the neo-Marxist theorist and revolutionist Guy Debord, one of the iconic figures of French libertarian thinking, who became the standard-bearer of a new strand of progressive hopelessness. In his classic *La société du spectacle* (*The Society of the Spectacle*, 1967), a work largely influenced by Barthes, Debord had argued that capitalist domination of society had become more pervasive through the forces of mass media, advertising, and popular culture.

By the late 1980s, a melancholic Debord believed this collective alienation to have become so widespread that, he concluded, "there is no such thing as collectivity or community anymore." After this nod to neoconservative thinking, he bowed out with this dejected—and appropriately mystifying—aphorism: "General decadence is an instrument in the service of the empire of servitude; and it is only in this capacity that it allows itself to be called progress." He shot himself in 1994.[28]

Yet this post-political moroseness was tempered for a while by the continuing presence of the Left in government. The end of Mitterrand's reign was followed in 1997 by Lionel Jospin's *gauche plurielle* government, which was formed after the Left's victory in the legislative elections. The turning point came with Jospin's defeat in the 2002 presidential elections, which provoked his retreat from public life and his later embittered diagnosis that France was crippled by a "*mal napoléonien.*" Particularly traumatic for the *peuple de gauche* was the socialist candidate's failure even to reach the second ballot—a result all the more devastating in that the hapless Jospin was beaten by Jean-Marie Le Pen. April 21 became a mythical date on the Left, a shorthand for a calamity of epic proportions. The depth of the wound could still be felt years later. Remembering it, left-wing sympathizers spoke of their incomprehension and anger, and their belief that the French had "voted like sheep." Some confessed to a sense of "guilt" for not voting for Jospin, while others expressed their "shame" that the Left had let the country down; one militant declared that he "no longer recognized France." The general sentiment, repeated in many different voices, was that the French were becoming more "closed" as a nation, thanks to the insidious propagation of the National Front's ideas about immigration and security (*lepénisation des esprits*). The wider prognosis was bleak: the Left was in "intellectual decomposition."[29]

One of the most conspicuous measures of the intellectual closure of the French Left was the dissipation of its international (and internationalist) outlooks. At a time when progressive political philosophers in the United States and Europe were coming up with broad and innovative frameworks for confronting the challenges to democratic power and civil liberties in Western societies (for example, Michael Hardt and Antonio Negri's notion of empire, and Giorgio Agamben's concept of the state of exception), their Gallic counterparts were indulging in mindless word games in the style of Derrida and Baudrillard. True, there were still some ambitious attempts to define the zeitgeist of the contemporary era, such as Luc Boltanski and Eve Chiapello's *Le nouvel esprit du capitalisme* (*The New Spirit of Capitalism*), which was grandiosely billed as a modern distillation of Max Weber's classic work. Yet this book was in fact largely based on an analysis of French managerial texts.[30]

Such an approach was, *en passant*, an expression of two classics in the Gallic repertoire: that something really became significant only when it happened in France, and that whatever occurred in France had universal significance. Most progressive thinkers simply threw their hands up in despair. Political scientists Gérard Grunberg and Zaki Laïdi concluded that the culture of the French Left had been transformed with the new millennium, and that its emotional and intellectual representation of reality was now dominated by "social pessimism." This negativity was not merely the product of the bleakness in the French outlook, but the result of a conception of politics in which change and transformation were no longer believed to be possible—especially in the management of globalization. Unable to look forward or outward, the Left was thus turning into itself: hence its anti-European vote in 2005, which symbolized its nationalist retreat (*repli identitaire*). Hence, also, the Left's paradoxical metamorphosis as it became the principal defender of the (French) state, causing it to embrace a conservative utopia that would seek "not to bring about a new society but . . . prevent the emergence of tomorrow's world."[31]

Even more spectacular was the philosophical pessimism of Jean-Claude Michéa, for whom modern progressivism was incapable of offering a viable alternative to capitalism because it had cut itself off from its popular roots and embraced the Enlightenment's liberal individualism. The "new order" promised by this liberal civilization was a dehumanized, Orwellian world where men were "resigned to become poor egoistic monads, condemned to produce and consume, each fighting without mercy against all the others."[32]

This sense of melancholy became widespread among progressive intellectuals. Marcel Gauchet, one of the major figures of the "antitotalitarian" Left, declared that democracy itself was facing a "foundational" crisis that featured a general sense of civic "dispossession" and "oligarchical appropriation" and the "disappearance of the collective political subject." Gauchet believed that the weakening of governance across democratic polities was evidence of a spiritual crisis, which could potentially lead to the "decomposition of the City" (though the formula was classically universalistic, this was probably also an unconscious allusion to the fact that his beloved École des Hautes Études was about to be moved from the upmarket Boulevard Raspail in the city center to the outer darkness of the Parisian *banlieue*). Gauchet believed that the outlook for the short term was "pessimistic," because "the downward movement of our societies is so marked that a correction of trajectory cannot be envisaged in the immediate future." At the end of a long-winded polemic against those on the Left who rejected "declinism" in the name of progress, the sociologist Pierre-André Taguieff concluded that "the prophets of doom were, in certain situations, the true voices of wisdom."[33]

The solutions to this malaise were unclear, to say the least. Affirming that progressive ideology had become a "cerebral straitjacket," Régis Debray invited his comrades to seek comfort in the past and recognize that human beings would always have a "vital need of belonging" (so much for internationalism, then); he ended on a Nietzschean note by calling for a "tragic Left" that traded the metaphysical universalisms of old for "the energy of despair" and a "progressivism without optimism." In 2010, Debray took this line of reasoning about the necessity of enclosure to its logical conclusion in his *Éloge des Frontières* (Praise for national borders). Never one to turn down an opportunity for self-flagellation, Bernard-Henri Lévy contributed his own necrology, comparing the Left to a putrefying corpse and upbraiding it for its antiliberalism, anti-Europeanism, anti-Americanism, and anti-Semitism, as well as for its celebration of the work of the Nazi philosopher Carl Schmitt. The philosopher Guy Hermet, for his part, saw in the rise of populism across France and other advanced industrial societies the intimations of the end of democracy itself.[34]

The most emphatic statement of this left-wing pessimism was Jacques Julliard's *Le Malheur français* (The French misfortune), which revealed the extent to which the progressive mindset had been captured by the general declinist mood. Julliard's account of the state of France was unrelentingly desolate: the national feeling was one of discouragement, abandonment, and closure, and the sense of unhappiness was so deeply entrenched that it had become part of the French "collective subconscious." He shared Baverez's analysis of the nation's economic decline as well as the belief that France had irreversibly lost ground to the "Anglo-Saxons" in the cultural arena. If anything, Julliard's analysis of French failings here was even more scathing, as he noted that standards had fallen catastrophically, not only in literature and in secondary education, but also in the humanities and social sciences and in the universities, where France was no longer globally competitive. Like Peyrefitte, he found that part of the problem lay in the "schizophrenic" expectations of the French—their love of equality, on the one hand, and their passion for privileges, on the other. But the real measure of the crisis, according to Julliard, was that it had corroded the Left's ability to think in universal categories: French progressivism had imbibed the xenophobic Right's conspiratorial schemes and its populist rejection of Europe. It now defined itself by its denial of the outside world, its paralysis, and its blind faith in the redemptive attributes of the state—in short, by its "resistance to change."[35]

Even François Hollande's victory in the 2012 presidential election did little fundamentally to alter this negativity, as illustrated by the self-explanatory title of a pamphlet published by the philosopher Philippe Corcuff: *La Gauche est-elle en état de mort cérébrale?* (Is the Left in a state of brain death?). This closed vision was perhaps best illustrated in the work of Alain Soral, whose Égalité et Réconciliation movement, founded in 2007, sought to build a platform around the values of fraternity, anticapitalism, and anti-Europeanism. A former member of the Communist Party and then the National Front, Soral captured attention through his exotic combination of extreme beliefs and strong profile on the Internet: his monthly online videos have been accessed by more than 15 million (mostly young) viewers. He defines himself by his fierce opposition to the "official" Left, which he argues has betrayed its popular traditions, and his belief in the need for a moral and spiritual regeneration of France; hence the priority he assigns to the "defense of the nation."[36]

The Turn Toward Ethnic Nationalism

Summing up the pessimistic French mood in an article in *Le Débat* in 2011, political scientist Pascal Perrineau highlighted many of the features mentioned thus far—the demise of grand narratives, the nostalgia for golden eras, the crisis of the French "model," the contestation of elites, the dysfunctions of the educational system, and the generalized loss of political and cultural references. All of these factors, he argued, not only reinforced each other but also served to reignite one of France's oldest fears: that of the breakdown of its sense of collective identity. The emergence of a powerful strand of French ethnic nationalism was perhaps the most visible translation of this anxiety. Advocates of a "return to the nation" gained considerable ground in republican political and cultural circles during the first decade of the new millennium, increasingly echoing the racialist rhetoric and imagery of the National Front. This movement was represented at the institutional level by Nicolas Sarkozy's Ministry of National Identity, under the influence of presidential adviser Patrick Buisson. Sarkozy's party, Union for a Popular Movement (UMP), also adopted an aggressive posture toward Islam. Leading figures in the party stigmatized the cultural practices of French Islam, claiming that the natives were becoming the victims of a form of "anti-French racism." Their denunciations of immigration and "Islamism" as threats to national cohesion became commonplace in the mainstream conservative press (*Le Figaro* and weeklies such as *Valeurs actuelles*). They also became common in the writings of "culturalist" intellectuals, such as the journalists Éric Zemmour, Elisabeth Lévy, and Éric Brunet.[37]

An example of this sort of republican ethnocentrism could be found in Zemmour's *Mélancolie française* (French melancholy, 2010). Presenting France's historical vocation as the continuation of its Roman heritage, Zemmour analyzed the nation's decline as a consequence of its failure to contain its "Anglo-Saxon" rivals, Britain and Germany. After some conventional observations about the Napoleonic and Gaullist eras, and some fairly eccentric suggestions (notably, that France should reannex Wallonia), Zemmour's presentation climaxed in an analogy with the fall of Rome, as given in Edward Gibbon's account. Just as Rome had collapsed because of its failure to assimilate its barbarian peoples, France, likewise, was destined to decadence because of its incapacity to integrate its immigrant populations. Although he was generally critical of the opening of borders to Europeans, the real "barbarian" menace he perceived was the one that came from the former French colonies of the Maghreb, whose migrants he claimed were "swamping" the country and leading to its "de-Christianization and de-Francification" (the parallels with the arguments of the extreme right-wing conservative politician Enoch Powell in Britain in the 1970s were striking).[38]

This process of national dispossession was the product of cultural and demographic factors, which Zemmour detailed with a characteristic combination of sweeping formulas, selective quotations, and dubious "statistics." He cited the non-assimilation of immigrants and their refusal to speak French ("the language of the devil") at home; the high rate of foreign marriages among French-born migrants and the immigrants' higher fertility rates; the weakening of traditional French civilization through multiculturalism and intermarriage; and the wholesale "substitution" of native French populations by Arab immigrants in certain suburban towns. His conclusion was that France was threatened with the prospect of enduring civil strife and the disintegration of its traditional cultural heritage. Zemmour regularly depicts the French Muslim population as an "enemy within," suggesting that its values are alien to the nation's culture. He thus described the perpetrators of the January 2015 attacks in Paris as the "advance party of a fifth column that is poised to strike at our country."[39]

These efforts to promote an ethnic conception of the French collective self were also relayed through an increasingly buoyant conservative nationalist historiography. This phenomenon had its roots in the Sarkozy era's "bling-bling history," as the historian Nicolas Offenstadt described it—an attempt by public authorities to reimpose a patriotic national narrative that would officially celebrate French greatness. As we saw in the previous chapter, the centerpiece of this ideological project to create a *roman national*—a Maison de l'Histoire de France—was abandoned in 2012. But the wider effort to promote a sanitized narrative of France's past, shorn of its most somber episodes and any notion of "repentance," continued—and, in many respects, flourished. It was spearheaded by figures such as Jean Sévillia, the deputy editor of the

Figaro Magazine, whose works sought to provide a counternarrative to the (alleged) historical misrepresentations of France's past by professional historians on such subjects as the monarchy, religion, colonialism, the world wars, and immigration. In his *Historiquement incorrect* (Historically incorrect, 2011) he offered an original solution to the problem of minority integration, suggesting that France's Islamic populations should be "evangelized" (though he magnanimously added that this should not be done forcibly). His *Histoire passionnée de la France* (A passionate history of France, 2013) offered an unapologetic return to the *roman national*, with an emphasis on the celebration of France's Christian roots and charismatic leaders; he concluded that this kind of history was necessary to fortify "the love of France."[40]

The most successful exponent of this cultural conservative vision was the actor and writer Lorànt Deutsch. His best-selling *Métronome*, an exploration of the history of Paris through its Métro stations, published in 2009, had sold 800,000 copies by the end of 2013; it was sponsored by the municipality of Paris and later serialized on French television. His subsequent *Hexagone* (2013), a travel history of France from the founding of Marseille to the construction of the Channel Tunnel, was also a major commercial success. Deutsch's monarchist and Catholic beliefs inform his conception of history. Although this is of course an entirely legitimate point of view, it is put across in a hyperbolic fashion, as when he declared in an interview that the execution of the king by the revolutionaries in 1793 had marked "the end of French civilization": "Since that moment, we were cut off from our roots, and we are still seeking them."[41]

Deutsch's narrative of the revolutionary era drew on the classic demonology of the counterrevolutionary tradition, presenting the French people in revolt as a menacing entity, prone to irrational surges of violence and destructiveness. His hostility toward radical republicanism was evident in his negative portrayal of the Paris Commune, which he (inaccurately) accused of seeking to destroy the Bastille column, and in the absence of any reference to the French Resistance in *Hexagone*. He fortified his ethnic nationalist reading of French history by stressing the significance of episodes of cultural conflict, such as Charles Martel's victory in the Battle of Poitiers in AD 732 against the "Arab aggressors of the French nation": there were obvious contemporaneous undertones to his celebration of "the sacred union of Christians and pagans against the Muslim invader."[42]

In contrast with these attempts to promote a relatively consensual version of the *roman national*, there also emerged a more strident and aggressive strand of this French ethnic nationalism. For the writer Renaud Camus, France was faced with a "Great Deculturalization" that had been induced by the "massive" presence of immigrants on national soil. Camus, who supported Marine Le Pen's presidential candidacy in 2012, embraced Samuel Huntington's "clash of civilizations" thesis with gusto, contending that Frenchness was an essentially ethnic concept and that there was no possibility of peaceful cohabitation among different races—only conquest and assimilation. The latter point was of course made without discussing, or even mentioning, any evidence that might point in the opposite direction. In any event, Camus believed that the notion of France as a land of immigration was a "myth" that had been fabricated by the ideologues of the establishment for the sake of promoting multiculturalism and the "decivilized" utopia of a global village. According to the author, the strategy was succeeding: the sacred concepts of patriotism, patrimony, and heritage had been emptied of their substance, and France was facing a "replacement" of its native populations by immigrants from the Maghreb—an Islamic invasion that Camus described as a "counter-colonization." This idea was repeated in Éric Zemmour's 2014 best-seller *Suicide français* (French suicide), in which he concluded that post–de Gaulle France had become a "decultured" nation, and its elites were "spitting on its grave and trampling over its smoldering corpse."[43]

This lament at the demise of a French sense of collective self was conveyed even more bleakly in Hervé Juvin's *La Grande Séparation*. The diagnosis from this conservative essayist was in many respects similar to Zemmour's: the French found themselves in an increasingly hostile world and no longer enjoyed the sense of spiritual unity they had possessed when they were a white Christian nation. Frenchness, Juvin asserted, had been destroyed by multiculturalism and also by globalization, which had separated the state from the nation and turned it into a passive agent of Anglo-Saxon corporate interests. Hence (this is where the argument makes an extreme leap) the advent of a "denaturalized" man, uprooted from his traditions and alienated from any genuine attachments to history and geography.[44]

The centerpiece of Juvin's argument is that, while destroying the local sense of community, globalization has led to the development of new patterns of migration, with vast population movements across international borders. Paradoxically, this trend has reinforced ethnic sentiment, Juvin claimed, forging new lines of physical division within post-national societies. The main agent of the "new totalitarianism" was the capitalist mode of production, which needed a global reserve army of labor to service its requirements. Unless they can find ways of reinstituting effective frontiers, European societies with large immigrant populations, such as France, are thus faced with an apocalyptic prospect: the continuing "invasion" of the nation by foreign migrants, with the "major problem" being the one posed by Islam, whose followers, Juvin said, consider European territory to be "theirs." In addition, these societies are in danger of establishing a social "apartheid" in which natives and new populations live in separate territories but share a "common misery." The people will be "trapped in a morose and inescapable alienation, at the heart of the unfulfilled promises of modernity."[45]

A Stranger in His Own Land

Perhaps the most significant exposition of this new ethnic nationalism was the one offered by Alain Finkielkraut in *L'Identité malheureuse* (The unhappy identity), among the best-selling nonfiction books in France in the autumn of 2013. It is fitting that the pessimistic ideas and modes of reasoning described thus far reached their culminating point in this short book, as Finkielkraut is the ultimate example of this narrow-minded and parochial way of thinking—both in terms of its legitimation by the elite (he was elected to the Académie Française in April 2014) and in terms of his own intellectual evolution. He is a disillusioned ex-Maoist whose *oeuvre* is suffused with images of death, disease, and decay; he has a fondness for schematism, for cultivating paradoxical propositions (such as the eccentric idea that antiracism is more pernicious than racism itself), and for pursuing particular *idées fixes* (notably, the pervasiveness of anti-Semitism in contemporary France). He has also become absorbed by threats to French integrity, in particular the menace of "Islamism" (about which he is all the more eloquent because he has no firsthand knowledge of how French immigrant communities live).[46]

Finkielkraut's passion for hyperbole is irrepressible, as shown by his capacity to find signs of the disintegration of the French sense of collective self everywhere: in the destructive cultural effects of new technologies ("National identity is crushed, as is everything durable, by the instantaneous and interactive nature of electronic media"); in the erosion of France's humanist traditions and the abandonment of the nation's cultural heritage by its "overbooked and hyperconnected" elites; in the corruption of the French language by the debasement of grammatical rules and the widespread pedagogical use of English (Finkielkraut described the socialists' decision to allow courses to be taught in English in French universities in 2013 as the "final nail in the coffin"); in the breakdown of the education system ("French schools have not cultivated the people, they have defeated those with culture"); in the encroachments of multiculturalism into national life, as symbolized by the (alleged) refusal of children of immigrant origin to eat in school cafeterias and the impossibility of conducting a dispassionate discussion about the meaning of French "national identity"; and in the "deconstruction" of Frenchness itself, a process that had its origins in the triumph of a purely civic conception of Europe in the post-Hitlerian age, fortified by the anti-European cosmopolitanism of progressive thinkers such as Fanon.[47]

Finkielkraut often repeats his time-honored themes. (His most dismissive critics accuse him of writing the same book every few years, a claim not entirely without foundation.) What is striking, though, is the language and tone of his book, and the extent to which his nationalism has now become completely emptied of any republican substance. His earlier struggle to safeguard the principle of educational *laïcité*, for example, had been waged in the name of traditional republican ideals of equality and moral autonomy. In *L'Identité malheureuse*, equality is firmly rejected as producing both sterilizing uniformity and "boorishness"; Finkielkraut instead embraces a hierarchical conception of cultural and social order—for example, in his curious justification of the ban on the Islamic veil in the name of "French gallantry." His ultimate purpose here is not to work toward a community of shared values, but to rehabilitate the notion of "common identity" by retrieving the "national" culture of the French majority while at the same time denouncing the appropriation of Frenchness by immigrant minorities and the (alleged) "self-effacement" of natives.[48]

The driving force behind Finkielkraut's nationalism, in short, is no longer civic but ethnic. This ideological turn is reflected in his celebration of the nationalist writer Maurice Barrès's "racialized" conception of French identity and his lament at the abandonment of the concept of race in modern political discourse. Barrès belonged to a tradition of closed nationalism that Finkielkraut himself had criticized in the past, as we saw earlier—but consistency was clearly no longer a priority. Indeed, despite a convoluted attempt to enlist the anthropologist Claude Lévi-Strauss as a defender of Western singularity, Finkielkraut's intellectual references underline the extent of his own abandonment of the French humanist terrain. His conception of human respect is drawn from Thomas Hobbes, his ideal of cultural conservatism from the political philosopher Leo Strauss, and his postulate that national elites have developed a hatred of their own culture (*oikophobia*) from the conservative thinker Roger Scruton. His overall conclusion that the French are "becoming strangers in their own land," and are threatened with "national disintegration," is a pure echo of his friend Renaud Camus's rhetoric of dispossession and deculturation. In his drift toward this self-pitying and xenophobic nationalism, Finkielkraut illustrates how far the declinist obsession has pushed much of mainstream French thought away from its Rousseauist and republican heritage.[49]

CONCLUSION

Anxiety and Optimism

The scale of France's contemporary loss of self-confidence becomes apparent when set against the zeitgeist of national elites for most of the twentieth century. This, for example, is how the academician and political scientist André Siegfried spoke about his country's place in the world in the immediate aftermath of World War II:

> Absent France from the stage, [and] a certain way of approaching problems is lost: everything becomes commercial, administrative, practical, but one then looks for something more fundamental, without which Europe would not be herself, nor the Western world the cradle of human civilization. France may not find better solutions to the problems of our time, but she best knows how to define them. Her classical formation allows her to take the right measure of things, to put each object in its place, and then to combine them judiciously, thus illuminating the issue at hand. Wherever she goes, France introduces clarity, intellectual ease, curiosity and, at the end of the day, a subtle and necessary form of wisdom.[1]

The last time this sort of Cartesian aplomb was paraded on the international stage was in Dominique de Villepin's speech at the United Nations in 2003, with which this book opened. With the benefit of hindsight, his speech now appears as a last piece of French bravado, the dying echo of a tradition of confident universalism whose constitutive elements have slowly dissolved. French public institutions of course deny that such a retrenchment has occurred, and their claims about the nation's ongoing *rayonnement*—a characteristically untranslatable term that combines the sense of a wide impact with a notion of benevolent radiance—are expressed in glossy publications such as the *Atlas de l'influence française au XXIe siècle* (Atlas of French influence in the twenty-first century), which asserts that France's unique role "is to offer an alternative, an autonomous path, in comparison with other great centers of power." Pointing to the estimated 220 million French speakers across the world, the *Atlas* also highlights France's global networks of diplomatic and economic power as well as its cultural institutions, in particular the Alliance Française and the Organisation Internationale de la Francophonie (OIF) representing French-speaking countries and regions. Yet the OIF provides a good example of how the appearance of French grandeur can be misleading. Despite the celebration of the community of French-speaking peoples around the world by governmental institutions and the Académie Française, Francophonia remains a symbolic and essentially neocolonial ideal with no intellectual or emotional resonance in contemporary French thought.[2]

France's diminishing cultural imprint across the globe can be measured by the overall decline in the number of books translated into English, especially in the humanities and social sciences, and by a phenomenon that would have startled the likes of Rousseau, Victor Hugo, and Sartre: the absence of interest in contemporary French thought among progressives around the world. It is especially notable in this context how little the democratic revolutions of the post–Cold War era—in particular, the Arab Spring—were shaped by French critical thinking. In his homage to Mohamed Bouazizi, whose self-immolation launched the protest movement in Tunisia, the writer Tahar Ben Jelloun concluded pointedly, "The story of Mohamed belongs to no one." Indeed, the French government of the time continued the established pattern of preferring familiar despots to the uncertainties of democratic change: two days before the fall of the Ben Ali regime in 2011, Sarkozy's foreign minister, Michèle Alliot-Marie, offered to share French security knowhow with the Tunisian police.[3]

Pessimism thus broadened out from a confined sense of anxiety to become one of the entrenched features of the contemporary French mindset. Especially prominent were the ethnic and nationalist undertones of this declinism, as we saw in the previous chapter, and the extent to which its rhetoric and imagery penetrated ways of thinking that used to constitute bastions of Gallic collective self-assurance—not only the projection of French values across the world, as noted by Siegfried, but also high culture, the model of the state, the republican educational system, and progressive social thought. Even the new Astérix book, released amid a blaze of publicity in the autumn of 2013, was found by many to be a disappointment, a feeble reflection of the series' past glory.[4]

This bleak situation was noted in the regional press. The *République des Pyrénées*, for example, observed that France's "closure upon itself" had become a "profound disease." Sibylle Vincendon, a journalist from the left-wing daily *Libération*, observed, "The discourse of decline has effectively colonized our national narrative"—and, in a perverse symbolic confirmation of this downward trend, the newspaper itself, losing money, came under threat of closure in early 2014, when its owners floated a plan to convert it into a social network. According to the director of France's leading polling institute, public opinion has been consistently pessimistic about the nation's future since the mid-1990s; during the second half of 2013 alone, the percentage of optimists among poll respondents fell from 44 to 30 percent.[5]

Still Cultured, Still Happy

But it would be premature to condemn France to a new trilogy (as *Le Monde* had it in June 2013) of liberty, equality, and moroseness. By any reasonable yardstick, and despite the periodic predictions of its impending demise, the French continue to manifest a strong attachment to their culture. Around 3,000 major cultural festivals are held every year in France: most of them (60 percent) occur in the summer, and preponderantly in coastal regions—but they can be found in every metropolitan *département*. And how else but as an expression of cultural pride could we explain the extraordinary success of the Journées du Patrimoine (Heritage Days), which draw 12 million visitors to France's heritage sites each year? Although the budget of the Ministry of Culture has been regularly shaved in recent years, it is still considerable compared to that of most European countries, with the provision of sizable public subsidies to a wide range of artistic and cultural activities, from museums, theaters, symphonic orchestras, and educational associations to the Charles de Gaulle Foundation.[6]

In the literary sphere, the ministry supports (through grants and tax incentives) France's large network of 3,500 independent bookshops, which are granted the special title "Librairie Indépendante de Référence" (Independent Reference Bookshop) if they undertake to maintain a large selection of books and organize readings and cultural events in their communities (though the wonderfully French conception of autonomy is interesting: in order to be recognized as "independent," these bookshops have to be funded by the state). As an editorial in *Le Monde* noted, the French passion for books is still robust: surveys indicate that at least half the population reads a book every day—and, contrary to what might be expected, the figure rises to 80 percent among those between the ages of fifteen and twenty-four. The Paris Salon du Livre, the largest book fair in France, welcomes around 200,000 visitors each year, and in 2013 more intimate gatherings of book-lovers were held in picturesque provincial settings on such topics as correspondence (Grignan), mountaineering (Passy), short stories (Muret), detective stories (La Canourgue), Corsican thrillers (across the island, starting in Ajaccio), poetry (Sète and Le Chambon-sur-Lignon), contemporary fiction (Île de Ré, Cap Ferret, and Chanceaux-près-Loches), and theater (Alès).[7]

Declinists often point to the fall in readership of books and newspapers in France and the difficulties faced by the publishing industry, and it is undeniable that these sectors have been steadily contracting. The more militant defenders of the French language would also note disapprovingly that translations of American fiction tend to top the literary charts: in 2013, the two best-selling titles were French versions of E. L. James's *Fifty Shades of Grey* and Dan Brown's *Inferno*. (These books had topped the charts in Britain, too, where the best-seller that year was the autobiography of Sir Alex Ferguson.) Yet distinctive French approaches and styles of thinking continue to survive, notably through the enduring presence of leading publishers such as Flammarion, Gallimard, Plon, Grasset, and Fayard, which have adapted to the changing national and international market while retaining a distinct cultural philosophy.[8]

Intellectuals continue to occupy a significant position in the French public sphere. Not only is there a greater concentration of them in France than anywhere else in the developed world, but the sheer volume of their published work is remarkable. Their visibility is further enhanced by their participation in radio and television programs, their contributions to newspapers and journals, and the strategic role they play in shaping the agenda of major publishers in Paris. Even though they are not as globally famous as their predecessors of the postwar era, intellectuals thus continue to matter in France, and their activities (and social functions) are topics of regular discussion in the national press and in periodicals such as *Le Nouvel Observateur*.[9]

Writing is still widely viewed as an important activity, a means of connecting the elite and the people, and as being crucial in many ways to strengthening the sense of citizenship: it is no accident that the main French history festival, the annual Rendez-Vous de l'Histoire in Blois, has been described as a "republican pilgrimage." And while the academic study of philosophy in French universities is stagnating, the more profound legacy of Descartes in contemporary France lies in the way his work continues to inspire wider cultural practices and norms—from the pedagogical ideal of the philosophy *baccalauréat*, centered around the notions of abstract rationalism and critical individual judgment, to the collective reflections and recollections that emerge every summer in France when the *baccalauréat* examination questions become publicly known.[10]

The creed that *la philo* should be enjoyed by a general audience is, among other things, reflected in the growth of popular events and products, from philosophical summer schools, bistros, cruises, festivals, comic strips, CDs, and DVDs to radio programs such as France-Culture's *Nouveaux Chemins*, one of the station's most notable successes in recent years. Likewise, the market for books on general culture aimed at a nonacademic audience is still strong. This is borne out in the excellent sales of books such as Érik Orsenna's *La Grammaire est une chanson douce* (*Grammar Is a Sweet, Gentle Song*, 2003), Charles Dantzig's *Dictionnaire égoiste de la littérature française* (An egoist dictionary of French literature, 2005), François Reynaert's *Nos ancêtres les gaulois et autres fadaises* (Our ancestors the Gauls and other nonsense, 2010), and the *Pour les nuls* (For Dummies) series, a collection of engagingly written introductory texts aimed, as its title indicates, at the intellectually challenged. Over nine hundred titles have been published in the series since 2001 in France, and they have sold more than 14 million copies. One of the iconic pre-presidential photographs of François Hollande, taken while he was on holiday in 2006, shows him reading a copy of *L'Histoire de France pour les nuls* (French history for dummies).[11]

The pessimistic turn among the nation's cultural elites discussed in the previous chapter was expressed through a very familiar conceptual repertoire—and many of its elements continue to inform the French style of thinking today: the presentation of ideas through overarching frameworks; a preference for considering questions in their essence, rather than in their particular manifestations; a fondness for apparent contradictions; and a tendency to frame issues around binary oppositions. Even a figure as untypical as Bruno Latour, whose sociology is committed to the very un-French notions of pluralism and relativism, and who has jettisoned the notion that human behavior can be explained in terms of general concepts such as class, power, and gender, has labeled his alternative approach "a practical metaphysics."[12]

This is not, of course, to deny that there have been substantive changes in the French intellectual landscape: the notions of revolution and rupture appear much less frequently in public discussions than in the past, and conversations about the good life no longer revolve around such idealized abstractions as reason, the general will, or the proletariat. But these entities have disappeared only to be replaced by other, equally metaphysical concepts. One powerful theme that has emerged in this context is the notion of a more privatized individualism, or an "apotheosis of personal singularities," as one observer put it. Here we have another classic French paradox: its people may have become overwhelmingly negative about their collective outlook as a nation, and more so than the people of almost any other European country. Yet when asked whether they are *personally* happy, the vast majority (around 80 percent) of French men and women consistently respond in the affirmative. An explanation may perhaps be found in a 2013 article published in *Le Point* on "why one should not despair of France," which noted that one of the "constant features of the French genius" has been its "idea of happiness and *douceur de vivre*"—an echo of Cioran's elegiac prophecy: "When Europe will be draped in shadows, France will remain its *most living* sepulcher."[13]

This contrast marks the resurgence of a classic strand of French individualism, both cerebral and frivolous, and oriented toward what the philosopher Benjamin Constant once called "the peaceful enjoyment of private independence." It is not only alive and well, but flourishing: its spirit appears in the gently ironic worldview of contemporary novelists such as Benoît Duteurtre, in the literary historian Antoine Compagnon's rediscovery of Montaigne's nonchalance, and in writings about happiness that stress self-fulfillment and the pursuit of sensuous pleasures. In his illustration of the ontology of happiness, philosopher Bertrand Vergely celebrated "the joy of living, of breathing, of inhaling the fresh morning air, of looking at the sun, of hearing the wind rustling the trees." In the same vein, lifestyle guru Luc Deborde defined bliss as "the maximization of joy and pleasure and the minimization of pain and sorrows." For opera director Jérôme Deschamps, the heart of modern Frenchness lies in its capacity to produce "a form of happiness that is distinctively ours, and which is a singular combination of the popular and the refined." This utilitarian pleasure can at times, however, be bounded by an ineffable sense of foreboding, as when a historian quoted Albert Camus's expression of anxious contentment as he basked in the heat of the Algerian sun: "There is no shame in being happy."[14]

The Weight of the Past

This resurgence of hedonistic individualism demonstrates not just the continuity of certain attitudes toward life but also the lasting capacity of the French to construct and then immerse themselves in soothing mythologies. For most of the post-Liberation decades, the threat of decadence was countered by the reassuring Gaullist assertion that the French had behaved heroically during the war, and that France represented an alternative force in world politics, thanks to its messianic leadership and its distinct political and cultural values (as the general once observed, "I prefer uplifting lies to demeaning truths"). This myth was largely intended as a replacement of the (equally fabulous) ideal of the French *mission civilisatrice* in the colonies. Yet this sense of collective confidence was damaged by the unraveling of the myth of the Resistance and the emergence of a "Vichy syndrome," which in the last two decades of the twentieth century shone a light on the darker side of the years of Occupation, prompting a growing mood of historical unease.[15]

As historian Henry Rousso has observed, the notion of contemporaneity in France changed at this juncture. Ideological battles around the revolutionary legacy faded away and the debate shifted to the catastrophes of the twentieth century, especially World War II. In this sense, France's current intellectual trough might be seen as a perverse by-product of its fixation with the 1940–1944 period. The historian Robert Frank has argued that the French have been "haunted by decline" not only because of their defeat in 1940, but because this calamity was followed by two more catastrophes that were not fully internalized: the loss of Indochina and the withdrawal from Algeria.[16]

There are frequent references, in the writings of older generations of French men and women, to the May 1940 debacle as the psychological foundation of national pessimism. Reflecting on the French malaise in 2006, the late René Rémond thus wondered whether his compatriots had ever "come to terms with 1940"; he sensed a "collective resurgence of the memory of the disaster, of the defeat that still weighs heavily on our conscience." Marcel Gauchet made the same point in an interview with the *Journal du dimanche*: the year 1940, he said, marked "the moment when France ceased to be a great power. . . . [W]e are still bearing the cross of this trauma, which we have never really confronted." This syndrome partly explains the extraordinary literary success in France of Jonathan Littell's *Les Bienveillantes* (*The Kindly Ones*), a tale of Nazi atrocities told through the eyes of a fictionalized SS officer: widely celebrated for its graphic realism and its portrayal of the banality of evil, the novel was also pilloried for its historical inaccuracies and its implicit relativization of violence.[17]

The other much-noted change to the French collective outlook is the disintegration of the progressive eschatology (a mixture of Cartesian rationalism, republicanism, and Marxism) that dominated the mindset of the nation's elites for much of the modern era. As France (soberly) celebrated the fortieth anniversary of May 1968 in 2008, former leaders of the movement reflected nostalgically about their dreams of "another life, and another type of social relations." Not coincidentally, the French penchant for utopianism also disappeared in the late twentieth century, at least for the time being; as communism imploded, Parisian thinkers turned away from the kind of sweeping visions that had so long typified the constructs of the Left Bank.[18]

Although it remains the primary source of the nation's cultural life, Paris is no longer a site of major intellectual innovation on a global scale. This is partly, as we saw in Chapter 10, a reflection of the increasing closure of French thought: its retreat from universalist concerns to narrower horizons. A more parochial but equally significant factor is that, largely as a result of the blind alley of Derridian deconstructionism, philosophy has lost its commanding position as the dominant discipline in the French humanities or social sciences. If a French book receives international attention these days, it is much more likely to be in a technical field such as economics—Thomas Piketty's study of global capitalism, for example, was widely discussed, with Paul Krugman describing it in the *New York Review of Books* as "a book which will change both the way we think about society and the way we do economics." Whether this prediction comes to pass remains an open question; nevertheless, it is hard to think of any other French work published in the social sciences since the 1980s that has earned comparable international accolades.[19]

Institutionally, the center of gravity, in terms of the training of French elites, has shifted from the École Normale Supérieure to the more technocratic Grandes Écoles, such as the École Nationale d'Administration and the École Polytechnique. The reign of the humanist (whose last representative was the mercurial, enigmatic bibliophile François Mitterrand) has given way to that of the "expert." As discussed in Chapter 4, this change has come at a price: according to Ezra Suleiman, one of the leading comparative specialists in the study of elites, graduates from the technocratic Grandes Écoles have two primary intellectual characteristics: a sense of corporatism, and a resistance to unconventional thinking.[20]

Yet this does not mean that the French no longer write serious, intellectually ambitious books. Indeed, the predilection for grand theory survives in a number of fields of inquiry—most notably, in attempts to explain the major changes in the fabric of French society since the 1960s. In a work that became a classic, the sociologist Henri Mendras coined the expression "second French revolution" to characterize the transformation of French society in the aftermath of May 1968. Mendras showed how, as the nation turned away from Catholicism, its values became more socially liberal and individualistic; the peasantry and the working class also decreased significantly as a proportion of the population, and the middle class expanded. This tradition of grand theorizing was reaffirmed in Hervé Le Bras and Emmanuel Todd's *Le Mystère français* (*The French mystery*), a cartographic representation of the key social and cultural transformations in France between 1980 and 2010. Its 120 maps chart France's transition into postindustrialism during these years, showing that the negative social and economic effects were compounded by clashes between conflicting value systems in different parts of the territory: on the one hand, a declining revolutionary and egalitarian core concentrated around the Parisian basin, and on the other an increasingly assertive periphery shaped by the latent Catholic legacy of social solidarity, associational activity, and educational achievement.[21]

While recognizing the depth of French social unease, Le Bras and Todd found evidence of more positive outlooks in their compatriots' collective mores: a decline in suicide and homicide rates, rising levels of fertility, higher educational achievements (reflected, among other things, in the growing number of high-school graduates, or *bacheliers*), a continuing trend toward the emancipation of women, and the successful assimilation of immigrants. Le Bras and Todd's conclusions about the "French mystery" thus take us back to the earlier paradox between collective and individual outlooks. For the authors, this contrast was the product of the underlying tension between a conscious pessimism and an unconscious optimism. By taking this broader (and deeper) view, the authors dispelled some of the fallacies surrounding the notion of decline—notably, the assertion that immigrants were failing to integrate and that a civilizational clash between Islam and Christianity was brewing in France. The social underpinnings of contemporary French pessimism were found to lie instead in a sense of the economic and cultural fragility of the middle classes, and in the disappearance of the secular faith represented by communist culture, which had formerly provided de-Christianized parts of the country with the promise of better horizons. This "massive depletion of social and cultural energy" was deemed to be one of the major causes of the "depression" of the French working classes.[22]

The Great Divide

Beneath the apparently placid surface of French pessimism thus lurk more complex intellectual and cultural undercurrents. It might be concluded that a new division between the confident nation and the anxious nation has replaced the old divisions of class, religion, ideology, and regional identity. The confident France consists primarily of mainstream political and business elites, and of the younger and more educated sections of the community. It feels materially secure (often because it enjoys the guarantees afforded by public-sector employment), has a positive and cosmopolitan outlook, embraces the English language (and often speaks it fluently), and has a buoyant view of the nation's future in a more economically integrated world. This is the France that recognizes itself in the quiet optimism of the writings of the academician Jean d'Ormesson, and in the frothy novels of Marc Lévy and Guillaume

Musso. According to a poll conducted in April 2014, this optimism is particularly visible in young people: 66 percent of those between the ages of eighteen to twenty-five are confident in their personal prospects for success; they agree with the statement that France is still a great power (80 percent) and believe in *la douce France*, with 82 percent celebrating the country for its excellent quality of life.[23]

The anxious France is typically older, more provincial, and more nationalistic than this group, and feels much more economically fragile; it is warier of the outside world and apprehensive of its impacts (both material and cultural) on society and on the "French way of life." Its phobias and resentments are given voice in the populist narratives of the Right and the Left, and it expresses itself in a vague anti-European sentiment; in the rising levels of support for Marine Le Pen's National Front; and in intense surges of protest that cut across party lines, from the egalitarian and regionalist tax revolt of the Breton "recaps" to the socially conservative demonstrations of the Manif pour Tous movement against gay marriage.[24]

This anxious France is also virulently anti-Parisian: in an article in *Le Figaro*, the conservative writer Natacha Polony blamed the capital for the "arrogance, certainty and complacency" of its elites; the nation, he said, was becoming an "undifferentiated global village," and the "authentic" France was being destroyed (we may note not only the appeal to essentialism again, but also the wonderful French touch of an anti-Parisian tirade being published in a quintessentially Parisian newspaper). In the same context, the graduates of the École Nationale d'Administration occupying top positions in politics and in the government bureaucracy have become a frequent object of ire in the provincial press: in a frustrated outburst, the president of a local football association in Deux-Sèvres said, "I am fed up with these rotten énarques who keep making absurd decisions." For a pensioner from Brittany, the énarques were driving France to ruin because they were so convinced that they were "the sole bearers of the truth."[25]

In a sense, this is merely the latest version of the eternal battle between the "two Frances." The ongoing confrontation between the confident and the anxious France takes place in debates about the integration of immigrant minorities from the North African Maghreb. This problem straddles issues of social equality and justice in the suburban *banlieues*, and appears in discussions relating to secularism and the preservation of *laïcité*; in the divisions over the use of political violence by a small minority of French-born Islamist extremists; and in clashes over historical memories of France's colonial legacy. In the words of one of the leading French specialists on these colonial issues: "No other European country has a relationship with its ex-colonies which is both so intense and violent, made of passion and resentment in equal measure, thus perpetuating the misunderstandings to the present day."[26]

As we saw earlier, French elite thinking has drifted toward a strident form of ethnic nationalism, often accompanied by a demonization of immigrants. But away from the inflated rhetoric, and despite the absence of hard data (as noted in Chapter 8, it remains illegal to collect official statistics about race or ethnicity in France), the reality of what the French call *intégration* is indisputable. The fact that assimilation is taking place at least to some extent can be seen in the rejection of religious-based politics by the overwhelming majority of immigrants from the Maghreb, and the harmonious coexistence of different communities in most urban areas. *Intégration* is visible, too, in the number of mixed marriages announced in the regional press, and in the growth of a Maghrebi middle class—particularly in such occupations as health, education, and banking. Also worthy of note is the consistently high ranking of couscous in the list of the most popular French dishes.

At the political level, the same trend is apparent in the increasing presence of men and women of immigrant origins among candidates standing in municipal elections. This sense of belonging was powerfully expressed in the wake of the 2015 Paris attacks, notably in a widely circulated petition among French Muslims that asserted: "We are Muslims but also fully-fledged French and European citizens." Despite its advocacy by some public intellectuals, however, this tempered multiculturalism has yet to be reflected in French public discourse. This lag bears witness to the ongoing power of the Cartesian philosophical myth of a homogeneous, unchanging, and undivided self in the nation's collective imagination. It also points to a wider phenomenon in French intellectual culture that we have seen demonstrated throughout this book: the gap between dominant categories of thought in France and the social realities they seek to describe. As another expert in French integration has said, "there is a complete disjunction between the real sociability of people and their ideological rhetoric."[27]

It would be wrong to end by giving the impression that xenophobia and intellectual closure have become the exclusive traits of the French today, or that they are destined to be dominant forever. In more specialized arenas, such as university presses and research institutes, in parts of the national daily and weekly press, and in publications such as the literary magazine *Books*, French culture is in many respects more open and transnational than ever. And there is movement in the world of creative fiction, too: in 2007, in the wake of the award of the nation's most prestigious literary prizes to authors from outside France, a distinguished group of novelists (including J. M. G. Le Clézio, Amin Maalouf, Érik Orsenna, Patrick Rambaud, and Ananda Devi) published a petition in *Le Monde* welcoming the demise of the ideal of Francophonia (or, as Derek Walcott put it, "franco-phoney"). They called instead for a new style of fictional writing that would reengage with "the most egregious absence in contemporary French literature: the world."[28]

But French-speaking artists are still capable of reaching international audiences. The rapper MC Solaar, for example, who sees himself as a latter-day Baudelairean *flâneur*, and borrows freely from the works of Rimbaud, Descartes, and Rousseau, has even been known to pose as an heir to the structuralist tradition: "I pose, compose, recompose, decompose new prose like a structural linguist." This greater engagement with the wider world is also physical: since 2000, the number of French nationals living in other countries has risen by 60 percent, and currently stands at over 1.6 million; nearly 80,000 students travel abroad to study each year, including the entire third-year cohort at the Institut d'Études Politiques (aka Sciences Po).[29]

France is of course not alone in experiencing an unsettled intellectual and cultural transition into the new century. In some respects, the tension between greater openness and closure is present in all major industrialized nations. But it is striking that this particular Gallic mixture of pessimism and optimism has few echoes in Britain and Germany or, for that matter, in the United States, where the new lines of social and intellectual fracture are very different. This observation brings home the uniqueness of the French way of seeing the world. The deep roots of French communism in the nation's history and culture were discussed in Chapter 3, but the point could be made more broadly. The French "republican model," as it has evolved since the later nineteenth century, remains noteworthy for its holistic way of thinking, which can be seen both in its civic ideals and in its fervent adhesion to the Rousseauist notion of popular sovereignty. Gaullism, the inheritor of the Bonapartist tradition, which decisively reshaped French political culture in the modern era, is likewise unique to France: through its appeal to providential leadership and collectivist notions of the general interest and national grandeur, it differed in key respects from British conservatism and European Christian democracy. The French Left's powerful strain of anticapitalism and its cultural hostility to the bourgeoisie have no other real European equivalent, whether in British Labourism or Scandinavian social democracy. And even though these French ideologies have become frayed in recent decades, they continue to cast a long shadow over national political culture—if only because of their debilitating impact on liberalism, which has yet to develop into a coherent political and intellectual force in France, and their appeal to powerful mythologies such as the division of the world between friends and enemies, the fear of dispossession, and the sense that the refusal of fatalism is an inherent characteristic of Frenchness.

So, as the new millennium unfolds, and despite their increasing frailty, the French remain a recognizably intellectual people, lyrical and pugnacious, energetic and impatient, filled with generosity, pride, and an insatiable yearning for perfectibility—but riven, too, with contradictions: instinctively attached to the ideal of democratic governance, but vulnerable to the temptation of the providential hero; clinging to a belief in the enabling capacities of the state, but forever complaining about its distance from the citizenry and rebelling against its decisions; ready to take up the "social critique" provided by intellectuals, but obstinately wedded to an educational system that rewards conventional thinking; dissatisfied with the performance of their elites, but faithful, and even deferential, to their faded old glories (especially the *immortels* of the Académie Française and the indestructible rock star Johnny Hallyday); averse to communitarian conceptions of society, which might unleash the socially destructive force of "groups," yet willing to devolve ever greater freedoms to regional political institutions; scornful of the power of "technocracy" (among the most reviled terms in the French language), yet finding no greater fulfillment for their progeny than entry into the gilded ranks of the Grandes Écoles; decisive architects of an economically liberal Europe, but profoundly contemptuous of capitalism; increasingly retreating from the public sphere, and more suspicious than ever of their leaders, yet capable of turning out in their millions on the streets of Paris to reaffirm their republican values. Seen in this light, the current wave of French diffidence expresses a Gallic contestation of a world perceived to be both ever more chaotic and at the same time dominated by Anglo-American mercantilism. One thing is certain, however: as they face the challenges of the twenty-first century, the French will remain the most intellectual of peoples, continuing to produce elegant and sophisticated abstractions about the human condition.

ACKNOWLEDGMENTS

Every book is in some sense a collective venture, a work that rests on the intellectual endeavors and accumulated wisdom of present and past generations. I am especially aware of this debt with this work and would like to start by paying tribute to all of those—friends, colleagues, and students—who have molded my way of thinking about France over the past three decades. I would particularly like to single out two remarkable figures who are, sadly, no longer with us: Tony Judt, whose brilliant lectures on French politics captivated me when I first arrived in Oxford as an undergraduate in the early 1980s, and Vincent Wright, who supervised my doctorate and from whom I inherited (among other oddities) an abiding obsession with the history of Bonapartism. Both Tony and Vincent became dear friends, inspiring me with their encyclopedic understanding of French ideas and practices and their belief that, ultimately, there is no meaningful difference between history, politics, and political thought.

My approach has also been shaped by exchanges with French friends and colleagues. I cannot name them all, of course, but I would like to mention the following in particular for their intellectual generosity and their readiness to engage in discussion about the rich treasures of French thought: Jean-Pierre Azéma, Marc-Olivier Baruch, Gilles Candar, Jean-Claude Caron, Jean-Claude Casanova, Vincent Duclert, Patrice Gueniffey, Patrice Higonnet, Jacqueline Lalouette, Thierry Lentz, Emmanuelle Loyer, Jean-Pierre Machelon, Pierre Nora, Natalie Petiteau, Christophe Prochasson, Pierre Rosanvallon, Philippe Roussin, and Jean-François Sirinelli. Special thanks to Henri Bovet for his unstinting *fidélité* and his ever-stimulating insights into the latest twists in the French dialectic.

This book has hugely benefited from the comments of a group of dedicated readers. For their unceasing encouragement, their invaluable suggestions, and their eagle eyes, my warmest thanks go to David Bell, Henri Bovet, Alain Chatriot, Robert Darnton, Laurent Douzou, Emmanuel Fureix, Chloé Gaboriaux, Cécile Laborde, Marc Lazar, Michel Leymarie, Karma Nabulsi, Olivier Postel-Vinay, Graham Robb, Anne Simonin, Adam Swift, Abdel Takriti, Max Thompson, and Robert Tombs.

I have also had the good fortune of working with three outstanding editors: Sophie Berlin at Flammarion, Lara Heimert at Basic Books, and Stuart Proffitt at Allen Lane. They all carefully read through early drafts of the book and provided precious feedback, both on presentational and substantive issues, as well as on specific points. It is a great honor to join the distinguished list of authors at Basic Books, and I am very grateful to Lara for welcoming me into the fold. My warmest thanks, too, to Leah Stecher at Basic Books for all her help, to Roger Labrie for his timely and efficient line-editing of the manuscript, and to Kathy Streckfus for her excellent work with the copy-editing.

I am indebted to the Master and Fellows of Balliol College and the Department of Politics and International Relations at Oxford for granting me two terms of sabbatical in 2013, during which I carried out the bulk of the research for this book and completed its first draft. My literary agent, James Gill, has been a pillar of support, as always, and I cannot thank him enough for his efficiency and steadfastness.

Above all, I am grateful to Karma, whose illuminating comments have helped make this a better book than it would otherwise have been. Her boundless energy and radiant spirit fill me with admiration, and I am forever thankful for the miracle of our shared life, full of intellectual excitement, expansive horizons, and sheer joy. I dedicate this book to her.

SUDHIR HAZAREESINGH
Paris, January 2015

NOTES

Preface

1. The term *rentrées littéraires* refers to the dramatic opening of the publishing season in France following the August holidays each year. Hundreds of books are published and the top literary prizes are awarded during this time amid much fanfare and media coverage.

2. Edgar Morin, *Autocritique* (Paris, 1975), 97; Alfred Fouillée, *Psychologie du peuple français*, 3rd ed. (Paris, 1903), 379.

Introduction: A Yearning Toward Universality

1. For a full analysis of Villepin's speech, see Frédéric Bozo, *Histoire secrète de la crise irakienne* (Paris, 2013), 249–250. All translations from the French within the text are by the author unless otherwise noted.

2. Blaise Pascal, *Pensées* (1669), ed. A. J. Krailsheimer (London, 1995), no. 82; Antoine Rivarol, *De l'universalité de la langue française* (1784) (Clermont-Ferrand, 2009), 43; Hippolyte Taine, *La Fontaine et ses fables* (Paris, 1875), 15; Montesquieu, *De l'esprit des lois* (Paris, 1973), Book 19, chap. 5; Ernest Lavisse, "L'État d'esprit qu'il faut," *La Revue de Paris*, January 1915; Jules Michelet, *Le Peuple* (Paris, 1974), 160; Émile de Montégut, *Libres opinions morales et historiques* (Paris, 1858), 3; Julien Benda, *Du style d'idées: Réflexions sur la pensée* (Paris, 1948), 45.

3. Axelle Choffat, "Métaphysique du pain quotidien," *L'Est républicain*, August 17, 2014; Philippe Corcuff, "Qui a tué l'esprit à gauche?," *Libération*, December 27, 2012; Michel Lacroix, *Éloge du patriotisme: Petite philosophie du sentiment national* (Paris, 2011), 19; Bruno Frappat, "Mots de France," *La Croix*, May 3, 2014; Le Festival du Mot, www.festivaldumot.fr/.

4. "*Thèse, antithèse, synthèse!*," *L'Est républicain*, June 17, 2014; Louis Pinto, *Le Café du commerce des penseurs* (Broissieux, 2009), 142.

5. Quoted in Stuart Macintyre, *A Proletarian Science: Marxism in Britain, 1917–1933* (London, 1980), 1; Rifa'a Rafi' al-Tahtawi, *An Imam in Paris: Account of a Stay in France by an Egyptian Cleric, 1826–1831* (London, 2011), 176; *Instructions for British Servicemen in France* (1944) (Oxford, 2005). Césaire's remains stayed on his native island, but a fresco in his honor was inaugurated in the Panthéon in 2011 by President Sarkozy. See "Hommage national à Aimé Césaire," *L'Express*, April 6, 2011. Tillion, whose remains will enter the Panthéon in May 2015, was among a group of four Resistance figures chosen by President François Hollande. See "Germaine Tillion, une grande femme bientôt au Panthéon," *Libération*, February 19, 2014.

6. Jacques-Bénigne Bossuet, *Lettres sur l'éducation du Dauphin* (Paris, 1920), 128; Nicolas de Condorcet, *Cinq mémoires sur l'instruction publique* (Paris, 1994), 61; David Caute, *Communism and the French Intellectuals* (London, 1964), 212; Ben Macintyre, "The Bare-chested Cheek of a French Thinker," *The Times*, March 29, 2011; Pierre Bourdieu, *The State Nobility: Elite Schools in the Field of Power* (Stanford, 1996).

7. Louis-Sébastien Mercier, *Tableau de Paris*, vol. 2 (Amsterdam, 1783), 145; Patrice Higonnet, *Paris: Capital of the World* (Cambridge, MA, 2002), 144; Charles Dupont-White, *L'Individu et l'état*, 3rd ed. (Paris, 1865), lxvii.

8. Letter of February 24, 1878, quoted in Gilles Candar and Vincent Duclert, *Jean Jaurès* (Paris, 2014), 62.

9. See Benedetta Craveri, *L'Âge de la conversation* (Paris, 2002).

10. Ernest Lavisse, *Études et étudiants* (Paris, 1890), 89; Jean d'Ormesson, "Être français," *Le Point*, January 13, 2011.

11. See the chapters by Raoul Girardet and Michel Vovelle in Pierre Nora, ed., *Les Lieux de mémoire*, vol. 1 (Paris, 1984).

12. See the chapter on the republican tradition in Sudhir Hazareesingh, *Political Traditions in Modern France* (Oxford, 1994).

13. See Jack Hayward, *Fragmented France: Two Centuries of Disputed Identity* (Oxford, 2007); Jean Picq, *Il faut aimer l'état: Essai sur l'état en France à l'aube du XXIe siècle* (Paris, 1995).

14. For the classic analysis of Gaullism as a form of Bonapartism, see René Rémond, *Les Droites en France* (Paris, 1998).

15. Laurent Martin, *Le Canard enchaîné: Histoire d'un journal satirique, 1915–2005* (Paris, 2005), 341; "L'Homme qui voulait être roi," *Le Nouvel Observateur*, February 2, 1981; Jean Guitton, "Le Philosophe, le président et la mort," *Libération*, December 16, 1994; Alain Duhamel, *La Marche consulaire* (Paris, 2009); Louis XIV, *Mémoires*, ed. Joël Cornette (Paris, 2007), 65, 337.

16. On this theme, see Jean-Marc Largeaud, *Napoléon et Waterloo: La défaite glorieuse de 1815 à nos jours* (Paris, 2006); entry of October 13, 1950, in Julien Green, *Journal, 1950–1954* (Paris, 1955), 33–34.

17. Norman Hampson, *The Enlightenment* (London, 1968); Patrice Higonnet, *Goodness Beyond Virtue* (Cambridge, MA, 1998); Theodore Zeldin, *France, 1848–1945*, rev. ed. (Oxford, 1979); Tony Judt, *Past Imperfect* (Berkeley, 1992); Jeremy Jennings, *Revolution and the Republic: A History of Political Thought in France Since the Eighteenth Century* (Oxford, 2013); David A. Bell, *The Cult of the Nation in France*

(Cambridge, MA, 2003); Marc Lazar, *Le Communisme, une passion française* (Paris, 2005).

18. See Quentin Skinner, *Liberty Before Liberalism* (Cambridge, UK, 1997); Alfred Delvau, *Histoire anecdotique des cafés et cabarets de Paris* (Paris, 1862), 2; "Réfugiés," *Libération*, April 19–20, 2014.

19. On the *salon* and seventeenth-century society, see Dena Goodman, *The Republic of Letters: A Cultural History of the French Enlightenment* (Ithaca, NY, 1994); Erica Harth, *Cartesian Women: Versions and Subversions of Rational Discourse in the Old Regime* (Ithaca, NY, 1992), 4. The diplomat is quoted in Steven Kale, *French Salons: High Society and Political Sociability from the Old Regime to the Revolution of 1848* (Baltimore, 2006), 6.

20. Quoted in Vincent Laisney, *L'Arsenal romantique: Le salon de Charles Nodier, 1824–1834* (Paris, 2002), 66.

21. Entry of January 19, 1832, in Heinrich Heine, *De la France* (Paris, 1994), 51.

22. It was published in the posthumous collection edited by Michael Otsuka and G. A. Cohen, *Finding Oneself in the Other* (Princeton, NJ, 2013).

23. Alain Duhamel, "François Hollande et le pessimisme français," *Libération*, June 26, 2013; Patrice Bollon, "La France pense-t-elle encore?," *Magazine Littéraire*, September 7, 2012.

24. Hampson, *Enlightenment*, 146.

25. Arno Mayer, *The Furies: Violence and Terror in the French and Russian Revolutions* (Princeton, NJ, 2000); Alice L. Conklin, Sarah Fishman, and Robert Zaretsky, *France and Its Empire Since 1870* (New York, 2010). On Comte's influence in Brazil, see Paul Arbousse-Bastide, Annie Petit, and Francis Utéza, *Le Positivisme politique et religieux au Brésil* (Turnhout, 2010); and Isabel di Vanna, "Reading Comte Across the Atlantic: Intellectual Exchanges Between France and Brazil and the Question of Slavery," *Journal of the History of European Ideas*, July 2012.

26. On the folk song, see J. Collin de Plancy, *La Vie et la légende intime des deux Empereurs Napoléon Ier et Napoléon II* (Paris, 1867), 405. On Giáp, see Bui Diem, *In the Jaws of History* (Bloomington, IN, 1999), 13. I am grateful to Pierre Brocheux for bringing this memoir to my attention.

27. Jonathan I. Israel, *Democratic Enlightenment, Philosophy, Revolution and Human Rights, 1750–1790* (Oxford, 2011); Letter to Laure de Gasparin, September 1857, cited in Laurent Theis, *François Guizot* (Paris, 2008), 273; Tocqueville letter to Kergorlay, October 18, 1847, quoted in Lucien Jaume, *Tocqueville* (Paris, 2008), 14; Jules Michelet, *Légendes démocratiques du Nord* (Paris, 1877), 12; Olivier Todd, *André Malraux, une vie* (Paris, 2001), 491.

28. "I am not a Marxist" is quoted in Leslie Derfler, *Paul Lafargue and the Founding of French Marxism, 1842–1882* (Cambridge, MA, 1991), 207. Talleyrand is quoted in Philippe Roger, *L'Ennemi américain* (Paris, 2002), 70. On "tact and charm," see Ernest Renan, *La Réforme intellectuelle et morale* (Paris, 1872), x. On England as a political model, see Aurelian Craiatu, *A Virtue for Courageous Minds: Moderation in French Political Thought, 1748–1830* (Princeton, NJ, 2012), 2. On Hugo, and French exiles more generally, see Sylvie Aprile, *Le Siècle des exilés: Bannis et proscrits, de 1789 à la Commune* (Paris, 2010).

29. Flora Tristan, *Promenades dans Londres* (Paris, 2003), 72; Jean Guiffan, *Histoire de l'anglophobie en France: De Jeanne d'Arc à la vache folle* (Rennes, 2004); "La Perfide Albion," in G. Faurie, *Le Réveil populaire, chants et poèmes* (Paris, 1888), 5; Jean-Louis Crémieux-Brilhac, *La France Libre de l'appel du 18 juin á la Libération* (Paris, 1996), 310; Christophe (pseud. of Georges Colomb), *La Famille Fenouillard* (Paris, 1893).

30. Jean-François Revel, *Le Style du Général* (1959) (Brussels, 1988), 118.

Chapter 1: The Skull of Descartes

1. Since 1967, La Haye–Descartes has been known simply as "Descartes." An excerpt of Dumayet's interview was broadcast on the program *Concordance des temps*, presented by Jean-Noël Jeanneney: "Descartes, symbole national et mythe universel," France Culture, May 14, 2011.

2. On "remarkable advances," see Abbé de Saint-Pierre, "Discours sur les différences du grand homme et de l'homme illustre," in Abbé Seran de la Tour, *Histoire d'Epaminondas* (Paris, 1739), xliv. On Descartes's place in modern French thought, the seminal work is François Azouvi's *Descartes et la France: Histoire d'une passion nationale* (Paris, 2002). On "passion for solitude," see Anthony Kenny, *Descartes: A Study of His Philosophy* (New York, 1968), 5.

3. René Descartes, *Discourse on Method* and *The Meditations*, ed. and trans. F. E. Sutcliffe (London, 1968), 53–54.

4. Marcelle Joignet, *La Solitude de M. Descartes* (Paris, 1940). For an example of Cartesian feminist writings from the late seventeenth century, see François Poullain de la Barre, *Three Cartesian Feminist Treatises*, ed. Marcelle Maistre Welch, trans. Vivien Bosley (Chicago, 2002).

5. Voltaire, *Lettres philosophiques* (Paris, 1734), 151; Jean-François Revel, *Descartes inutile et incertain* (Paris, 1976); Colleen Boggs, "Humans That Harm Animals Should Be Held Accountable," *Guardian*, April 17, 2013.

6. Charles Péguy, "Note conjointe sur M. Descartes et la philosophie cartésienne," in *Oeuvres complètes de Charles Péguy, 1873–1914*, vol. 9 (Paris, 1924), 61–62; Fernand Giraudeau, *Nos moeurs politiques: Lettres au rédacteur du "Constitutionnel"* (Paris, 1868), 100.

7. Stéphane Van Damme, "Restaging Descartes: From the Philosophical Reception to the National Pantheon," *Les Dossiers du Grihl*, Blumenthal Lectures, Colorado, October 8, 2002. On the scientific disputes around Descartes's remains, see Russell Shorto, *Descartes' Bones: A Skeletal History of the Conflict Between Faith and Reason* (New York, 2008). On the Jardin des Plantes skull, see Philippe Comar, *Mémoires de mon crâne: René Des-Cartes* (Paris, 1997), 61.

8. Convention Nationale, *Rapport fait à la Convention Nationale au nom du Comité d'Instruction Publique et des inspecteurs, par Marie-Joseph Chénier*, Paris, October 2, 1793, p. 3; Louis Lavelle, "L'Esprit cartésien," *Le Temps*, January 26, 1936.

9. Paul Valéry, "Seconde Vue de Descartes," in Paul Valéry, *Variété V* (Paris, 1944), 258; Émile Durkheim, *L'Éducation morale* (Paris, 1925), 290.

10. Theodore Zeldin, *France, 1848–1945: Intellect and Pride* (Oxford, 1980), 225.

11. Auguste Comte, *Discours d'ouverture du cours de philosophie positive de M. Auguste Comte* (Paris, 1829), 33; Auguste Comte, *Discours sur l'ensemble du positivisme* (Paris, 1907), 238; Georges Cantecor, *Le Positivisme* (Paris, 1904), 103–104.

12. François Guizot, *Cours d'histoire moderne* (1829), cited in Azouvi, *Descartes et la France*, 174; Descartes, *Discourse*, 45; Charles de Rémusat, "Descartes," in *Essais de philosophie*, vol. 1 (Paris, 1842), 102.

13. Broglie speech during parliamentary debate (1844), quoted in Lucien Jaume, *L'Individu effacé, ou Le Paradoxe du libéralisme français* (Paris, 1997), 258. On the reinvention of French conceptions of the subject, see Jan Goldstein, *The Post-Revolutionary Self: Politics and Psyche in France, 1750–1850* (Cambridge, MA, 2008).

14. On the "absence of chimeras," see Victor Cousin, *Histoire générale de la philosophie* (Paris, 1884), 365. For "reveal known truths," see Cousin speech to Chambre des Pairs on the teaching of philosophy (1844), in Claude Bernard, ed., *Victor Cousin, ou La Religion de la philosophie* (Toulouse, 1991), 80.

15. Jules Michelet, *Ma jeunesse* (Paris, 1884), 204; Claude Husson, *Philosophie de la république, ou Exposition des principes républicains d'après la raison pure* (Paris, 1848), 17–18.

16. Étienne Vacherot, *Essais de philosophie critique* (Paris, 1864), 305; Jules Simon, *La Politique radicale* (Paris, 1868), 2; Ferry speech during parliamentary debate on education (December 1880), quoted in Azouvi, *Descartes et la France*, 223.

17. Jules Steeg, *La Vie morale: Recueil de lectures choisies et annotées* (Paris, 1889), 81–82. On Descartes and the Freemasonry, see Léo Taxil, *Supplément à "la France maçonnique"* (Paris, 1889), 66.

18. Maurice Barthélemy, *La Libre pensée et ses martyrs: Petit dictionnaire de l'intolérance cléricale* (Paris, 1904), 56; Léon Blum, "Souvenirs sur l'affaire," in *L'Oeuvre de Léon Blum* (Paris, 1965), 540.

19. P.-Félix Thomas, "De l'individualisme," *Revue de l'enseignement primaire et primaire supérieur* 9, no. 3 (1898): 18.

20. Hippolyte Taine, *Les Origines de la France contemporaine*, vol. 1 (Paris, 1901), 315, 316.

21. Claude Nicolet, *L'Idée républicaine en France* (Paris, 1982), 55; Henri Bergson, "Message au Congrès Descartes" (1937), in Henri Bergson, *Mélanges* (Paris, 1972), 1579; Gérard Milhaud, "Descartes vu par la génération française contemporaine," *Revue de Synthèse* 14, no. 1 (1937): 67.

22. Charles Adam, "Descartes: Ses trois notions fondamentales," in *Descartes*, special tricentenary issue of *Revue philosophique* (1937): 14; Charles Adam, *Descartes: Sa vie et son oeuvre* (Paris, 1937), 173, 175; Maxime Leroy, *Descartes social* (Paris, 1931).

23. Alain, "Étude sur Descartes," in René Descartes, *Discours de la méthode* (Paris, 1927), 2–3; "La Vie intérieure," June 21, 1932, Alain, *Propos*, vol. 1 (Paris, 1956), 1089; untitled article dated January 28, 1914, *Propos*, vol. 2 (Paris, 1970), 343; "Se penser soi-même," April 15, 1930, *Propos*, 1:929; untitled article dated November 1931, *Propos*, 2:881; untitled article dated January 1934, *Propos*, 2:1000–1001; "Contre les nouveautés," January 10, 1936, *Propos* 1:1302; "Le Fanatisme," January 24, 1928, *Propos*, 1:755.

24. On the analogy with Descartes, see "La Vraie République," April 1, 1914, *Propos*, 1:186. For "power of refusal," see article of November 25, 1922, *Propos*, 2:524.

On the individuality of thought, see Alain, *Le Citoyen contre les pouvoirs* (Geneva, 1979), 159.

25. On "movement and rhythm," see Henri Petit, *Images: Descartes et Pascal* (Paris, 1930), 33, 50. On "swordsmanship," see, for example, "Le Dieu cruel," November 5, 1927, *Propos*, 1:749.

26. On the comparison with Foch, see Jacques Chevalier, *Descartes* (Paris, 1921), 347; on the common good, ibid., 5; on the dualities, ibid., 3–4; on the "liberation" from "German thinking," ibid., 2.

27. Georges Duhamel, "Ligne Maginot et Ligne Descartes," *Le Figaro*, November 5, 1938; Henri Berr, *Machiavel et l'Allemagne* (Paris, 1939), 30.

28. On the masked nature of Cartesianism, see "La Dissolution des sociétés secrètes," *Le Journal des débats*, August 4, 1940. On the need to discard Descartes, see Marc Bernard, "La Foi est nécessaire," *Le Figaro*, November 23, 1940. The Bonnard quotation is cited in Marcelle Barjonet, "Ce qui mourait et ce qui naissait chez Descartes," *La Pensée*, no. 32 (1950): 23.

29. Paul Masson-Oursel, "Francs et raison," *La Nouvelle Revue Française*, December 1941, 665–666, 669.

30. On time for action, see Henri Michel, *Les Courants de pensée de la Résistance* (Paris, 1962), 763. On "rationalism in movement," see Georges Politzer, "Qu'est-ce que le rationalisme?," *La Pensée* 1, no. 2 (1939): 19. On logical consequence, see Georges Canguilhem, *Vie et mort de Jean Cavaillès* (Paris, 1996), 36. On the lecture, see Yves Soulignac, *Les Camps d'internement en Limousin, 1939–1945* (Saint-Paul, 1995), 37 (my thanks to Laurent Douzou for this information). On the communist citation in celebration of Descartes, see André Voguet, "Souvenirs de l'année universitaire, 1940–1941," *La Pensée*, no. 89 (1960): 25.

31. On the "undoing of all norms," see Pierre Bourdan, *Carnet des jours d'attente* (Paris, 1945), 12. On the appeal to conscience, see Alya Aglan, *Le Temps de la Résistance* (Paris, 2008), 39. On de Gaulle's "straight path," see Albert Hall speech, June 18, 1942, in Charles de Gaulle, *Discours et messages*, vol. 1 (Paris, 1946), 198. On "weak reasons," see Descartes, *Discourse*, 46.

32. On Descartes's explosiveness, see Jean-Paul Sartre, *Carnets de la drôle de guerre: Septembre 1939–Mars 1940* (Paris, 1995), 284–285. On Camus's notion of the absurd, see Albert Camus, *Le Mythe de Sisyphe* (Paris, 1942), 37. On the weight of the world, see Jean-Paul Sartre, *L'Être et le Néant* (Paris, 1943), 598.

33. On Descartes as the architect of democracy, see Jean-Paul Sartre, *Descartes* (Paris, 1944), 19; for "absolute autonomy," ibid., 47. On *cogito*, see Jean-Paul Sartre, *L'Existentialisme est un humanisme* (Paris, 1996), 57.

34. On spruced-up version of Cartesianism, see Sartre, *L'Existentialisme est un humanisme*, 86. On "never more free," see Jean-Paul Sartre, *The Republic of Silence*, ed. A. J. Liebling (New York, 1947), 498. On "we are alone," see Sartre, *L'Existentialisme est un humanisme*, 39.

35. Jean-Paul Sartre, *Qu'est-ce que la littérature?* (Paris, 1948), 27, 72, 283.

36. Albert Camus, *L'Homme révolté* (Paris, 1951), 36, 292–299.

37. On the positive ethic, see Simone de Beauvoir, "L'Existentialisme et la sagesse des nations" (1945), in Simone de Beauvoir, *L'Existentialisme et la sagesse des nations*

(Paris, 2008), 37. On the "morality of ambiguity," see Simone de Beauvoir, *Pour une morale de l'ambiguité* (Paris, 1947), 196–197.

38. For "act without . . . guarantees," see Simone de Beauvoir, *Le Sang des autres* (1945) (Paris, 1979), 212. On the need to choose, see Simone de Beauvoir, "Idéalisme moral et réalisme politique" (1945), in de Beauvoir, *L'Existentialisme et la sagesse des nations*, 68. On the limitations of this approach, see Simone de Beauvoir, *La Force des choses* (Paris, 1963), 79–80.

39. Simone de Beauvoir, *Le Deuxième Sexe*, trans. H. M. Pashley as *The Second Sex* (London, 1984), 295.

40. Georges Cogniot, "Chronique politique," *La Pensée*, no. 13 (1947): 76.

41. On "eminent representatives," see Marcel Cachin, "Les Communistes célèbrent la mémoire du philosophe et du savant," *L'Humanité*, May 11, 1937. On Descartes as the "glory of France," see "La Grandiose Manifestation du mur," *L'Humanité*, May 31, 1937. On the tradition of excellence, see *L'Humanité*, September 27, 1944.

42. *Discours de la méthode*, with preface and commentary by Marcelle Barjonet (Paris, 1950); Jean-Louis Lecercle, "La Réforme de l'enseignement et les humanités classiques," *La Pensée*, no. 62 (1955): 17. On mass education, see, for example, "Importantes interventions des élus communistes," *L'Humanité*, December 17, 1938.

43. "Le Discours de Maurice Thorez," *L'Humanité*, May 3, 1946.

44. On the "unity of thought," see Henri Mougin, "L'Esprit encyclopédique et la tradition philosophique française," Part I, *La Pensée*, no. 5 (1945): 16. For "the installation of thought in the world," see Henri Mougin, "L'Esprit encyclopédique et la tradition philosophique française," Parts II and III, *La Pensée*, no. 6 (1946), and no. 7 (1946). See also Henri Lefebvre, *Descartes* (Paris, 1947), 309; Karl Marx, "Descartes et les sources du matérialisme français," *La Pensée*, no. 28 (1950).

45. "Les Voyageurs et la terre," *L'Humanité*, March 4, 1937.

46. Jean Cassou, "Le Oui de Descartes," *Les Lettres françaises*, 1946; see Jean Cassou, *Une vie pour la liberté* (Paris, 1981), 273–274; Jean-Richard Bloch, *L'Homme du communisme: Portrait de Staline* (Paris, 1949), 13.

47. André Glucksmann, *Descartes, c'est la France* (Paris, 1987), 275.

48. Pierre Guenancia, *Descartes et l'ordre politique* (Paris, 2012 [1983]); Denis Moreau, *Dans le milieu d'une forêt: Essais sur Descartes et le sens de la vie* (Paris, 2012); Bruno Latour, *Cogitamus: Six lettres sur les humanités scientifiques* (Paris, 2010), 101.

49. On Descartes's remains, see "Le Crâne de Descartes au Panthéon?," *Le Figaro*, January 10, 2011. On "being at home in . . . Europe," see Jean-Claude Brisville, *L'Entretien de M. Descartes avec M. Pascal le jeune* (Paris, 1986), 13. Premiered in 1985 in Paris, this play was performed again at the Théâtre de Poche in Montparnasse in the autumn of 2014. On Descartes's devotion to God, see Brigitte Hermann, *Histoire de mon esprit: Le Roman de la vie de René Descartes* (Paris, 1996). On his love for his daughter, see Jean-Luc Quoy-Bodin, *Un amour de Descartes* (Paris, 2013), 112. On his "virtuous humility," see Huguette Bouchardeau, *Mes nuits avec Descartes* (Paris, 2002), 196–201, 213. On his ability to inspire "pathological doubt," see Frédéric Schiffter, *Sur le blabla et le chichi des philosophes* (Paris, 2002), 24. For "a knight of the impossible," see Alexandre Astruc, *Le Roman de Descartes* (Paris, 1989), 245.

50. "'Terre de Breizh: Révélation' en tournage au temple de Lanleff," *Ouest-France*, August 14, 2014; Frédéric Pagès, *Descartes et le cannabis: Pourquoi partir en Hollande?* (Paris, 1996); "René Descartes, c'est aussi le nom d'une rose," *La Nouvelle République du Centre-Ouest*, May 14, 2012. On the Lorient Football Club, see *Le Progrès* (Lyon), May 17, 2014. On the artist Brigitte Clamon, see "L'Art géométrique de Brigitte Clamon," *Ouest-France*, July 3, 2013. The mystery novel is Frédéric Serror and Herio Saboga, *L'Échelle de Monsieur Descartes* (Paris, 1999).

Chapter 2: Darkness and Light

1. For an excellent biography, see Philip Short, *Mitterrand: A Study in Ambiguity* (London, 2013).

2. Élizabeth Teissier, *Sous le signe de Mitterrand: Sept ans d'entretiens* (Paris, 1997), 78, 168–169.

3. The title of her thesis was *The Epistemological Situation of Astrology Through the Fascination-Rejection Ambivalence in Postmodern Societies*. On "forces of the spirit," see "Je crois aux forces de l'esprit et je ne vous quitterai pas," *Libération*, January 2, 1995.

4. On the "Robespierre constellation," see Jules Michelet, *Les Femmes de la Révolution* (Paris, 1855), 284, 287. On Napoleon's star, see *Mémoires du Général Rapp, aide-de-camp de Napoléon* (Paris, 1823), 23–24. On Home, see Georges Lacour-Gayet, *L'Impératrice Eugénie* (Paris, 1925), 48.

5. On fortune-tellers, see, for example, "Jaurès spiritualiste," *Annales du spiritisme*, March 1925. On Auriol and Pinay, see Georges Minois, *Histoire de l'avenir: Des prophètes à la prospective* (Paris, 1996), 576–577. Professionally known as Regulus, Vasset revealed his role in an interview in 2000. See Josette Alia, "L'astrologue de de Gaulle parle," *Le Nouvel Observateur*, no. 1865, August 3, 2000; Charles de Gaulle, *Mémoires de guerre*, vol. 3 (Paris, 1999), 344.

6. On the enduring fascination with the work of Nostradamus, see Stéphane Gerson, *Nostradamus: How an Obscure Renaissance Astrologer Became the Modern Prophet of Doom* (New York, 2012). On occultism in 1934, see Theodore Zeldin, *France 1848–1945: Taste and Corruption* (Oxford, 1980), 49–52, 55. On contemporary occultism, see Cyril Hofstein, "La France occulte," *Le Figaro*, October 30, 2013. On books, see *L'Édition en Perspective 2010–11* (Paris, 2011). In 2011, esoteric literature represented 1 percent of the overall market in France (history represented 1.1 percent), but the average sales for a title on esotericism was 5,077 copies per title, just below literature (5,362), and considerably ahead of history (967). More recent figures (for the year 2012–2013) show a drop in the volume of sales for both history and esoteric literature. See *L'Édition en Perspective 2012–13* (Paris, 2013), 67–68. See also Edgar Morin, *La Croyance astrologique moderne* (Lausanne, 1982), 145.

7. Quoted in Girolamo Imbruglia, "Raison," in Vincenzo Ferrone and Daniel Roche, eds., *Le Monde des Lumières* (Paris, 1999), 88.

8. *Encyclopédie, ou Dictionnaire raisonné des sciences, des arts et des métiers*, vol. 12 (Neuchâtel, n.d.), 509.

9. On cow urine, see ibid., 1:612. On "infected this world," see Letter [D13805] to King Frederick II, January 5, 1767, in *Les Oeuvres complètes de Voltaire*, W. H. Barber and T. Besterman, eds., vol. 31 (Geneva, 1974), 184. On Voltaire's view of sorcery,

see Margaret Libby, *The Attitude of Voltaire to Magic and the Sciences* (New York, 1935), 222. On occult causes, see "Occultes" entry in *Dictionnaire philosophique*, in Voltaire, *Oeuvres complètes*, vol. 19 (Paris, 1876), 86. On the heavenly city, see Carl Becker, *The Heavenly City of the Eighteenth-Century Philosophers* (New Haven, CT, 1974), 31.

10. Abbé de Saint-Pierre, "Discours sur les différences du grand homme et de l'homme illustre," in Abbé Séran de la Tour, *Histoire d'Epaminondas* (Paris, 1739), xxvii; Jean-Jacques Rousseau, *Émile, ou de l'Éducation*, rev. ed. (Paris, 1924), 313; Nicolas de Condorcet, *Esquisse d'un tableau historique des progrès de l'esprit humain* (Paris, 1970), 201, 239.

11. Abbé Barruel, *Memoirs Illustrating the History of Jacobinism*, vol. 3 (New York, 1799).

12. On Illuminism, see Louis-Claude de Saint-Martin, *Lettre à un ami, ou Considérations politiques, philosophiques et religieuses sur la Révolution française* (Paris, 1795), 13, 59, 73. On the living dead, see Louis-Claude de Saint-Martin, *Le Cimetière d'Amboise* (Paris, 1913), 1. For "most knowledgeable," see Joseph de Maistre, *Les Soirées de Saint-Petersbourg* (Paris, 1895). On Mme. de Staël, see Germaine de Staël, *De l'Allemagne*, new ed., vol. 5 (Paris, 1960), 96, and Nicole Jacques-Chaquin and Stéphane Michaud, "Documents sur Saint-Martin dans l'entourage de Mme de Staël et de Baader," *Cahiers de Saint-Martin* (1978): 59–119. On the Martinist Order, see Robert Ambelain, *Le Martinisme, histoire et doctrine* (Saint Martin de Castillon, 2011), 149–151. On the history of Martinism more generally, see David Allen Harvey, *Beyond Enlightenment: Occultism and Politics in Modern France* (DeKalb, IL, 2005).

13. On Mesmerism, see Robert Darnton, *Mesmerism and the End of the Enlightenment in France*, new ed. (Harvard, 1986), 45. On Lafayette, see *Mémoires, correspondance et manuscrits du Général Lafayette* (London, 1837). Brissot quotation cited in Darnton, *Mesmerism*, 97. On "moral solidarity," see Louis Blanc, *Histoire de la Révolution française*, vol. 2 (Paris, 1869), 100.

14. Fabre is quoted in Pierre Rosanvallon, *Le Modèle politique français: La Société civile contre le jacobinisme de 1789 à nos jours* (Paris, 2004), 36. On republican and Catholic rituals, see Albert Mathiez, *Les Origines des cultes révolutionnaires (1789–1792)* (Paris, 1904), 144. On the 1789 Declaration as catechism, see Mona Ozouf, *La Fête révolutionnaire, 1789–1799* (Paris, 1976), 450–451. On Napoleonic catechism, see André Latreille, *Le Catéchisme impérial de 1806* (Paris, 1935). On the symbolism of the mountain, see Monique Mosser, "Le Temple et la montagne: généalogie d'un décor de fête révolutionnaire," *Revue de l'Art* 83 (1989): 21–35. For "yes, obviously," see Bias Parent, *Cathéchisme français, républicain, enrichi de la Déclaration des Droits de l'Homme, et de maximes de morale républicaine, par un sans-culotte* (Paris, 1794), 14. On Bias Parent more generally, see Nicole Bossut, "Bias Parent curé jacobin, agent national du district de Clamecy en l'an II," in *Annales historiques de la révolution française* 274 (1988): 444–474.

15. On the cult of human remains, see Clémentine Portier-Kaltenbach, *Histoire d'os et autres illustres abattis* (Paris, 2007). Robespierre is quoted in Ruth Scurr, *Fatal Purity: Robespierre and the French Revolution* (London, 2006), 173. On the cult of Rousseau, see Gordon McNeil, "The Cult of Rousseau and the French Revolution,"

Journal of the History of Ideas 4, no. 6 (1945): 207. On Rousseau as "the first god," see *Voyage à Ermenonville, ou Lettre sur la translation de J. J. Rousseau au Panthéon* (Paris, 1794), 24.

16. On David's painting of Marat, see Antoine Schnapper, *David, la politique et la Révolution* (Paris, 2013), 237. On the cult of Marat and patriotic saints, see Albert Soboul, "Sentiment religieux et cultes populaires pendant la Révolution: Saintes patriotes et martyrs de la liberté," in *Archives des sciences sociales des religions*, no. 2 (1956): 76, 78–80. On Sainte-Pataude, see Joël Bigorgne, "La Tombe à la Fille, lieu de culte populaire," *Ouest-France*, August 18–19, 2007. On the contemporary phenomenon of popular cults more generally, see Dominique Camus, *Dévotions populaires et tombes guérisseuses en Bretagne* (Rennes, 2011).

17. Ernest Marré, *Comment on parle avec les morts: Guide complet et abrégé de spiritisme pratique* (Paris, 1910), 48, fig. 10.

18. On "supernatural qualities," see Philippe Muray, *Le XIXe Siècle à travers les âges* (Paris, 1999), 482. Napoleonic visions and rumors are mentioned in French local administrative reports and cited in Sudhir Hazareesingh, *The Legend of Napoleon* (London, 2004), 62, 68, 70.

19. For the "Red Man," see Honoré de Balzac, *Le Médecin de campagne* (Paris, 1974), 228–229. On Louis-Napoléon Geoffroy-Château, see his *Napoléon et la conquête du monde, 1812–1832: Histoire de la monarchie universelle* (Paris, 1836), 51. On Chateaubriand's Napoleonic obsession, see Jean Boorsch, "Chateaubriand and Napoleon," *Yale French Studies*, no. 26 (1960): 55–62. For Gérard de Nerval, see his *Selected Writings* (London, 1999). On Towiański, see Gustave Vapereau, *Dictionnaire universel des contemporains*, 3rd ed. (Paris, 1865), 1738.

20. For the former surgeon's book, see Jean-Claude Bésuchet de Saunois, *Réflexions sur la mort de Napoléon, suivies de quelques considérations sur l'empoisonnement par les substances introduites dans l'estomac* (Paris, 1821). On the conspiracy theories more generally, see Thierry Lentz and Jacques Macé, *La Mort de Napoléon: Mythes, légendes et mystères* (Paris, 2009). *Monomanie orgueilleuse* is a form of monomania that is expressed in obsession with one particular person. See also Laure Murat, *L'Homme qui se prenait pour Napoléon* (Paris, 2011), 17, 187.

21. *Apothéose de Napoléon, poème traduit de l'arabe par Victor Lavagne* (Paris, 1829), 24.

22. See the "Evadisme" entry in Pierre Larousse, *Grand Dictionnaire universel du XIXe siècle* (Paris, 1873). The 1840 pamphlet citations are from Simon Vanneau, *Retour des cendres de Napoléon en France* (Paris, 1840), 3, 5. On republican devotees of Evadism, see Jean Wallon, *La Presse de 1848, ou Revue critique des journaux publiés à Paris depuis la Révolution de février jusqu'à la fin de décembre* (Paris, 1849), 133. The Alexandre Dumas citation is from *Mémoires d'Alexandre Dumas*, vol. 8 (Paris, 1884), 48.

23. On the séance, see Gustave Simon, *Chez Victor Hugo: Les Tables tournantes de Jersey* (Paris, 1923), 33. Based on the notes taken by Hugo and other participants (notably, his son Charles), these are the official transcripts of the Marine Terrace sessions. For an English translation of some of the material, see Victor Hugo, *Conversations with Eternity*, trans. John Chambers (Boca Raton, FL, 1998). See also Auguste Vacquerie, *Les Miettes de l'histoire* (Paris, 1863), 408.

24. "Vex not the bard: his lyre is broken / His last song sung, his last word spoken," Simon, *Les Tables tournantes*, 288. "Tu as la clé d'une porte du fermé," ibid., 39.

25. On Faure and on the Hugo library, see Claudius Grillet, *Victor Hugo spirite* (Paris, 1929), 12, 14. See, more generally, Lynn L. Sharp, *Secular Spirituality: Reincarnation and Spiritism in Nineteenth-Century France* (Lanham, MD, 2006). For "existence of spirits," see Victor Hugo, December 1853 comment, reported in Adèle Hugo, *Le Journal d'Adèle Hugo*, vol. 2 (Paris, 1971), 409. On narcissism, see Simon, *Les Tables tournantes*, 370.

26. Simon, *Les Tables tournantes*, 71–72 (Napoleon), 107 (Marseillaise).

27. Ibid., 64 ("bottle-feeding republicans" [*des républicains au biberon*]), 67–68 (Danton), 120 (Chénier), 114 (prophet Muhammad).

28. Adèle Hugo, *Le Journal d'Adèle Hugo*, vol. 3 (Paris, 1984), 291; Simon, *Les Tables tournantes*, 370 (egalitarianism), 303 ("onward journey"), 77 (Moses), 307 (apotheosis of being).

29. On Kardec's doctrine, see Guillaume Cuchet, *Les Voix d'outre-tombe: Tables tournantes, spiritisme et société au XIXe siècle* (Paris, 2012), 107–170. By 1912, the *Livre des esprits* had reached its fifty-second edition. See Nicole Edelman, *Voyantes, guérisseuses et visionnaires en France, 1785–1914* (Paris, 1995), 110. On occultist dance, see Maxime du Camp, *Souvenirs littéraires* (Paris, 1906), 116. On occultist beliefs, see Jacques Lantier, *Le Spiritisme, ou L'Aventure d'une croyance* (Paris, 1971), 110. On Barrès, see Maurice Barrès, *La Grande Pitié des églises de France* (Lille, 2012), 88.

30. André Breton, *Premier manifeste du surréalisme* (1924), in *Manifestes du surréalisme* (Paris, 1962), 41; Simon, *Les Tables tournantes*, 369.

31. For "powerful wings," see Édouard Charton, *Mémoire d'un prédicateur Saint-Simonien* (Paris, 1832), 23. For an analysis of Charton's Saint-Simonism, see Marie-Laure Aurenche, *Édouard Charton et l'invention du "Magasin pittoresque," 1833–1870* (Paris, 2002), 83–120. See also Georges Weill, *L'École Saint-Simonienne: Son histoire, son influence jusqu'à nos jours* (Paris, 1896), 290–291.

32. Charton's intellectual legacy is evident in his memoirs, published in the late nineteenth century; see Édouard Charton, *Le Tableau de Cébès* (Paris, 1882). Founded by Désirée Véret, Marie-Reine Guindorf, and Suzanne Voilquin in August 1832, *La Femme libre* changed its name to *La Femme de l'avenir*, and then to *La Femme nouvelle*; the collection is held at the Bibliothèque de l'Arsenal in Paris (8-JO-20530).

33. Quoted in Antoine Picon, *Les Saint-Simoniens: Raison, imaginaire et utopie* (Paris, 2002), 39; Barthélemy-Prosper Enfantin et al., *Doctrine Saint-Simonienne: Exposition* (Paris, 1854).

34. Sébastien Charléty, *Histoire du Saint-Simonisme, 1825–1864* (Paris, 1896), 143.

35. Jules Michelet, *L'Insecte* (Paris, 1858), 306; Barthélemy-Prosper Enfantin, *Lettre du Père à Charles Duveyrier sur la vie éternelle* (Paris, 1830), 11; Pierre Leroux, *De l'humanité, de son principe et de son avenir*, 2 vols. (Paris, 1845); Alphonse Esquiros, *De la vie future au point de vue socialiste* (Paris, 1850); Jean Reynaud, *Philosophie religieuse: Terre et ciel* (Paris, 1854). The full quotation by Enfantin was "Ma vie est indéfinie, une et multiple, elle se manifeste en moi, hors de moi, et par l'union du moi et du non-moi."

36. Camille Flammarion, *La Pluralité des mondes habités* (Paris, 1877), 320; Louis-Auguste Blanqui, *L'Éternité par les astres* (Paris, 1872), 74 (body doubles), 76 (infinity).

37. Entry of April 1898, *Journal inédit de Ricardo Viñes*, ed. Suzy Levy (Paris, 1987), x; André Breton, "Lettre aux voyantes" (1925), in *Manifestes du surréalisme*, 233; Mircea Eliade, *Occultism, Witchcraft and Cultural Fashions: Essays in Comparative Religions* (Chicago, 1976), 53.

38. Élisée Reclus, *La Terre*, vol. 2 (Paris, 1869), 747; Ruth Harris, *Lourdes: Body and Spirit in the Secular Age* (London, 1999), 59.

39. For meetings of spiritualist groups, see Anne Osmont, *Mes souvenirs: 50 années d'occultisme* (Paris, 1941), 40. On progressive ambitions of spiritism, see Anna Blackwell, *De l'effet probable des idées spirites sur la marche sociale de l'avenir* (Paris, 1877). On the Coué method, see Hervé Guillemain, *La Méthode Coué: Histoire d'une pratique de guérison au XXe siècle* (Paris, 2010), 11.

40. For "because he is reasonable," see Eugène Pelletan, *Heures de Travail*, vol. 2 (Paris, 1854), 355. For "arrive at faith," see Charles Fauvety, *La Question religieuse* (Paris, 1864), 2. On Palladino authentification, see Christine Blondel, "Eusapia Palladino: La Méthode expérimentale et la 'diva des savants,'" in Bernadette Bensaude-Vincent and Christine Blondel, eds., *Des savants face à l'occulte, 1870–1940* (Paris, 2002), 143–144. For Charles Richet, see his *Traité de métapsychique* (Paris, 1922), 2.

41. For an example of occultist influences on radical thought, see Louis Dramard, "L'Occultisme" and "La doctrine ésotérique," *Revue Socialiste*, vols. 8 and 9 (1885). For Lermina Monte-Cristo sequels, see Jules Lermina, *Le Fils de Monte-Cristo* (Paris, 1881); *Le Trésor de Monte-Cristo* (Paris, 1885). On sublime intuitions, see Jules Lermina, "Le Congrès de 1889," in *La Religion de l'avenir*, no.1, November 1, 1889. On dazzling illuminations, see Jules Lermina, *La Science occulte: Magie pratique, révélation des mystères de la vie et de la mort* (Paris, 1890), 267. For Kardec message from the dead, see "Communication de l'esprit Allan Kardec," *Annales du spiritisme*, November 1921, 5.

Chapter 3: Landscapes of Utopia

1. Louis-Sébastien Mercier, *L'An deux mille quatre cent quarante, rêve s'il en fut jamais*, ed. Raymond Trousson (Paris, 1971), 170. The first English translation was published in 1772 in London; curiously, it was entitled *Memoirs of the Year Two Thousand Five Hundred*. See Robert Darnton, *The Forbidden Bestsellers of Pre-revolutionary France* (New York, 1995).

2. Mercier, *L'An deux mille quatre cent quarante*, 338.

3. Raymond Trousson, *Voyages aux pays de nulle part* (Brussels, 1975), 175; Alain Touraine, *Le Mouvement de mai, ou Le Communisme utopique* (Paris, 1968). For a recent reassessment, see Julian Jackson, Anna-Louise Milne, and James S. Williams, eds., *May 68: Rethinking France's Last Revolution* (Basingstoke, UK, 2011).

4. Louis-Sébastien Mercier, *De Jean-Jacques Rousseau considéré comme l'un des premiers auteurs de la Révolution*, vol. 1 (Paris, 1791), 4.

5. For a more comprehensive account of Rousseau's republican political thought, see Karma Nabulsi, *Traditions of War: Occupation, Resistance and the Law* (Oxford,

UK, 1999), 177–204; Jean-Jacques Rousseau, *Discourse on the Arts and Sciences* (1750), in *The Social Contract and Discourses*, ed. P. D. Jimack, trans. G. D. H. Cole (London, 1993), 5–6; Jean-Jacques Rousseau, *Discourse on the Origin of Inequality*, in ibid., 117.

6. See Jean Fabre, "Réalité et utopie dans la pensée politique de Jean-Jacques Rousseau," *Annales de la société Jean-Jacques Rousseau* 35 (1959–1962): 181–221. The most comprehensive analysis of Rousseau is Antoine Hatzenberger's *Rousseau et l'utopie* (Paris, 2012). On transparency, see Jean Starobinski, *Jean-Jacques Rousseau: Transparency and Obstruction* (Chicago, 1988), 15. For "conferred on us all," see Jean-Jacques Rousseau, *The Social Contract*, in *Social Contract and Discourses*, 195, 214.

7. On Rousseau's impact on the political thought of the early revolutionary era, see James Swenson, *On Jean-Jacques Rousseau, Considered as One of the First Authors of the Revolution* (Stanford, CA, 2000). On "Panthéon," see Saint-Just, "Fragments d'institutions républicaines," in *Théorie politique* (Paris, 1976), 295. Rousseau wrote, "Sovereignty, for the same reason as makes it inalienable, cannot be represented: it lies essentially in the general will, and will does not admit of representation: it is either the same or other, there is no intermediate possibility. The deputies of the people, therefore, are not and cannot be its representatives: they are merely its stewards, and can carry through no definitive acts" (*The Social Contract*, in *The Social Contract and Discourses*, 266).

8. Jean Starobinski, *L'Invention de la liberté, 1700–1789* (Paris, 2006), 187; Mercier, *L'An deux mille quatre cent quarante*, 232.

9. "Without . . . confusion": ibid., 90; "vegetation": ibid., 114; "scientific advances": ibid., 300.

10. "Natural equality": ibid., 101; "disproportion" and "luxury": ibid., 9, 102; clergy: ibid., 174; diet: ibid., 385–386; politeness and consideration: ibid., 414.

11. "Depraved souls": ibid., 186; natural frontiers: ibid., 234–235.

12. "Intimate" ally: ibid., 236; "universal reason": ibid., 133–134; English melancholy: ibid., 236; suicide in Japan: ibid., 392.

13. Laws: ibid., 327–328, 331; absolute sovereignty: ibid., 333; corpses: ibid., 142.

14. Ordinary people: ibid., 342; "perfection of human nature": ibid., 225; "public lesson": ibid., 108; "avenger of the new world": ibid., 205.

15. Mona Ozouf, *L'Homme régénéré: Essais sur la Révolution française* (Paris, 1989), 14; Mercier, *L'An deux mille quatre cent quarante*, 220; Rousseau, *Social Contract*, in *Social Contract and Discourses*, 297.

16. Discussion: Mercier, *L'An deux mille quatre cent quarante*, 151, 366, 124; "soul": ibid., 319; bonfire: ibid., 250; Rousseau preserved: ibid., 265–266.

17. Cited in Michèle Riot-Sarcey, *Le Réel de l'utopie: Essai sur le politique au XIXe siècle* (Paris, 1998), 146.

18. Mona Ozouf, "La Révolution française au tribunal de l'utopie," in *L'Homme régénéré*, 234; cited by Louis Reybaud, *Étude sur les réformateurs sociaux*, vol. 1 (Paris, 1844), 42.

19. Charles Fourier, *Théorie des quatre mouvements et des destinés génerales* (Leipzig, 1808), 283, 369; Charles Fourier, *Hiérarchie du cocuage* (Paris, 2000).

20. Satisfaction of passions: Fourier, *Théorie des quatre mouvements*, 116; hearty snacks: ibid., 251n1.

21. On "perfectibility," see Nicolas de Condorcet, *Esquisse d'un tableau historique des progrès de l'esprit humain* (Paris, 1970), 236. For "Citizen of the Globe," see Fourier, *Théorie des quatre mouvements*, 211; Suez and Panama canals: ibid., 246; *aigresel*: ibid, 66. For number of years, see Fourier, *Traité de l'association domestique-agricole*, vol. 1 (Paris, 1822), 243.

22. The definitive work on the subject is by Bernard Desmars, *Militants de l'utopie? Les Fouriéristes dans la seconde moitié du XIXe siècle* (Dijon, 2010).

23. Fourier, *Théorie des quatre mouvements*, 180; Charles Bergeron, *Le Chemin de fer sous-marin entre la France et l'Angleterre* (Paris, 1873).

24. The first article of the Declaration of the Rights of Man and of the Citizen is "Men are born and remain free and equal in rights."

25. Godefroy Cavaignac, "La Force révolutionnaire," in G. Cavaignac, ed., *Paris révolutionnaire* (Paris, 1848), 9; "Petit catéchisme républicain," in *Les Révolutions du XIXe siècle*, 1st ser., vol. 3; "Association des Amis de l'égalité: Déclaration" (1830), in ibid., 1st ser., vol. 1; Jules Ferry, *La Lutte électorale en 1863* (Paris, 1863), 105; Adolphe Rion, "Droits et devoirs du républicain," *Les Révolutions du XIXe siècle*, 1st ser., vol. 9; "Société des droits de l'homme et du citoyen: De l'égalité," in *Les Révolutions du XIXe siècle*, 1st ser., vol. 3; "De la misère des ouvriers et de la marche à suivre pour y remédier," in *Les Révolutions du XIXe siècle*, 1st ser., vol. 4.

26. Olympe de Gouges, *Déclaration des droits de la femme et de la citoyenne*, in *Oeuvres* (Paris, 1986), 102; "Sur l'admission des femmes au droit de cité," July 3, 1790, in *Oeuvres de Condorcet*, A. Condorcet O'Connor and F. Arago, eds., vol. 10 (Paris, 1847), 121; Jeanne Deroin, *Association fraternelle des démocrates socialistes des deux sexes pour l'affranchissement politique et sociale des femmes* (Paris, 1849), 3.

27. On nineteenth-century women writers, see Sarah Kay, Terence Cave, and Malcolm Bowie, *A Short History of French Literature* (New York, 2003), 239–241. On Sand and Flaubert, see Gustave Flaubert and George Sand, *Correspondance*, ed. A. Jacobs (Paris, 1981). On Sand's politics, see the collection of her articles edited by Michelle Perrot, *George Sand, politique et polémique, 1843–1850* (Paris, 1996). On Adam, see Anne Hogenhuis-Seliverstoff, *Juliette Adam (1836–1936), l'instigatrice* (Paris, 2002); Aldo d'Agostini, "L'Agency de Juliette Adam," *Rives méditerranéennes* 41 (2012): 101–115.

28. Louis Blanc, *L'Organisation du travail* (Paris, 1839); Pierre-Joseph Proudhon, *Qu'est-ce que la propriété?* (Paris, 1840).

29. Philippe Buonarroti, *History of Babeuf's Conspiracy for Equality*, trans. James Bronterre O'Brien (London, 1836), 10; *Almanach de la communauté* (1843), in *Les Révolutions du XIXe siècle, 1835–1848*, 2nd ser., vol. 8; Jean-Jacques Pillot, *Histoire des égaux, ou moyens d'établir l'égalité absolue parmi les hommes* (Paris, 1840), in *Les Révolutions du XIXe siècle, 1835–1848*, 2nd ser., vol. 6.

30. Étienne Cabet, "Comment je suis communiste," in *Les Révolutions du XIXe siècle, 1835–1848*, 2nd ser., vol. 5; Étienne Cabet, *Le Vrai Christianisme suivant Jésus-Christ* (Paris, 1847), 165.

31. Equality: Étienne Cabet, *Voyage en Icarie*, 4th ed. (Paris, 1846), Preface; provisions cart: ibid., 56; "perfect proportions": ibid., 42; physicians: ibid., 112; "underwater boats" (*bateaux sous-marins*), ibid., 73.

32. Popular committees: ibid., 176; religion: ibid., 168; machines: ibid., 100–101.

33. Art: ibid., 48; clothing: ibid., 57; menus: ibid., 51; "respected couples": ibid., 141, 143; "Perfection Commission": ibid., 122; local tribunals: ibid., 132; "consent": ibid., 125, 127.

34. Crespy-Noher (pseud. of Alexis Manières), *Les Prières républicaines du citoyen Xiléas* (Bordeaux, 1875).

35. Maximilien Robespierre, *Discours sur l'organisation des gardes nationales* (Besançon, 1791), 56. On active citizenship, see Anne Simonin's remarkable study, *Le Déshonneur dans la République: Une histoire de l'indignité, 1791–1958* (Paris, 2008).

36. *Déclaration des droits de l'homme et du citoyen, avec des commentaires par le citoyen Laponneraye* (Paris, 1832), 8. On the impact of Poland on European revolutionary politics more generally, see Karma Nabulsi, "Patriotism and Internationalism in the 'Oath of Allegiance' to Young Europe," *European Journal of Political Theory* 5 (2006). On "*European republic*," see *La Tribune*, January 31, 1833.

37. Gaëtan Delmas, *Curiosités révolutionnaires: Les Journaux rouges. Histoire critique de tous les journaux ultra-républicains publiés à Paris depuis le 24 février jusqu'au 1er octobre 1848* (Paris, 1848).

38. Quoted in Philippe Darriulat, *Les Patriotes: La Gauche républicaine et la nation* (Paris, 2001), 239; Émile Littré, "République occidentale," *Le National*, September 24, 1849; Jean-Joseph Brémond, *Plan de la confédération européenne et universelle du livre précurseur* (Paris, 1867); *Aux républicains: Appel de Kossuth, Ledru-Rollin et Mazzini*, September 1855. On cosmopolitan fraternity, see "Système de Fraternité," *Le Populaire*, July 1850. On progressive youth, see Gustave Flourens et al., *Appel de la Rive Gauche à la jeunesse européenne* (Brussels, 1864).

39. On the International, see the volume of pamphlets gathered in "L'Association Internationale des Travailleurs," *Les Révolutions du XIXe siècle*, 3rd ser., vol. 5. For the full list of 1867 delegates, see Auguste Scheurer-Kestner, *Souvenirs de jeunesse* (Paris, 1905), 108–109; Charles Lemonnier, *Les États-Unis d'Europe* (Paris, 1872).

40. Jules Barni, *La Morale dans la démocratie*, 2nd ed. (Paris, 1885), 116.

41. See Claudine Rey, Annie Limoge-Gayat and Sylvie Pépino, *Petit dictionnaire des femmes de la Commune: Les Oubliées de l'histoire* (Paris, 2013).

42. For Blanqui, see Gustave Geffroy, *L'Enfermé* (Paris, 1897), 243. On the political thought of the Commune, see Charles Rihs, *La Commune de Paris 1871: Sa structure et ses doctrines* (Paris, 1973). The "new page" quotation is from a speech by Arthur Ranc, March 29, 1871, in Georges Bourgin and Gabriel Henriot, *Procès-verbaux de la Commune de 1871*, vol. 1 (Paris, 1924), 42. Jules Vallès's novel was *L'Insurgé* (Paris, 1975), 257. On the Commune more generally, see Robert Tombs, *The Paris Commune, 1871* (London, 1999); and John Merriman, *Massacre: The Life and Death of the Paris Commune* (New York, 2014).

43. Émile Littré, *De l'établissement de la Troisième République* (Paris, 1880), x.

44. Cabet is quoted in Raoul Girardet, *L'Idée coloniale en France, de 1871 à 1962* (Paris, 1972), 40. The Ferry speech at the National Assembly, March 27, 1884, is in Jules Ferry, *Discours et opinions*, ed. Paul Robiquet, vol. 5 (Paris, 1897), 159. On negative representation of blacks, see Carole Reynaud Paligot, *La République raciale 1860–1930* (Paris, 2006), 140, 235. On abandonment of revolutionary equality, see Olivier Le Cour Grandmaison, *La République impériale: Politique et racisme d'État* (Paris, 2009).

45. On the *grand soir*, see Maurice Tournier, "Le Grand Soir: Un mythe de fin de siècle," *Mots* 19 (1989): 79–94. For Paul Adam's communist utopia, see *Lettres de Malaisie* (Paris, 1898). Jaurès is cited in Gilles Candar and Vincent Duclert, *Jean Jaurès* (Paris, 2014), 285. On "destructive power," see *L'Humanité*, March 31, 1912. The defense of Islamic civilization is quoted in Gilles Manceron, "La Gauche et la colonisation," in Jean-Jacques Becker and Gilles Candar, eds., *Histoire des Gauches en France*, vol. 1 (Paris, 2004), 543.

46. Maurice Thorez, speech at Ivry Central Committee meeting of the French Communist Party, in *L'Humanité*, May 20, 1939.

47. Communism as purest ideal: Maurice Thorez, *Fils du peuple* (Paris, 1949), 101; Promethean reason: ibid., 241, 248; "real" democracy: ibid., 50.

48. Cited in Jean-Marie Goulemot, *Pour l'amour de Staline: La Face oubliée du communisme français* (Paris, 2009), 85–86.

49. Herriot is cited in Fred Kupferman, *Au pays des Soviets: Le Voyage français en Union Soviétique, 1917–1939* (Paris, 1979), 87. For Charles Vildrac, see *Russie neuve* (Paris, 1937), 206.

50. For ideology of happiness, see Sophie Coeuré, *La Grande Lueur à l'Est: Les Français et l'Union Soviétique, 1917–1939* (Paris, 1999).

51. The envelope containing the letter was addressed to "Monsieur Picasso, grand peintre"; both are reproduced in *Les Archives de Picasso* (Paris, 2003), 308–309. *L'Humanité*, November 26, 1949; Annette Wieviorka, *Maurice et Jeannette: Biographie du couple Thorez* (Paris, 2010), 647.

52. Anatole de Monzie, *Du Kremlin au Luxembourg* (Paris, 1924), 125; Roger Vailland, *Drôle de jeu* (Paris, 1945), 15. On "positive utopia," see François Furet, *Le Passé d'une illusion: Essai sur l'idée communiste au XXe siècle* (Paris, 1995), 243. Sartre is quoted in François Hourmant, *Au pays de l'avenir radieux: Voyages des intellectuels français en URSS, à Cuba et en Chine populaire* (Paris, 2000).

53. The Daniel quotation is in Jean Daniel, "Avec Castro à l'heure du crime," *L'Express*, November 28, 1963. On fraternal internationalism, see Catherine Simon, *Algérie, les années pieds-rouges: Des rêves de l'indépendance au désanchantement* (Paris, 2011). Kristeva is quoted in Richard Wolin, *The Wind from the East: French Intellectuals, the Cultural Revolution and the Legacy of the 1960s* (Princeton, NJ, 2010), 274.

54. Louis Aragon, *La Pensée*, May-August 1952; Romain Rolland, *Voyage à Moscou, juin-juillet 1935* (Paris, 1992); speech by Jacques Duclos, *Cahiers du Bolchevisme*, July 1939; *L'Humanité*, March 4, 1939; Goulemot, *Pour l'amour de Staline*, 94.

55. Jean Guéhenno, *Journal des années noires, 1940–1944* (Paris, 2014), 454.

56. Alexis de Tocqueville, *The Old Regime and the Revolution* (New York, 1856), 172. On Foucault's critique of Enlightenment rationality, see Lois McNay, *Foucault: A Critical Introduction* (Oxford, 1994), 26–31. On Lefort's political thought, see, more generally, Bernard Flynn, *The Philosophy of Claude Lefort: Interpreting the Political* (Evanston, IL, 2005).

57. See, for example, Emmanuel Le Roy Ladurie, *Paris-Montpellier: P.C.-P.S.U., 1945–63* (Paris, 1982); Mona Ozouf, *Composition française: Retour sur une enfance bretonne* (Paris, 2009).

58. Paul Nizan, *La Conspiration* (Paris, 1938), 22; Mona Ozouf, "L'Idée républicaine et l'interprétation du passé national," *Annales* 53, no. 6 (1998): 1087.

59. Laura Lee Downs, *Childhood in the Promised Land: Working-Class Movements and the "Colonies de Vacances" in France, 1880–1960* (London, 2002); Hervé Hamon and Patrick Rotman, *Génération* (Paris, 1988), 287; Furet, *Le Passé d'une illusion*, 134.

Chapter 4: The Ideals of Science

1. Abbé Louis-Mayeul Chaudon, *Bibliothèque d'un homme de goût*, vol. 2 (Avignon, 1772), 335.

2. On the "Republic of Sciences," see Stéphane van Damme, *Paris, capitale philosophique, de la Fronde à la Révolution* (Paris, 2005). On the Cassinis, see Jerry Brotton, *A History of the World in Twelve Maps* (London, 2012).

3. On the expansion of science more generally, see the "La République des sciences," ed. Irène Passeron, special issue of *Dix-huitième siècle*, no. 40 (2008). On the development of scientific learned societies in provincial France, see Daniel Roche, *Les Républicains des lettres: Gens du culture et lumières au XVIIIe siécle* (Paris, 1988), 205–216; Daniel Mornet, "Les Enseignements des bibliothèques privées, 1750–1780," *Revue d'histoire littéraire* 27 (1910); and Daniel Mornet, *Les Sciences de la nature en France au 18e siècle* (1911) (Geneva, 2001), 182.

4. The full title for the Abbé Pluche's work in English translation is *Spectacle de la nature: Or, Nature Displayed. Being Discourses on Such Particulars of Natural History as Were Thought Most Proper to Excite the Curiosity, and Form the Minds of Youth*; it has been published in various editions. On the Leyden jar experiment, see Colm Kiernan, *The Enlightenment and Science in Eighteenth-Century France* (Oxford, 1973), 154; René Antoine Ferchault de Réaumur, *Mémoires pour servir à l'histoire des insectes*, 7 vols. (Paris 1734–1742). On Gersaint, see Guillaume Glorieux, *À l'enseigne de Gersaint: Edme-François Gersaint, marchand d'art sur le pont de Notre-Dame, 1694–1750* (Seysell, 2002), 279–281.

5. Quoted in Mornet, *Les Sciences de la nature*, 3.

6. Peter Gay, *The Science of Freedom* (London, 1977), 126–133; Jean-Jacques Rousseau, *Confessions* (Paris, 1931), book 5, 53–54.

7. On the body as a clock: Aram Vartanian, ed., *La Mettrie's "L'Homme machine": A Study in the Origins of an Idea* (Princeton, NJ, 1960), 186; machine: ibid., 154; hidden first causes: quoted by Aram Vartanian, "Interpretation of *l'Homme machine*," in Vartanian, *La Mettrie's "L'Homme machine*," 29; "potent effect of Meals": ibid., 155. In a letter to Madame Denis (November 14, 1751), Voltaire claimed it was "eagle paté stuffed with bad lard, minced pork and ginger." See Pierre Pénisson, "La Mettrie à Berlin," in Sophie Audidière et al., eds., *Matérialistes français du XVIIIe siècle* (Paris, 2006), 98.

8. For the full list of titles, see Mornet, "Les Enseignements des bibliothèques privées," 489–490. The tales are cited in Mornet, *Les Sciences de la nature*, 15–17.

9. Kiernan, *Enlightenment and Science*, 145; Jessica Riskin, *Science in the Age of Sensibility: The Sentimental Empiricists of the French Enlightenment* (Chicago, 2002), 7.

10. Mornet, *Les Sciences de la nature*, 32–33, 49–50.

11. On Montesquieu, see Kiernan, *Enlightenment and Science*, 132–136. On Rousseau, see ibid., 58. On the heavenly city, see Carl Becker, *The Heavenly City of the Eighteenth-Century Philosophers* (New Haven, CT, 1974), 44–45.

12. Nicole Dhombres and Jean Dhombres, *Naissance d'un nouveau pouvoir: Sciences et savants en France, 1793–1824* (Paris, 1989), 30–31; Jean-Paul Marat, *Les Charlatans modernes* (Paris, 1791), 290.

13. On the academies as symbols of despotism, see article in *L'Auditeur national,* August 9, 1793, cited in Joseph Fayet, *La Révolution française et la science, 1789–1795* (Paris, 1960), 132. On speculative sciences as poison, see Gabriel Bouquier, *Rapport et projet de décret formant un plan général d'instruction publique* (1793), cited in Fayet, *La Révolution française,* 199. On Montesquieu and the imagination, see *Pensées et fragments inédits de Montesquieu, publiés par le Baron Gaston de Montesquieu,* vol. 2 (Bordeaux, 1901), 182.

14. "A Catalogue of the Library of the Late Emperor Napoleon Removed from the Island of Saint Helena by Order of His Majesty's Government (London, 1823)," in Victor Advielle, *La Bibliothèque de Napoléon à Sainte Hélène* (Paris, 1894), 22.

15. Emmanuel de Las Cases, *Mémorial de Sainte-Hélène,* vol. 1, ed. Marcel Dunan (Paris, 1951), entry dated November 25, 1815, and p. 264; Étienne Geoffroy Saint-Hilaire, *Sur une vue scientifique de l'adolescence de Napoléon Bonaparte* (Paris, 1835), 7.

16. On differential equations, see Dhombres and Dhombres, *Naissance d'un nouveau pouvoir,* 667. "Resolve the problem of life in the universe" is quoted in Étienne Geoffroy Saint-Hilaire, *Études progressives d'un naturaliste* (Paris 1835), 183.

17. On the Egyptian expedition, see Patrice Gueniffey, *Bonaparte, 1769–1802* (Paris, 2013), 334–339. On gunpowder, see Robert Solé, *Les Savants de Bonaparte* (Paris, 1998), 37. The Monge article is "Mémoire sur le phénomène d'optique connu sous le nom de mirage, par le citoyen Gaspard Monge," *La Décade égyptienne* 2, no. 7 (1798–1799): 37–46.

18. Eric Sartori, *L'Empire des sciences: Napoléon et ses savants* (Paris, 2003), 9.

19. On the prestigious Institut prizes, see Georges Barral, *Histoire des sciences sous Napoléon Bonaparte* (Paris, 1889), 81. Rousseau is quoted in Dhombres and Dhombres, *Naissance d'un nouveau pouvoir,* 684. On the Musée, see ibid., 685.

20. Napoleon's statement about exploring the New World is quoted in Barral, *Histoire des sciences sous Napoléon Bonaparte,* 275. See also "A Catalogue of the Library of the Late Emperor Napoleon," 27.

21. On "Brutus Bonaparte," see Georges Dumas, *Psychologie de deux messies positivistes, Saint-Simon et Auguste Comte* (Paris, 1905), 144–145. For "definitive stage of human intelligence," see Auguste Comte, *Cours de philosophie positive,* vol. 1 (1830) (Paris, 1968), 10. For apogee of Encyclopedic tradition, see letter of August 7, 1852, in *Auguste Comte, correspondance générale et confessions,* vol. 6 (Paris, 1973–1990), 325.

22. On "mechanical romanticism," see John Tresch, *The Romantic Machine: Utopian Science and Technology after Napoleon* (Chicago, 2012). On three stages of positivism, see Comte, *Cours,* 1:3, 4. For night's meditation, see Henri Gouhier, *La Vie d'Auguste Comte* (Paris, 1965), 102.

23. On "pressing need," see Comte, *Cours,* 1:18. On "spiritual reorganization," see Auguste Comte, *Discours sur l'ensemble du positivisme* (1848) (Paris, 1907), 112. On "new class," see Comte, *Cours,* 1:24.

24. On Comte's new religion, see Andrew Wernick, *Auguste Comte and the Religion of Humanity* (Cambridge, UK, 2001). Jowett is quoted in Mary Pickering,

Auguste Comte: An Intellectual Biography, vol. 3 (Cambridge, UK, 2009), 580. On J. S. Mill, see *Auguste Comte et la philosophie positive* (Paris, 1890), 197.

25. On ethical values, see Mary Pickering, *Auguste Comte: An Intellectual Biography*, vol. 1 (Cambridge, UK, 1993), 5. On suspicion of scientists, see Pickering, *Auguste Comte*, 3:319.

26. On priority of affection, see 1846 letter, quoted in Pickering, *Auguste Comte: An Intellectual Biography*, vol. 2 (Cambridge, UK, 2009), 224. For *vivre au grand jour*, see Auguste Comte, *Catéchisme positiviste* (1852) (Paris, 1891), 297. On tobacco, see ibid., 574. For annual confession, see *Testament d'Auguste Comte, avec les documents qui s'y rapportent: Pièces justificatives, prières quotidiennes, confessions annuelles, correspondance avec Mme de Vaux, publiés par ses exécuteurs testamentaires, conformément à ses dernières volontés*, ed. Pierre Laffite (Paris, 1884). On the dead governing the living, see Comte, *Catéchisme*, 67.

27. On animal comparisons in Comte's sociology, see Jean-François Braunstein, *La Philosophie de la médecine d'Auguste Comte: Vaches carnivores, Vierge Mère et morts vivants* (Paris, 2009), 95. On "vital force," see Pascal Nouvel, ed., *Repenser le vitalisme: Histoire et philosophie du vitalisme* (Paris, 2011).

28. On functions of the brain, see Auguste Comte, *Système de politique positive* (1851), vol. 1 (Paris, 1969), 726–727. On "biocracy," see Braunstein, *La Philosophie de la médecine d'Auguste Comte*, 175–181. On "eternal widowhood," see Comte, *Système*, 1:238–239.

29. Gustave Flaubert, *Dictionnaire des idées reçues* (Paris, 1988), 454; Pierre Macherey, *Comte: La Philosophie et les sciences* (Paris, 1989), 6.

30. On Collège de France, see *Cours sur l'histoire générale des sciences: Discours d'ouverture prononcé par M. Pierre Laffitte* (Paris, 1892). On the positivist religion in the post-Comtian era, see Annie Petit, "Les Disciples de la religion positiviste," *Revue des sciences philosophiques et théologiques* 87 (2003): 75–100.

31. On Durkheim and Comte, see Steven Lukes, *Émile Durkheim: His Life and Work* (Stanford, CA, 1985), 67–68. On the suppression of the column, see the *Système*, 4:397, where Comte had called for the destruction of this "oppressive monument," of which the French capital had to be "purified." On Maurras and Comte, see Charles Maurras, *Romantisme et révolution* (Paris, 1922), 101. On Barrès and Comte, see Maurice Barrès, *Mes Cahiers*, vol. 1 (Paris, 1929), 129. On Houellebecq and Comte, see Bruno Viard, *Houellebecq au scanner: La Faute à mai '68* (Nice, 2008), 36–37, 49–50.

32. On Freemasons, see Sudhir Hazareesingh and Vincent Wright, *Francs-maçons sous le Second Empire* (Rennes, 2001), 168–172. Gambetta is cited in Pierre Barral, "Ferry et Gambetta face au positivisme," *Romantisme* 8, nos. 21–22 (1978): 152. For Ferry, see Jules Ferry, "Marcel Roulleaux et la philosophie positive," *La philosophie positive*, September-October 1867, in *Discours et opinions de Jules Ferry*, ed. P. Robiquet, vol. 1 (Paris, 1893), 586. Bert is quoted in Anne Rasmussen, "Science et progrès, des mythes pour la République?," in M. Fontaine, F. Monier, and C. Prochasson, eds., *Une contre-histoire de la IIIe République* (Paris, 2013), 263.

33. On monuments to scientists, see June Hargrove, *Les Statues de Paris* (Paris, 1989). On the scientific aspects of colonial expansion, see Emmanuelle Sibeud, *Une*

science impériale pour l'Afrique? La construction des savoirs africanistes en France, 1878–1930 (Paris, 2002), 275–276.

34. Louis Pasteur, "Pourquoi la France n'a pas trouvé d'hommes supérieurs au moment du péril" (1871), in Louis Pasteur, *Pour l'avenir de la science française* (Paris, 1947), 63; Charles Moureu, *Maurice Barrès et la science française* (Paris, 1925), 21. Biot is quoted in Robert Fox, "Scientific Enterprise and Patronage of Research in France, 1800–1870," in Robert Fox, *The Culture of Science in France, 1700–1900* (Aldershot, UK, 1992), 455. On Bernard and Pasteur, see Theodore Zeldin, *France, 1848–1945: Taste and Corruption* (Oxford, 1980), 233–236.

35. On "human nature": Ernest Renan, *L'Avenir de la science* (Paris, 1890), 150–151; progress: ibid., vii; perfectibility: ibid., 433; explain man to himself: ibid., 23; "religion": ibid., 108; "multiplicity": ibid., 314; preserve of elite: ibid., ix; error: ibid., xix.

36. On Zola, see Sarah Kay, Terence Cave, and Malcolm Bowie, *A Short History of French Literature* (New York, 2003), 249. On Verne's scientific imagination, see Jean-Jacques Bridenne, *La Littérature française d'imagination scientifique* (Paris, 1950). For "shoot the socialists," see letter of November 1870, in *Correspondance inédite de Jules Verne à sa famille* (Lyon, 1988), 454.

37. On Verne and religion, see Jean-Paul Dekiss, "Jules Verne et le futur," in Phillipe de la Cotardière et al., *Jules Verne, de la science à l'imaginaire* (Paris, 2004), 173. On legends, see Michel Serres, *Jouvences sur Jules Verne* (Paris, 1974), 14. On Franceville, see Michel Clamen, *Jules Verne et les sciences* (Paris, 2005), 107–120.

38. Jules Verne, *Paris au XXe siècle* (Paris, 1994), 60 (oxygen), 196 (electricity).

39. Gaston Palewski, *La Science clé de l'avenir français* (Paris, 1963), 16 ("sphere of politics"), 19 ("fortitude"), 20 (spiritual elevation).

40. On the "scientific state" in France, see Robert Gilpin, *France in the Age of the Scientific State* (Princeton, NJ, 1968). See also Alain Chatriot and Vincent Duclert, eds., *Le Gouvernement de la recherche: Histoire d'un engagement politique, de Pierre Mendès France à Charles de Gaulle, 1953–1969* (Paris, 2006). "No oil but . . . ideas" is quoted in Jean-Marie Domenach, *Enquête sur les idées contemporaines* (Paris, 1970). On the rationalist critique of science, see Edgar Morin, *Science avec conscience* (Paris, 1982), 65; Jean Baudrillard, *La Société de consommation* (Paris, 1970), 312; René Dumont, *L'Utopie ou la mort!* (Paris, 1973).

41. Jacques Bernot, *Gaston Palewski: Premier baron du gaullisme* (Paris, 2010), 234–235, 302–303.

42. On nineteenth-century conceptions of the administrative state, see Hippolyte Carnot, *D'une école d'administration* (Versailles, 1878), 26. See, more generally, Guy Thuillier, *L'ENA avant l'ENA* (Paris, 1983); Renan, *L'Avenir de la science*, 350. On the rise of technocratic ideas during post-Liberation, see Philip Nord, *France's New Deal* (Princeton, NJ, 2010), 8–10. On rationale for ENA, see Michel Debré, *Réforme de la fonction publique* (Paris, 1945), 23–25. For "desire to succeed," see ibid., 16. On the displacement of ENS by ENA, see Ezra Suleiman, *Les Élites en France: Grands corps et grandes écoles* (Paris, 1979), 41. On the consistent presence of *énarques* on the staff of the French executive, see Luc Rouban, "L'État à l'épreuve du libéralisme: Les Entourages du pouvoir exécutif de 1974 à 2012," *Revue française d'administration publique*, no. 142 (2012): 467–490.

43. On the sociological critique of French decision-making, see, in particular, Michel Crozier, *La Société bloquée*, 3rd ed. (Paris, 1994). On the funding of scientific research, see Olivier Postel-Vinay, *Le Grand Gâchis: Splendeur et misère de la science française* (Paris, 2002). For "sexual maturity," see Jacques Mandrin (pseud. of J.-P.Chevènement, D. Motchane, and A. Gomez), *L'Énarchie, ou Les Mandarins de la société bourgeoise* (Paris, 1967). Madelin is quoted in Luc Rouban, *La Fin des technocrates?* (Paris, 1998), 13. On "conformism," see Saint-Preux, *À l'ENA, y entrer, [s']en sortir* (Paris, 2013), 51. On "sterility," see Olivier Saby, *Promotion Ubu Roi: Mes 27 mois sur les bancs de l'ENA* (Paris, 2012), 274. For a broader analysis of the inadequacies of the French system of elite education, see Peter Gumbel, *Élite Academy: Enquête sur la France malade de ses grandes écoles* (Paris, 2013). For a vigorous defense of the ENA, see Jean-François Kesler, *Le Pire des systèmes, à l'exception de tous les autres: De l'énarchie, de la noblesse d'état et de la reproduction sociale* (Paris, 2007). On "parallel world," see "Chômage, c'est la faute à Voltaire," *Le Figaro*, March 1, 2014.

44. See Martin Leprince, *Le Roman de la promotion Voltaire* (Paris, 2013); Bernard Domeyne, *Petits meurtres entre énarques* (Paris, 2011), 386.

Chapter 5: To the Left, and to the Right

1. "Manifeste de la gauche," Paris, April 20, 1870, in *Les Révolutions du XIXe siècle, 1852–1872*, 4th ser., vol. 10.

2. On Napoleon III, see Bordeaux speech, October 9, 1852, in Napoleon III, *Discours, messages et proclamations de l'empereur* (Paris, 1860). On the Cartesian character of the Left-Right distinction, see Maurice Agulhon, "La Droite et la gauche," in *Histoire vagabonde*, vol. 2 (Paris, 1988), 222.

3. On left-wing Bonapartism, see Gilles Candar, "La Mémoire d'un bonapartisme de gauche," in Jean-Jacques Becker and Gilles Candar, eds., *Histoire des Gauches en France*, vol. 1 (Paris, 2004), 152–160. On the Bonapartist influence on the Third Republic, see Sudhir Hazareesingh, "La Fondation de la République: Histoire, mythe, et contre-histoire," in Marion Fontaine, Frédéric Monier, and Christophe Prochasson, eds., *Une contre-histoire de la IIIe République* (Paris, 2013), 243–256.

4. On the nineteenth-century clash between royalists and Bonapartists, see Pierre Triomphe, "La Contribution paradoxale du légitimisme à l'enracinement de la République dans le Midi de la France de 1830 à 1870," in Luis P. Martin, Jean-Paul Pelligrinetti, and Jérémy Guedj, eds., *La République en Méditerannée* (Paris, 2012). On the conflict between Gaullists and Algerian colonial settlers, see Jeannine Verdès-Leroux, *Les Français d'Algérie, de 1830 à nos jours* (Paris, 2001). Mollet is quoted in Jean-Jacques Becker, "L'Homme de Gauche au XXe siècle," in Jean-Jacques Becker and Gilles Candar, *Histoire des Gauches en France*, vol. 2 (Paris, 2004), 729. The pamphlet by Étienne Fajon, *L'Union est un combat*, was published in Paris in 1975.

5. Patrice Gueniffey, *Le Nombre et la raison: La Révolution française et les élections* (Paris, 1993); Marcel Gauchet, "La Droite et la Gauche," in Pierre Nora, ed., *Les Lieux de mémoire*, vol. 3, no. 1 (Paris, 1992); Marc Crapez, "De quand date le clivage Gauche/Droite en France?," *Revue française de science politique* 48, no. 1 (1998): 42–75.

6. Speech at the National Assembly, January 29, 1891, quoted in Pierre Barral, *Les Fondateurs de la IIIe République* (Paris, 1968), 114; Marie-Pierre-Henri Durzy, *Guerre aux passions! Ou dictionnaire du modéré* (Paris, 1821), 73. *Gauche* was similarly defined as "democracy / new interests" (p. 73).

7. Charles Morazé, *Les Français et la République* (Paris, 1956), 252; François-Joseph Liger, *La Souveraineté du peuple* (Rouen, 1848), 3, 4.

8. On monarchy as tyranny, see *Déclaration des droits de l'homme et du citoyen, avec des commentaires par le citoyen Laponneraye* (Paris, 1833). On virtue, see Ernest Richard, ed., *Le catéchisme des droits de l'homme et du citoyen* (Sceaux, n.d.), 4. For "people are good," see *Pourquoi nous sommes républicains et ce que nous voulons, par le citoyen Guérineau, ouvrier, membre de la Société des droits de l'homme* (Paris, n.d.), 2. On "perfectibility," see Société des Droits de l'Homme et du Citoyen, *De l'instruction* (Paris, n.d.).

9. Joseph de Maistre, *Considérations sur la France* (Paris, 1877), 79 ("regeneration"), 176 ("never met one").

10. Marc Fumaroli, *Chateaubriand: Poésie et terreur* (Paris, 2003); Louis de Bonald, *Théorie du pouvoir politique et religieux*, in Louis de Bonald, *Oeuvres completes*, Jacques Paul Migne, ed., vol. 1 (Paris, 1859), 305; Louis de Bonald, *Législation primitive* (Paris, 1802), 25.

11. Louis de Bonald, *Pensées sur divers sujets, et discours politiques*, vol. 1 (Paris, 1817), 360; Albert O. Hirschman, *The Rhetoric of Reaction: Perversity, Futility, Jeopardy* (Cambridge, MA, 1991); A. Clozel de Boyer, *Monarchie ou anarchie* (Paris, 1851), 23–24.

12. Louis Gaston Adrien de Ségur, *La Révolution* (Paris, 1861), 12; Gabriel de Belcastel, *La Citadelle de la liberté* (Toulouse, 1867), 27; Jean-Baptiste-Victor Coquille, *Politique chrétienne* (Paris, 1868), vi.

13. For "respect for authority," see E.S., *Causeries avec mes concitoyens des villes et des campagnes* (Compiègne, 1869), 6. On the Constitution as tradition, see Antoine-Eugène de Genoude (pseud.) and Henri de Lourdoueix, *La Raison monarchique* (Paris, 1838), vi. For "restores him to goodness," see Antoine Blanc de Saint-Bonnet, *Politique réelle* (Paris, 1858), 49. For "leads on to death," see Louis Veuillot, *L'Illusion libérale* (Paris, 1866), 18.

14. See Emmanuel Fureix, *La France des larmes: Deuils politiques à l'âge romantique, 1814–1840* (Paris, 2009).

15. On cafés, see Jérôme Grévy, "Les Cafés républicains de Paris au début de la Troisième République," *Revue d'histoire moderne et contemporaine*, April-June 2003, 52. On Saint-Gilles celebration, see police report, Saint-Gilles, May 2, 1900, Archives Nationales, Paris, F7 12529. On Perdiguier's white rosette, see Agricol Perdiguier, *Mémoires d'un compagnon* (Paris, 1992), 87–88. On the red menu, see Maurice Dommanget, *Histoire du drapeau rouge* (Paris, 1967), 460. On the French Left's contrasting gastronomical cultures, see Thomas Bouchet, *Les Fruits défendus: Socialismes et sensualité du XIXe siècle à nos jours* (Paris, 2014).

16. The quotation in French was: "Mon agitation ne fut jamais une course vers quelque chose, mais une fuite vers un ailleurs." It appears in Maurice Barrès, *Mes cahiers*, vol. 1 (Paris, 2010). See also Daniel Stern (pesud. for Marie d'Agoult), *Esquisses morales et politiques* (Paris, 1849), 205.

17. For "robust athlete," see A.-F Lacroix, "Au scrutin!," *Le Père Duchesne*, 1849.

18. "Let us smash the old systems" ("Brisons les vieux engrenages") is featured in Charles Perussaux, ed., *Les Affiches de mai '68, ou L'Imagination graphique* (Paris, 1982). The Mitterrand quotation is from speech at Épinay, June 11, 1971, in Jacques Julliard and Grégoire Franconie, eds., *La Gauche par les textes, 1762–2012* (Paris, 2012), 414.

19. The distinction of the four main "families" is offered in Jacques Julliard, *Les Gauches françaises: Histoire, politique, imaginaire, 1762–2012* (Paris, 2012). The Briand quotation is from ibid., 491.

20. See the contributions in M. Agulhon, ed., *Le XIXe Siècle et la Révolution française* (Paris, 1992).

21. Léon Blum, "Anniversaire de la Révolution de 1848" (conference at Sorbonne, February 24, 1948), in *L'Oeuvre de Léon Blum*, vol. 8 (Paris, 1963).

22. On "common enemy," see Jules Simon, *Souvenirs du 4 Septembre* (Paris, 1874), 251. On de Gaulle as a Bonapartist, see Jacques Duclos, *De Napoléon III à de Gaulle* (Paris, 1964).

23. On the Radical Party manifesto, see Jean Touchard, *La Gauche en France depuis 1900* (Paris, 1977), 48. On communists as allies of the bourgeoisie, see Annie Kriegel, *Les Communistes français* (Paris, 1968), 246. The Jean Rony quotation is from *Trente ans de parti: Un communiste s'interroge* (Paris, 1978), 114.

24. Jules Michelet, *Introduction à l'histoire universelle* (Paris, 1897), 446; Philippe Darriulat, *Les Patriotes: La Gauche républicaine et la nation, 1830–1870* (Paris, 2001), 281.

25. Henri Martin, *De la France, de son génie et de ses destinées* (Paris, 1847), 24. The Lafargue citation is from an article in *Le Socialiste*, June 10, 1893, quoted in Michel Winock, *Le Socialisme en France et en Europe* (Paris, 1992), 369. For Mollet as symbol of the Left's bankruptcy, see Julliard, *Les Gauches françaises*, 746.

26. See Robert Tombs, ed., *Nationhood and Nationalism in France: From Boulangism to the Great War, 1889–1918* (London, 1991); Bertrand Joly, *Nationalistes et conservateurs en France 1885–1902* (Paris, 2008); Zeev Sternhell, *La Droite révolutionnaire* (Paris, 1978).

27. Jules Barbey d'Aurevilly, *L'Ensorcelée* (Paris, 1916), 2; Charles Maurras, *L'Idée de décentralisation* (Paris, 1898); Carole Reynaud-Paligot, "Maurras et la notion de race," in Olivier Dard, Michel Leymarie, and Neil McWilliam, eds., *Le Maurrassisme et la culture*, vol. 3 (Villeneuve-d'Ascq, 2010).

28. On Poitiers, see *La Voix de Jeanne d'Arc*, November-December 1934. On "the cruelty of the English," see Yvonne Pirat, *Jeanne d'Arc devant ses juges* (Lyon, 1942), 123. On "national preference," see Michel Winock, "Jeanne d'Arc," in Pierre Nora, ed., *Les Lieux de mémoire*, vol. 3 (Paris, 1992).

29. On family, see Christophe Capuano, *Vichy et la famille: Réalités et faux-semblants d'une politique publique* (Rennes, 2009). On regional dialects, see R. de Verduillet, "La Décentralisation sous l'ancien régime et la centralisation révolutionnaire," *L'Action française*, no. 212, May 15, 1908, 140. For the cookbook, see Pampille (pseud. of Marthe Daudet), *Les Bons Plats de France* (Paris, 2008).

30. For "backbone of the Nation," see speech by Poujade, May 9, 1955, quoted in Romain Souillac, *Le Mouvement Poujade* (Paris, 2007), 92. "Brothel" is quoted

in Jean Touchard, "Bibliographie et chronologie du poujadisme," *Revue française de science politique* 6, no. 1 (1956). "Defecations" is cited in Thierry Bouclier, *Les années Poujade* (Paris, 2006), 100.

31. See Jean Charlot, "Le Gaullisme," in Jean-François Sirinelli, ed., *Histoire des Droites en France*, vol. 1 (Paris, 1992), 653–689. On the Left and the market, see Alain Bergounioux and Gérard Grunberg, *L'Ambition et le remords: Les Socialistes français et le pouvoir, 1905–2005* (Paris, 2005), 458. For "pullover over his shoulders," see Frédéric Beigbeder, *L'Égoïste romantique* (Paris, 2005), 21.

32. On denouncing Freemasons, see Abbé Augustin Barruel, *Mémoires pour servir à l'histoire du jacobinisme*, vol. 1 (Paris, 1974), 422. For pernicious theories, see Armand Neut, *Attentats de la franc-maçonnerie à l'ordre social* (Gand, 1868), 32. The Vichyist publication is quoted in Pierre Birnbaum, "Accepter la pluralité: Haines et préjugés," in Jean-François Sirinelli, ed., *Histoire des Droites en France*, vol. 3 (Paris, 1992), 449. For "universal conspiracy," see Georges Bernanos, *La France contre les robots* (Paris, 1947).

33. Auguste Romieu, *Le Spectre rouge de 1852* (Paris, 1851). On this theme, see Dominique Lejeune, *La Peur du rouge en France: Des partageux aux gauchistes* (Paris, 2003).

34. Sarrault is cited in Sophie Coeuré, "Communisme et anticommunisme," in Jean Jacques Becker and Gilles Candar, eds., *Histoire des Gauches en France*, vol. 2 (Paris, 2004), 489. On carrier pigeons, see "Rapport d'expertise," June 3, 1952, signed by Professor Letard of the Veterinary School of Alfort, Captain Lefort of the French Army, and M. Poulain, Archives Jacques Duclos 293 J/1 (42), PCF archives, Archives départementales de la Seine-Saint-Denis. On the post-1981 conservative panic, see Pierre Favier, *Dix Jours en mai* (Paris, 2011), 26.

35. On Jews as foreigners, see Malcolm Bowie, *Proust Among the Stars* (London, 1998), 141–147; Jérôme and Jean Tharaud, *Quand Israel n'est plus roi*, quoted in Michel Leymarie, *La Preuve par deux: Jérôme and Jean Tharaud* (Paris, 2014), 169. For the AF oath of allegiance, see Rémond, *Les Droites en France* (Paris, 1998), 287.

36. On *La France juive*, see Pierre Birnbaum, *Le Peuple et les gros: Histoire d'un mythe* (Paris, 1979), 40, 74. On the National Front, see James Shields, *The Extreme Right in France: From Pétain to Le Pen* (London, 2007).

37. For "out of the abyss," see Pierre-Jean de Béranger, *Ma biographie* (Paris, 1868), 68. Guizot is quoted in Adrien Dansette, *Louis-Napoléon à la conquête du pouvoir* (Paris, 1961), 280.

38. The Thiers quotation is in Jules Simon, *Le Gouvernement de M. Thiers, 1871–1873*, vol. 1 (Paris, 1878), 67. On Pétain as a father figure, see Jean Garrigues, *Les Hommes providentiels: Histoire d'une fascination française* (Paris, 2012), 89. The quotation about Lyautey is in Edward Berenson, *Heroes of Empire: Five Charismatic Men and the Conquest of Africa* (Berkeley, CA, 2011), 238, 261.

39. Jules Michelet, *Le Peuple* (Paris, 1974), 160.

40. For "sickening . . . exploiters," see Eugène Pottier, "L'Insurgé," *Le Cri du peuple*, March 19, 1886. On the Commune as liberation from exploitation, see "En avant pour les 8 heures!," CGT poster (1906).

41. On the representations of the proletarian myth in French communist literature, see Bernard Pudal, "Récits édifiants du mythe prolétarien et réalisme socialiste en

France," *Société et représentations*, no. 15 (2003): 77–96. The Jean Daniel quotation is from *Les Miens* (Paris, 2009), 24.

42. Robespierre speech of February 7, 1794; François Mitterrand, *Le Coup d'état permanent* (Paris, 1964).

43. Béranger and Blanc are cited in Jacqueline Lalouette, *La République anticléricale* (Paris, 2002), 27. The Gambetta speech, May 4, 1877, is cited in Pierre Barral, *Les Fondateurs de la IIIe République* (Paris, 1968), 176. "J'ai enculé le pape" from *Charlie Hebdo* is quoted in Stéphane Mazurier, *Bête, méchant, et hebdomadaire: Une histoire de Charlie Hebdo, 1969–1982* (Paris, 2009), 463.

44. On bourgeois greed, see Albert Laponneraye, *Catéchisme démocratique* (Paris, 1837), 12–13. On "bourgeois Norm," see Roland Barthes, 1970 preface to *Mythologies* (Paris, 1970), 8. For "merely conditional," see François Mitterrand, *Mémoires interrompus* (Paris, 1996), 168. On Furet, see François Furet, *Le Passé d'une illusion: Essai sur l'idée communiste au XXe siècle* (Paris, 1995), 34–35.

45. Pierre Mauroy, *Ce jour-là* (Paris, 2012), 43.

46. On French opinion, see the contributions in Jacques le Bohec and Christophe Le Digol, eds., *Gauche-Droite: Genèse d'un clivage politique* (Paris, 2012). On the National Front, see Julien Licourt, "Quand le FN reprend Jaurès," *Le Figaro*, July 31, 2014. More generally, on the attempted appropriation of Jaurès by the extreme right, see Alexis Corbière, *Le Parti de l'étrangère: Marine Le Pen contre l'histoire républicaine de France* (Brussels, 2012), 96–108.

47. *Le Monde*, June 5–6, 2006, quoted in Robert and Isabelle Tombs, *That Sweet Enemy: Britain and France* (London, 2006), 691. For a wider discussion of the concept of the "Anglo-Saxon" in French public discourse, see Émile Chabal, "The Rise of the Anglo-Saxon: French Perceptions of the Anglo-American World in the Long Twentieth Century," *French Politics, Culture and Society* 31, no.1 (2013).

48. François Hollande, *Changer de destin* (Paris, 2012), 50; Jean-Luc Mélenchon, *Qu'ils s'en aillent tous!* (Paris, 2011), 10; Stéphane Hessel, *Time for Outrage!* (New York, 2011), 22; Olivier Dard, *La Synarchie, ou Le Mythe du complot permanent* (Paris, 1998), 226; Laurent Joffrin, "Béquille intellectuelle," *Libération*, January 20, 2015.

49. On Sarkozy as a "protector," see "Nicolas Sarkozy adopte la ligne gaulliste de l'homme providentiel," *Le Monde*, July 10, 2013. The tweet of September 19, 2014, is quoted in *Libération*, September 20–21, 2014. For "tellement cool," see Alain Auffray, "Carla joue la carte usée de l'homme providentiel," *Libération*, May 2, 2014. The de Villiers quotation was reported in *Le Figaro*, August 18, 2014.

50. Marine Le Pen, *Pour que vive la France* (Paris, 2012); "Pour la présidente du FN, les résultats des Bleus sont liés à 'l'ultralibéralisme,'" *Le Monde*, November 18, 2013; quoted in Touchard, *La Gauche en France depuis 1900*, 35.

Chapter 6: The Sum of Their Parts

1. Report of the Mayor of Foix to the Prefect of Nord, August 17, 1866, Archives Départementales du Nord (Lille), M 141 (95), *Fête du 15 août*, 1864–1870.

2. Alexis de Tocqueville, *L'Ancien régime et la Révolution* (1856), in *Oeuvres complètes*, Georges Lefebvre and André Jardin, eds., vol. 2, no. 1 (Paris, 1952), 74.

3. Ernest Renan, *Qu'est-ce qu'une nation?* (Paris, 1882).

4. Louis Veuillot, *L'Illusion libérale* (Paris, 1866), 128.

5. Quoted in Graham Robb, *The Discovery of France* (London, 2007), 20–21; see Thomas Dodman, "Un pays pour la colonie: Mourir de nostalgie en Algérie Française, 1830–1880," *Annales*, July–September 2011, 743–784; Report of prefect of Var, July 7, 1856, quoted in Bernard Le Clère and Vincent Wright, *Les Préfets du Second Empire* (Paris, 1973), 132.

6. On Mérimée, see January 1836 letter, cited in Fanch Morvannou, *Le Breton: La Jeunesse d'une vieille langue*, 3rd ed. (Lannion, 1994), 20. On "people from another world," see Alain Corbin, "Paris-Province," in Pierre Nora, ed., *Les Lieux de mémoire*, vol. 3, no. 1 (Paris, 1992), 778. On Charles Dupont-White, see his *La Centralisation: Suite de l'individu et l'état* (Paris, 1861), 270; see also his *Le Progrès politique en France* (Paris, 1868), 52. On Hippolyte Taine, see Taine's *Carnets de voyage: Notes sur la province, 1863–1865* (Paris, 1897), 33. On Breton folk dances, see Denise Delouche, "De l'image au mythe, la caractérisation d'une province: La Bretagne," in *Du provincialisme au régionalisme* (Montbrison, 1989), 38. For "deflowered," see Pierre Durand (pseud. of Eugène Guinot), *Physiologie du provincial à Paris* (Paris, 1842), 7.

7. On romantic travel writings, see Odile Parsis-Barubé, *La Province antiquaire: L'invention de l'histoire locale en France, 1800–1870* (Paris, 2011). Michelet is quoted in Raoul Girardet, *Mythes et mythologies politiques* (Paris, 1986), 156. On "contemplation," see Dorothée de Courlande, Duchesse de Dino, *Chronique de 1830 à 1862* (Paris, 1910), 46. On "perfectibility," see Alfred de Falloux, *Mémoires d'un royaliste*, vol. 2 (Paris, 1888), 241–242. On "fortifying consciences," see Pierre-Joseph Proudhon, *Du principe fédératif*, in *Oeuvres complètes*, vol. 15 (Paris, 1959), 549.

8. Émile Boutroux, "La Pensée française et l'idéal classique," *Revue bleue*, January 1915.

9. Stéphane Gerson, *The Pride of Place: Local Memories and Political Culture in Nineteenth-Century France* (Ithaca, NY), 34–35.

10. On Balneolum, see preface by M. H. Monin, in Eugène Toulouze, *Histoire d'un village ignoré (Balneolum)* (Paris, 1898), cited in François Ploux, *Une mémoire de papier: Les Historiens de village et le culte des petites patries rurales, 1830–1930* (Rennes, 2011), 211. On attendance at municipal festivals, see Gerson, *Pride of Place*, 53.

11. Letter of Napoleon III to Eugène Rouher, June 27, 1863, Archives Nationales, Papiers Rouher, 45 AP 11.

12. Ernest Pinard, *Mon Journal*, vol. 1 (Paris, 1892), 223–224; Auguste Pougnet, *Hiérarchie et décentralisation* (Paris, 1866), 130 (liberal view); Charles Muller, *La Légitimité* (Paris, 1857), 147; Gustave Chaudey, *L'Empire parlementaire est-il possible?* (Paris, 1870), 48 (federalist view).

13. The Bondues ceremony list is cited in F. Nazé, "Maires et municipalités de mon village, Bondues," in "Jacobus, bulletin du club d'histoire locale de Bondues," special issue, 1984. On Doubs music, see Vincent Petit, *La Clef des champs: Les Sociétés musicales du Haut-Doubs horloger au XIXe siècle* (Maiche, 1998), 31. The musician's quotation is in *L'Orphéon*, May 1, 1867, quoted in Pierre Rosanvallon, *The Demands of Liberty: Civil Society in France Since the Revolution* (Cambridge, MA, 2007), 188.

14. On Masonic values, see Sudhir Hazareesingh and Vincent Wright, *Francsmaçons sous le Second Empire* (Rennes, 2001), 125. The journalist's quotation is in "Bulletin du Grand Orient de France," July-August 1870, 339. On Masonic freedom,

see *La Liberté: Discours d'un F.M.* (Aix-en-Provence, 1872), 3. On "whole of humanity," see André Rousselle, "Des scissions en maçonnerie," *L'Action maçonnique*, no. 27, December 15, 1868.

15. Quoted in Gerson, *Pride of Place*, 230.

16. See James Lehning, *To Be a Citizen: The Political Culture of the Early French Third Republic* (Ithaca, NY, 2001).

17. On "grateful thoughts," see Edmond Groult, *Annuaire des musées cantonaux* (Lisieux, 1880), 13. On "conquest of the universe," see Daniel Stern (pseud. of Marie d'Agoult), *Esquisses morales et politiques* (Paris, 1849), 7. On "mayor already exists," see Eugène Pelletan, *Droits de l'homme* (Paris, 1867), 281–282. On municipal institutions, see Alexandre Laserve, *La République et les affaires* (Paris, 1875), 10.

18. On the Commune, see Dionys Ordinaire, *La République c'est l'ordre* (Paris, 1875); Hippolyte Maze, *La Fin des révolutions par la République* (Paris, 1872). Sixty-one percent of the French population was engaged in agriculture in 1851; this figure fell to 45 percent in 1891 and to 32.5 percent by the late 1930s. See Theodore Zeldin, *France 1848–1945: Ambition and Love* (Oxford, 1979), 171. Gambetta's speech of May 24, 1878, and Ferry's speech of August 30, 1885, are quoted in Chloé Gaboriaux, *La République en quête de citoyens* (Paris, 2010), 306–307. The speech by Minister of Agriculture Albert Viger at Rouen, 1910, is cited by Pierre Barral, *Les Agrariens français de Méline à Pisani* (Paris, 1968), 137.

19. The 1906 school inspector is quoted in Jean-François Chanet, *L'École républicaine et les petites patries* (Paris, 1996), 150. The schoolbook is G. Bruno (pseud. of Augustine Fouillée), *Le Tour de la France par deux enfants: Devoir et patrie* (Paris, 1889), iv, 153, 217. For "bedrock of the nation," see "Un poète du sol et du foyer," *Le Figaro*, July 5, 1905.

20. Hippolyte Taine, *La Fontaine et ses fables* (Paris, 1875), 16; Jean-Pierre Bois, *Histoire des 14 juillet, 1789–1919* (Rennes, 1991), 10; Renan, *Qu'est-ce qu'une nation?* (1882).

21. For "consecration," see Henri Martin, speaking at a Senate debate on the Republic's national day, June 29, 1880, *Journal officiel de la République Française* (1880): 7236–7237. "Sense of duty" is quoted in Rosemonde Sanson, *Les 14 juillet 1789–1975: Fête et conscience nationale* (Paris, 1976), 65. On the flag hanging from window, see Maurice Agulhon, *Marianne au combat: L'Imagerie et la symbolique républicaines de 1789 à 1880* (Paris, 1979), 223.

22. On open-air banquets, see Olivier Ihl, "Convivialité et citoyenneté: Les Banquets commémoratifs dans les campagnes républicaines à la fin du XIXe siècle," in A. Corbin et al., eds., *Les Usages politiques des fêtes aux XIXe–XXe siècles* (Paris, 1994), 144. On Marianne, see Olivier Ihl, *La Fête républicaine* (Paris, 1996), 160. For the report of the mayor of Soubise (Charente-Maritime), see July 15, 1885, ibid., 145. For the report of the mayor of Vinon (Cher), see July 15, 1882, ibid., 177.

23. The D'Ormes priest incident is cited in Rémi Dalisson, *Célébrer la nation: Les Fêtes nationales en France de 1789 à nos jours* (Paris, 2009), 279.

24. On anarchists, see "Fête du 14 juillet," pamphlet by Groupe Avant-Garde de Londres (1889), AN F7–12518. On Brittany, see *Le réveil de l'esclave*, anarchist pamphlet, Paris (1913), AN F7–13055.

25. On Vendée royalists, see Pascal Ory, *Une nation pour mémoire: 1889, 1939, 1989, Trois Jubilés révolutionnaires* (Paris, 1992), 116. On Yann Sohier, see Mona Ozouf, *Composition française* (Paris, 2009), 43. On Paris socialist students, see Alexandre Zevaès, *Notes et souvenirs d'un militant* (Paris, 1913), 87–88. On flags on buildings, see police report, July 14, 1900, APP DA-289 (manifestations 14 juillet 1886–1913).

26. On the execution of the king, see Philippe Dujardin, "D'une commémoration à l'autre: Lyon 1889, 1939," in Jean Davallon, Philippe Dujardin, and Gérard Sabatier, eds., *Politique de la mémoire: Commémorer la Révolution* (Lyon, 1993), 171. On patriotism and internationalism, see Jean-William Dereymez, "Le patron, l'ouvrier, la République: fêtes patronales, fêtes ouvrières et fêtes républicaines au Creusot et à Montceau-les-Mines (fin XIXe–début XXe siècles)," in M. Agulhon, ed., *Cultures et folklores républicains* (Paris, 1995), 135–136.

27. On socialism and patriotism, see Paul Lafargue, *Le Patriotisme de la bourgeoisie* (Paris, 1895). On the perversion of 1789, see Jean Lardennois, "Critique socialiste des principes de '89," *Revue socialiste* 8 (1888): 501–516. The Jules Delmorès quotations are from his *Du quatorze juillet* (Montbrison, 1887), 5–6.

28. On the anarchist critique, see *La Révolte*, July 1893. The trade unionist was Jacques Toesca, in "Le 14 juillet," *Le Fonctionnaire syndicaliste*, April 1930.

29. On "socialist Easter," see Benoît Malon, "Le Congrès de Marseille," *Revue socialiste*, July-December 1886, 1080. See, more generally, Danielle Tartakowski, *Nous irons chanter sur vos tombes: Le Père Lachaise, XIX–XXe siècle* (Paris, 1999). On the Blanquists, see Patrick Hutton, *The Cult of the Revolutionary Tradition: The Blanquists in French Politics, 1864–1893* (Berkeley, CA, 1981), 15, 168–169.

30. On "cry of social revolt," see article in *Action*, January 23, 1905. On the Lyon revolts of the early 1830s, see Ludovic Frobert, *Les Canuts, ou La Démocratie turbulente, Lyon, 1831–1834* (Paris, 2009). On "Commune was killed," see speech by anarchist delegate Dumas at May 1 meeting, Union des Syndicats Ouvriers, Saint-Étienne (1898), AN F7-12528. On "bourgeois centralized state," see "La Commune," *La Bataille syndicaliste*, May 28, 1911.

31. On "intense struggle," see Édouard Vaillant, "La Commune," *Le Socialiste*, March 15–22, 1903. On the socialist program of the Commune, see Jules Guesde, "Le 18 mars," *Le Socialiste*, March 15–22, 1903. On the Commune not being a socialist model, see Jean Jaurès, "Hier et demain," *L'Humanité*, March 18, 1907.

32. "Le Réveil des travailleurs de l'Aube," May 1, 1900.

33. Police report on Louise Michel speech, Rouen, May 30, 1897, AN F7–12505.

34. Vincent Auriol, *Souvenirs sur Jean Jaurès* (Algiers, 1944), 4.

35. Quoted in Robert Gildea, *The Past in French History* (New Haven, CT, 1994), 170.

36. Sudhir Hazareesingh, "Republicanism, War and Democracy: The Ligue du Midi in France's War Against Prussia, 1870–1871," *French History* 17, no.1 (2003): 48–78; Jean Estèbe, *Les Ministres de la République* (Paris, 1982), 53, 67–68.

37. On Charles de Gaulle, see Comte de Charencey, H. Gaidoz, and Charles de Gaulle, *Pétition pour les langues provinciales au Corps Législatif de 1870* (Paris, 1903), 18–19. On Breton nationalism, see "Manifeste du parti national breton" (October 1911), cited in Michel Nicolas, *Histoire de la revendication bretonne* (Spézet, 2007),

321. On regionalism, see Caroline Ford, *Creating the Nation in Provincial France: Religion and Political Identity in Brittany* (Princeton, NJ, 1993).

38. On flexibility of Jacobinism, see Alain Chatriot, "French Politics, History, and a New Perspective on the Jacobin State," in Julian Wright and H. S. Jones, eds., *Pluralism and the Idea of the Republic in France* (New York, 2012), 249. On "irritations of politics," see Mistral letter to A. Dumas, October 3, 1859, in Frédéric Mistral, *Correspondance de Frédéric Mistral et Adolphe Dumas* (Gap, 1859), 55. On Mistral as a monarchist, see conversation with J. Ajalbert, cited in R. Jouveau and P. Berengier, eds., *Frédéric Mistral: Écrits politiques* (Marseille, 1989), 159. On regionalism fortifying national culture, see Sextius Michel, *La Petite Patrie: Notes et documents pour servir à l'histoire du mouvement félibréen à Paris* (Paris, 1894).

39. On Ricard, see Fernand Clerget, *Louis-Xavier de Ricard* (Reims, 1906), 29. On Clovis Hugues, see Jean-Claude Izzo, *Clovis Hugues, un rouge du Midi* (Marseille, 1978), 107. His Provençal poems can be found in Tricío Dupuy, *Clovis Hugues* (Marseille, 2013).

40. On regional assemblies, see Maurice Barrès, "Notes sur les idées fédéralistes," *La Quinzaine*, December 15, 1895. On "vitality," see Maurice Barrès, *Scènes et doctrines du nationalisme* (Paris, 1925), 492–493. On resistance to Germanic influences, see Zeev Sternhell, *Maurice Barrès* (Paris, 1872), 333.

41. On concentric communities, see Jean Charles-Brun, *Le Régionalisme* (Paris, 2004), 133. On republicanism of Charles-Brun, see Julian Wright, *The Regionalist Movement in France, 1890–1914: Jean Charles-Brun and French Political Thought* (Oxford, 2003), 195. On the folkloric writings of Charles-Brun, see his *Intérieurs rustiques* (Paris, 1928), *Costumes des provinces françaises* (Paris, 1932), and *Costumes de notre terroir* (Paris, 1945). On the Poincaré-Mistral lunch, see Maurice Agulhon, "Conscience nationale et conscience régionale en France," in M. Agulhon, *Histoire vagabonde*, vol. 2 (Paris, 1988), 150.

42. On Guesde, see Maurice Dommanget, *Histoire du premier mai* (Paris, 1972), 130. On Fourmies, see Madeleine Rébérioux, ed., *Fourmies et les premier mai* (Paris, 1994), 15.

43. In June 1906, National Assembly member Adolphe Maujan tabled a motion demanding that May 1 be recognized as a legal holiday, "given that since 1789 festivals have been established to promote fraternity among citizens." On slavery, see "1893: 1er Mai–1 May," anarchist placard (1893), AN F7–12518. On Bordeaux celebrations, see police report, Bordeaux, April 28, 1899, AN F7–12528; police report, Lorient, May 2, 1898, AN F7–12528.

44. On Fourmies, see, for example, the police report from Anor (Nord), May 2, 1898, where local socialists marked the anniversary by laying a wreath for the victims of Fourmies, AN F7–12528. On the 1891 Lyon police violence, see Dommanget, *Histoire du premier mai*, 155.

45. On the Italians being invited, see Prefect of Isère report, May 2, 1900, AN F7–12529. On Thizy, see police report, Cahors, May 2, 1898, AN F7–12528. On Besançon, see police report, Besançon, May 2, 1898, AN F7–12528.

46. Prefect report, Nevers, May 2, 1901, AN F7–12529; police report, Dijon, May 2, 1908, AN F7–12533; police report, Calais, June 1, 1891, AN F7–12527; Dommanget, *Histoire du premier mai*, 155.

47. Fernand Braudel, *The Identity of France*, vol. 1 (London, 1988), 23.

48. Péguy is cited in Raoul Girardet, *Le Nationalisme français: Une anthologie, 1871–1914* (Paris, 1983), 23. On the Digne schoolteacher, see "La Petite Patrie," speech by M. Aubin at prize ceremony, Lycée Gassendi, Digne, July 12, 1919.

49. Joseph de Maistre, *Considérations sur la France* (Paris, 1797), 11; Edgar Quinet, *Le Christianisme et la Révolution*, in Joseph de Maistre, *Oeuvres complètes*, vol. 3 (Lyon, 1891), 272; Gambetta speech at Annecy, October 1, 1872, in Pierre Barral, *Les Fondateurs de la IIIe République* (Paris, 1968), 164–165; Renan speech given to the Alliance for the Propagation of the French Language, February 2, 1888, in Ernest Renan, *Feuilles détachées* (Paris, 1892), 257. The *Le Parisien* votes were as follows: Pasteur 1,338,425; Hugo 1,227,103; Gambetta 1,155,672, and Napoleon 1,118,034. *Le Parisien*, January 13, 1907, quoted in Alain Corbin, *Les Héros de l'histoire de France expliqués à mon fils* (Paris, 2011), 193–194.

50. On "return to the land," see Gérard de Puymège, *Chauvin, le soldat-laboureur: Contribution à l'étude des nationalismes* (Paris, 1993), 236–238. On the monuments built, see Rémi Dalisson, *Les Guerres et la mémoire* (Paris, 2013), 110–111. On the Marchampt priest, see Abbé E. Montaland, *Petite Patrie dans la mère patrie* (Lyon, 1919), 77. On "religious indifference," see E. Jeanne and P. Ruel, "Aux jeunes," *La Petite Patrie*, no.1, January 1922. For Daniel Halévy, see his *Visites aux paysans du Centre* (Paris, 1978). On the novelists, see Sarah Kay, Terence Cave, and Malcolm Bowie, *A Short History of French Literature* (New York, 2003), 268. Mauriac is quoted in Anne-Marie Thiesse, *Écrire la France: Le Mouvement littéraire régionaliste de langue française entre la Belle Époque et la Libération* (Paris, 1991), 99.

51. On communists, see Marc Lazar, "Damné de la terre et homme de marbre: L'Ouvrier dans l'imaginaire du PCF du milieu des années trente à la fin des années cinquante," *Annales: Economies, sociétés, civilisations* 45, no. 5 (1990): 1078–1079. On Colonial Exposition, see Herman Lebovics, *True France: The Wars over Cultural Identity, 1900–1945* (Ithaca, NY, 1992). Pétain is quoted in Anne-Marie Thiesse, *Ils apprenaient la France: L'Exaltation des régions dans le discours patriotique* (Paris, 1997), 71.

52. On culinary excellence, see Vincent Martigny, "Le Goût des nôtres: Gastronomie et sentiment national en France," *Raisons politiques*, no. 37 (2010): 39–52. According to a poll conducted in November 2013, 57 percent of French men and women had a positive view of mayors. See the article by Denis Daumin, *La Nouvelle République du Centre-Ouest*, November 19, 2013.

53. Jean-Marie Domenach, *Regarder la France: Essai sur le malaise français* (Paris, 1997), 173.

54. For a discussion of these themes, see "Astérix: Un mythe et ses figures," special issue of *Ethnologie française*, June-September 1998; and Nicolas Rouvière, *Astérix, ou Les Lumières de la civilisation* (Paris, 2006).

Interlude: New Paths to the Present

1. "Flame of French Resistance" is cited in Jonathan Fenby, *The General: Charles de Gaulle and the France He Saved* (London, 2010), 38. "Lady de Gaulle" is cited in Philippe de Gaulle, *De Gaulle: Mon père*, vol. 1 (Paris, 2003), 162. For "man sent by

providence," see Ludovic Bron, *Le Général de Gaulle: L'Homme providentiel* (Le Puy, 1945).

2. Charles de Gaulle, *Mémoires de guerre*, vol. 1 (Paris, 1989), 9.

3. Romain Gary, *Ode à l'homme qui fut la France* (Paris, 1997), 112; "Bal tragique à Colombey: 1 Mort," *Hara-kiri*, no. 94, November 16, 1970. This irreverence was not appreciated by the French government, which promptly banned the magazine, and it immediately renamed itself *Charlie Hebdo*.

4. Letter of August 11, 1884, quoted in Thierry Paquot, *Les Faiseurs de nuages: Essai sur la genèse des marxismes français, 1880–1914* (Paris, 1980), 57. See Isabelle Gouarné, *L'Introduction du marxisme en France: Philosoviétisme et sciences humaines, 1920–1939* (Rennes, 2013).

5. See Jeannine Verdès-Leroux, *Au service du parti: Le Parti communiste, les intellectuels et la culture, 1944–1956* (Paris, 1983).

6. For "cannonball," see Régis Debray, *Loués soient nos seigneurs* (Paris, 1996), 45. On right and wrong, see Sudhir Hazareesingh, *Intellectuals and the French Communist Party* (Oxford, 1991), 151. On Althusser, see his letter (1955) to his wife, Hélène, in Louis Althusser, *Lettres à Hélène, 1947–1980* (Paris, 2011), 283.

7. The petit-bourgeois quotation is from Althusser's interview with the Italian communist daily *L'Unità*, reproduced in Louis Althusser, *Positions* (Paris, 1976), 37. On "philosophy of order," see Jacques Rancière, *La Leçon d'Althusser* (Paris, 1974), 9. On "proud to be communist," see Daniel Lindenberg, *Le Marxisme introuvable* (Paris, 1975), 26. On *se faire althusser*, see François Dufay and Pierre-Bertrand Dufort, *Les Normaliens, de Charles Péguy à Bernard-Henri Lévy* (Paris, 1993), 200.

8. On philosophical abstractions, see Tony Judt's illuminating account of the intellectual evolution of French Marxism between 1945 and 1975 in *Marxism and the French Left* (Oxford, 1986), 169–238. For "failure of the philosophy of history," see Maurice Merleau-Ponty, *Les Aventures de la dialectique* (Paris, 1955), 321. For Raymond Aron, see his *The Opium of the Intellectuals* (London, 1957).

9. Quoted in Alain Peyrefitte, *C'était de Gaulle* (Paris, 2002), 57; André Malraux, *Les Chênes qu'on abat* (Paris, 1971), 32, 108.

10. I am grateful to Madame Agnès Callu, former curator of the de Gaulle papers at the Archives Nationales in Paris, for this information.

11. André Gorz, *Adieux au prolétariat* (Paris, 1980), 18.

Chapter 7: Freedom and Domination

1. *Tristes Tropiques* was translated into English as *A World on the Wane*.

2. Claude Lévi-Strauss and Didier Eribon, *De près et de loin* (Paris, 2008), 47.

3. On best travel book, see François Dosse, *Histoire du structuralisme*, vol. 1 (Paris, 1992), 164. Lévi-Strauss turned down the prize. For "comfortable in its universe" and myths, see Claude Lévi-Strauss, *Tristes Tropiques* (Paris, 1990), 192, 227.

4. James Boon, "Claude Lévi-Strauss," in Quentin Skinner, ed., *The Return of Grand Theory in the Social Sciences* (Cambridge, UK, 1990), 161; Lévi-Strauss, *Tristes Tropiques*, 529.

5. "Ethnographic . . . philosophers": Lévi-Strauss, *Tristes Tropiques*, 499; "tenderness": ibid., 373; not patriarchy: ibid., 403; "fraternity": ibid., 501; "start afresh": ibid., 502.

6. "Metaphysics for shop girls" (*une sorte de métaphysique pour midinettes*): ibid., 77.

7. On "new man," see Frantz Fanon, *Les Damnés de la terre* (1961) (Paris, 1991), 376; "negation of humanity": ibid., 372–373.

8. Ibid., 126; Ronald Walters, "The Impact of Frantz Fanon on the Black Liberation Movement in the United States," in *Mémorial international Frantz Fanon* (Paris, 1984), 210.

9. Alice Cherki, *Frantz Fanon: Portrait* (Paris, 2011), 25.

10. Fanon, *Les Damnés de la terre*, 71, 83.

11. Sartre, preface to Fanon, *Les Damnés de la terre*, 52.

12. Cherki, *Frantz Fanon*, 273. See Albert Memmi, "La Vie impossible de Frantz Fanon," *Esprit*, September 1971.

13. See David Macey, *Frantz Fanon, une vie* (Paris, 2011), 505; François Bondy, "The Black Rousseau," *New York Review of Books*, March 31, 1966.

14. The cartoon was by Maurice Henry, in *La Quinzaine littéraire*, July 1, 1967. On disease, see G. Lapouge, "Encore un effort et j'aurai épousé mon temps," *La Quinzaine littéraire*, March 16, 1986. On soccer, see Dosse, *Histoire du structuralisme*, 1:9.

15. On "immutable character," see Roland Barthes, *Mythologies* (Paris, 1957), 206. On scavenger (*fouilleur de bas-fonds*), see Foucault interview with Jacques Chancel, *Radioscopie*, Radio France, March 10, 1975. For "I think where I am not," see Jacques Lacan, "L'Instance de la lettre dans l'inconscient," in *Écrits* (Paris, 1966), 276–277.

16. On "experimenter," see "Interview with Michel Foucault" (1980), in James D. Faubion, ed., *The Essential Works of Michel Foucault, 1954–1984*, vol. 3 (New York, 2000), 239–240. For "Do not ask," see Michel Foucault, *The Archaeology of Knowledge* (New York, 1972), 17. On "liberties with chronology," see Lévi-Strauss, *De près et de loin*, 105.

17. Michel Foucault, *Madness and Civilization* (New York, 1965), 257–258.

18. Michel Foucault, *The Order of Things* (London, 1970), xiv.

19. Michel Foucault, "What Is the Enlightenment?," in *The Foucault Reader*, ed. P. Rabinow (London, 1984), 42.

20. Michel Foucault, "Confinement, Psychiatry, Prison," in L. Kritzman, ed., *Michel Foucault: Politics, Philosophy, Culture: Interviews and Other Writings, 1977–1984* (New York, 1988), 197.

21. Claude Lévi-Strauss, *Le Cru et le cuit* (Paris, 1964), 26; Roland Barthes, "The Death of the Author," in Roland Barthes, *Image Music Text* (London, 1977); Foucault, *The Order of Things*, 387.

22. Didier Eribon, *Michel Foucault* (Paris, 2011), 49; Roger Crémant, *Les Matinées structuralistes* (Paris, 1969), 41.

23. Jacques Derrida, "From Moscow and Back" (1992), quoted in Mark Lilla, "The Politics of Jacques Derrida," *New York Review of Books*, June 25, 1998.

24. Benoît Peeters, *Derrida: A Biography* (London, 2012). On the formative influences on Derrida's thought, see Edward Baring, *The Young Derrida and French Philosophy* (Cambridge, UK, 2011).

25. David Hoy, "Jacques Derrida," in Skinner, ed., *The Return of Grand Theory*, 44.

26. François Dosse, *Histoire du structuralisme*, vol. 2 (Paris, 1992), 36–45, 52.

27. Jacques Derrida, *The Politics of Friendship* (London, 2005), 306.

28. On "Revolution," see Jacques Derrida, "L'Esprit de la révolution," in Jacques Derrida and Elisabeth Roudinesco, *De quoi demain . . .* (Paris, 2001), 138.

29. On "ghost," see Jacques Derrida, *Spectres of Marx* (London, 1994), 10. On "nothing outside the text" (*Il n'y a pas de hors-texte*), see Jacques Derrida, *Of Grammatology* (1967), trans. Gayatri Chakravorty Spivak (Baltimore, 1976), 163.

30. Andrew Boyd, *Life's Little Deconstruction Book* (New York, 1999).

31. For further discussion of the dissemination of French structuralism in the United States, see Michèle Lamont and Marsha Witten, "Surveying the Continental Drift: The Diffusion of French Social and Literary Theory in the United States," *French Politics and Society* 6, no. 3 (1988). See also Michèle Lamont, "How to Become a Dominant French Philosopher: The Case of Jacques Derrida," *American Journal of Sociology* 93, no. 3 (1987), 584–622. Derrida held the post at Irvine until his death in 2004. His papers have been deposited at UCI and include material from his student days at the École Normale; teaching, seminar, and conference material covering four decades; and audio and video recordings from the mid-1980s to the late 1990s.

32. On deconstruction and America, see Jacques Derrida, *Mémoires: For Paul de Man* (New York, 1986), 18. On mystification, see Anselm Haverkamp, "Deconstruction is/as Neopragmatism?," in A. Haverkamp, ed., *Deconstruction is/in America: A New Sense of the Political* (New York, 1995), 3.

33. On irreverence: Edward Said, "The Franco-American Dialogue: A Late-Twentieth-Century Reassessment," in I. van der Poel and S. Bertho, eds., *Travelling Theory: France and the United States* (Cranbury, NJ, 1999), 143–144.

34. For Edward Said, see his *Orientalism* (New York, 1979), 3. The quotation about *Orientialism* is from Conor McCarthy, *The Cambridge Introduction to Edward Said* (Cambridge, UK, 2010), 48. On feminism, see Jane Gallop, "French Theory and the Seduction of Feminism," in Alice Jardine and Paul Smith, eds., *Men in Feminism* (New York, 1987), 111.

35. On suppression of minorities, see Emily Eakin, "Derrida: The Excluded Favourite," *New York Review of Books*, March 25, 2013. On sadomasochism, see Jim Miller, *The Passion of Michel Foucault* (New York, 1993).

36. Camille Paglia, "Junk Bonds and Corporate Raiders," in Camille Paglia, *Sex, Art and American Culture* (New York, 1992), 174, 211.

37. The French sociologist Pierre Bourdieu was the second most quoted author. See "Most Cited Authors of Books in the Humanities," *Times Higher Education Supplement*, March 26, 2009. See also Wendy Brown, "Neo-liberalism and the End of Liberal Democracy," *Theory and Event* 7, no. 1 (2003); François Cusset, *French Theory: Foucault, Derrida, Deleuze & Cie et les mutations de la vie intellectuelle aux États-Unis* (Paris, 2005), 136.

38. John M. Ellis, *Against Deconstruction* (Princeton, NJ, 1989), 101, n. 5; Alan Sokal, "Transgressing the Boundaries: Towards a Transformative Hermeneutics of Quantum Gravity," *Social Text*, Spring/Summer 1996. On the moral and political

impasses of postmodernism, see Alan Sokal and Jean Bricmont, *Intellectual Impostures: Postmodernist Philosophers' Misuse of Science* (London, 1998), 193–196.

39. Jean Monnet, *Mémoires* (Paris, 1976), 35; quoted in Tony Judt, *Postwar: A History of Europe Since 1945* (London, 2005), 154–155.

40. For "type of man," see Monnet, *Mémoires*, 441. For "enemy of the French people," see 1943 memorandum, cited in Eric Roussel, *Jean Monnet* (Paris, 1996), 335–336. For "general ideas," see Monnet, *Mémoires*, 610, 273.

41. For "in the shadows," see Monnet, *Mémoires*, 273. For "man of silence," see François Mitterrand, *Allocution lors du transfert des cendres de Jean Monnet au Panthéon, 9 novembre 1988* (Paris, 1988). On pragmatism, see Monnet, *Mémoires*, 615; "lawyers and journalists": ibid., 321.

42. On states being moralized, see Monnet, *Mémoires*, 460; benefits of cooperation: ibid., 461; "interests converge": ibid., 459.

43. Maria Grazia Melchionni, "Le Comité d'Action pour les États-Unis d'Europe: Un réseau au service de l'Union Européenne," in Gérard Bossuat and Andreas Wilkens, eds., *Jean Monnet: L'Europe et les chemins de la paix* (Paris, 1999). See also Pascal Fontaine, *Jean Monnet: L'Inspirateur* (Paris, 1988).

44. Monnet, *Mémoires*, 478 ("intellectual power"), 574 ("equality"). See also Marc Joly, *Le Mythe Jean Monnet: Contribution à une sociologie historique de la construction européenne* (Paris, 2007).

45. On the communitarian method, see Jacques Delors, *Mémoires* (Paris, 2004), 456–457. On brandy-makers, see Laurent Lessous, *Jean Monnet bâtisseur d'Europe* (Poitiers, 2006); Jean-Pierre Chevènement, *La Faute de M. Monnet: La République et l'Europe* (Paris, 2006), 30, 40–41, 58. The "America's man" comment, made in early 1963, is quoted in Alain Peyrefitte, *C'était de Gaulle* (Paris, 2002), 370. For François Duchêne, see his *Jean Monnet: The First Statesman of Interdependence* (New York, 1994), 384. On baked beans, see Sherrill Brown Wells, *Jean Monnet: Unconventional Statesman* (Boulder, 2011), 233.

46. Quoted in Andrei Markovits, *Uncouth Nation: Why Europe Dislikes America* (Princeton, NJ, 2007), 207.

47. On anti-Americanism, see Jean-François Revel, *L'Obsession anti-américaine: Son fonctionnement, ses causes, ses inconséquences* (Paris, 2002), 102.

48. Maurras is quoted in Pierre Rigoulot, *L'Anti-américanisme: Critique d'un prêt-à-penser rétrograde et chauvin* (Paris, 2004), 56. Thorez is quoted in Alessandro Brogi, *Confronting America: The Cold War Between the United States and the Communists in France and Italy* (Chapel Hill, NC, 2011), 158.

49. On civilizational construct, see Philippe Roger, *L'Ennemi américain* (Paris, 2002), 441–443. On "French way of life," see Yves Roucaute, *Éloge du mode de vie à la française* (Paris, 2012), 302. On "aftertaste," see Georges Duhamel, *Scènes de la vie future* (Paris, 1930), 211. On Coca-Cola, see Richard Kuisel, *Seducing the French: The Dilemma of Americanization* (Berkeley, CA, 1993). On "the vanguard," see *Témoignage chrétien*, March 3, 1950, cited in Rigoulot, *L'Anti-américanisme*, 45.

50. José Bové and François Dufour, *Le Monde n'est pas une marchandise* (Paris, 2000), 24; Tony Caron, "Why Courts Don't Deter France's Anti-McDonald's Astérix," *Time*, February 15, 2001; Paul Ariès, *Petit Manuel anti-MacDo à l'usage des petits et des*

grands (Villeurbanne, 1999), 12; Noël Mamère and Olivier Warin, *Non merci, Oncle Sam!* (Paris, 1999), 186.

51. On the "Anglo-Saxon Diet," see Emmanuel Godin and Tony Chafer, "Introduction," in E. Godin and T. Chafer, eds., *The French Exception* (New York, 2004), xiii. Mélenchon is quoted in Jennifer Fuks, *L'Anti-américanisme au sein de la Gauche socialiste française* (Paris, 2010), 176. For "absolutely not French," see Roucaute, *Éloge du mode de vie à la française*, 84.

52. René Étiemble, *Parlez-vous franglais?* (Paris, 1973), 344.

53. Robin Adamson, *The Defence of French: A Language in Crisis?* (Clevedon, UK, 2007), 28; Alfred Gilder, *En vrai français dans le texte: Dictionnaire franglais–français* (Paris, 1999).

54. Jacques Derrida, *Monolinguism of the Other* (Stanford, CA, 1998), 46.

55. Dominique Noguez, *La Colonisation douce* (Paris, 1998), 49; Dominique Noguez, *Comment rater complètement sa vie en onze leçons* (Paris, 2003), 140; Jean Dutourd, *À la recherche du français perdu* (Paris, 1999), 21, 26, 91; Jacques Myard, "*Non!*," in Jacques Myard, *Langue française en colère: Manifeste pour une résistance* (Paris, 2000), 109.

56. On "agents," see Albert Salon, *Colas colo, Colas colère: Un enfant de France contre les empires* (Paris, 2007), 14. Michel Serres is quoted in Catherine Girard-Augry, *Langue française en péril* (Paris, 2011), 118. On "clash of civilizations," see Jean-Philippe Immarigeon, *American parano* (Paris, 2006), 230.

57. On slavishness, see Claude Duneton, *La Mort du français* (Paris, 1999), 132–133. On globalization, see Albert Salon, "Preface," in Girard-Augry, *Langue française en péril*, 12. On "markets," see Claude Hagège, *Combat pour le français: Au nom de la diversité des langues et des cultures* (Paris, 2008), 82, 232. On Chirac, see Nicholas Watt, "Chirac Leaves EU Summit as Frenchman speaks English," *Guardian*, March 24, 2006. On CIA plot, see Girard-Augry, *Langue française en péril*, 115.

58. Étiemble, "Vive le franglais, crève la France!," *Cahiers laïques*, no. 180, November-December 1981, 198; "Jean-François Copé, Carpette Anglaise 2011," www .avenir-langue-francaise.fr/news, December 17, 2011; "'I Loches You': nuit-il à la langue française?," *La Nouvelle République du Centre-Ouest*, February 1, 2014.

59. On Marc Fumaroli, see his *Quand l'Europe parlait français* (Paris, 2001), 23 (published under the title *When the World Spoke French* in English).

60. On "Frenchies," see Alain Schifres, *My Tailor Is Rich but My Franglais Is Poor* (Paris, 2014), 130. For "speaking in slogans," see Dutourd, *À la recherche du français perdu*, 11. On salted butter, see Noguez, *La Colonisation douce*, 278. On cancer deaths, see *Avenir de la Langue Francaise*, no. 32, October 2007.

61. Claude Hagège, "Refusons le sabordage du français!," *Le Monde*, April 25, 2013; "Ne nous laissons pas submerger par la 'langue des affaires,'" *L'Humanité*, May 15, 2012; "Je lance un appel pour faire la grève de l'anglais," *La Dépêche du Midi*, October 20, 2013.

Chapter 8: Writing for Everybody

1. Jean-Paul Sartre, "Itinerary of a Thought," in Jean-Paul Sartre, *Between Existentialism and Marxism* (London, 1974), 59.

2. Jean-Paul Sartre, "L'Espoir, maintenant . . . ," in *Le Nouvel Observateur*, no. 802, March 24–30, 1980, 134. There was some debate as to whether Sartre was in full control of his intellectual faculties at the time.

3. On Voltaire's influence among French writers in the nineteenth century, see Michel Winock, *Les Voix de la liberté: Les Écrivains engagés au XIXe siècle* (Paris, 2001). On the consecration of the writer, see Paul Bénichou, *Le Sacre de l'écrivain, 1750– 1830: Essai sur l'avènement d'un pouvoir spirituel laïque dans la France moderne* (Paris, 1973), 470. See also his *Le Temps des prophètes* (Paris, 1977) and *Les Mages romantiques* (Paris, 1988). On the history of intellectuals, see Pascal Ory and Jean-François Sirinelli, *Les Intellectuels en France, de l'Affaire Dreyfus à nos jours* (Paris, 1986).

4. On "writing for everybody," see Jean-Paul Sartre, *What Is Literature?* (London, 1967), 257. On "oppressed," see Jean-Paul Sartre, *Plaidoyer pour les intellectuels* (Paris, 1972), 12, 61; "in order to change it": ibid., 68.

5. Cited in Jonathan Fenby, *The General: Charles de Gaulle and the France He Saved* (London, 2010), 453.

6. On "mistress," see *Les Lettres françaises* (clandestine edition), April 1943. On "complicit with the oppressors," see Jean-Paul Sartre, "La Nationalisation de la littérature," *Les Temps modernes*, no. 1 (1945), reprinted in *Situations*, vol. 2 (Paris, 1948), 51; dog: Jean-Paul Sartre, *Situations*, vol. 4 (Paris, 1964), 248–249.

7. On "existentialism," see Annie Cohen-Solal, *Sartre* (Paris, 1985), 33–35. On "valuable in every man," see Albert Camus, *Carnets, mai 1935–février 1942* (Paris, 2013), 152.

8. Albert Camus, *L'Homme révolté* (Paris, 1951), 302; Jean-Paul Sartre, "Réponse à Albert Camus," in *Les Temps modernes*, no. 82, August 1952, reprinted in *Situations*, 4: 90.

9. On "Truth," see Jean-Paul Sartre, *Critique of Dialectical Reason*, vol. 1 (London, 1991), 822. On explaining away Stalinism, see Tony Judt, "French Marxism, 1945–1975," in Tony Judt, *Marxism and the French Left* (New York, 2011), 235. On putrefaction, see "Le seul [parti] qui vive, qui grouille de vie, quand les autres grouillent de vers," in Jean-Paul Sartre, "Les Communistes et la paix," in *Situations*, vol. 6 (Paris, 1964), 259.

10. For an illuminating discussion of Sartre's rise to prominence in the immediate postwar years, see Patrick Baert, "The Sudden Rise of French Existentialism: A Case Study in the Sociology of Intellectual Life," *Theory and Society* 40 (2011): 619–644.

11. Régis Debray, "Cela s'appelait un intellectuel," *Le Nouvel Observateur*, no. 806, April 21–27, 1980, 105. On the evolution of Sartre's political thought, see Sunil Khilnani, *Arguing Revolution: The Intellectual Left in Post-war France* (New Haven, CT, 1993).

12. Althusser later wrote a memoir that opened with his account of the killing. See Louis Althusser, *L'Avenir dure longtemps* (Paris, 2007). For "silent," see Philippe Boggio, "Le Silence des intellectuels de Gauche," *Le Monde*, July 27–28, 1983. For "perverted his thinking," see Jean-François Lyotard, "Tombeau de l'intellectuel," *Le Monde*, October 8, 1983, in Jean-François Lyotard, *Tombeau de l'intellectuel et autres papiers* (Paris, 1984), 20–21.

13. Hervé Hamon and Patrick Rotman, *Les Intellocrates* (Paris, 1981), 221–225.

14. Simone de Beauvoir, *La Cérémonie des adieux* (Paris, 1981), 15. Sartre's correspondence with Beauvoir was also published in 1983, in two volumes, as *Lettres au Castor et à quelques autres* (Paris, 1983). See also Benny Lévy, *Le Nom de l'homme* (Paris, 1984); Olivier Todd, *Un fils rebelle* (Paris, 1981), 263–276.

15. Claude Roy, "Le 'Colloque' permanent," in Claude Lanzmann, ed., *Témoins de Sartre* (Paris, 2005), 134; Jean Cau, "Croquis de mémoire," ibid., 61; Claude Imbert, "Sartre: La passion de l'erreur," *Le Point*, January 14, 2000; Denis Moreau, *Dans le milieu d'une forêt: Essais sur Descartes et le sens de la vie (Paris, 2012)*, 48 n. 21.

16. Jacques Julliard and Michel Winock, eds., *Dictionnaire des intellectuels français* (Paris, 1996; rev. ed., 2002); Jean-François Sirinelli, *Sartre et Aron: Deux Intellectuels dans le siècle* (Paris, 1999), 376.

17. Gilbert Joseph, *Une si douce occupation: Simone de Beauvoir et Jean-Paul Sartre, 1940–1944* (Paris, 1991); Tony Judt, *Past Imperfect: French Intellectuals, 1944–1956* (Berkeley, CA, 1992).

18. On "collective action," see Pierre Bourdieu, "For a Corporatism of the Universal," in Pierre Bourdieu, *The Rules of Art* (Stanford, CA, 1996), 399. On "destruction," see Pierre Bourdieu, "Contre la destruction d'une civilisation," in *Contre-feux* (Paris, 1998), 30–33. On "dominant intellectual," see *Le Magazine littéraire*, no. 369, October 1998.

19. Pierre Grémion, "Écrivains et intellectuels à Paris," *Le Débat*, no. 103, January-February 1999, 82; Bernard Fauconnier, *L'Être et le géant* (Paris, 2000) (the title is a play on words, referring to Sartre's early philosophical work *L'Être et le néant* [*Being and Nothingness*]; Bernard-Henri Lévy, *La Barbarie à visage humain* (Paris, 1977), 222; Bernard-Henri Lévy, *Éloge des intellectuels* (Paris, 1987), 122; Bernard-Henri Lévy, *Le Siècle de Sartre* (Paris, 2000), 33.

20. Raymond Aron, *L'Opium des intellectuels* (Paris, 1955); Raymond Aron, *Le Spectateur engagé* (Paris, 1981), 331 ("Je me retrouve probablement isolé et opposant, destin normal d'un authentique liberal"); Jean-Luc Barré, "Preface," in Jean Mauriac, *Le Général et le journaliste: Conversations avec Jean-Luc Barré* (Paris, 2008), 7.

21. François Denord, *Néo-libéralisme version française: Histoire d'une idéologie politique* (Paris, 2007), 302; Guy Sorman, *La Solution libérale* (Paris, 1984); Édouard Balladur, *Je crois en l'homme plus qu'en l'état* (Paris, 1987).

22. "Entretien avec Marcel Gauchet," *Esprit*, no. 195, October 1993, 89.

23. On "intellectual-oracle," see Pierre Nora, "Que peuvent les intellectuels?," *Le Débat*, no. 1, May 1980, 7. On Furet, see Christophe Prochasson's intellectual biography, *François Furet: Les Chemins de la mélancolie* (Paris, 2013). For two notable examples of French liberal thought, see Pierre Rosanvallon, *Le Moment Guizot* (Paris, 1985), and Marcel Gauchet, *La Révolution des droits de l'homme* (Paris, 1989). On Tocqueville, see Pierre Manent, *Tocqueville et la nature de la démocratie* (Paris, 1982), 181.

24. François Furet, Jacques Julliard, and Pierre Rosanvallon, *La République du centre* (Paris, 1988), 10 (post-ideological age); 51, 54 (democratic normality); 129 ("passions"); 137 ("boredom"); 181 ("diagnoses").

25. For a full list, see *Les Notes de la Fondation Saint-Simon, 1983–1998: Cent Textes pour réfléchir le monde contemporain* (Paris, 1998).

26. On Europe, see Antoine Winckler, *Europe: La Nostalgie du modèle impérial*, September 1991; Pierre Bouretz, *Les Formes politiques de l'Europe après Maastricht*, October 1992; Thierry Chopin, *Fédération et Europe*, April 1998. For comparisons, see Patrick Weil, *Les Politiques d'immigration: Une comparaison internationale*, February 1991; Thomas Piketty, *Les Créations d'emploi en France et aux États-Unis*, December 1997. On the dysfunctions, see Pierre Rosanvallon, *La Nouvelle Crise de l'État-Providence*, September 1993; Lucile Schmid, *Crise et réforme de la haute fonction publique*, May 1997; Denis Olivennes, *La Préférence française pour le chômage*, February 1994; *Le Modèle social français*, January 1998. On the state, see *L'État impartial*, October 1995.

27. For "Tocquevillian moment," see special issue of the journal *Raisons politiques*, no. 1, February 2001. On the 1989 bicentenary, see Steven Kaplan, *Adieu 89* (Paris, 1993). On "spirit of the times," see Pierre Nora, "Dix Ans de Débat," *Le Débat*, no. 60, May-August 1990, 5. On moving away from grand theorizing, see Pierre Rosanvallon, "La Fondation Saint-Simon: Une histoire accomplie," *Le Monde*, June 23, 1999.

28. François Furet, Jacques Julliard, and Pierre Rosanvallon, *La République du centre*, January-February 1995, 23; Aron, *Le Spectateur engagé*, 317.

29. "Splendeurs et misères de la vie intellectuelle," *Esprit*, March-April 2000 and May 2000; Daniel Lindenberg, *Le Rappel à l'ordre: Enquête sur les nouveaux réactionnaires* (Paris, 2002).

30. On the negative mythologization of May 1968 by Sarkozist intellectuals, see Serge Audier, *La Pensée anti-'68: Essai sur une restauration intellectuelle* (Paris, 2008), 23–38.

31. On the conservative turn among French intellectuals, see Serge Halimi, *Les Nouveaux chiens de garde* (Paris, 2005); Gérard Noiriel, *Les Fils maudits de la République: L'Avenir des intellectuels en France* (Paris, 2005); and Pascal Boniface, *Les Intellectuels faussaires: Le Triomphe médiatique des experts en mensonge* (Paris, 2011). On Perry Anderson, see his *La Pensée tiède: Un regard critique sur la culture française* (Paris, 2005); also included was Nora's reply to Anderson ("La Pensée réchauffée").

32. "Une Europe au pluriel," *Esprit*, July 2005, 5; Yves Bertoncini and Thierry Chopin, "Impressions de campagne," *Le Débat*, no. 137, November-December 2005, 191.

33. See Nicolas Sauger, Sylvain Brouard, and Emilio Grossman, *Les Français contre l'Europe? Le Sens du référendum du 29 mai 2005* (Paris, 2007); *Libération*, April 30, 2005; *Le Monde*, May 12, 2005.

34. On "simulation," see Jean Baudrillard, *Simulacra and Simulation*, trans. Sheila Glaser (Ann Arbor, MI, 1984). On the shattering of grand narratives, see Jean Baudrillard, *The Illusion of the End* (Stanford, CA, 1994), 263. On the Gulf War, see Jean Baudrillard, *The Gulf War Did Not Take Place* (Bloomington, IN, 1995).

35. On "ghost-events," see Jean Baudrillard, *À l'ombre du millénaire, ou Le Suspens de l'an 2000* (Paris, 1999), 34. On 9/11, see Jean Baudrillard, *The Spirit of Terrorism* (London, 2003).

36. The subject remains a focus of periodic controversy among experts since the 1990s; see Patrick Simon, "The Choice of Ignorance: The Debate on Ethnic and Racial Statistics in France," *French Politics, Culture & Society* 26, no. 1 (2008).

37. See Jeremy Jennings, "Citizenship, Republicanism and Multiculturalism in France," *British Journal of Political Science* 30 (2000).

38. On Dominique Schnapper, see his *La Communauté des citoyens* (Paris, 1994). See also Patrick Weil, *La République et sa diversité* (Paris, 2005). On French multiculturalism, see, in particular, Françoise Gaspard and Farhad Khosrokhavar, *Le Foulard et la République* (Paris, 1995); Jean-Loup Amselle, *Vers un multiculturalisme français: L'Empire de la coutume* (Paris, 1996); and the contributions in the collection edited by Michel Wieviorka, *Une société fragmentée? Le Multiculturalisme en débat* (Paris, 1996). See also Cécile Laborde's ambitious attempt to reconcile French republicanism and Anglo-American liberalism in her *Critical Republicanism: The Hijab Controversy and Political Philosophy* (Oxford, 2008). On "cultural affirmation," see Sophie Heine, "The *Hijab* Controversy and French Republicanism: Critical Analysis and Normative Propositions," *French Politics* 7, no. 2 (2009): 177.

39. "Profs, ne capitulons pas!," *Le Nouvel Observateur*, November 2–8, 1989; Christian Jelen, "La Régression multiculturaliste," *Le Débat*, no. 97, November-December 1997, p. 139; Pierre Manent, "Le Sentiment national en déshérence," *Le Figaro*, May 23, 2002.

40. On "archaic modernity," see Régis Debray, *Que vive la République* (Paris, 1989), 117. On classroom discipline, see "Républicains, n'ayons plus peur!," *Le Monde*, July 10, 1998. On support for Milošević, see Régis Debray, "Lettre d'un voyageur au président de la République," *Le Monde*, May 13, 1999. On "group effects," see Régis Debray, *Ce que nous voile le voile* (Paris, 2004), 34, 38. On "community of destiny," see ibid., 52, 57–58, 71. On "contraception," see Régis Debray, *Le Moment fraternité* (Paris, 2009), 105. On republican fundamentalists, see Jean Baubérot, *L'Intégrisme républicain contre la laïcité* (Paris, 2006).

41. Pierre Rosanvallon, *La Contre-démocratie: La Politique à l'âge de la défiance* (Paris, 2006); *La Légitimité démocratique* (Paris, 2008); *La Société des égaux* (Paris, 2011).

42. Rosanvallon, *La Contre-démocratie*, 322.

43. For a strong critique of Rosanvallon from this perspective, see the article by Frédéric Lordon in *Le Monde diplomatique*, February 7, 2014.

44. Alain Badiou, *De quoi Sarkozy est-il le nom?* (Paris, 2007). On history, see, in particular, his pamphlet *L'Hypothèse communiste* (Paris, 2009); and his *Le Réveil de l'histoire* (Paris, 2011). On the vacuousness of republican rhetoric, see Alain Badiou, *Le Siècle* (Paris, 2005), as well as his *Circonstances, 3: Portées du mot "juif"* (Paris, 2005); Alain Badiou, "Foulard," *Le Monde*, February 22–23, 2004, reproduced in *Circonstances, 2: Irak, foulard, Allemagne/France* (Paris, 2004), 109–125.

45. On Camus as a high-school philosopher, see Jean-Jacques Brochier, *Albert Camus: Philosophe pour classes terminales* (Paris, 2001). On the dilemma concerning his mother, see Tony Judt, *The Burden of Responsibility: Blum, Camus, Aron and the French Twentieth Century* (Chicago, 1998), 134–135. On "Stéphane Camus," see *Le Nouvel Observateur*, May 2, 2012. Sarkozy also confused Roland Barthes with the goalkeeper of the World Cup–winning French national football team, Fabien Barthez.

46. Olivier Todd, *Albert Camus: Une vie* (Paris, 1996), 756–760; "Camus, le nouveau philosophe," *Le Nouvel Observateur*, November 19, 2009; André Comte-Sponville,

"L'Absurde dans 'Le Mythe de Sisyphe,'" in his *Camus, de l'absurde à l'amour* (Vénissieux, 1995), 10; Alain Finkielkraut, *Un coeur intelligent* (Paris, 2009); Jean Sarocchi, *Camus le juste?* (Biarritz, 2009); Michel Onfray, *L'Ordre libertaire: La Vie philosophique d'Albert Camus* (Paris, 2012); Stéphane Giocanti, *Une histoire politique de la littérature* (Paris, 2009), 145; Jean-Louis Saint-Ygnan, *Le Premier Homme, ou Le Chant profond d'Albert Camus* (Paris, 2006), 144; "Abd al Malik slame Albert Camus," *Le Point*, March 13, 2013; François Hollande, Le Bourget speech, in *Le Journal du dimanche*, January 22, 2012; Bernard-Henri Lévy, *Ce grand cadavre à la renverse* (Paris, 2007), 411; Bernard-Henri Lévy, *La Guerre sans l'aimer* (Paris, 2011), 180–182.

47. Bertrand Rothé, "La Fin de Saint-Germain-des-Près," *Marianne*, no. 826, February 16, 2013.

48. On "baggage train," see Bruno Latour, "Why Has Critique Run Out of Steam?," *Critical Inquiry* 30 (2004). On Depardieu, see Giampiero Martinotti, "Où sont passés les intellos français?," *Courrier international*, April 19, 2012. On intellectuals and political parties, see Marion van Renterghem and Thomas Wieder, "Intellectuels et politiques, une planète en recomposition," *Le Monde*, April 29, 2012. On Chagos Islanders, see J. M. G. Le Clézio, "Les Îlois des Chagos contre le Royaume-Uni, suite et fin?," *Libération*, May 15, 2013.

49. Pierre Rosanvallon, *Le Parlement des invisibles* (Paris, 2014), 63. The series is available at http://raconterlavie.fr/.

50. See, for example, the recent book by the socialist writer and journalist Serge Moati, *Le Pen, vous et moi* (Paris, 2014). On the incapacity of present-day French intellectuals to confront the National Front effectively, see the editorial and series of articles in *Libération*, March 20, 2015: "FN: l'éclipse des intellectuels."

51. For the poll, see "L'Influence des intellectuels sur l'opinion publique," Institut CSA–*Marianne*, June 2010. For "shrinking of horizons," see Pierre Nora, "Continuer 'Le Débat,'" *Le Débat*, no. 160, May-August 2010, 3.

Chapter 9: The End of History

1. There was a keen French interest in events in postindependence Haiti, with a number of writings on the subject by writers, poets, and chroniclers. See, for example, Pamphile de Lacroix's *Mémoires pour servir l'histoire de la Révolution de Saint-Domingue* (Paris, 1819).

2. Charles de Rémusat, *L'Habitation de Saint-Domingue, ou L'Insurrection* (1824) (Paris, 1977), 52–60.

3. Augustin Thierry, *Dix Ans d'études historiques* (Paris, 1835), 321; François-René de Chateaubriand, *Études, ou Discours historiques* (Paris, 1831), "Preface"; see, more generally, Patrick Garcia and Jean Leduc, *L'Enseignement de l'histoire en France, de l'ancien régime à nos jours* (Paris, 2003).

4. François Guizot, *The History of the Origins of Representative Government in Europe*, trans. A. R. Scoble (Indianapolis, 2002), 5.

5. Thierry, *Dix Ans d'études historiques*, 324; Thierry, "Histoire véritable de Jacques Bonhomme" (1820), in ibid., 311.

6. François Mignet, *Histoire de la Révolution française depuis 1789 jusqu'en 1814* (Paris, 1824), 4, 436. For a taste of these debates, see the documents gathered in François Furet, *La Gauche et la Révolution au milieu du XIXe siècle* (Paris, 1986).

7. François Guizot, *History of Civilization in Europe*, trans. William Hazlitt (New York, 1899), 2–3.

8. Guizot's 1789 quotation appears in Ceri Crossley, *French Historians and Romanticism* (London, 1993), 77. On the bourgeoisie, see François Guizot, *Histoire de la civilization en France*, vol. 1, no. 4 (Paris, 1846), cited in Pierre Rosanvallon, *Le Moment Guizot* (Paris, 1985), 196.

9. Laurent Theis, *François Guizot* (Paris, 2008), 367.

10. For "either of men or of nature," see Adolphe Thiers, *Histoire du consulat et de l'Empire*, vol. 20 (Paris, 1862), 606; "vast genius": ibid., 613.

11. Alexis de Tocqueville, *The Old Regime and the Revolution*, eds. François Furet and Françoise Mélionio (Chicago, 1998), 118–124.

12. Pierre Guiral, *Adolphe Thiers* (Paris, 1986), 287.

13. Tocqueville, *Old Regime and the Revolution*, 246.

14. *Défense du citoyen Laponneraye, prononcée aux assises du département de la Seine, le 21 avril 1832* (Paris, 1832), 2–4.

15. Entry for September 2, 1850, in Jules Michelet, *Journal*, vol. 2, *1849–1860*, ed. P. Viallaneix (Paris, 1962).

16. Paul Viallaneix, *La Voie royale: Essai sur l'idée de peuple dans l'oeuvre de Michelet* (Paris, 1959), 218; Crossley, *French Historians and Romanticism*, 222.

17. Jules Michelet, 1869 preface, in Jules Michelet, *Histoire de France*, vol. 1 (Paris, 1869), 3; Viallaneix, *La Voie royale*, 313–314; Jules Michelet, *Introduction à l'histoire universelle* (Paris, 1831), 5, 49.

18. Michelet, *Histoire de la Révolution française*, vol. 1 (Paris, 1847), 38, 88–89.

19. Louis Blanc, *Histoire de dix ans*, vol. 5 (Paris, 1844), 507; Victor Hugo, *Napoléon le petit* (London, 1852), 368; Taxile Delord, *Histoire du Second Empire*, vol. 1 (Paris, 1869), 1–2.

20. On Louis-Antoine Garnier-Pagès, see his *Histoire de la Révolution de 1848*, vol. 1 (Paris, 1866), 4. On the White Terror, see A. de Rolland, *Histoire populaire de la terreur blanche* (Paris, 1873). On tales of heroism, see Édouard Rastoin-Brémond, *Histoire populaire de la Révolution de 1830* (Paris, n.d.). A list of civilian victims was published in the appendix of Eugène Ténot's *Paris en décembre 1851* (Paris, 1868), 293–297.

21. For "easy to memorize," see Prosper Lissagaray, *Jacques Bonhomme: Entretiens de politique primaire* (Paris, 1870), 5. On Bonhomme, see Jean-Baptiste Jouancoux, *Jacques Bonhomme: Histoire des paysans français*, vol. 2 (Paris, 1876), 70.

22. See Suzanne Citron, *Le Mythe national: L'Histoire de France en question* (Paris, 1987).

23. On Renan, see Viallaneix, *La Voie royale*, 278. On July 14, see Olivier Ihl, *La Fête républicaine* (Paris, 1996), 124. On Jean Jaurès, see his *Histoire socialiste de la Révolution Française*, ed. A. Mathiez (Paris, 1922–1924), "Introduction."

24. Ernest Lavisse, *Histoire de France: Cours élémentaire* (Paris, 1913), 168.

25. Charles-Olivier Carbonell, *Histoire et historiens: Une mutation idéologique des historiens français, 1865–1885* (Toulouse, 1976), 297; Ernest Renan, *Vie de Jésus* (Paris, 1863), 32.

26. "Impartial history" is cited in James Friguglietti, "La Querelle Mathiez-Aulard et les origines de la Société des études Robespierristes," *Annales historiques de la Révolution française*, no. 353, July-September 2008. On "positive science," see *Revue historique*, no. 1, January-June 1876, 36. On "objectivity," see Gérard Noiriel, "Naissance du métier d'historien," *Genèses*, no. 1, September 1990, 58–95.

27. For a thorough critical evaluation of the *école méthodique*, see Isabel DiVanna, *Writing History in the Third Republic* (Newcastle, UK, 2010).

28. Febvre is cited in André Burguière, *L'École des Annales: Une histoire intellectuelle* (Paris, 2006), 29. On "origins," see Sylvain Venayre, *Les Origines de la France: Quand les historiens racontaient la nation* (Paris, 2013), 205. On the social sciences, see Jacques Revel, "Histoire et sciences sociales: Les Paradigmes des Annales," *Annales* 34, no. 6 (1979): 1362.

29. Fernand Braudel, *La Méditerranée et le monde méditerranéen à l'époque de Philippe II* (Paris, 1949) (the English version, translated by Siân Reynolds, was published between 1972 and 1975); Fernand Braudel, "Histoire et sciences sociales: La Longue Durée," *Annales*, no. 4, October-December 1958, 725–753; Peter Burke, *The French Historical Revolution: The Annales School, 1929–1989* (Cambridge, UK, 1990), 54–55. See also Lynn Hunt, "French History in the Last Twenty Years: The Rise and Fall of the Annales Paradigm," *Journal of Contemporary History* 21, no. 2 (1986).

30. Marc Bloch, *L'Étrange Défaite* (Paris, 1990), 31–32.

31. See the letter from Febvre to Bloch, April 13, 1941, in Marc Bloch and Lucien Febvre, *Correspondance*, vol. 3, *1938–1943* (Paris, 2003), 115–119. In his reply three days later, Bloch refused: "The suppression of my name would be an abdication." Ibid., 123. For "not a law," see Lecture of December 2, 1942, in Lucien Febvre, *Michelet et la Renaissance* (Paris, 1992), 17. On lecture series, see Marleen Wessel, "'Honneur ou Patrie?' Lucien Febvre et la question du sentiment national," *Genèses*, no. 25 (1996).

32. "Positions de l'histoire en 1950," in Fernard Braudel, *Écrits sur l'histoire* (Paris, 1969), 21; Furet and Richet are quoted in Richard Cobb, "Nous des Annales," in *A Second Identity* (Oxford, 1969), 79.

33. On "the gap," see Pierre Bourdieu, *Homo academicus* (Paris, 1984), 148. On Marxist theory, see Hervé Coutau-Bégarie, *Le Phénomène nouvelle histoire: Grandeur et décadence de l'école des Annales* (Paris, 1989), 214–215. On the peasantry, see Krzysztof Pomian, "L'Heure des Annales," in Pierre Nora, ed., *Les Lieux de mémoire*, vol. 2, no. 1 (Paris, 1986). On "Thirty Glorious Years," see Fernand Braudel, *L'Identité de la France: Les Hommes et les choses*, vol. 2 (Paris, 1986), 430.

34. See Jacques Le Goff and Pierre Nora, eds., *Faire de l'histoire* (Paris, 1974); Emmanuel Le Roy Ladurie, *Montaillou, village occitan* (Paris, 1975).

35. Louis Aragon, *La Semaine sainte* (Paris, 1958), 600.

36. De Gaulle, *Mémoires de guerre*, vol. 1 (Paris, 1954–1959), 82, 128.

37. Pierre Nora, "Les Mémoires d'État: De Commynes à de Gaulle," in *Les Lieux de mémoire*, vol. 1 (Paris, 1997), 1417; Charles de Gaulle, *Mémoires de guerre*, vol. 3

(Paris, 1954–1959), 883; Charles de Gaulle, *Mémoires de guerre*, vol. 2 (Paris, 1954–1959), 576 (presence), 425 ("revolutionary").

38. De Gaulle, *Mémoires*, 583–585.

39. Quoted in André Malraux, *Les chênes qu'on abat* (Paris, 1971), 37; Henry Rousso, *Le Syndrome de Vichy* (Paris, 1990), 19; Maurice Agulhon, *De Gaulle: Histoire, symbole, mythe* (Paris, 2000), 127; quoted in André Malraux, *Les Chênes qu'on abat* (Paris, 1971), p. 37.

40. François Furet, *La Révolution française*, vol. 2 (Paris, 1988), 467.

41. On Robert Paxton, see *Vichy France: Old Guard and New Order, 1940–1944* (New York, 1972). On the complex history of the Resistance, see Laurent Douzou, *La Résistance française, une histoire périlleuse* (Paris, 2005). On disorientation, see François Hartog, "Le Temps désorienté," *Annales* 50, no. 6 (1995). On "crisis," see Gérard Noiriel, *Sur la "crise" de l'histoire* (Paris, 1996).

42. On the history of colonialism, see N. Bancel et al., eds., *La Fracture coloniale* (Paris, 2005); Raphaelle Branche, *La Guerre d'Algérie: Une histoire apaisée?* (Paris, 2005). On the history of women, see the work of Michelle Perrot, such as *Les Femmes, ou Les Silences de l'histoire* (Paris, 1998). For biographies, see, for example, Eric Roussel, *Jean Monnet* (Paris, 1996); Grégoire Kauffmann, *Édouard Drumont* (Paris, 2008); Annette Wieviorka, *Maurice et Jeannette: Biographie du couple Thorez* (Paris, 2010). Since 1987, the Académie Française has created an annual prize for the best biography.

43. Pierre Rosanvallon, *Le Modèle politique français* (Paris, 2004).

44. Roger Chartier, "Le Monde comme représentation," *Annales* 44, no. 6 (1989); Maurice Agulhon, *Marianne au combat* (Paris, 1979); *Marianne au pouvoir* (Paris, 1989); *Les Métamorphoses de Marianne* (Paris, 2001).

45. Pierre Nora, "General Introduction," in Pierre Nora, ed., *Rethinking France: Les Lieux de mémoire* (Chicago, 1999), xv; Pierre Nora, "Lavisse, instituteur national: Le 'Petit Lavisse,' évangile de la République," in *Les Lieux de mémoire*, vol. 1 (Paris, 1984); "Gaullistes et communistes," in Pierre Nora, ed., *Les Lieux de mémoire*, vol. 3, no. 1 (Paris, 1992). The English translations consist of a series of three volumes entitled *Realms of Memory*, published by Columbia University Press (1996–1998), and four volumes entitled *Rethinking France*, published by the University of Chicago Press in 1999, 2006, 2009, and 2010.

46. Steven Englund, "The Ghost of Nation Past," *Journal of Modern History* 64, no. 2 (1992); Perry Anderson, "Union Sucrée," *London Review of Books* 26, no. 18 (2004).

47. Pierre Nora, "Patrimoine," in *Le Débat*, no. 160, May-August 2010, 244; François Hartog, *Croire en l'histoire* (Paris, 2013), 31.

48. For a subtle account of the controversies surrounding these laws, see Marc-Olivier Baruch, *Des Lois indignes? Les Historiens, la politique et le droit* (Paris, 2013). On the theme of colonial nostalgia generally, see Kate Marsh and Nicola Frith, eds., *France's Lost Empires: Fragmentation, Nostalgia and "la fracture coloniale"* (Lanham, MD, 2011). On the museum, see "Lettre ouverte de Pierre Nora à Frédéric Mitterrand sur la Maison de l'Histoire de France," *Le Monde*, November 11, 2010. Nora denounced the *lois mémorielles* as an "abusive and perverse radicalization of memory." See Pierre Nora and Françoise Chandernagor, *Liberté pour l'histoire* (Paris, 2008), 15.

49. Charles de Gaulle, *Mémoires d'espoir*, vol. 2 (Paris, 1996), 239.

50. There are, of course, excellent historians outside Paris, notably, in French provincial universities. But they would be the first to accept (and deplore) that the institutional, intellectual, and editorial centers of power remain firmly in the hands of Parisian elites. For "deification," see Lucien Febvre, *Combats pour l'histoire* (Paris, 1992), 9. Some recent examples of books by politicians would include Philippe Séguin, *Louis Napoléon le Grand* (Paris, 1990); Nicolas Sarkozy, *Georges Mandel: Le Moine en politique* (Paris, 1994); François Bayrou, *Ils portaient l'écharpe blanche* (Paris, 1998); Dominique de Villepin, *Les Cent-Jours, ou L'Esprit du sacrifice* (Paris, 2001); Jean-François Copé, *La Bataille de la Marne* (Paris, 2013); Philippe de Villiers, *Le Roman de Saint-Louis* (Paris, 2013); and Lionel Jospin, *Le Mal napoléonien* (Paris, 2014).

51. There is, of course, nothing exceptional about the fact that the past shapes a nation's collective identity. France is distinctive because its political culture does not rest on an appeal to a collective ethnic identity—hence the need to rely more heavily on history.

52. Alexis Jenni, *L'Art français de la guerre* (Paris, 2011), 161; Fernand Braudel, *The Identity of France*, vol. 1 (London 1990), 15.

53. Michelet, *Histoire de France*, 1:11; Braudel, *Identity of France*, 18.

54. Pierre Nora, ed., *Essais d'ego-histoire* (Paris, 1987); Stéphane Audoin-Rouzeau, *Quelle histoire: Un récit de filiation, 1914–2014* (Paris, 2013), 141.

55. Jean-François Sirinelli, *L'Histoire est-elle encore française?* (Paris, 2011), 21 (less likely to read French), 46 (demographic crisis), 48 ("necrosis").

Chapter 10: The Closing of the French Mind

1. For opinion polls, see "La France, championne d'Europe du pessimisme," *Le Monde*, May 6, 2013; "Le Pays décline," *La Croix*, November 19, 2013. For "shipwrecked," see "La France naufragée," *Le Figaro*, November 18, 2013. For "all we have left," see Eric Le Boucher, "La Préférence pour le déclin," *Les Echos*, November 8, 2013.

2. On "too much thinking," see Christel Peticollin, *Je pense trop: Comment canaliser ce mental envahissant* (Paris, 2010). On *mal du vivre*, see Georges Minois, *Histoire du mal de vivre* (Paris, 2003), 429. On "losing its substance," see François Fillon, "La France est en train de perdre sa substance," *Paris Match*, August 2013. On the socialist seminar, see "Le Progrès face aux idéologies du déclin," Agence France-Presse report, November 18, 2013. On "veering . . . to the right," see Gaël Brustier, interview in *Libération*, November 13, 2013.

3. For the editorials, see "L'État face à la désindustrialisation inacceptable," *Le Monde*, November 6, 2013; "L'Inexorable déclin de la production automobile française," *L'Usine nouvelle*, November 20, 2013. On the piano manufacturer, see "Grandeur et décadence des pianos Pleyel," *Le Temps*, November 15, 2013. On Caen, see "L'Inexorable Déclin?," *L'Express*, September 18, 2013. On deindustrialization, see "L'Inquiétante Fracture territoriale française," *Le Point*, November 9, 2013. On the dying rural world, see Jean-Pierre Le Goff, *La Fin du village* (Paris, 2012), 39. The dystopian novel is Michel Houellebecq, *La Carte et le territoire* (Paris, 2010), 416.

4. For "collective realization," see Pierre Nora interview in *Le Figaro*, November 11, 2013. On "idiots," see Jean-Marie Paul, *Du pessimisme* (Paris, 2013), 283. On *marinisation*, see Franz-Olivier Giesbert, "La Marinisation des esprits," *Le Point*, September 21, 2013.

5. On antimodernism, see Antoine Compagnon, *Les Antimodernes, de Joseph de Maistre à Roland Barthes* (Paris, 2005). For "deluded myself," see Proudhon letter to Gustave Chaudey, September 11, 1863, in Pierre-Joseph Proudhon, *Correspondance de Pierre-Joseph Proudhon*, vol. 7 (Geneva, 1971), 147.

6. On "agony," see Robert Aron and Arnaud Dandieu, *Décadence de la nation française* (Paris, 1931), 188. On the theme of decadence in the 1930s, see Debbie Lackerstein, *National Regeneration in Vichy France: Ideas and Policies, 1930–1944* (Farnham, UK, 2011). For "the thirties are back," see François-Guillaume Lorrain, "Au secours, les années 30 sont de retour!," *Le Point*, April 8, 2013. For "smell," see *L'Humanité*, November 8, 2013. For "global visions," see *Le Nouveau Marianne*, September 21, 2013. For Gaspard Koenig, see his "Pour un réveil libéral de la philosophie française," *Libération*, November 1, 2013.

7. For "national disease," see Michel Winock, *Parlez-moi de la France* (Paris, 1995), 288.

8. On "without haloes," see Emil Cioran, *Précis de décomposition*, in Emil Cioran, *Oeuvres* (Paris, 2011), 52. On "great affirmation," see Cioran, *La Tentation d'exister* (1957), ibid., 416. On "fear of death," see Cioran, *De l'inconvénient d'être né*, ibid., 732.

9. Emil Cioran, *De la France* (Paris, 2009), 31 ("narrow perfectionism"), 36 ("terrified of the future"); Frédéric Schiffter, *Traité du cafard* (Bordeaux, 2007), 11, 27.

10. Alain Peyrefitte, *Le Mal français* (Paris, 2006), 100.

11. Ibid., 450 ("convulsionary immobilism"), 445 (idolatry of tradition and "spasmophilia"), 480 (refusal of difference), 492 ("magical spirit"), 503 (simple dichotomies), 505 ("not . . . at ease").

12. On state interventionism, see Peyrefitte, *Le Mal français*, 9.

13. On "decadence," see Pierre-Henri Taguieff, "Les Droites radicales en France," *Les Temps modernes*, no. 465, April 1985, 1783. On ideological inspiration, see Michel Winock, "L'Éternelle Décadence," in *Nationalisme, antisémitisme et fascisme en France* (Paris, 2004), 101. See also Jacques du Perron, *Décadence et complot*, vol. 2 (Paris, 1998), 9 (corruption), 5 (alienation).

14. Quoted in Gabriel Goodliffe, *The Resurgence of the Radical Right in France: From Boulangisme to the Front National* (Cambridge, UK, 2012), 40, n. 34.

15. Alain Finkielkraut, *La Défaite de la pensée* (Paris, 1987), 165; Jean-François Mattéi, *La Barbarie intérieure: Essai sur l'immonde moderne* (Paris, 1999).

16. Jean-Marie Domenach, *Le Crépuscule de la culture francaise?* (Paris, 1995), 15, 37; Michel Crépu, "Le Roman français est-il mort?," *L'Express*, March 29, 2001; Patrick Besson, "La Littérature française est-elle morte?" (Is French literature dead?), *Le Point*, December 12, 2013. (His answer was yes.)

17. The translation statistics are from Laurence Marie, "Mais bien sûr que si, les livres français se vendent à l'étranger!," *Le Nouvel Observateur*, January 1, 2014.

18. Stanley Hoffmann, "Paradoxes of the French Political Community," in Stanley Hoffmann et al., eds., *In Search of France* (Cambridge, MA, 1963), 1–21.

19. Nicolas Baverez, *La France qui tombe* (Paris, 2003), 72 (investment), 18 ("decline").

20. Jacques Marseille, *Du bon usage de la guerre civile en France* (Paris, 2006), 166.

21. Christian Saint-Etienne, *L'Incohérence française* (Paris, 2012), 47; Philippe Manière, *Le Pays où la vie est plus dure* (Paris, 2012); Simone Wapler, *Pourquoi la France va faire faillite* (Brussels, 2012); Nicolas Baverez, *Réveillez-vous!* (Paris, 2012), 56.

22. See, most notably, Roger Fauroux and Bernard Spitz, eds., *Notre état: Le Livre vérité de la fonction publique* (Paris, 2000). For a broader view of the phenomenon, see John Micklethwait and Adrian Wooldridge, *The Fourth Revolution: The Global Race to Reinvent the State* (London, 2014). For "cry of alarm," see Marc Le Bris, *Et vos enfants ne sauront pas lire . . . ni compter! La Faillite obstinée de l'école française* (Paris, 2004), 323, 328. This notion of a "cultural catastrophe" was echoed by Fanny Capel, *Qui a eu cette idée folle un jour de casser l'école?* (Paris, 2006), 34.

23. Jean-Paul Brighelli, *La Fabrique du crétin: La Mort programmée de l'école* (Paris, 2005), 43, 153; also 46 (underclass), 91 (ZEP failure), 164 (equality of opportunity).

24. On the cultural gap, see Paola Mattei, "The French Republican School Under Pressure: Falling Basic Standards and Rising Social Inequalities," *French Politics* 10, no. 1 (2012): 84–95. On the interests of global capitalism, see Jean-Claude Michéa, *L'Enseignement de l'ignorance et ses conditions modernes* (Paris, 2006). On "neoliberal ideology," see Alain Planche, *L'Imposture scolaire* (Bordeaux, 2012), 232.

25. Speech at Tours, January 15, 2011.

26. Peter Gumbel, *On achève bien les écoliers* (Paris, 2010), 14 ("mediocrity"), 27 (failure); Anne Muxel, *Avoir 20 ans en politique: Les Enfants du désenchantement* (Paris, 2010), 201; Claudia Senik, "La Dimension culturelle du bonheur . . . et du malheur français," *Le Monde*, October 28, 2011; Yann Algan, Pierre Cahuc, and André Zylberberg, *La Fabrique de la défiance* (Paris, 2012), 11.

27. Michel Charzat, *La France et le déclin* (Paris, 1988), 5, 12 (masochism), 34 ("malaise"), 51, 53 (nostalgia), 55 ("closure").

28. Guy Debord, *Commentaires sur la société du spectacle* (Paris, 1988), 29; Guy Debord, *Panégyrique*, vol. 1 (Paris, 1993), 84.

29. Lionel Jospin, *Le Mal napoléonien* (Paris, 2014); Marie Radović and Loïc Rivalain, *21 Avril, les lendemains qui déchantent* (Paris, 2007), 45 ("sheep"), 28 ("no longer recognized France"), 29 (*lepénisation*), 51, 75 ("intellectual decomposition").

30. Michael Hardt and Toni Negri, *Empire* (Cambridge, MA, 2000); Giorgio Agamben, *State of Exception* (Chicago, 2005); Luc Boltanski and Eve Chiapello, *The New Spirit of Capitalism* (London, 2007).

31. Gérard Grunberg and Zaki Laïdi, *Sortir du pessimisme social: Essai sur l'identité de Gauche* (Paris, 2006), 8 ("social pessimism"), 11 (nationalist retreat), 10 (conservative utopia).

32. Jean-Claude Michéa, *Impasse Adam Smith: Brèves Remarques sur l'impossibilité de dépasser le capitalisme sur sa gauche* (Paris, 2006), 16; Jean-Claude Michéa, *L'Empire du moindre mal: Essai sur la civilisation libérale* (Paris, 2010), 203.

33. On "disappearance of . . . subject," see Marcel Gauchet, "Les Tâches de la philosophie politique," in *La Condition politique* (Paris, 2005), 540. On "decomposition,"

see Marcel Gauchet, *Un Monde désenchanté?* (Paris, 2007), 312. On "pessimistic," see Marcel Gauchet, *La Condition historique* (Paris, 2003), 415–416. On "prophets of doom," see Pierre-André Taguieff, *Les Contre-réactionnaires: Le Progressisme entre illusion et imposture* (Paris, 2007), 558.

34. Régis Debray, *Supplique aux nouveaux progressistes du XXIe siècle* (Paris, 2006), 44 ("belonging"), 61, 65 ("despair," "without optimism"); Bernard-Henri Lévy, *Ce grand cadavre à la renverse* (Paris, 2007); Guy Hermet, *L'Hiver de la démocratie ou le nouveau régime* (Paris, 2007).

35. Jacques Julliard, *Le Malheur français* (Paris, 2005), 13, 14 ("collective subconscious"), 72 (lost ground), 99–100 (globally competitive), 139 (passion for privileges), 19 ("resistance to change").

36. Philippe Corcuff, *La Gauche est-elle en état de mort cérébrale?* (Paris, 2012) (His answer was yes); Evelyne Pieiller, "Alain Soral tisse sa toile," *Le Monde diplomatique*, October 2013; Égalité et Réconciliation, www.egaliteetreconciliation.fr/.

37. Pascal Perrineau, "Le Pessimisme français: Nature et racines," *Le Débat*, no. 166, September-October 2011, 85–86; see Cécile Laborde, *Français, encore un effort pour être républicains!* (Paris, 2010); see Marika Mathieu, *La Droite forte année zéro* (Paris, 2013), 298.

38. Éric Zemmour, *Mélancolie française* (Paris, 2010), 221 (integration), 224, 244 ("swamping" and "de-Christianization").

39. Ibid., 245 ("language of the devil"), 226 (fertility), 233 (intermarriage), 241 ("substitution"), 250–251 (disintegration); interview on RTL radio station, January 22, 2015.

40. Nicolas Offenstadt, *L'Histoire bling-bling: Le Retour du roman national* (Paris, 2009); Jean Sévillia, *Historiquement incorrect* (Paris, 2011), 335; Jean Sévillia, *Histoire passionnée de la France* (Paris, 2013), 530.

41. Interview in *Le Figaro*, March 5, 2011.

42. Loràant Deutsch, *Métronome: L'Histoire de France au rhythme du métro parisien* (Paris, 2009), 348–349 (irrationality), 353 (Resistance); Loràant Deutsch, *Hexagone: Sur les routes de l'histoire de France* (Paris, 2013), 231–232.

43. Renaud Camus, *Le Grand Remplacement* (Paris, 2011), 19 (immigrants), 23 ("clash of civilizations"), 30, 44–45 (global village), 56 ("counter-colonization"); Éric Zemmour, *Le Suicide français* (Paris, 2014), 527.

44. Hervé Juvin, *La Grande Séparation* (Paris, 2013), 12–13, 51 (white Christian nation), 268 (corporate interests), 18–19 (history and geography).

45. Ibid., 65–66 (post-national societies), 187, 192 ("new totalitarianism"), 371 ("invasion"), 130 (Islam), 277 (social "apartheid"), 143 ("common misery").

46. Alain Finkielkraut, *L'Identité malheureuse* (Paris, 2013).

47. Ibid., 147 ("national identity is crushed"), 153 ("hyperconnected"), 156 ("final nail"), 156 ("defeated"), 106–108 (meaning of "national identity"), 97, 101 (Fanon).

48. For Finkielkraut's critics, see, for example, Aude Lancelin, "L'Identitaire national," *Le Nouveau Marianne*, October 12, 2013. See also Finkielkraut, *L'Identité malheureuse*, 206 ("boorishness"), 65 ("gallantry"), 83 ("common identity"), 115 ("self-effacement").

49. Finkielkraut, *L'Identité malheureuse*, 92 (race), 169 (Hobbes), 211 (Strauss), 104–105 (Scruton), 123, 214 ("national disintegration").

Conclusion: Anxiety and Optimism

1. André Siegfried, "Preface," in Cristobal de Acevedo, *Valeurs spirituelles françaises* (Paris, 1946), vi.

2. Michel Foucher, *Atlas de l'influence française au XXIe siècle* (Paris, 2013), 17. This view is commonly expressed in the French press at the time of the annual summit of the organization. For recent examples, see Jean-Baptiste Piriou, "La Francophonie pour quoi faire?," *Le Spectacle du monde*, no. 598, March 1, 2013; "Francophonie: La France fait-elle cavalier seul?," *Le Monde*, March 11, 2014.

3. Gisèle Sapiro, "Conclusion," in Gisèle Sapiro, ed., *Traduire la littérature et les sciences humaines: Conditions et obstacles* (Paris, 2012), 378; Tahar Ben Jelloun, *Par le feu* (Paris, 2011), 50; "Michèle Alliot-Marie et la Tunisie, retour sur une polémique," *Le Monde*, February 7, 2011.

4. Jacques Drillon, "Alors, ce nouvel album?," *Le Nouvel Observateur*, October 31–November 6, 2013.

5. Gérard Cazalis, "La République des Pyrénées," June 28, 2013; Sibylle Vincendon, *Pour en finir avec les grincheux: Contre le discours du déclin* (Paris, 2013), 148; Frédéric Dabi (director of the Institut Français d'Opinion Publique), "Le Pessimisme des français est une réalité," *La Croix*, March 6, 2014.

6. On new trilogy, see Anne Chemin, "Liberté, égalité, morosité," *Le Monde*, June 22, 2013. For a recent exchange about the decline of French culture between an American journalist and a French literary historian, see Donald Morrison and Antoine Compagnon, *The Death of French Culture* (London, 2010). On cultural festivals, see Sophian Fanen, "Peut-on aller quelque part en France sans tomber sur un festival?," *Libération*, July 28, 2014. On cultural subsidies, see Jules Bonnard, Samuel Laurent, and Jonathan Parienté, "Associations: À qui profitent les subventions?," *Le Monde*, July 1, 2013. The Ministry of Culture is the most generous ministry in terms of subsidies: in 2011, it distributed 228 million euro to more than 5,000 recipients.

7. "Et pourtant les français lisent," editorial, *Le Monde*, March 21, 2014; Mohammed Aïssaoui, "La France des festivals littéraires," *Le Figaro*, July 4, 2013. A full list of *librairies labellisées* in each French *département* is available on the website of the Centre National du Livre.

8. Alain Beuve-Méry, "Le Secteur du livre ne veut pas céder à la morosité," *Le Monde*, March 20, 2014; "Bestselling Books of 2013," *Guardian*, December 27, 2013. See also Jean-Yves Mollier, *Édition, presse et pouvoir au XXe siècle* (Paris, 2008), 439–440.

9. See, for example, the editions of October 9–15, 2008, "Le Pouvoir intellectuel en France," and of May 9–15, 2013, "Les Penseurs qui comptent."

10. On the Blois festival as a republican pilgrimage, see Gaïdz Minassian, "L'Histoire globale peine encore à supplanter le 'roman national' en France," *Le Monde*, October 19, 2011. On philosophy teaching, see Amandine Schmitt, "Bac de philo: Si je comprends pas ce que j'écris, c'est bon!," *Le Nouvel Observateur*, June 17, 2013.

11. Nathalie Brafman and Nicolas Weill, "Les Nouveaux Clients de la philo," *Le Monde*, June 25, 2012; Nicolas Truong, "La Philo contre la philosophie?," *Le Monde*, July 28, 2014; Macha Séry, "Les Français accros à la culture gé," *Le Monde*, February 1, 2013.

12. Bruno Latour, *Reassembling the Social: An Introduction to Actor-Network Theory* (Oxford, 2005).

13. On "personal singularities," see François Miquet-Marty, *Les Nouvelles Passions françaises* (Paris, 2013), 195. On personal happiness, see, for example, the opinion polls in *La Tribune*, June 5, 2013, and *Figaro Magazine*, November 29, 2013. On *"douceur de vivre,"* see François-Guillaume Lorrain, "Pourquoi il ne faut pas désespérer de la France," *Le Point*, August 15, 2013. For "draped in shadows," see Cioran, *De la France*, 60.

14. Benjamin Constant, "De la liberté des anciens comparée à celle des modernes" (1819), in Benjamin Constant, *Écrits politiques*, ed. Marcel Gauchet (Paris, 1977), 602; Antoine Compagnon, *Un été avec Montaigne* (Paris, 2013); Frédéric Lenoir, *Du bonheur: Un Voyage philosophique* (Paris, 2013), 206–207; Bertrand Vergely, *Dictionnaire philosophique et savoureux du bonheur* (Paris, 2011), 249–250; Luc Deborde, *Douze sentiers vers le bonheur + Un treizième en bonus!* (Paris, 2013), 14; Deschamps, quoted in "Culture: Y a-t-il encore un style français?," *Le Figaro*, April 8, 2013; Albert Camus, *Les Noces*, quoted in Michel Faucheux, *Histoire du bonheur* (Paris, 2007), 222.

15. Quoted in Pierre Assouline, "L'Esprit du 18 juin," *La République des livres*, June 18, 2010; see Olivier Wieviorka, *La Mémoire désunie: Le Souvenir politique des années sombres, de la Libération à nos jours* (Paris, 2010).

16. Henry Rousso, *La Dernière Catastrophe: L'Histoire, le présent, le contemporain* (Paris, 2012), 22; Robert Frank, *La Hantise du déclin* (Paris, 1994); see also his interview on the resurgence of the themes of decline and decadence in contemporary France in *Libération*, July 12, 2014.

17. René Rémond, "Le Temps du marasme," *Le Débat*, no. 141, September-October 2006, 5–6; Marcel Gauchet, "La France est inquiète," *Journal du dimanche*, September 16, 2013. For more discussion of the literary and historical dimensions of the novel, see Emmanuel Bouju, "La Transcription de l'histoire dans le roman contemporain," *Annales* 65, no. 2 (2010): 421–425.

18. Alain Geismar, *Mon mai 1968* (Paris, 2008), 247.

19. Thomas Piketty, *Capitalism in the Twenty-First Century* (Cambridge, MA, 2014), reviewed by Paul Krugman in "Why We're in a New Gilded Age," *New York Review of Books*, May 8, 2014.

20. Ezra Suleiman, "La France est championne du monde dans le gaspillage des talents," *Les Echos*, July 4, 2014.

21. Henri Mendras, *La Seconde Révolution française, 1965–1984* (Paris, 1988); Hervé Le Bras and Emmanuel Todd, *Le Mystère français* (Paris, 2013), 70–72.

22. Le Bras and Todd, *Le Mystère français*, 226 (assimilation of immigrants), 39–40 (rejection of civilizational clash), 194–195 ("depletion").

23. According to a recent poll, these three writers were "the best representatives of optimism" in contemporary French literature. See *Le Point*, May 14, 2014; Aline Gérard, "Plus optimistes qu'on croit," *Aujourd'hui en France*, April 10, 2014.

24. For a version of this distinction between the confident and anxious France, see Emiliano Grossman and Nicolas Sauger, eds., *France's Political Institutions at Fifty* (London, 2009), chap. 8. On populist protests, see Ronan Le Coadic, "Les 'Bonnets rouges,' la Bretagne et l'écotaxe," *Le Nouvel Observateur*, November 7, 2013. On the

movement against same-sex marriage, see "Génération 'Manif pour tous,'" *Le Figaro*, May 27, 2013.

25. On "arrogance," see Natacha Polony, "Qu'est-ce que Paris a fait de la France?," *Le Figaro*, August 16, 2014. For ENA criticisms, see interview with Pierre Lacroix, *La Nouvelle République du Centre-Ouest*, October 10, 2012, and "Ça va et ça vient," *Le Télégramme*, April 6, 2014.

26. Gilles Kepel, *Passion française: Les Voix des cités* (Paris, 2014), 252.

27. On the Muslim petition, see Yamna Chrirra, Felix Marquardt, Tareq Oubrou, and Omero Marongiu-Perria, "Français de confession musulmane: 'Khlass' (ça suffit) le silence!," *Libération*, January 22, 2015. On tempered multiculturalism, see Alain Renaut, "La France doit faire le choix d'un multiculturalisme tempéré," *Le Monde*, January 14, 2015. On "disjunction," see interview with the sociologist Olivier Roy, *Le Monde*, May 30, 2014.

28. "Pour une 'littérature-monde' en français," *Le Monde*, March 15, 2007. In 2006, the Franco-American Jonathan Littell won the Goncourt and the Grand Prix du Roman de l'Académie Française for *Les Bienveillantes*; the Congolese-born Alain Mabanckou won the Renaudot prize for *Mémoires de porc-épic*; the Franco-Canadian Nancy Huston won the Prix Femina for *Lignes de faille*; and the Cameroonian author Léonora Miano won the Goncourt des Lycéens for *Contours du jour qui vient*.

29. Quoted in Alison Finch, *French Literature: A Cultural History* (Cambridge, 2010), 219. The overall figures are from France Diplomatie, www.diplomatie.gouv .fr/en/french-overseas/.

INDEX

SUDHIR HAZAREESINGH is a fellow of politics at Balliol College, Oxford, a fellow of the British Academy, and author of the prize-winning books *The Legend of Napoleon* and *In the Shadow of the General*. He divides his time between Paris and Oxford.